Adventures in Auteurism

Adventures in Auteurism

A Crusade for the Critically Neglected

Daniel Kremer

Foreword by Joe Dante
Afterword by Daniel Waters

Sticking Place Books
New York

© Sticking Place Books 2025
© Daniel Kremer

Cover design Scott Saslow

www.stickingplacebooks.com

ISBN 979-8-89976-027-3

Contents

Dedicated to Wendel Meldrum (1959–2021),
who is greatly missed—
a dear friend, a brilliant artist, and a proud Canadian woman

Dedicated to Ted Kotcheff (1931–2025),
one of the greatest of all Canadian directors

And to my husband, Evan,
truly the light of my life
(who is not Canadian, and that's cool too)

When it came to certain directors, I was, for some time, too much under the influence of people like François Truffaut. The worst thing for a critic is a lack of real curiosity, and following the general fashion. We did not investigate some directors enough ten or twenty years ago. For instance, we let somebody like Anatole Litvak die without ever meeting him—and he lived in Paris! But in the Sixties, Truffaut, in order to boost the 1958 Otto Preminger film *Bonjour Tristesse*, which he loved, knocked other directors who had adapted Françoise Sagan. One of them was Litvak. And stupidly, we followed Truffaut.

Because Litvak's later films were bad, we refused to investigate his career. And his career had started in Russia; then he went to Germany and France, where he made masterpieces in the Thirties, one of which contains scenes and a use of sound as imaginative as Renoir, and another which seems to me less dated than [Howard Hawks's 1930 film] *The Dawn Patrol*. So the lack of not being open—being prejudiced—is the worst thing. Film history suffered a lot from that.

In John Huston's case, it's true, I was a little like Truffaut—aloof about Huston. I admired some of his films, but I remember being aloof about *Red Badge of Courage* and some others. When I see *Red Badge of Courage* today, I realize it was not an easy film to do. There are shots in it that now, I say to myself, "My God, I wish I could do that!"

Even as a film buff, I hated clans—chapelles—groups of critics thinking all the same. [...] I think we are just starting the story of the cinema. A lot of territory still has to be explored.

Bertrand Tavernier
in a 1992 interview
with Patrick McGilligan

Foreword by Joe Dante

Most dyed-in-the-wool film buffs nurture their own private lists of movie directors they feel have been unappreciated, neglected, and/or underrated. These are our underdogs, our "pet causes" in cinema. But very few of us are moved to write an entire book about them. Daniel Kremer steps into the void with this sprawling volume that enthusiastically sings the praises of these cinematic warhorses, heavy on the Canadians he loves, and divided into three categories: Canucks, Americans, and Brits. Few of them are household names, but all have contributed memorable works whose titles still ring bells with many filmgoers.

Titles like *Georgy Girl*, *The Ipcress File*, *Wake in Fright*, *The Ruling Class*, *The Blue Max*, *Papillon*, *Now, Voyager*, *The Incident*, *Crossing Delancey*, *Blue Thunder*, and many others are certainly familiar to viewers, or at least "movie people." But what of their directors? Rarely do we speak of guys like Sidney Furie or John Guillermin or Ted Kotcheff, though there are certainly worthwhile conversations to be had. Other titles, such as *In Praise of Older Women*, *Fortune and Men's Eyes*, *Reach for Glory*, *They Might Be Giants*, *Deception*, *Papillon*, *The Incident*, and *Rattle of a Simple Man* likely don't ring the same bells, but they're worthy of some recognition and discussion, which is what Daniel provides for us here.

Of course herein, Daniel can only scratch the surface of the roster of unjustly neglected filmmakers. I, for one, was especially pleased to see dancer-turned-director Wendy Toye on his list. On my own "unsung list" would be names like Val Guest (*Yesterday's Enemy*, *The Quatermass Xperiment*, *The Day the Earth Caught Fire*), John Farrow (*Alias Nick Neal*, *The Big Clock*, *Night Has a Thousand Eyes*), Roy William Neill (*The Black Room*, *Frankenstein Meets the Wolf Man*, the film noir *Black Angel*), Servando Gonzales (one of my longtime favorites, *The Fool Killer*), and Robert Enrico (*The Last Adventure*, *An Occurrence at Owl Creek Bridge*). All have done memorable work across genres, but for various reasons, their cinematic identities haven't resonated as much within the mainstream. But each has stood the test of time—that is, if people these days ever get around to seeing their films.

With the morass of movies out there in the world, it's very difficult to curate such titles in a way that people can really relate to it all. This is one of the reasons I opened my Trailers from Hell site: to create bite-size film lectures aimed at inspiring viewers to seek out older and more overlooked films, as well as the people who made them, of course. You can find Daniel among the numerous industry creatives who contribute there. Other gurus include Guillermo Del Toro, Allison Anders, Roger Corman, Illeana Douglas, Luca Guadagnino, John Landis, Patton Oswalt, Eli Roth, Edgar Wright, John Sayles, Ernest Dickerson, and many more.

In 1983, I wrote in *Film Comment*, "Film appreciation has opened up to a point where, happily, J. Hoberman can attempt a serious analysis of Edward D. Wood and nobody bats an eye. So let's face it, the search for the obscure, the forgotten, and the disreputable has become a lot more difficult." The truth is, there's always going to be stuff out there that needs to be uncovered by people like Daniel and our roster of Trailers from Hell gurus. I will always continue encouraging others to seek out buried treasure, in whatever ways I can.

But in the end this isn't *my* book, it's Daniel's. And his choices are all worth your time. I can only hope this impassioned tome will engender a lot more interest in the often elusive works that lie within. In any case you'll learn a lot of things you didn't know about these movies and their makers. His Trailers from Hell selections are certainly some of the most unique.

Joe Dante is the director of Gremlins *(1984),* The Howling *(1981),* Innerspace *(1987), and others. A protégé of Roger Corman, he is also a passionate film historian and founder of the cinephile site Trailers from Hell.*

Introduction, With My "Sarris List"

This book is a curious collection of case studies. I wish to define it immediately as a window into an entire philosophy via a closer understanding of an unlikely cast of filmmaking "characters."

John Boorman has it that filmmaking is translating "money into light." As a synagogue-attending Jew, I prefer a Jewish mystical template, an ever so slightly more nuanced iteration: Filmmaking is translating "gashmiyus" into "ruchnius" (i.e. turning the material world into the spiritual), a very Chabad Lubavitch outlook on things, within the realm of Jewish thought. In this context: You take this cold, inert substance of cellulose acetate (or these days, ones and zeroes on a hard drive) and translate it into something emotional, spiritual, reflective of dreams and dream-states, immediate to one's experience of the world, and most of all, something unique about the way a principal creator—a director, as the hardened auteurists (myself included) would have it—sees the world. Sometimes, yes, moviemaking can be cynical, simply a commercial gambit, to latch onto trends, and/or only suited for the purpose of going on an enjoyable but forgettable little amusement park ride, but for the filmmakers that matter, you find the schools of spirituality, the "churches" (or in my case, "synagogues") you like to attend and you keep attending. The hope is that, there, one finds one's community. The stately movie palaces of the day were, after all, glittering temples more than anything else.

As a practical exercise and as a brief diversion, let's build this out. What, for instance, would the "church of John Ford" look like? I have it as: "He would be the most ritually-oriented Catholic priest y'ever did meet, one who does truly believe all the dogma. But his true self only emerges at the church socials, where the women leave early and the men stay all night, sit around in their uniforms, get blotto drinking tear-infused beer while rhapsodizing their mothers one at a time. It's... a scene. Not mine, but knock yourself out."

Or how about Terrence Malick, a bête noire of mine: "A strict, humorless, forbidding Calvinist minister who is ostensibly 'New

Age' but gives cold, albeit flowery, sermons, and never cracks a smile let alone a laugh. Keep him away from moi. He may 'mean it,' and he utters beautiful, poetic phrases from time to time, but he'll always be a step away from charlatan in my book."

(I have probably lost a few readers by now, but I do encourage you of open mind to carry on.)

How about a more favorable one: "Jacques Rivette is a non-denominational minister who tells you, 'It's all performance, and it gets complicated, but don't worry too much.' And why? 'The play is the play, but nothing about that is ever set in stone." I'd attend every week.

Or another for a favorite director of mine: "Joan Micklin Silver as rabbi will always remind you, 'It's a modern world, and as much as many of you are attached to tradition and the past, and as much as I am too, I'm here to tell you how funny the lot of us are.' I'll likewise turn up to services every week."

Finally, a short, tongue-in-cheek entry: "George Cukor pauses his services in the middle for a fashion show." (For the record, I love George Cukor, so hurrah!)

Somewhat similarly, *New Yorker* film critic Richard Brody has likened seeing a given film or the work of a given filmmaker as close or akin to "reading a book of philosophy," while Jonathan Rosenbaum has described "the art of film as a way to learn how to live." In the November-December 1979 edition of *Film Comment*, the esteemed William K. Everson writes, "The juxtaposition of personal experience *with* film is a curious thing that must have affected everybody in differing ways."

To Everson's observation, I would add another factor: indi-vidual—and sometimes very customized—cultural sensibility, which plays a too often unrecognized but outsized role in how we personally receive films and filmmakers (and by extension, art in general). This is never something to be standardized, streamlined, or homogenized by designated tastemakers, either the ones we have groomed, or those who have groomed themselves for us as such.

Veteran film scholar David Thomson, for instance, deplores John Ford's "Irish vaudeville" humor and deemed him a sort of "non-intellectual" and "bully"—even a racist. "The community of drunken sergeants in some of his films is not one that I wish to belong to," he once stated in an interview. He also rues the "very Irish and very Catholic" paternalistic sexual politics in Ford-landia, as well as the "print the legend" ethos as expressed in *The Man Who Shot Liberty Valance*. He asserts that the latter is a benighted (and unfortunately prevailing) attitude that has ensnared America in any number of geopolitical hornets' nests. On these fronts and more, I'm inclined to agree (though, knowing Thomson personally, I differ with him on any number of other fronts, especially the British New Wave). But on this count, it would seem he and I would much rather run from Ford into the arms of a Hawks and an Anthony Mann, whose females were much sturdier, among other virtues.

But are we *supposed to* tip the hat to the likes of Ford and others so knighted or canonized? Is there an obligation here, spoken or unspoken? I, for one, am far more inclined to wander elsewhere to seek my own cinematic priests, preachers, and rabbis, per my metaphor—and this is informed by a personal, mostly culturally inflected philosophy or belief construct. We are all primed for life and for cinemagoing by a variety (or, maybe more aptly, litany) of factors.

Case in point: Sydney Pollack's *Jeremiah Johnson* (1972) and Alejandro G. Iñarritu's *The Revenant* (2015) may very well assay similar material (i.e. rugged man in the wilderness brushing up against the elements, often distressingly), but I personally connect far more with the former than the latter. I believe it's the cultural infusion that tips the scale. Iñarritu's implicit, vaguely Christian "dark night of the soul," purification-through-defilement imprint on the material fails to resonate, while Pollack's Jewishness, his carefully humorous pilpul, emerges even in a picture that has nothing to do with Jewishness. Non-Jewish "Man of Cinema" Pierre Rissient famously championed *Jeremiah Johnson*, for whatever that's worth. Good or noteworthy directors inevitably emboss themselves onto their material, no matter the ease of authorial detection. This was all the subject of an actual conversation I had with my best friend and cinematographer upon leaving a special early screening of the Iñarritu film, one that had been introduced by a top-tier, elite film scholar who was very effusive—and rather inscrutable—in his praise for it. In attempting to determine why the both of us disliked it so intensely, we started speculating around these theories.

Mind you, the vector of culture is certainly not the only determiner, but a crucial one. Beyond that, though, the idea is not to constrain (or limit) oneself to the preordained, sanctioned, or unassailably kosher. There is no such thing as cinematic kashrus (i.e. kosher certification) vis-à-vis. A friend once told me, "You're the last door at the end of a hallway of university religious scholars.

Walk that hallway and you'll get your experts in Christianity, Islam, Hinduism, all the majors, all the well-documented and widely observed dogmas and disciplines we expect from such a department. They teach the rigorously studied and mostly defined. But if you keep on walking down that hallway, you're the one with the scraggly beard and wild eyes who will profess on feral, rarefied sects at the far edges of the world. And your door is the one that's always open. The rest don't much like keeping office hours." Not to pat myself on the back, but I liked the analogy. My stance is that auteurism is everywhere, never to be confined to exclusionary, country-club-style preciousness.

My antipathy toward figures like Ford and Malick tends to land me in the doghouse with not merely the more hidebound traditionalists, but also fair-weather cinephiles. The reflex is to deem it a kind of heresy. They're shocked that so seemingly "worldly" or "sophisticated" a viewer as I could be so dismissive and indifferent toward artists who are, as they see it, objectively and unassailably important. My answer to that is, it's possible to hold some basic respect for artists without personally connecting with their work. Indeed, it is also possible for that respect to undergird cultivated outright distaste. The problem lies in how some modern film scholarship and discourse has turned too many into Leonard Zelig types (methinks, anyway). Conformity has bred a posse that I call "Orthodox cineastes," those who disdain the heterodox and engage in what I call "critic-proofing," a circle-the-wagons-and-launch-the-nukes censoriousness that manufactures a pariah class. "We renounce you, goo-boo ga-boo, *not* one of us!" With some zealots to the cause, they do everything short of pointing and shrieking like the alien replacements in Philip Kaufman's *Invasion of the Body Snatchers*.

My skepticism of the Church (or Cult) of Hitchcock, which is no different than the aforementioned Rissient's, likewise banishes me to the doghouse. But this is simply an aversion to its slavish dogmatism. Any civil, reasonable criticism of *Vertigo*, for instance, is simply too much for a breed of smug, hypersensitive muck-ety-mucks run amok. This brand of censoriousness... how did we get this way? Partly it is our very human need to go with the flow, or any number of "flows," but none of this stops me from finding the true pleasure, thrills, and stimulation elsewhere, for myself, with the themes and aesthetics *I* value.

I tend to hijack the spotlight trained on more popular films and filmmakers, and I try to turn it into a searchlight—one directed toward the overlooked and neglected. I turn the searchlight into its own limelight. There are thousands of filmmakers and millions of films, far too many potential subjects for further study and research to perpetuate a focus on those who have already received more-than-ample coverage. "Auteur socialism" as I call it, is another kind of fight for the "oppressed," one that is not intrinsically political in nature, but (if anything) spiritual and (above all) personal. The philosophy involves closer readings of marginalized films and film-makers who were never afforded the critical heft or scholarly bene-fits that the "1%" in this analogy received. In a way, it's a "comfort the afflicted and afflict the comforted" ethic, and a stab at liberating *la politique des auteurs* from many of the rigid strictures and struc-tures of its roots.

The label "journeyman" is among the most cruelly abused words in any discourse on film, and its deployment has gotten worse over time. It would seem, on the whole, that the thematic earmarks and stylistic flourishes that cement a given authorship/auteurship must loudly—and even cacophonously—announce themselves to avoid the brandishing of the "journeyman" label. This is the laziest of tendencies. But there is more comfort, I suppose, in reducing even slightly more covert cases to a quick-and-ready label than there is in looking closer and doing the work. Tasteful subtlety and covertness to much of any degree, in conjunc-tion with genre-hopping, would seem a cardinal sin in auteur study heretofore (Hawks being a notable outlier), and that's for shame. I blame exclusivity (the cognoscenti just love their "boys clubs," read into that what you will) and, in all candor, an intellectual laziness cloaked in a militant and occasionally belligerent non-curiosity. Astoundingly, even in modern contexts wherein cinema consumers have the privilege of access and immediate playback, the viewership at large tends to miss too much. Ultimately, maybe that's because they're just not prepared to really see these under-valued works, all for the way that that long-in-the-tooth scholarly class, the aforementioned tastemaker contingent, has primed them to see only what they see, and not what *you* see.

We can be grateful that Andrew Sarris brought the *politique des auteurs* to America, but no one truly built off the foundations he had lain, nor academically challenged his assumptions or his pronounce-ments (at least enough to make a lasting impression, or approach forming any rival critical canon). Most live to reinforce, in varying strides, many if not most of his 1968 verdicts in *The American Cinema*, which—though formative and significant—have become fossilized by now. Those who came in his wake built fortresses around directors with a resolutely masculine purview (especially in appraisal of classic Hollywood directors). Auteurism developed a masculinity complex, one that revolved around the idea that assertive, very old-world masculinity computed to pure artistic voice beyond reproach. American critics didn't like their icons sullied by any pesky sexual ambiguity, lest it be filtered through a compulsory layer of grit and muscle and manly protectionism.

A class of sclerotic, superannuated scholar will contend that the canons are written, the dice are cast, and the ships have sailed. I challenge that entirely, and my defiance is a studied one. Sacred cows are one thing, but steak is my favorite meal.

I respond most of all to the "phantom threads" left behind by those working across multiple genres and narrative forms, which are not merely arcane patterns. I resist any intimation that these individuals are, at best, metteurs en scène. My own principal dark horses— Sidney J. Furie, Irving Rapper, Silvio Narizzano, Philip Leacock— did their share of genre-hopping, but there's "a way of seeing," an expression I often use. On a personal and cultural level, my gayness and Jewishness is soothed by each and every one of them. Many missed consistent styles and thematic patterns because they couldn't withstand consistent shifts in narrative trappings. When I started writing my volume on Furie, published by University Press of Kentucky's Screen Classics Series in 2015, it was deemed an "unserious" pursuit by a majority of critical dignitaries. Quite frankly, I was scorned. In approaching the editor of a major film journal about the possibility of writing an article to prime readers for my book's publication, he sniffed, "Why would you do a book on Sidney Furie? Why not do something on so-and-so instead?" (I forget the alternative he floated, but this is likely because I was miffed at his breathtaking condescension.)

Cut to about twelve years later. While Furie may not be on everyone's lips, he's on a great many more. I see him popping up in serious conversation, mentioned more and more with reverence and, at the very least, respect. After years of being the butt of obtuse jokes in some quarters, Furie films now sit next to Sam Fuller titles in special director sections at the Los Angeles video stores I visit. His stock has risen, especially as many of his most important pictures have become available anew. It's notable what a little insistence and perseverance can do in reviving a body of work and reversing course in favor of reappraisal. Of course, I'm on the very far opposing end of the critical slander and shortsightedness, because I'm mystified how so many scholars missed the eloquence and stylistic mastery of Furie for so long. Blindness, perhaps? Yes, of a kind. I might call it a stubborn blindness.

This is not a struggle for equity for its own sake. I'm here to say that there is intellectual, aesthetic, emotional, and historical significance to studying—and even favoring—such forgotten cinematic classes over what I will refer to as the "overstudied," which foster an identity homogeneity and genericism when the approach is, by design, exclusionary. I cling to something that film historian Tim Lucas once said: "I feel lists should dispense with any fantasies of objectivity right away; such a list should serve as an X-ray snapshot of the individual curator and be exchangeable with others like a mix tape. It should tell others, 'This is who I am.'"

A bifurcation of the universal vs. the personal, coupled with a "visual literacy" (specifically favoring directors who lean into the plasticity of the form), and a voracious appetite for buried treasure, is the essence of my ethic. Discernment, knowing yourself enough to understand what speaks to you (and how), is vital above all. Are Sidney Furie, Irving Rapper, Silvio Narizzano, Philip Leacock, and my other dark horses—my "pet causes"—as important as Ford or Hitchcock? To me, they are, and that's enough. These and the others in my personal pantheon, especially The Archers (Powell and Pressburger), Claude Jutra, Jacques Rivette, Joseph Losey, Joan Micklin Silver, are with me always. I both recognize and realize aspects of myself, and open a window to a wider world, thanks to each of them.

My various subjects for further study (catalogued later in this introduction) animate me as a historian and, more basically, as a watcher and appreciator. I await the first book on, for instance, Michael Ritchie, or Peter Medak, or Peter Collinson, or Muriel Box, rather than the n-thousandth volume on Kubrick.

Mainly, I feel that no one should be beholden to exalting something or someone merely because they are universally venerated, nor should they feel obligated to include them in every cinema-lover's favorite exercise (listmaking, oh listmaking!) merely because the cognoscenti have done the peremptory sanctioning on each selection. One should be free to omit fetishized and (as I see it) over-indexed works like *Vertigo* and *The Searchers* as one pleases. There is a class of people who, no matter where a conversation started, always steer it back to those two titles in particular. I call them Searchigos. With that in mind, I have fashioned a Sarris-esque and Sarris-inspired catalogue of directors under self-defined categories. With this, you peer into my taste, and the particulars which most connect with the "ways of seeing" I personally cherish.

My life has been one in pursuit of what I call "pregnant films"—not "good" or "bad" in any reductive sense, but works that are both front-loaded and back-loaded with the beguiling traces of eccentricity capable of stoking even the most outlandish debates. In other words, films that play not merely as they present themselves, but that can be broken down in a variety of ways, depending on the set of eyes that behold them. It's crucial to remember that putatively "successful" films can still be passionless, and perceived "failures" can be quite passionate. I intend to carve out a theory around why auteurism does not need constriction but rather expansions (plural). What follows is not a collection of paeans to mediocrities (or, if you like, panegyrics for patzers), as some might see it. I'm not out to cast myself as another boring and boorish non-conformist. These are profiles of real artists who require more serious reckoning—and for cineastes to favor them with, at the very least, a "day in court." I intend this book as evidence for the defense, and for perhaps a prosecution.

MY SO-CALLED "SARRIS LIST"

Presented here are my classifications and rankings of as many filmmakers as I believe deserve some level of serious discussion. Those who have pored over Sarris' The American Cinema *text will recognize categories similar to his, but I've gingerly redefined some, while inventing some of my own, and otherwise customizing or totally overhauling others. In any event, I believe these types of exercises, above all, at least should present a snapshot of the individual.*

○ ○ ○

THE PERSONALS / MY PANTHEON
These are my personal favorite directors, the ones who hit me right in my solar plexus, who speak to me, as me and myself, rather than being "great" or "good" in some more general or objective (or objectivized, as in "made dogma") sense. These define who I am as a cinephile and as an individual. These speak to the Tim Lucas sentiment recounted earlier, amen and amen.

Michael Powell/Emeric Pressburger (The Archers), Sidney J. Furie, Claude Jutra, Jacques Rivette, Irving Rapper, Joseph Losey, Philip Leacock, Otto Preminger, Luchino Visconti, Silvio Narizzano, Ritwik Ghatak, Robert Altman, George Cukor, Mitchell Leisen, Frank Borzage, Vincente Minnelli, Rainer Werner Fassbinder, Joan Micklin Silver, John Cassavetes, Nicolas Roeg, Max Ophüls, William Wyler, Shohei Imamura, Ted Kotcheff, Morris Engel

o o o

THE SHOULD-BES

The next rung down, my "Far Side of Paradise" in a way, but also not. Directors I love who I wish were on more peoples' lips and minds, who should be studied and discussed more, and who I feel deserve the spotlight more than some who actually get spotlit. My second class of pet cause filmmakers.

Michael Ritchie, Ettore Scola, Delmer Daves, Charles B. Pierce, Jerry Schatzberg, Michael Schultz, Peter Watkins, Jules Dassin, Frank Perry, Allan Moyle, Peter Medak, Franklin J. Schaffner, Paul Bartel, Philip Kaufman, Robert M. Young, Anthony Harvey, Jon Jost, Marcel L'Herbier, Abel Gance, Julien Duvivier, Anatole Litvak, Eldar Ryazanov, Andrzej Zulawski, John G. Avildsen (specifically pre-*Rocky*), Jerzy Kawalerowicz, Eloy de la Iglesia, Krzysztof Zanussi, Haile Gerima, Francesco Rosi, Stanley Donen, Richard Quine, Muriel Box, Wendy Toye, Harvey Hart

o o o

THE SOLIDS

The generally unassailable filmmakers. All are great, and they don't need me to cheerlead for them. We know they're great, I'd never deny it, so hooray for them. But this volume really isn't about them.

Orson Welles, Peter Bogdanovich, Martin Scorsese, Francis Ford Coppola, Roman Polanski, Howard Hawks, Alan J. Pakula, Bernardo Bertolucci, Michelangelo Antonioni, Blake Edwards, John Huston, Robert Bresson, George Stevens, Federico Fellini, Billy Wilder, Preston Sturges, William Friedkin, Jean Renoir, Ernst Lubitsch, John Frankenheimer, Ingmar Bergman, John Carpenter, François Truffaut, Bertrand Tavernier, Charles Chaplin, Buster Keaton, Fritz Lang, Michael Curtiz, Carol Reed, Joe Dante, Chantal Akerman, Anthony Mann, John Schlesinger, Peter Weir,

Radley Metzger, F. W. Murnau, Akira Kurosawa, Ida Lupino, Oscar Micheaux, Paul Verhoeven, Raoul Walsh, Budd Boetticher, Kenji Mizoguchi, Dario Argento (along with many of the giallo superstars)

This category could run on and on indefinitely.

○ ○ ○

DESERVING OF A CLOSER LOOK
I'm not ready to include these guys in my Should-Bes or Solids categories, but they are just expressive enough that I want to take deeper analytical dives.

Robert Mulligan, Seth Holt, Clive Donner (one of Sarris' biggest pet causes), Richard Rush, Jean Negulesco, Waris Hussein, Peter Sasdy, Larry Peerce, Lance Comfort, Peter Collinson, Ernest Pintoff, Richard C. Saraffian, Hugo Haas, Paul Williams, Spencer Williams, Ralph Nelson, David Greene, Ivan Passer, Peter Yates, Richard Franklin, Jean Delannoy, Jeremy Paul Kagan, Claude Autant-Lara (a bête noire of the *Cahiers* crowd), Larry Cohen, Lino Brocka

○ ○ ○

THE OEUVRETTES (OR, WISH THEY'D DONE MORE)
In other words, the tiny oeuvres. The "Oeuvritos" if you must. These are simply filmmakers whose outputs are limited in quantity, but not in quality (or at least interest). There is evidence of brilliance and/or individuality in the few films they managed to finish. In order of quantity. Italics indicate extra special interest.

Daniel Bourla (1), Charles M. Conner (1), Richard Crawford (1), François de Menil (1), *Phillip Fenty* (1), Wendell Franklin (1), *Edward Folger* (1), *James William Guercio* (1), *Christine Hornisher* (1), Jordan Leondopoulos (1), *Barbara Loden* (1), *Patrick Loubert* (1), *Nelson Lyon* (1), *Gordon Sheppard* (1), *Robert Thom* (1), Ralph Waite (1), *Yong-Kyun Bae* (2), Allen Baron (2), *Kathleen Collins* (2), *Milton Moses Ginsberg* (2), *Peter Emmanuel Goldman* (2), Stuart Hagmann (2), *Jack Hazan* (2), *Robert J. Kaplan* (2), *Stanton Kaye* (2), *Kent Mackenzie* (2), Alex Matter (2), Conrad Rooks (2), *Jean Vigo* (2), *Jean Eustache* (3), *Bill Gunn* (3), *Abraham Polonsky* (3), Aram Avakian (4), *Daryl Duke* (4), *Morris Engel* (4), *Elaine May* (4), Barney Platts-Mills (4), William Richert (4), *Michael*

Roemer (5), *Barry Shear* (4), Theodore J. Flicker (5), *James B. Harris* (5), *Floyd Mutrux* (5), *Wendy Toye* (5), George Armitage (6), Noel Black (6)

○ ○ ○

LIKE BUT WISH I LOVED (Adjacent to "Lightly Likable")
My "Lightly Likable" à la Sarris. These make/made perfectly respectable, likable work, but they never "popped" for me like others have.

David Lynch, Nicholas Ray, Samuel Fuller, Arthur Penn, Robert Aldrich, Michael Haneke, John Sturges, Jim Jarmusch, Jean Rollin, Jane Campion

○ ○ ○

THE FLUCTUANTS
Depending on the day and the mood, I'll feel one way or the other about these guys. But I do still respect them.

Brian De Palma (I tend to much prefer the earlier stuff), Douglas Sirk (I'll watch him for color and staging more than his stories or characters), David Lynch (I have unbounding respect for him, but the films don't quite land for me), Sam Peckinpah (though I love *Ride the High Country* unconditionally), Claude Chabrol, Joel and Ethan Coen, Carl Th. Dreyer

○ ○ ○

THE FLATULANTS
The overbearing bloviators and blowhards who, ironically considering the category name, abjectly fail "the fart test" (which a friend of mine originated). "In any of a filmmaker's works, could a character let one rip without throwing off or ruining the entire movie?" The majority of good directors pass this. Bergman passes it, for crying out loud! Fellini certainly passes it. Bresson would too if you ask me. Even a quieter inoffensive rectal toot with a tried and tested musicality would mean nothing short of armageddon for, for instance, Terrence Malick. I can't abide humorless filmmakers.

Terrence Malick, Denis Villeneuve, Alex Garland, Darren Aronofsky (he's still somehow palatable on the whole)

O O O

THE TOUCHABLE UNTOUCHABLES
The scholarly ruling class seem intent on ruining these filmmakers for me, by "critic-proofing" them, by building fortresses around them, and treating any true critical interaction with them as heretical or philistinish. I'm not having it.

Stanley Kubrick, John Ford (I despise *The Searchers* more than any other classic movie), Alfred Hitchcock, Andrei Tarkovsky (though *Andrei Rublev* is indeed untouchable and unassailable)

O O O

THE PLUS-SIGN DIVISIVES
Divisive or controversial filmmakers I admire, in so much that I understand what they pursue, why they pursue it, and also understand why they elicit the uproar or debate they often do.

Henry Jaglom, Steven Spielberg, Alan Rudolph, Michael Cimino, Claude Lelouch (the French themselves seem to hate him)

Note: Spielberg is "controversial" in relation only to the "is he a confectioner hack or a real artist?" argument. Spielberg is more the latter than someone like George Lucas ever was (or could be) to me. Lucas is the former in my book. [See Spielberg's entry in this book's appendix.]

O O O

THE MINUS-SIGN DIVISIVES
Divisive or controversial filmmakers that I'm not keen on. Shapeless provocateurs don't rouse my passions.

Gaspar Noé, Lars Von Trier (comes off too much like a practical joker more than a filmmaker sometimes)

O O O

THE NON-CONNECTS
These filmmakers don't speak to me much, and never did. In most of the cases below, they just alienate me.

Jean-Luc Godard, Claire Denis, John Ford, Ridley Scott, George Lucas (never was a Warsy, and other than some of the visuals in *THX 1138*, the rest doesn't impress me), Christopher Nolan (I like pretty much nada), Alejandro D. Iñarritu (I've liked only one of his films, and it was the one that everyone seemed to hate), Krzysztof Kieslowski (I like *Camera Buff* and two in the *Dekalog*, kind of cold on the rest), Abbas Kiarostami (*Close Up* is the only one that got to me), Yorgos Lanthimos (too much snarky smugness)

○ ○ ○

THE BETE NOIRES
I simply don't like those listed here. My "shit list," if you like. In the case of someone like Lumet, only a very small handful passes my smell test, and they're often not the ones others go for.

Terrence Malick (*Badlands* excepted), Sidney Lumet (a few select, and sometimes unexpected, titles excepted), James Toback, Damien Chazelle, Taika Waititi, Adam McKay, David Mamet, David O. Russell, Abel Ferrara, Nicolas Winding Refn, Ridley Scott (in late career), Cooper Raiff (recent addition)

○ ○ ○

AGNOSTIC
Hard for me to feel one way or the other, definitively or in the overall. It always always always depends on a given individual film. Doesn't mean they're not auteurs, it's simply that the returns vary. I think it's that a number of them feel philosophical in much too "dude-ish" a way for my taste.

Monte Hellman, Cecil B. DeMille, Alain Resnais, Walter Hill, Richard Fleischer, Richard Lester, Eric Rohmer, John Boorman

○ ○ ○

THE VANILLA POPS
These guys get pretty vanilla, especially as they age. They did their best work early on, but occasionally their later work can be compelling. They're normally entertaining.

Mike Nichols (in particular, got caught up in the well-heeled, "Nora Ephron cocktail humor" clique, a New York cultural power elite, and it paled his imprint), Richard Attenborough

O O O

THE POLEMICISTS
No one likes being screamed or barked at. I feel that way when I watch the work of these filmmakers, and it's often not pleasurable or even edifying. Their angry politics tend to override their craft on too many occasions.

Ken Loach (*Kes* is fantastic, but I waver on much of the rest, too sanctimonious overall, and his socialism is instrumentalized to make audiences feel like they're good people for having appreciated the work), Jean-Luc Godard, Adam McKay (aggressive, zealous, smug Bernie Bro™ smart-assery makes for the absolute worst cinema), Oliver Stone (who's become an outright lunatic)

O O O

THE TRANSCENDENT POLEMICISTS
They're often/mostly very political, but rarely or never obnoxiously so. They convey a political purview without shouting or smarming.

Peter Mettler, Chris Marker, Marcel Ophuls, Costa-Gavras (with certain exceptions), John Sayles, Peter Watkins, Spike Lee (for the most part), Robert Kramer

O O O

AVANT-GARDE PLUS
Experimental film and video artists with whom I do connect.

Jonas Mekas, Adolfas Mekas, Bruce Conner, Ken Jacobs, Kenneth Anger, Chantal Akerman, Yvonne Rainer, James Benning, Jon Jost, Mark Rappaport

O O O

AVANT-GARDE MINUS
Experimental film and video artists with whom I fail to connect.

Nathaniel Dorsky, Mario Peixoto, Andy Warhol (variable)

O O O

THE HOPENIKS
The few contemporary filmmakers who give me hope for the future of the form.

Paul Thomas Anderson, Jeff Kao, Josh & Benny Safdie, Greta Gerwig, Laura Citarella, Albert Serra, Alice Rohrwacher, Sky Hopinka, Patrick Wang, Andrew Haigh, Kenneth Lonergan, Brady Corbet, Onur Tukel (one of our best contemporary satirists)

○ ○ ○

Everyone's favorite impossible task, my constantly evolving and changing list of favorite films, as of time-of-publication (including many by filmmakers covered herein):

The Life and Death of Colonel Blimp (1963, Powell/Pressburger), *Céline and Julie Go Boating* (1974, Rivette), *The Leather Boys* (1964, Furie), *Puzzle of a Downfall Child* (1970, Schatzberg), *Kamouraska* (1973, Jutra), *The Ipcress File* (1965, Furie), *Mon Oncle Antoine* (1971, Jutra), *Now, Voyager* (1942, Rapper), *Innocent Sinners* (1958, Leacock), *Dear Mr. Wonderful* (1982, Lilienthal), *A Star is Born* (1954, Cukor), *Crumb* (1995, Zwigoff), *Rocco and His Brothers* (1960, Visconti), *Kings and Desperate Men* (1981, Kanner), *An Affair of the Skin* (1963, Maddow), *The Brave One* (1956, Rapper), *Zabriskie Point* (1970, Antonioni), *Rosemary's Baby* (1968, Polanski), *New York, New York* (1977, Scorsese), *Montreal Main* (1974, Vitale), *A Matter of Life and Death* (1946, Powell/Pressburger), *Chilly Scenes of Winter* (1979, Silver), *A Woman Under the Influence* (1974, Cassavetes), *Midnight Cowboy* (1969, Schlesinger), *Little Fugitive* (1953, Engel, plus Engel's others), *Hannah and Her Sisters* (1986, Allen), *Targets* (1968, Bogdanovich), *Young Shoulders* (1984, Narizzano), *They Shoot Horses, Don't They?* (1969, Pollack), *Blue* (1968, Narizzano), *Mr. Klein* (1976, Losey), *The Cloud-Capped Star* (1960, Ghatak), *A tout prendre* (1963, Jutra), *Johanna d'Arc of Mongolia* (1989, Ottinger), *Edvard Munch* (1973, Watkins), *The Earrings of Madame de...* (1953, Ophüls), *A Double Life* (1947, Cukor), *La belle noiseuse* (1991, Rivette), *Odd Man Out* (1947, Reed), *The Unbearable Lightness of Being* (1988, Kaufman), *The Profound Desires of the Gods* (1972, Imamura), *L'Atalante* (1934, Vigo), *Short Cuts* (1993, Altman), *Hester Street* (1975, Silver), *The Clock* (1945, Minnelli), *The Long Goodbye* (1973, Altman), *The Leopard* (1963, Visconti), *Chimes at Midnight* (1967, Welles), *The Moment of*

Truth (1965, Rosi), *Sheila Levine is Dead and Living in New York* (1975, Furie), *The Best Years of Our Lives* (1946, Wyler), *3 Women* (1977, Altman), *Margaret* (2011, Lonergan), *The Boys in Company C* (1978, Furie), *Someone to Love* (1987, Jaglom), *Umberto D.* (1952, De Sica), *The Year-Long Road* (1958, De Santis), *I Know Where I'm Going* (1945, Powell/Pressburger), *Hit!* (1973, Furie), *Eros Plus Massacre* (1969, Yoshida), *Hold Back the Dawn* (1941, Leisen), *Georgy Girl* (1966, Narizzano), *Something for Everyone* (1970, Prince), *The Late Mathias Pascal* (1925, L'Herbier), *The Bad and the Beautiful* (1952, Minnelli), *Marjorie Morningstar* (1958, Rapper), *Andrei Rublev* (1966, Tarkovsky), *The Last Detail* (1973, Ashby), *The Christian Licorice Store* (1971, Frawley), *Fortune and Men's Eyes* (1971, Hart), *To Each His Own* (1946, Leisen), *Quackser Fortune Has a Cousin in the Bronx* (1970, Hussein), *Wake in Fright* (1971, Kotcheff), *Bad Timing* (1980, Roeg), *The Sky is Falling* (1975, Narizzano), *Remember the Night* (1940, Leisen), *Bonjour Tristesse* (1958, Preminger), *Berlin Alexanderplatz* (1980, Rainer Werner Fassbinder), *Gambling, Gods and LSD* (2001, Mettler), *Los Angeles Plays Itself* (2003, Andersen), *Sunrise* (1927, Murnau), *Ulysses' Gaze* (1995, Angelopoulos), *Blue Collar* (1978, Schrader), *La Dolce Vita* (1960, Fellini), *Signal 7* (1985, Nilsson), *Hand in Hand* (1961, Leacock), *Barry Lyndon* (1975, Kubrick), *The Bicycle Thieves* (1947, De Sica)

PART ONE
MY DARLING CANADIANS

I. Clear Lines of Sight
The Sidney J. Furie Vision

In a manner of speaking, Sidney J. Furie was my "patient zero" for the philosophy that this book explicates and advocates. Presented here is a hodge-podge of multiple Furie-themed pieces I've written and published, in both print and video form, reorganized and repackaged for readability. For more of my writings on Sidney J. Furie, consult my 2015 book Sidney J. Furie: Life and Films *(University Press of Kentucky, 2015).*

On the evening of Saturday, November 23, 1968, film students filed into the Academy Award Theatre for a special screening of Sidney J. Furie's *The Leather Boys* (1964) as part of the Directors Choice series, hosted by the Academy of Motion Picture Arts and Sciences. Other guests throughout the season included George Cukor, Frank Capra, King Vidor, Richard Brooks, Alfred Hitchcock, John Frankenheimer, and a young Francis Ford Coppola. The Academy instructed each filmmaker to select one of their own films to screen, then engage a group of film students afterward. As a quick aside, Coppola elected to open his show with a short documentary entitled *Filmmaker*, about the making of *The Rain People*, directed by a young man named George Lucas. Transcripts still exist for all question-and-answer sessions; Coppola's transcriber spells Lucas' name L-U-K-A-S. (Who says historical record can't be amusing?)

Furie and Coppola were noticeably the young guns amid an old guard of august Hollywood veterans programmed alongside them. At one point in Furie's session, a student rose to tell him, "You're somewhat of a legend for a young man in the business. By that I mean, Sidney J. Furie shots or angles are getting to be well-known and they're usually low shooting up." Furie retorted, "That's 'cause I'm praying all the time." The quip drew the expected laughs. This is the Sidney Furie that I have personally come to know: self-deprecating but charming, energetic to a fault, hesitant to participate in such events but disarming and charismatic when he does.

The film student deployed the word "legend" in this instance. Considering the other directors who shared the stage with Furie, it's clear that many if not most have forgotten just how much of a name director he once was, and could be again. He is more than a mere cog, journeyman, or metteur en scène.

One of Furie's favorite films is William Wyler's *The Best Years of Our Lives* (1946), and it's not difficult to understand why, in terms of both content and style. Wyler's stacked, deep-focus compositions, which became a directorial trademark as pioneered by cinematographer Gregg Toland, set Furie's pace on the visual plane. Critic and theorist André Bazin once expressed his affinity for Wyler's compositions in *The Best Years of Our Lives*, writing in *Cahiers du Cinéma*: "The action in the foreground is secondary, although interesting and peculiar enough to require our keen attention since it occupies a privileged place and surface on the screen. Paradoxically, the true action, the one that constitutes at this precise moment a turning point in the story, develops almost clandestinely in a tiny rectangle at the back of the room—in the left corner of the screen. Thus the viewer is induced actively to participate in the drama planned by the director." The Wyler visual DNA is present and perceptible in (especially) the first three decades of Furie's work, with maybe slightly different "genetic sequencing," if you will.

Furie's early experiments with refracted views of action, chiefly in the Caine-Brando-Sinatra headlined "Wild Angles Trilogy," incited a furor in their day. The youth tuned into their sheer visual audacity, while elders took potshots (or, in the case of Billy Wilder, cheap shots in which the master exaggerated Furie's radicalism for comic effect). In *The American Vein*, Christopher Wicking and Tise Vahimagi recount how Furie "was on the bête noire rankings of most critics with his willful style." While the authors concede that "those critics have a point," they recognize Furie as a "resolute original" and maintain that "it's hard not to have a soft spot for his attempts to redefine the visual horizons of the modern screen." But the director's critical opponents "beat that style out of me," in Furie's own words, so he adjusted and tempered its audacity to favor slightly clearer lines of sight in his Seventies Paramount titles—a run that ranged from *The Lawyer* (1970) through *Sheila Levine is Dead and Living in New York* (1975), as well as his masterpiece *The Boys in Company C* (1978), which was produced by Golden Harvest. Furie, at this point, was content to just let shots and dialogues play uninterrupted and

Furie has named William Wyler as an influence, and *The Best Years of Our Lives* has long been one of his favorite films. Wyler packed and layered his compositions with stagings that worked on multiple planes of action. Where the eye looks at any moment is a source of information or suspense. Furie visually tips his hat to Wyler throughout his career, but the influence is very evident in his *The Boys in Company C.*

unencumbered, in stagings that were often nothing if not unexpected and sometimes experimental. In many scenes during Furie's Paramount period, he favors extended single sustained shots ("one-ers"), his framing suggestive and dynamic, enhancing the performers' contributions by showing us what bristles at the edges of the drama.

Nothing is traditional about Furie's approach. His camera narrates by revealing. Blake Edwards once remarked that he preferred to choreograph or situate his camera strategically, rather than shoot for coverage, using the set like a proscenium. If you've dined out with Furie as many times as I have, you'd come to notice that he prefers a corner booth with a grandstand view of the entire establishment. On one of those occasions with me, the conversation led up to the subject of framing and staging, and he was in the perfect position to demonstrate the potential of anamorphic widescreen, his beloved canvas size.

Furie's first big breakthrough as a director was on *The Young Ones*, having first written his ticket as a pioneering independent filmmaker in Canada on two self-funded features, *A Dangerous Age* (1957) and *A Cool Sound from Hell* (1959), which are today recognized by many Canadian film scholars as Canada's first modern English-language dramatic feature films. In the Foreword of my book *Sidney J. Furie: Life and Films*, onetime TIFF director Piers Handling writes, "It remains a wonder to behold that [Furie] started making striking, bold, and of-the-moment feature films in Canada when the only game in town was the short films being made by the National Film Board. Furie and his films captured a country struggling to establish its identity."

He cemented his professional reputation with two horror quickies, *Doctor Blood's Coffin* (1960) and *The Snake Woman* (1961), the latter of which was shot in only six days. Amid this string of monster-mashes, and his Cliff Richard vehicles, are a trio of more personal projects that spoke more directly to his emerging sensibility: *During One Night* (1961), *The Boys* (1962), and *The Leather Boys* (1964). *During One Night* is an especially ripe text that most conspicuously manifests his favored themes of wounded masculinity and male anxiety, following a young, sexually impotent World War II bomber who frets over losing his virginity before his number his up. Will his number or his male anatomy rise first?

Very few if any of these threads and elements regarding masculinity tie into *The Young Ones* (1961) or *Wonderful Life* (1964),

Furie first experimented with screen width and Cinemascope on his career breakthrough *The Young Ones* (1961), with multi-panel split screen and red lens fog.

but what these Cliff Richard pop musicals do carve out is a slight detour, another line of Furie pictures which culminates in the late film *Global Heresy* (2002), starring Peter O'Toole, Joan Plowright, and Alicia Silverstone, about a rock band holed up in exile at a sprawling British estate. With his *Lady Sings the Blues* (1972) as a mid-career accent mark, the Furie pop musicals deliver the goods for fans of the artists who've come to see *them*, but hints at a broader worldview as well.

In *The Young Ones*, a spunky bubblegum musical to its core, Furie's visual personality, his distortions, his Dutch angles, his dynamic angular widescreen compositions, and even a dip into split-screen territory (arranged as a perfect eight-panel octave), are all a blueprint for a style that would boldly announce itself further in the Furie pictures that followed. In one key sequence, our filmmaker clouds the lens with red Vaseline during a solo love ballad. This echoes forward to the type of refracted imagery we see in the Wild Angles trilogy. Furie was, to some degree or another, writing some of the grammar for the British pop musical, and setting the pace for an emerging genre unto itself.

I'm of the perhaps unusual opinion that *Wonderful Life* is superior to *The Young Ones*. Movies are the essence of life itself in *Wonderful Life*, and the title reflects this. The eponymous "wonderful life" is clearly life as it exists in the movies, while the mission of our heroes, Cliff and the Shadows, is to make the "wonderful life" of the film-within-the-film even more wonderful by covertly musicalizing it. The knowingly affected Andy Hardy-esque narrative model of the previous Cliff Richard musicals is subverted, as the moviemaking dream factory and its irresistible magic assume almost religious heights in *Wonderful Life*.

With his exuberant pastiche of various movie musical number styles, Furie's game in *Wonderful Life* is the meta-meta. Though ostensibly a throwaway picture in the Furie filmography, *Wonderful Life* sees him at his most sly. An average British moviegoing audience in 1964 would be caught in a kind of inter or intra-dimensional web, all fueled or hopped up on cinema. Or more primally, the movies. There are multiple layers in *Wonderful Life*: there's the first layer, the setup reality, of Cliff and the Shadows, who row ashore on a lifeboat and unwittingly intrude onto a movie set under the rule of director Walter Slezak. There's the second-layer, Slezak's movie-within-the-movie, with Furie packaging Cliff and the Boys' surreptitious by-product movie-within-the-movie alongside it. There's the third-layer, the movie fantasies of Cliff and the gang, reflective of their own vision for the project they hope to commandeer for themselves. Then, in the fourth and final layer, especially in the "We Love the Movies" sequence, we crawl into the pre-existing cinematic worlds of classic movies, the "I-wish-we-weres" of their artistic desires.

Nearly forty years later, after Furie had fled the Hollywood studios to make a tentative filmmaking return to his native Canada, Furie saw to some unfinished business. *Global Heresy* is best seen as the late third entry in his cycle of Cliff Richard musicals. Whereas those films pitted age against youth in a classic *Babes in Arms*/Andy Hardy struggle, *Global Heresy* has age and youth joining forces against a more general class of users and abusers. As opposed to the "let's put on a show" or "let's make a movie" proclamations of *The Young Ones* and *Wonderful Life*, the young heroes in *Global Heresy* have settled for "Hey, let's have a jam session." The message is fairly loaded and the personal statement is there to be perceived. As the title band Global Heresy risks losing their artistic freedom, thanks to a more corporatized music business bent solely on profits and trends (and thanks to contracts that screw the artists in the smallest print between the lines), they escape civilization to regroup at a remote estate where they can work in peace without being relentlessly covered and judged by the press.

This falls right in line with Furie's view of his later Canadian non-studio pictures as "just a chance to go to work," without the pressure of being seriously reviewed or put under any kind of spotlight. His direct-to-video pictures are "jam sessions" with the time having been happily spent. Once the band arrives at the Foxley Estate, the servants maintaining the place are actually the masters in disguise. This is enough of a symbol already. Lord and Lady Foxley, played by O'Toole and Plowright, align with the Robert Morley and Walter Slezak presences in the previous films. Their characters are themselves in danger of losing everything near and dear to them, so they lower the bar, keep under the radar, and do what needs to be done to keep afloat amid difficult times.

Whereas the band's conflict speaks to Furie's artistic struggle, the Foxleys' struggle speaks to Furie's practical need to make a living. As *Wonderful Life* ends with the song "Youth and Experience," which celebrates the two forces joining for the greater good, *Global Heresy*'s final image is of the two elderly stars dancing to the music of the young. It is the perfect note on which to end, when one realizes that filmmaking, a demanding enterprise ostensibly fit only for the young, has kept the aging Furie full of vigor, long after his A-list status burned out. He himself dances to the music of the young, just as his younger self acutely understood the transitional rhythms of a band like Cliff and the Shadows.

Furie indulges in what I call "sly emasculations." In *A Cool Sound from Hell*, a street-smart Beatnik girl aptly named Steve remakes a nervous milquetoast in her image and continues wearing the pants in the relationship. As already noted, in *During One Night*, a sexually impotent young pilot agonizes over losing his virginity before possibly losing his life in combat. *The Boys* follows four juvenile delinquents asserting their masculinity by wreaking local havoc during a night out that ends in a senseless killing, while *The Leather Boys* probes the sexual elasticity of male camaraderie. How close is too close... for men as they prefer to define themselves, or as they are often scared into defining themselves? The latter was a groundbreaking work of queer cinema, then and for all time.

In *The Ipcress File* (1965), there is a gender reversal, with Sue Lloyd making the more aggressive sexual moves on bespectacled Michael Caine after he's the one to have cooked the meal they have just eaten. *The Ipcress File* is an extraordinary synthesis as a film because it can be appreciated and enjoyed as an espionage potboiler and as meditation on themes that its genre can often not afford. It's one of the best films about the existential dilemma and the existential frustration of being a cog in the system. The ending speaks to this, and establishes the trope of the "Furie professional." "That's what you're paid for," Ross tells Palmer after he has been driven nearly mad by a "brain drain," a regiment of rigorous, sadistic mental reprogramming, during which he is reduced to a laboratory rat (not unlike the way Barbara Hershey's character would later be rendered similar in the final act of Furie's masterpiece *The Entity* eighteen years later). The austerity of Ross' matter-of-factness suits the coded world that has been set up—one where even the park benches have soulless, arcane letter/number fixings. I have the distinct sense that Terry Gilliam took notes on all the weird esoteric, bureaucratic form names ("B-107," "TX-182," and so on) when he made his *Brazil* (1985).

Ipcress is a film about privacy; the camera is always hiding. As one scholar said, "It's as if the camera itself doesn't have security clearance." It's a film about secrets and what they propel or intimate, but more so, it's about the little kingdom that an easy-to-overlook man, the aforementioned "Furie professional," builds when he is discouraged from emotional commitment, not to mention the multitude of surprises he contains or signifies (Palmer being a gourmet, a lover of classical music, etc.) Coppola expresses his similar notion of the professional in *The Godfather Part II* with the iconic line "This is the business we've chosen." *The Ipcress File* emerges as a deeply personal film in a way that many if not most fail to realize, especially when seen within the broader context of Furie's filmography. He took a dime-novel piece of material and made it sing as cinema, and as personal testament. Its sequels cannot touch it, even with Ken Russell in the saddle.

When I initially interviewed Joe Dante, he thrilled at describing the way Furie redefined camera grammar and camera language itself in the three Wild Angles films. The "best cinema" isn't necessarily

Right: In the visually radical *The Ipcress File*,
the camera is always hiding, and the images are always filtered
through sometimes unlikely elements/items of the mise en scene.

"the most cinema" (in fact, many of the tastemakers will treat you to a fevered jeremiad on this very point)—but sometimes, it's at least some of the most interesting and groundbreaking. Dante's words in a video interview I shot: "Seeing *Ipcress*, *Appaloosa*, and *Naked Runner* when they were first out, I thought to myself, 'Wow, this guy is truly reinventing cinema!'" Pity too few others noticed, though as mentioned, he was very popular with the early film school generation. To call these compositions decorative is to imply that they are too schematic or clinical—tokens of an empty or self-indulgent formalism. To me, they are merely trying to say the unsaid using a purely visual language, showing us another way to see.

With Marlon Brando in *The Appaloosa* (1966) and Frank Sinatra in *The Naked Runner* (1967), Furie goes into familiar *Ipcress* territory vis-à-vis masculinity, especially the idea of men trapped by geometry. As much as Brando and Sinatra's characters attempt to act in *The Appaloosa* and *The Naked Runner*, more often they are acted upon. In *The Naked Runner*, the warehouse interrogation scene between Sinatra and Derren Nesbitt builds tension with cutting that jangles the nerves and framing that builds expectation and then disorients. In so doing, Furie places us squarely in the jumbled mind of Sinatra's character, who is manipulated and, for lack of a better word, mindfucked by virtually every single character in the film. It's the decoupage of the *Get Out* "sunken place" sequence extended on its own to feature length. The word "decoupage," the coalescing of montage and mise en scène, is central in any serious discussion of Furie. His sense of it is overt and almost grandly overstated, but he uses the concept of anamorphic eyescan to startle the viewer. As Karen (Nadia Grey) emerges from behind Sinatra's head, we observe in real time (and considerable "reel estate") her landing in the frame, standing relative to our protagonist in voided space. On an offscreen line of dialogue comes a hard, almost jump-scare cut to the interrogator, now fully occupying the part of the frame where Karen had stood in the previous shot. Strangely, somehow, this hyper-formalist scene (the approach of which might be seen as "clinical") is rendered subjective. How can wide open space feel claustrophobic?

As Furie ascended to the A-list of directors, he remained there for the better part of over two decades as Hollywood opened its doors to him. His first project at the outset of his new American life was *The Lawyer*, finished and copyrighted in 1969, but released in early 1970 amid Paramount's dire existential crises, when mega-

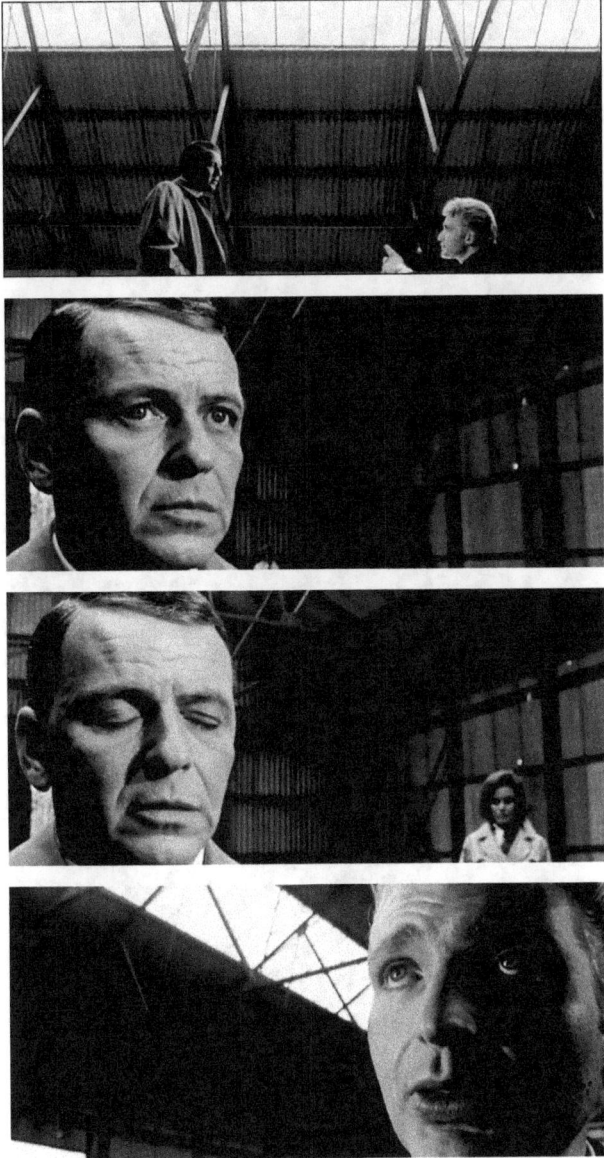

Above: Furie's images in *The Naked Runner* are often geometric. His editing sometimes shocks the system, as in this warehouse interrogation sequence. A line of dialogue almost becomes a spatial jump-scare.

Furie induces paranoia by making negative space prominent, altogether re-envisioning what an over-the-shoulder shot can convey. He also toys with mise en scene distortion in similar ways. For example, one memorable facial close-up favors a bright red lampshade.

budget flop musicals and old-guard extravaganzas were drowning the studio in untenable debt. Furie had wrapped production on *The Lawyer* a few months before his evening with film students at the Directors Choice event, telling them, "Now I've just finished a picture where I was terrified to do anything with my camera. And that's wrong. I was absolutely terrified because I told you, I'm like everyone else. Buckle under. No let's just have it straight. So the first four weeks of shooting, everything was straight. Then I say screw it, I'm going to do what I want to do within reason, and I did it, and it's going to be a hodge-podge picture. But maybe no one will know."

To what extent is *The Lawyer* a so-called "hodge-podge picture"? While elements of Furie's then-established trademark visual style are certainly present, it is decidedly more tempered. His heretofore preferred themes, of male anxiety and wounded masculinity, redefining—and often stripping down—the macho, were upstaged by a new thematic concern with notions of duty and commitment. In a distinctively man's world, one that men have codified strictly for themselves, this duty and commitment is both valorized and weaponized, sometimes as a surrogate for intimacy. In *The Lawyer*, attorney Anthony Petrocelli was born years before the character got his own television series. His method, motto, and mantra are recited in the film's very short theatrical trailer, which was specially filmed as a promotional rather than extracted from the feature itself.

> Petrocelli: I don't keep a cat or dog because they eat too much, little kids bore the pants off me, and when I go to a ball game, I root for the visitors. I never cried at a wedding or a funeral, I never sent a Christmas card, and I cheat on my wife, if I have the time. But I have one soft spot: a man is innocent until proven guilty.

Petrocelli is a creature not necessarily of habit, but of duty. His small Colorado cattle town has already, for all intents and purposes, tried and convicted his client before he's even gone to trial. The inquest scene, staged at a rodeo cum cattle auction ground with a grotesque, hooting-and-hollering public, is unmistakably a Furie creation, harsh, angular distortions and all. Yet Petrocelli remains duty-bound. As Andrew Sarris once wrote, "If John Ford's heroes are sustained by tradition, the Howard Hawks hero is upheld by an instinctive professionalism." This is true of most of Furie's duty-bound professional men. By doing, they exist.

This is certainly true of dirt bike racers Little Fauss and Halsy Knox in *Little Fauss and Big Halsy* (1970). They live in a world where one races first, then deals with the woman in labor afterward. The duo in *Little Fauss and Big Halsy* are a pair of rootless ruffians drifting around a "so what?" world, speed being their only need—defiant professional losers, in contrast to the professional winner in *The Lawyer*. In the latter case, by adhering to the type of professional code that Fauss and Halsy lack, Petrocelli can rest assured and enter his home justified. In two films, we see a juxtaposition of professional ethics.

One can also catch individual shots that rhyme with very specific earlier stagings in Furie's corpus. In the case of Fauss and Halsy, and Reg and Pete from *The Leather Boys*, two fraught reverse tracking shots visualize male interdependence. Furie becomes a king of parallel eyeline (i.e. unmet eyeline, with characters in dialogue looking the same direction, not at each other, but at or beyond the camera itself) with the prevalence of such shots. The earlier, British *The Leather Boys* and *Little Fauss and Big Halsy* are, in many ways, companion films. These are not your ordinary male buddy, or male bonding, films. In the words of Robert Redford's Halsy Knox, "Once is cool, twice is queer." *The Leather Boys* floated a number of questions about male intimacy and its contours, which echo forward with *Little Fauss and Big Halsy*:

How much can one effectively "stretch" the boundaries of a relationship that is, or at least seems, non-sexual and "innocent," especially as it exists between two men?

How much latitude does one have before the chaste and spiritual connection shared between friends, kindred spirits, and fellow travelers crosses an undefined line, to possibly become something else?

How much are we willing to give of ourselves to this other before the burdens of personal discomfort and social barriers prohibit further exploration?

How much is the notion of this gray area still taboo, even in a modern society that is progressive concerning matters of sexuality and sexual orientation?

Images that rhyme.
Above: *The Leather Boys*. Below: *Little Fauss and Big Halsy*.

Of course, the taboo persists because men, especially heterosexual men, are a guarded species. This code of behavior is especially souped-up in *Little Fauss and Big Halsy*, where male intimacy is sometimes achieved outside of what is defined by the clearer eros expressed in *The Leather Boys*. For Fauss, it is his porous emulation and hero worship of Halsy, and that sometimes manifests in coveting and sleeping with the same women. Fauss even tries to become Halsy in the final act, assuming the worst aspects of his identity, with his brazen devil-may-care swagger. Furie still visually frames both dynamics, of men sharing themselves with other men, in precisely the same way.

Appearing on a podcast to talk about *Restrepo* (2010), filmmaker Sebastian Junger recounts how his co-director on that film, Tim Heatherington, observed that war "might be the only situation where young men are free to love each other unreservedly without it being mistaken for something else." Heatherington ventured this theory while he and Junger rolled their documentary cameras amid a fusillade of gunfire. This idea is present in *The Boys*

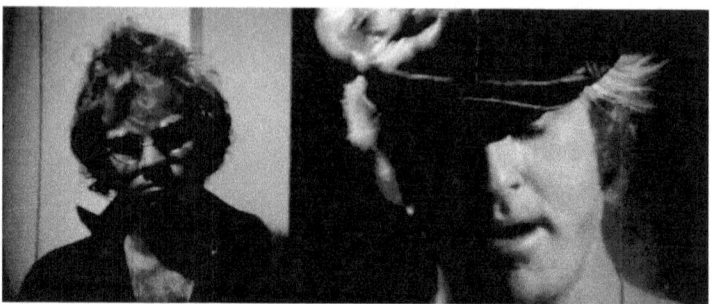

More examples of parallel eyelines.
Above: *Little Fauss and Big Halsy*. Below: *The Leather Boys*.

in Company C (1978) as the third manifestation of Furie's focus on male bonding, and the constant struggle against being misconstrued. *The Leather Boys*, *Little Fauss and Big Halsy*, and *The Boys in Company C* skillfully plumb a "median" realm of the human relationship. This informal trilogy is a capstone of Furie's long-running thematic preoccupation.

Lady Sings the Blues (1972) presents something of a left turn: Furie's first film with a female protagonist, and the first not directly assaying heretofore favored themes. They do emerge in a secondary sense, however, amid the film's primary fixation on artistic process. The men in this film aren't wounded or diminished. They're confident or gallant, with quick wits and million-dollar smiles. Some stoop to interfere with Billie Holiday's profession, and her professionalism. If you hear Furie discuss those with whom he most enjoyed collaborating, the first words out of his mouth are, "He/she was a pro," without fail. That's the highest compliment he pays those with whom he spent six decades of a creative life. Being a pro is exalted, and anything that impedes the professional ethic is to be skewered or outright vilified, as it tends to be in *Lady Sings the Blues*, in the guise of those feeding Holiday smack. The film happened to be one of the biggest hits of Sidney's career. Even the notoriously hard-to-please Pauline Kael loved it, unreservedly lauding it for, "personality—great quantities of personality."

The film that followed *Lady Sings the Blues* is the very definition of a "getting the band back together" picture, one that reconvened the cast and crew of a fresh success in the hope of recapturing lightning in a bottle. *Hit!* (1973) is Furie at his most Hawksian, a film that I call *Rio Bravo* for the *French Connection* era, designed with a kind of cinematic jazz language not far afield from what audiences experienced in *Lady Sings the Blues*. Richard Pryor manically improvises comic bits in both, within the contours of serious dramatic character parts. These are early dynamic showcases for his estimable talents as a performer. As in *Lady*, drugs play a central role in the story of *Hit!* An ad hoc, handpicked, assembled, "family" of haunted citizen professionals find common cause in the dirty task at hand, wiping out the fat-cat overlords of the Marseilles narcotics trade. Ringleader Billy Dee Williams and others in his ragtag special ops unit have seen family members die of overdoses.

Hit! is an uncommonly slow burn, focusing on the recruitment, formation of, and amity between, this motley crew hit squad, rather than the cheap-and-easy thrills one might associate with such an exploitation-flick premise. It's Furie's own crime family,

Again, a masterful use of widescreen. A hand lifting into frame from screen left affords our male lead (Billy Dee Williams) a dramatic and highly cinematic entrance into Furie's *Lady Sings the Blues*. The emergence of Williams' smiling face out from the shadows in the following shot is any photogenic star's idea of movie heaven.

Hit! is a film of meticulous ensemble shots, with its ragtag family of "amateur assassins" packed together in the same frame as much as possible.

his Dirty Half-Dozen. Stacked ensemble shots convey the power of collectives in ways that reflect the William Wyler frames that inspired Furie's kino-eye as a young man. The actual killings are reserved for the final movement of the 135-minute runtime, often executed at a passive distance. The film's only chase sequence is a subjective affair full of panicked, reactive handheld shots from respective backseats. *Hit!*'s raison d'être is all about the characters and how they interrelate. The sequence set on the eve of the assassinations resonates emotionally, and gets to Furie's humanism. Of course, humanism isn't a rarefied commodity, but again, films like *Hit!* normally cannot afford such luxuries. *Hit!*'s mix of genres and tones clashed with the expectations of the moviegoing public in 1973. These days, however, it has caught on with a growing number of admirers who praise how unclassifiable it is.

Furie's wild departures from film to film always put him at serious odds with any appraisal of his status as auteur, and no departure in his oeuvre was more radical than moving from the Mediterranean cloak-and-dagger of *Hit!* to the shadowy urban corridors of the romantic comedy melodrama *Sheila Levine is Dead and Living in New York* (1975), another Furie picture that defies easy categorization—as Furie once put it, "neither fish nor fowl." The Harrisburg born and bred Sheila Levine arrives in Manhattan to make her fortune, to both find a man and fulfillment in a creative career. In an affirmative return to themes of duty, commitment, and professionalism, there's strapping suitor Roy Scheider's evolving attitudes vis-à-vis monogamy, as well as Jeannie Berlin's efforts to realize her professional ambitions. Gail Parent's novel stands in dramatic contrast to the film that bears its title. Rarely has an adaptation had less in common with its source, likely in the whole of movie history.

For good or for ill—I say for good—the film of *Sheila Levine is Dead and Living in New York* is a vehicle for Furie's preoccupations, guided in part by a Jeannie Berlin script rewrite that he sanctioned and oversaw. This all sounds like a recipe for disaster, and it was at the time of release, but today, divorced from hyper-awareness of its vicissitudes and the public's affection for the Gail Parent bestseller, *Sheila Levine* can be experienced as one of Furie's finest, packed with the distinctive compositions and stagings and prevailing themes and ringing humanity that were his stock in trade. One prominent critic even called his shots "Ozu-like." One of the studio execs called the lighting "too dark" and "noirish." Just to recount, that's noirish Ozu-like shots in what is supposed to be a romantic comedy cum melodrama. Words that come to mind are experimental, risk-taking, sui generis.

Furie's spatial configuration motifs in this period are also of note. For instance, one can delight in *Hit!*'s ensemble shots while noticing an apropos penchant for threes in *Little Fauss and Big Halsy* and *Sheila Levine*. In the former, he fashions two-to-one and one-to-two configurations, to visually communicate the third-wheel tensions between his characters, while *Sheila Levine* revels in the imbalance of triangulation. Once again, as in his Wild Angles Trilogy, he traps his protagonist in his treacherous geometry. As in Wyler's films, we're invited to participate, and our eye can elect to focus on any element in these complex frames, and keep scanning for new information.

He directed one more romantic fantasy, the ignominious and ill-fated *Gable and Lombard* (1976), which frames the eponymous lovers as carrying on in secret to avoid bad publicity and possible

Sheila Levine is Dead and Living in New York is a film of extended takes and "one-ers." This shot runs six minutes and manages to hold every second of its screen time.

Furie heightens suspense and expectation with peripheral action. Foreground characters are pushed to right or left extremes, with background action vying for dominance in the rest of the frame, as in multiple shots from *The Boys in Company C.* Furie customized William Wyler's deep focus work to create a new graphic style tailored for his own sensibility.

career death. It's another Furie film to its core because it asks, does professional duty trump personal commitment? With the gleefully irreverent *The Boys in Company C* (1978), he turned his attention back to themes of, this time, very literal duty, in what is objectively one of the best films of his career, and one of the greatest of all war films. Furie and his co-writer Rick Natkin consciously lift the familiar archetypes of classic American war films, especially World War II movie models, and explode the tropes of those archetypes for a whole new era of doubt, disillusionment, and cynicism. The formulas have been re-adapted and reconstituted for a war no one really believed in fighting. Furie registers pre-established empathy with playfully diverse stock characters: Brooklyn Italiano, black, Southerner, and eccentric free spirit (newly manifested in Craig Wasson's hippie dude). Audiences had easily embraced such ensembles before, but amid the injustices of a new, highly criticized foreign conflict, Furie uses collective uncertainty to strip these stock types down to their barest humanity. All is accented with a biting, anarchic, but far more subtle humor than in Kubrick's later carbon copy picture *Full Metal Jacket* (1987). More accurately, Furie's unit recalls William Wellman's own Company C in *The Story of G.I. Joe* (1945). There is even a dash of *M*A*S*H* (1970) for good measure (with its kooky climactic soccer game).

He would triumph yet again with *The Entity* (1982), following two misbegotten projects—*Night of the Juggler* (1980) and *The Jazz Singer* (1980), which he quit and got fired off, respectively. He shot about a third of *Night of the Juggler*, and one can distinctly sense a Furie sensibility and imprint in the script he co-tailored with writing partner Rick Natkin; thus I include the final product in the Furie canon. The Furie professional and the wounded male are in conflict in *Juggler*, and they make their presences known in the ways we have by now come to recognize, using some of the same visual grammar. On the occasion of the film's rediscovery and major theatrical re-release in 2025, the film's star, James Brolin, told a journalist, "[Replacement director] Robert Butler is more like a basketball coach than a director. He doesn't have an understanding of actors and what they may need and what makes each one unique. It was a lot different than Sidney, who nurtured you." He also recalls that Furie had the shoot so well mapped-out with his cinematographer Vic Kemper that essentially Butler just followed his template. "Bob Butler couldn't really modify or minimize it. It was Sidney's vision."

Perhaps my favorite reading of *The Entity* is Michael Atkinson's: "There may not be, outside of David Cronenberg's wonder cabinet, a more nitro-powered horror-movie metaphor hell than that fueling this post-*Exorcist* remnant. It's like the movie is writing its own library of fiery feminist theory. It remains unnerving and savage, arguably the most eloquent movie ever made in Hollywood about the struggle of the sexual underclass." If Furie had, to this point, spent a career studying and probing the wounded male, with *The Entity* he pulls focus on a hapless female victim of wounded masculinity in extremis. Daniel Pirie in the *Time Out Film Guide* keenly observes, "The film's men are so uniformly creepy, and its heroine so strong and sympathetic, that apart from a couple of unpleasant moments the story often seems less like horror than feminist parable." It's a tough, terrifying summation—a crowning achievement—of a remarkably vigilant, clear-eyed run of pictures, prefiguring other similar successes like Todd Haynes' *Safe* (1995). It's no small wonder that Martin Scorsese named *The Entity* "one of the top ten scariest horror films of all time," or that experimental artist Peter Tscherkassky repurposed the film for his groundbreaking short *Outer Space* (1999).

The failure that followed *The Entity*, *Purple Hearts* (1984), gains with repeated viewings, standing as the middle entry in Furie's formal "Vietnam Trilogy" (2001's *Going Back* being the final), but is a flawed last outing for Furie the Artiste. As an unofficial updated treatment of Richard Brooks' wartime romance *Battle Circus* (1953), *Purple Hearts* occasionally retreats into memorably vivid combat set pieces and painterly battle landscapes that, when separated out from the larger film, showcase some of Furie's best work as tactician and scenarist. The popcorn-palooza *Iron Eagle* (1986) chronologically draws a distinctive line in the sand between Furie art and Furie junk, though *Ladybugs* (1992) can potentially be weighed as another entry in the director's fixation on wounded men, with a neutered Rodney Dangerfield dressing up his teenage stepson as a girl to win a soccer championship to earn the respect of his fiancée and boss. It's by no means anywhere near prime Furie, but it's there if one is open and wishes to further probe a director playing a rotten hand at a game that has altogether changed. It was his last studio picture; from there, he gratefully retired into the direct-to-video market.

If you are a Furie enthusiast, budding or otherwise, some of the direct-to-video pictures are highly entertaining and worth seeing, namely *Hollow Point* (1996), *In Her Defense* (1999), and *Global Heresy* (2002, released theatrically in some territories, released to

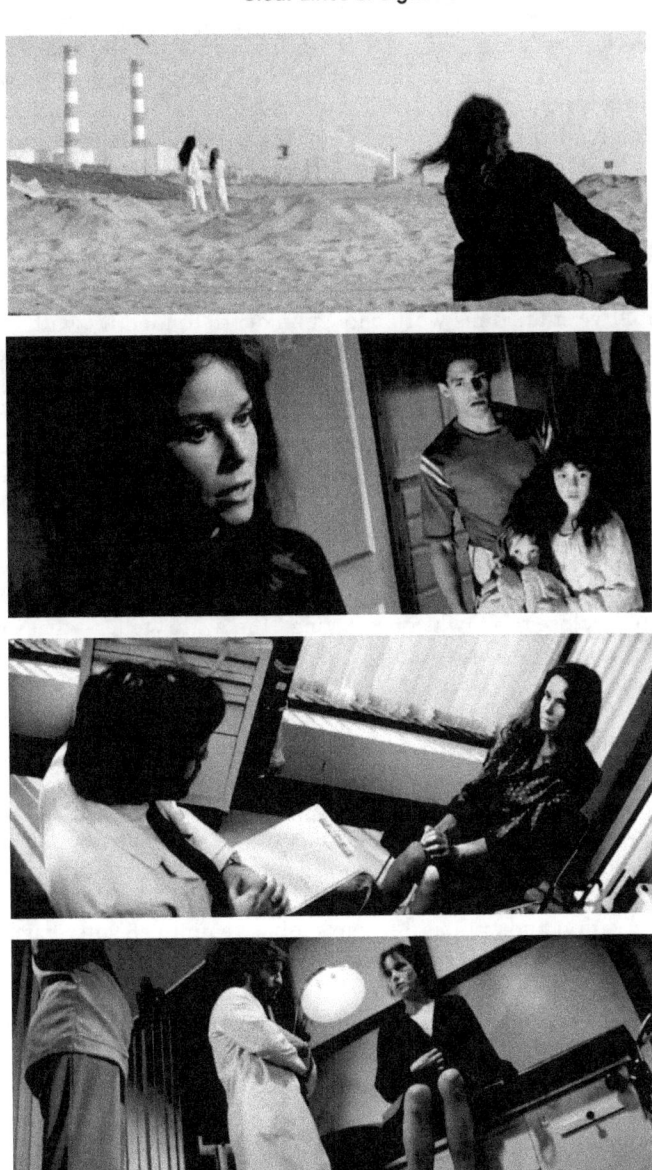

After fifteen years, Furie returned to the visual radicalism of his Wild Angles Trilogy. Though the films in between are tempered in comparison to these four, they are still visually audacious and often innovative.

American video as *Rock My World*), but most of the projects in this period telegraph a filmmaker who'd built himself up (with his brand) during a vital period of American studio moviemaking. Paramount, above all, offered Furie the freedom to operate mostly unmolested. His seven Seventies films all sport bittersweet endings that dangle interim success but signal long-term ambivalence, self-reflection, or cost. What becomes apparent, to me and to other surveyors who've cared enough to look closer at Furie's corpus to find one of our most exciting overlooked directors, is his authorship. I've studied his work enough in depth to identify, with ease, what I call Furie-isms, what you might call peculiarities of presentation that make him unique and confer on him that all-important component to auteurism: a voice, all his own.

As he told another film student on the night of November 23, 1968, "I think you can go out and do something on film that's very important. But I think even more important is to understand what a movie really is. You know most of us forget. It's not shots and it's not cameras and it's not all of that. And in a funny way it's not even acting. It's a story and we all forget that. It's a story." That sounds awfully close to Hawks once saying "I'm a storyteller—that's the chief function of a director. And they're moving pictures. Let's make 'em move!" In the case of Sidney J. Furie, his stories are all part of a picture, one with both literal and metaphorical clear lines of sight. And narrative arcs that rhyme, often with assonance, not unlike any auteur.

As Andrew Sarris concluded about Hawks, "That one can discern the same directorial signature over a wide variety of genres is proof of artistry. That one can still enjoy the genres for their own sake is proof of the artist's professional urge to entertain." This observation and appraisal to me sounds reminiscent of what I've expressed about Sidney J. Furie, ever in this sense the professional who's gone an unthinkable distance in eluding radar detection, by his own deliberate design as much as anyone's blind spots. He's covered literally every genre, but eyes wide open, one is bound to discover a treasure trove of *films maudits*, and classics that most never knew were so personal to their director. I'm a dedicated, unflappable Furie-ite, and a Furie-ite I shall remain. He's a great director, and the word, I'll repeat, is great.

Afterword: It recently came to my attention via still photographer Brian Hamill that Woody Allen discussed Sidney Furie "several times" through the decades as an "underrated director." Hamill has worked with Allen on twenty-six of his films and is still in touch with him—he is eagerly returning to Woody with news that there's a book on Furie. The influence of Sidney J. Furie is no longer something that can be belittled or mocked. Everyone from Vittorio Storaro, who almost worshipfully told Sidney that he cribbed visual ideas from *The Ipcress File* for *The Conformist* (and also lauded the impact his film made on the Italian film students of his generation), or Kubrick who cribbed his own *Full Metal Jacket* from *The Boys in Company C* (with Tarantino recently saying that the Kubrick film is "certainly no *Boys in Company C*, which is magnificent"), or Joe Dante who thought Furie was re-inventing movies when he saw his sixties work, or Philip Kaufman who waxed poetic about what *The Appaloosa* meant to him back in its day, or Peter Medak who marveled then and now at Sidney's innovative visual sense. Cinematographer Stephen Burum claimed that his three greatest director collaborations were with Coppola, De Palma, and Furie. All these people know that he used cinema *as* cinema. Whenever I've met name directors and tell them what I've done, Furie lovers and admirers crawl out of the woodwork. It's about time the critical establishment answered to just how beloved he is among the people who make the films they have long loved.

Theatrical Feature Films: *A Dangerous Age* (1957), *A Cool Sound from Hell* (1959), *During One Night* (1960), *Doctor Blood's Coffin* (1961), *The Snake Woman* (1961), *Three on a Spree* (1961), *The Young Ones* (1961), *The Boys* (1962), *The Leather Boys* (1964), *Wonderful Life* (1964), *The Ipcress File* (1965), *The Appaloosa* (1966), *The Naked Runner* (1967), *The Lawyer* (1970), *Little Fauss and Big Halsy* (1970), *Lady Sings the Blues* (1972), *Hit!* (1973), *Sheila Levine is Dead and Living in New York* (1975), *Gable and Lombard* (1976), *The Boys in Company C* (1978), *Night of the Juggler* (1980, with Robert Butler), *The Entity* (1982), *Purple Hearts* (1984), *Iron Eagle* (1986), *Superman IV: The Quest for Peace* (1987), *Iron Eagle II* (1988), *The Taking of Beverly Hills* (1991), *Ladybugs* (1992), *Hollow Point* (1996), *Top of the World* (1997), *In Her Defense* (1999), *Cord* (2000, a.k.a. *Hide and Seek*), *Going Back* (2001, a.k.a. *Under Heavy Fire*), *Global Heresy* (2002, a.k.a. *Rock My World*), *Drive Me to Vegas and Mars* (2018), *Finding Hannah* (2022, a.k.a. *Hannah Cohen*)

Other Notable Works: *American Soldiers* (2005), *The Four Horsemen* (2008), *Conduct Unbecoming* (2010)

Left to right: Author Daniel Kremer, Sidney J. Furie, and
Ted Kotcheff together at a Telluride Film Festival cocktail reception.

2. Looking to Get Out
The Ted Kotcheff Vision
(with a Peek into Michael Ritchie)

Presented is the voiceover script for the video essay "Looking to Get Out: A Comparative Analysis of the Ted Kotcheff Vision," as included on the North Dallas Forty *Blu-ray package. It has been slightly revised for this print edition.*

> I'm not the judge of my characters—I'm their best witness.
>
> Ted Kotcheff's directing motto,
> extrapolated from Anton Chekhov

If Ted Kotcheff had directed only *Wake in Fright* and *The Apprenticeship of Duddy Kravitz*, he would be a great filmmaker. That his filmography sports other great films like *North Dallas Forty* and *Edna the Inebriate Woman* should lay to rest any doubt.

No one was better at making films about social climbers than Ted Kotcheff. His characters only ever look in one direction: up. Whether it be catching up with Laurence Harvey's *Room at the Top*, Joe Lampton, character in *Life at the Top* (1965), cavorting through cockamamie scheme after cockamamie scheme with the ethically impaired but enterprising *Duddy Kravitz* (1974), or bumbling around a swarm of monied libertines with the so-called "two schmucks" in *Weekend at Bernie's* (1989), Kotcheff's heroes want to do more than merely "make it." In fact, there is one concise phrase that sums up pretty much all of their collective ambitions: "looking to get out." Yes, that is the title of a (rightly) much maligned Hal Ashby movie, but it could have also been the name of many Kotcheff pictures, because it best describes his characters' ultimate ambition, out of any number of other ambitions: to bust out, bust loose, or climb. Whatever the situation, his restless characters have internalized their first-act circumstances as a cage, a prison, sometimes of their own making, and they're pushed to varying outrageous extremes in their escape attempts. This makes

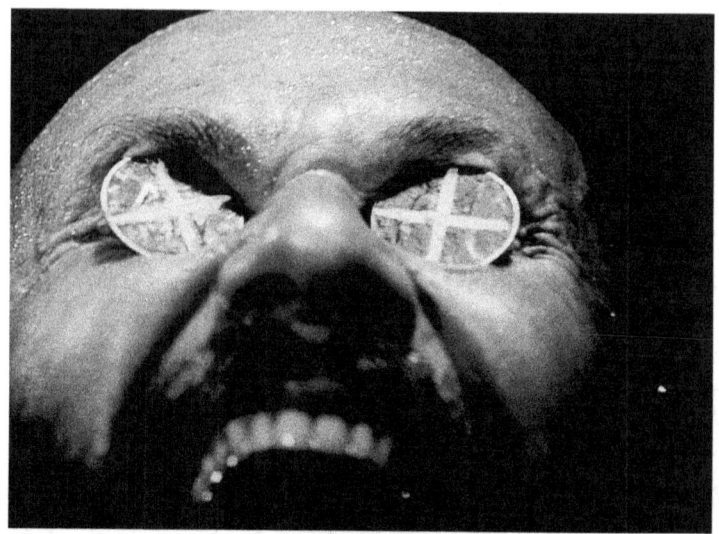

Wake in Fright

for a consummately Canadian vision of life and reality. The idea of escape, almost always through climbing, is as pervasive a theme, and trope, as the notion of "competition" is for Michael Ritchie. It also speaks to the influence of Kotcheff's best friend, and onetime roommate, author Mordechai Richler. Kotcheff heroes are creatures of undying shpilkes (Yiddish for "restless" or "on edge"), as Richler might have interpreted it.

In *Wake in Fright* (1971), a disenchanted and just plain stymied schoolteacher finds himself marooned in an Australian Outback town of hard-drinking degenerates who strip him of any last shreds of sanity and dignity. All he wants to do is get out of the Yabba, the town in the Outback where he is stranded. Or does he? In *Fun With Dick and Jane* (1976), the eponymous heroes played by Jane Fonda and George Segal are desperate to maintain their upwardly mobile lifestyle, despite major setbacks, so they break up the monotony of their middle-class existence and resort to outright criminal measures, re-inventing themselves as a bourgeois Bonnie and Clyde. In *North Dallas Forty* (1979), professional football wide receiver Phil Elliot, played by Nick Nolte, is sick of the game—and not just football. On some level, he can take the brutality of bone-crunching tackles and concussions, but another kind of gamesmanship is too much to bear. The corporation is mashing his body more than those tackles and concussions, and once again, he's looking to break out. In *First Blood* (1982), John Rambo takes the expression "busting out" to the nth degree, similar to Gene Hackman's character in *Uncommon Valor* (1983). Even the title character in his formative telefilm *Edna the Inebriate Woman* (1971), as well as the principals in *Two Gentlemen Sharing* (1969), a relatively early theatrical film, share an angst that fits within the Kotcheff parameter.

But that's never to say that Kotcheff is complacent, or that his work numbs you with this favored theme, or that his movies are ever predictable, because they're anything but. The auteur theory at least partly subsists on the idea that a filmmaker maintains an abiding philosophy, a vision of life, a unique way of looking at the world, over the course of multiple films. In essence, and in the best way, they make the same film again and again and again. Hollywood as a machine doing this is horrid, but a director working things out over the span of decades, that's the good stuff. Kotcheff is a director who proves this maxim, though he has never been recognized for it, nor has this unifying thematic concern and style been properly identified or examined either in print or in dialogue.

A film like *North Dallas Forty* tends to feel more thematically tied to the work of director Michael Ritchie. Ritchie, for his part, was obsessed with competition and the specifically American-born-and-bred competitive spirit. His picture of America was always one of a breakneck race for whatever brass ring was up for grabs. For Ritchie, America itself is dog-eat-dog competition, and it's further defined by the pageantry that surrounds those contests. The sins of fathers, who marinate the collective us in the overriding, overwhelming need to win, is the big red bow around Ritchie's carefully wrapped packages. So consumed with the idea of winning is the typical Ritchie character that he often does not know what to do or how to proceed when he actually does win, i.e. when he must exist beyond the contest itself. Therein lies the Ritchie protagonist's often comic, sometimes tragic flaw: victory is always only bittersweet because the victor is doomed to be haunted by the existentially fraught question of "What now?" evoking that Peggy Lee tune, "Is that all there is?"

Ritchie's major films—what I'll call his "primetime pictures"— about competition, most of which were made in the Seventies, namely *Downhill Racer* (1969), *The Candidate* (1972), *Smile* (1975), *The Bad News Bears* (1976), *Semi-Tough* (1977), and *An Almost Perfect Affair* (1979), revel in characters with a competitive edge, a drive to win, to come out on top at all costs, as others relish the spectacle. A few later movies in his filmography reflect this idea as well, especially *Diggstown* (1991).

But despite whatever threads exist between Kotcheff and Ritchie, at least in relation to *North Dallas Forty*, their sensibilities do not align much at all in terms of focus. If Ritchie had directed *North Dallas Forty*, it would have been a very different kind of picture, one about how a win seduces and overrides the need for personal betterment, and therein lies the power of a director. Ritchie would have constrained his lens to the games, the fandom, the integral, primal nature of gridiron thrills. The spectacle is the thing itself. *Semi-Tough* runs the closest to anomaly in the above lot, in that it strays most from the literal field of competition, revealing the "self-help" craze as a kind of competition of its own. "Who will reach enlightenment?"—custom nirvanas and enlightenment of whatever school or cult are the true Lombardi Trophy of *Semi-Tough*.

Kotcheff, however, wants us to consider why anyone within would ever dream of living without. While Ritchie's characters thrill in the race, the Kotcheff protagonist is always restless. Their resting state is restless. They are always striving for something better, tortured by the thought that somewhere, someone else has got it good, or better, or best. As intimated earlier, this "looking to get out" sentiment, or in some cases theme, is pervasive among a number of other Canadian artists. There might be an edge of animus, a sense of "get me out of here" in classic Canadian cinema, but it is this very animus, counterbalanced with a certain custom-designed warmth toward home and hearth and roots, that frames and invigorates the work of such Canadian artists. We explicitly get shades of that in Kotcheff's two Mordecai Richler adaptations, *The Apprenticeship of Duddy Kravitz* (1974) and *Joshua Then and Now* (1985). Duddy, for one, wants "home" to exist on his terms, with himself the king of the domain, namely St. Urbain's Street in Montreal and the majestic lake property over which he will one day reign and hold court, by any means necessary. It's not enough for these places to just be. The Kotcheff character, if he or she must stay and cannot wrestle loose from a detested status quo, must have their say, must have control as they alone define it.

Duddy Kravitz outlines the nature of his ambition in one key scene, when he reads his disdainful uncle the riot act. "You don't think I read? I've read books, big deal! They always make fun of guys like me... pushers, guys who want to get somewhere. You know, I'm going to have a place of my own one day. And when I

The Apprenticeship of Duddy Kravitz

do, there aren't going to be any superior shits like you to laugh at me or run me off."

Kotcheff characters are at their worst when they are forced to suffer the indignities and ignominy common to those who have simply surrendered. In this sense, social class regularly factors in. Things are tough all over. In the case of *Fun With Dick and Jane* and *Weekend at Bernie's*, the system seems to have failed his characters. The bureaucracy cripples the duo in the former, crushing their ambitions to the point that they must work around that system — I put that very euphemistically. When George Segal's character visits the unemployment office, he is confronted by a dowdy old lady, who berates him thus: "That's a pretty nice suit, mister. You've got some nerve coming in here dressed like that! People in here need this money. This ain't no damn joy ride!"

For the "two schmucks" in *Weekend at Bernie's*, that corporate ladder ain't for climbing. Not for them, anyway — until, that is, they unwittingly and inadvertently nail their well-heeled boss (who they see as a personal hero) for embezzlement. The window opens for them, they get their feet in the door, but to what end? In covering his tracks, Bernie intends to butter them up and then ice them at the first opportunity. Instead, he winds up iced himself, a corpse propped up as an insatiable party animal. "A fine mess," indeed. We're forgetting, though, that the two schmucks are Kotcheff characters. None of that is going to keep them down. What do they do? Look to escape the boss' idyllic island, taking Bernie with them and prolonging an increasingly awkward charade.

The Blake Edwards-adjacent, Bosch-like party sequences
of Kotcheff's films, seen here in *North Dallas Forty* (1979) (above) and
Weekend at Bernie's (1989) (below).

The film is an outrageous comic funeral for the Reaganite mega-yuppie, which literally beats the corpse of Gordon Gekko, or one who at least vaguely resembles him. *People* magazine described the film as having "aged into something close to respectability." In his memoir, Kotcheff himself writes, "The film's satirical edge about human behavior connected with audiences. These two guys want something so bad, something that they've never had and may never have again—a weekend of extravagant partying at the beach—that they don't care if their host is alive or dead. The people around them are so selfishly involved in their own needs that they don't notice Bernie is dead."

Weekend at Bernie's' foggy, maybe problematic reputation is the direct result of critics somehow, and almost absurdly, failing to recognize that it is a satire far more than it is slapstick farce. In *Fun*

With Dick and Jane and *Weekend at Bernie's* alone, you'll meet a formidable quartet of Kotcheff climbers. Kotcheff's last major studio release, *Folks*, written by *Bernie's* scribe Robert Klane, sees a self-satisfied yuppie living what he thinks is his best life, only to get his ass handed to him oh-so-royally by no less than his senile father, a kind of one-man geriatric demolition squad. Just fits right into the Kotcheff-verse, does it not? In terms of Canadian film-maker character archetypes, this text has defined and addressed two: the "Furie professional" and the "Kotcheff climber."

North Dallas Forty marks the first time Kotcheff directs a film shot in the 2.35:1 aspect ratio, one of only four out of a total nineteen theatrical features that uses this wider canvas. As in *Weekend at Bernie's*, Kotcheff presents big party scenes in a way not too far afield from Blake Edwards. I'd even venture to say that *Weekend at Bernie's* is a brat-pack Blake Edwards-style farce. Kotcheff's party sequence staging in both *North Dallas Forty* and *Bernie's* is like a Hieronymus Bosch painting. There is activity and constant motion across each frame, movement here, there, and everywhere. It isn't enough to simply mingle. Every performer's body must be fully engaged and "in it to win it," the "it" being our attention as viewers. In the context of the latter phrase, that certainly applies to the warrior jocks at the boisterous bacchanal in *North Dallas Forty*'s first act. Kotcheff uses the 2.35:1 widescreen canvas to paint a frenetic tableau of men behaving badly.

Five years prior, Paramount released Robert Aldrich's *The Longest Yard*, another beloved pigskin gridiron masterpiece. With Kotcheff's movie, Paramount delivered the flipside of *The Longest Yard*. In Aldrich's movie, the game is all his characters have, and they invest everything into it—more of a reflection of a Ritchie picture than a Kotcheff picture. In *North Dallas Forty*, the game is ancillary and dominates in a way beyond control. There is disquiet in Kotcheff's portrait of a football franchise, a coalition—I say coalition and not merely "team," just to be clear, as the corporation is part of this uneasy portrait. There is a weary cynicism here. Conflicting interests emerge, even brinksmanship. The vision is dark, far more satirical. There is a sense that the players are controlled, that they're muscle-bound marionettes, that the whole big damn muscle-mashing affair is engineered, manicured, clouded by that which is totally external to athletes huddled at a given yardline plotting their next big sweep. As Nick Nolte says in the climactic scene, "Team?! Oh, for Chrissake, we're not the team! [The owners and the corporation] are the team! These guys right here, they're the team! We're the equipment! We're the jock straps, the helmets, and they just depreciate us and take us off for their damn tax returns. That's what that is! But that was good when I played... because the only thing that's real in that game *is* me, and that's enough."

Methinks Nolte's Phil Elliot would appreciate sharing a cold can of Foster's with Gary Bond's character John Grant in *Wake in Fright*. Duddy Kravitz might enter the scene to try to hustle both of them. Meanwhile, Bernie is probably stashed in the john someplace. It's a picture.

In Kotcheff's 1982 drama *Split Image*, a young man from a fairly well-off family has never had to climb much of anything, apart from the high bar in gymnastics. His future is essentially predetermined and success is ensured. He grew up in a cushy neighborhood, where even the paper boy is chauffeured around in a Rolls. What is "up" for this character? Religion, of course, a literal "higher" calling—a Moonie-esque cult. This Kotcheff hero is born at the top, yet still climbs, albeit in a way we haven't seen in other Kotcheff pictures. If a Kotcheff character cannot ascend in any other way or form, well then reach for God, of course... in all the wrong ways. And even when he's rescued from the cult, it's still not enough for Kotcheff. Whereas the similar film *Ticket to Heaven* (1982) ends after a successful deprogramming, everything tied up neatly as if all is solved, Kotcheff mines further psychodrama.

After Michael O'Keefe is rescued, with the help of James Woods' skeezy cult-buster, a bitter confrontation ensues between the deprogramed son and his parents, who are concerned that he's not further along in recovery. Elizabeth Ashley, as mother, goes on an angry tirade in front of her husband and son: "Wait just one minute. See, I've sacrificed most of my life on that holy altar that they call motherhood, right? Always putting you first, your needs, your life. And I thought now that you were grown, maybe we can get on with our own lives. But did you ever think about that? No, you threw that away, you just scuttled that, but tell me something. What about me? What about me?! No, don't you see what's hanging him up, and us up, and turning our lives into some holy hell, is the young man's abdominal twitch over some small-change syphilitic hippie trash."

Even the mother is "looking to get out" in this profoundly Kotcheff-ian dramatic arrangement. If Kotcheff had directed *Ticket to Heaven*, we know he would have never let things rest at its deprogramming-as-panacea resolution, because chronic restlessness must manifest somehow in a Kotcheff picture.

There were many cult-themed films in its time, but *Split Image* mines the material for further psychodrama, even after our hero has been "cured."

It has become all too easy to enmesh *First Blood* (1982) with the rest of the blood-and-guts Rambo franchise. If the people behind the franchise told you they'd invented the word "jingoistic," you'd believe them. But people too often forget that the Kotcheff original has other things on its mind. There are two modes of Kotcheff bust-outs: literal and social. In some manner of speaking, he was an "escape artist" in all senses of the word "escape." *First Blood* ranks with *Uncommon Valor*, *Winter People* (1988), *Wake in Fright*, *Switching Channels* (1988), and the Western *Billy Two Hats* (1973, humorously dubbed "Shalom on the Range" for being shot in Israel but set on the American plains), as the literal breakout pictures. Others like *Life at the Top*, *Two Gentlemen Sharing* (1969), and *Duddy Kravitz* are the social breakout pictures. *Weekend at Bernie's* is the one mix of both literal and social, but *First Blood* at least hints at this mix as well.

The first act of *First Blood* sees John Rambo enter a town called Hope in a dissociative state. Treated, like many other grizzled Vietnam veterans, as the flotsam of society, he doesn't merely bust out of Hope (a bit of symbolic nomenclature if ever there was one) when the abuse gets impossible to bear, but he busts out of contemporary America itself by bringing the war home to his abusers—and to a society that merely wants to thoughtlessly move on. Novelist David Morrell could not have asked for a better interpreter of his novel than Ted Kotcheff, who, in infusing a high-octane Sylvester Stallone vehicle with social conscience, rendered a difficult-to-package message palatable and even entertaining, without sacrificing the hard, pointed edges. Rambo is a quintessential Kotcheff hero, an escapee who will never truly be free of the angst that irrevocably shackles him.

First Blood.

The idea that "A director makes only one movie in his life. Then he breaks it up and makes it again," originates from Jean Renoir. To build on that thought, with each iteration, with each new effort, a new dimension gets added. New depths are revealed and a sweeping picture of a career is built. Ted Kotcheff built a career on the steady dimensioning of themes and narratives centered around people obsessed with figuring out which way is up. Watching them figure it out, or not figure it out, to climb or not to climb, that is the question. That "slings and arrows of outrageous fortune" bit? For Ted Kotcheff, that's entertainment!

Theatrical Feature Films: *Tiara Tahiti* (1962), *Life at the Top* (1965), *Two Gentlemen Sharing* (1969), *Wake in Fright* (1971), *Billy Two Hats* (1973), *The Apprenticeship of Duddy Kravitz* (1974), *Fun With Dick and Jane* (1976), *Who is Killing the Great Chefs of Europe?* (1978), *North Dallas Forty* (1979), *Split Image* (1982), *First Blood* (1982), *Uncommon Valor* (1983), *Joshua Then and Now* (1985), *The Check is in the Mail...* (1986, uncredited), *Switching Channels* (1988), *Winter People* (1988), *Weekend at Bernie's* (1989), *Folks* (1992)

Other Notable Works: "The Greatest Man in the World" (1958, CBC-TV), "The Bird, the Bear, and the Actress" (1959, CBC-TV), "After the Show" (1959, CBC-TV), *The Human Voice* (1966), *Dare I Weep, Dare I Mourn* (1966), *Edna the Inebriate Woman* (1971), *Ackerman, Dougall and Harker* (1972)

3. Cruel, Usual, Necessary
The Silvio Narizzano Vision

This is the voiceover narration script of my documentary Cruel, Usual, Necessary: The Passion of Silvio Narizzano, *which was released in 2024. Though reading this as a printed essay paints a fairly exhaustive picture of the filmmaker, a viewing of the documentary only enhances one's understanding. Various talking-head interview subjects, not transcribed here, also make their own crucial points.*

> The demons are innumerable, appear at the most
> inconvenient times, and create panic and terror.
> But I have learned that if I master the negative forces,
> I can harness them to my chariot.
>
> Ingmar Bergman, *Images: My Life in Film*

The lyrics of the hit song "Georgy Girl" performed by The Seekers in the 1966 box office sleeper of the same name, could just as well exclaim "Hey there, Silvio!" in reference to the film's director, Silvio Narizzano. Any level of research into his life is forthcoming with the revelation that he suffered from lifelong, sometimes debilitating clinical depression, and once you recognize how that openly manifests in the work he left behind, it validates the question in these easily revised lyrics, "Hey there, Silvio, why do all the film buffs pass you by? Could it be you just don't try, or is it the pain you share?"

Silvio Narizzano's body of work haunts me. Images, moments, and even specific edits randomly flash in my mind over the course of a day. I've never encountered a director more ignored by the cognoscenti who so vigorously and even contentiously wrestled with his identity from project to project. In two mid-career movies especially, he does so extremely aggressively and even violently. The films so often feel like the work of a filmmaker who hated himself, but could only ever love himself through what he put on film. Each project was something like a step beyond exorcism, exploring human cruelty and modes of self-flagellation. Happy endings aren't really prevalent or prominent in the Narizzano-verse. Any break from suffering comes wrapped in newspaper and not glossy gift-paper. Nothing ever goes down easy, no gift has frills.

You might be thinking, Silvio Narizzano sounds like a name that could easily adorn the opening titles of a spaghetti Western or a *giallo* picture. But the altogether forgotten, long overlooked, and hence unexamined Narizzano worked in neither subgenre. He came close on some occasions, one might argue, helming an American studio Western uncommonly replete with dense arthouse symbolism, in a manner that feels very "European," at least from a commercially conscious vantage point. But if Narizzano's big-budget oater *Blue* (1968) is remembered at all today, it's for losing Paramount a pretty penny. This was a familiar story for its director. Looking at it now, it's so glaringly obvious that this queer-coded, visually fastidious, painterly-to-a-fault Western never had a shot at scoring the type of business it needed to justify its existence on the financially embarrassed studio's ledger, but as the psychological X-ray of a filmmaker who consistently, until his death in 2011, called it his best work, it shimmers with a pained and painful pathology both disquieting and beautiful. That phrase alone could sum up the entire filmography, the oeuvre, of Silvio Narizzano, that most Canadian of Canadian auteurs, and undoubtedly the most covert, the most hidden in plain sight.

He made only nine theatrical features, though I personally count eleven, because two of his later telefilms could, and should, have been rolled out theatrically, lest we forget that certain successful BBC films got playtime in U.S. arthouses. I'm referring specifically to his swan song *Young Shoulders* (1984), based on a novel by John Wain, and *Staying On* (1980), from a novel by Paul Scott, starring Trevor Howard and Celia Johnson, reunited 35 years after their timeless pas de deux in David Lean's *Brief Encounter* (1945).

Silvio's beginnings, in the early days of television, and his career behind the camera in general, resulted from first failing as an actor. On one fateful night, he forgot all his lines during a show, only to then run off to the newly formed Canadian Broadcasting Corporation to launch his directing career. His early television credits are far too numerous to fully account, but for now, let's begin with what I would argue as Narizzano's first substantial credit: *24 Hours in a Woman's Life*, a Stefan Zweig adaptation produced for live television,

Narizzano writes his early television productions in cinematic longhand.
This opening sequence from *24 Hours in a Woman's Life*,
starring Ingrid Bergman, plays with time and space in
unexpected ways, considering this was filmed and broadcast live.

starring Ingrid Bergman, Rip Torn, and Jerry Orbach. Stefan Zweig as adapted by John Mortimer was very much his bailiwick during his days as an in-house director at ITV. To this point, Narizzano had shepherded much in the way of sophisticated, you might say high-brow material to the small screen, having had his go at ace writers like Arthur Miller and Reginald Rose. This culminated in his production of the Paul Bowles translation of Jean-Paul Sartre's *No Exit* as a "Play of the Week," as well as an early screen rendering of *Death of a Salesman*.

24 Hours in a Woman's Life, broadcast on March 20, 1961, opens with an elaborate long take that appears difficult to have executed live, considering the need for a precision in timing, camera staging, and choreography. The camera begins as voyeur, framing five performers at some distance through an ajar parlor doorway. As the camera cranes away, in a wholly self-narrating move, meaning a move that the camera itself decides, rather than a move merely motivated by character mobility, Narizzano keeps us eavesdropping upon the offscreen conversation, still within earshot, while Ingrid Bergman slowly comes into view, and eventually into close-up. Our director takes extra time to foreground Bergman while he lays the expositional groundwork, further defining the space in the process. This is both elegant and efficient, even exquisite, and way beyond the paygrade of your average television director.

Narizzano is of course in the service of the writing here, and in live television, a director has only so much latitude, but be this any indicator, he was already thinking about the craft of directing through a cinematic prism. There's dimensionality in his craftsmanship, even at this point. And, much like in his later productions, a love story can never simply be a love story. Romance is unmasked and exposed in many guises, a beguiling lie, a head game, something that Narizzano's theatrical pictures would bear out further.

Ted Kotcheff, another Canadian émigré to England in the late Fifties, remembers in his memoir, "I sought out a former CBC drama director, a very good one named Silvio Narizzano. I had served as his assistant director in my early years at the CBC and learned a tremendous amount about directing from him." Sidney Furie, another in that same generation of Canadian filmmakers, credited Narizzano as his mentor, saying, "Silvio showed me the ropes. I don't know what I would have done without him." That school or clique, those I'll call the "Anglo-Canux" (i.e. the early crop of Canadian directors who left Canada for work in England) looked up to him. He pioneered their wilderness, in a manner of speaking.

Because Narizzano was content for years working in television, he transitioned into film later than those he mentored, including Kotcheff and Furie. Narizzano finally graduated from television to the movies when Hammer Studios came calling, debuting with *Fanatic* (1965), released stateside as *Die! Die! My Darling*, starring Tallulah Bankhead, making her withered and weary final bow in an unforgiving post-*Baby Jane* landscape. Long venerated female performers in their dotage, like Bankhead, Davis, Crawford, and De Havilland, could only hope for scraps of dignity smuggled between the lines of often demeaning material. But *Die! Die! My Darling* wasn't your average "hagsploitation" outing. Stefanie Powers plays a young woman who is terrorized and held captive by Bankhead, her deceased fiancé's domineering, religious fanatic mother, an oppressive gargoyle of a woman with a demented vendetta to cleanse souls in often the nastiest ways. It sounds lurid, but there's more here. While it's diverting on a pure surface level, under the surface, there are aspects and elements that unmistakably parallel Narizzano's later work. Narizzano himself said in an interview, "I liked it because it was mad, theatrical, weird, and I was very interested in working with Tallulah Bankhead."

With her imperious whiskey-and-cigarettes growl, Bankhead perfectly embodies the Puritan viper Mrs. Trefoile, whose invidious zealotry stifles, smothers, and subjugates not just the people around her, but the environment itself. The true pinnacle of that environment is not a crucifix or an altar, but the likenesses of Mrs. Trefoile's departed son Stephen which are enshrined around the estate, central in her superficially holy but thoroughly unholy domain. One particular painting of Stephen towers above the rest, and Mrs. Trefoile's fawning orbit is true as the sun and the moon, and best not tested. One is struck by Stephen's beauty—the word "strapping" doesn't fit, and the word "handsome" doesn't suffice, but "beautiful" certainly does. Film writer Ken Anderson writes that he was "anticipating a third act revelation that Stephen was gay," because as Stephen's presence is keenly felt throughout the film, we are often made to gaze upon a face that is acutely "too pretty." His very pretty shadow is cast over all from beyond.

Film historian David Del Valle expresses it more directly: "Stephen was obviously a big queen, and the film's alternate title should have been *My Son Was a Friend of Dorothy*." More to the point, though, everyone seems to skirt around something best left unsaid whenever they speak of Stephen. This culminates in Powers' defiant declaration that Stephen committed suicide, fronted by the

Tallulah Bankhead and the all-important portrait of her absent gay son, Stephen, in *Die! Die! My Darling*, a.k.a. *Fanatic*.

appearance of an auto accident. The obfuscations abound. Knowing that Narizzano was himself gay, and tracking the trajectory of his work from this debut film onward, this is no accident.

Narizzano's sensibility is unmistakably very gay, unabashedly so. Though he was quite evidently overcome with festering guilt, and armed with a prevailing sadness that was palpable on screen, he clearly believed in the concept of sin and penance, sometimes deadly penance. And though he remained a man who still needed to whisper the comforts and tell himself tales, as to keep passing the open windows, he never hid from himself or cowered from the truth of his essence. Upon his divorce from BBC performer Beatrice Lennard, he met writer, noted Beat poet, and drag performer Win Wells, and their live-in relationship lasted until Wells' death in 1983 at the age of 50. I could very well guess the cause, but for lack of official confirmation, I'll leave you to deduce the nature of my theory. (Editor Thom Noble recalls that Wells dreamed of one day opening a gay nightclub called Sissy's, and consistently pursued this ambition for many years.)

It is said that Narizzano never recovered from the loss of Wells—in fact, his lifelong clinical depression went into overdrive. His final film outing, *Young Shoulders*, a very internal, first-person chronicle of family tragedy, unflinchingly channels his own mourning and crystallizes his evergreen inability to cope. It distills his existence in his last 30 years of life. He'd find some solace at a Buddhist retreat in Chislehurst in southeast London, then at a Bible study enclave in Greenwich, where he spent his last years a recluse, long retired and shut off from television and cinema. Here, the biographical record, the life of the artist, does a great deal of heavy lifting in giving us clarity into the work and its voice.

Where do you channel grief when you can't forgive yourself for what you've lost, or what you feel like you've lost? Bearing this in mind, it's crucial to note the presence of religious fanaticism throughout many of his films. It's his favored accent mark, a prevalent trope and motif. The contrition of a bad Catholic is nestled between every cut. Part of this is Canadian as well, the national inferiority complex, the hankering fear of never measuring up, needing to atone for it. Hanging over all of it, as an umbrella, is the fragility of self-definition.

Mr. Narizzano was far from alone in these fixations. Religion is often trenchant in Canadian cinema, especially among those either *from* or working *in* Quebec, lest we forget a later hit Quebecois movie called *Jesus of Montreal*. But a useful point of contrast with Narizzano exists in yet another Montreal film with explicitly Catholic themes, *The Pyx* (1973), directed by Harvey Hart. A Magdalene-like sinner is redeemed through self-sacrifice in the face of desecration. In refusing to desecrate the host during a black mass, she hurls herself to her death to defy evil and realize eternal salvation. A prostitute, a woman whose life, in religious terms, is predicated upon sin, is martyred. A saint is born, in Montreal, Silvio's hometown. But though very Canadian and very Quebec in character, this certainly isn't Silvio's movie. There is no such salvation in Silvio Narizzano's movies. Not a whiff of it. What we get instead, all too often, is an almost systematic degradation. If Narizzano had directed *The Pyx*, we'd fade out on the desecration, on a woman broken, hollowed out by a distance from grace that's untraversable.

His film *The Sky is Falling* (1975) opens on heroin-addicted expat artist Dennis Hopper's cruel, racially charged humiliation of a visiting lady friend. It then hastily transitions, like a quicksilver escape hatch, to a vivid, drug-enhanced freakout in which Hopper, marooned at rock bottom, is tortured by memories of a hyper-religious mother wailing the hymn "Are You Washed in the Blood of the Lamb?"—an acute trauma that perversely stimulates. The film ends on the same hymn, once every cast member has been sufficiently defiled.

Christian hymns pop up in many of Narizzano's films. *Redneck* (1973), a.k.a. *Senza Ragione*, ends with little Mark Lester tearfully singing "Just As I Am" bloodied and depleted, aimlessly firing a pistol, signaling a messy complicity, a polluted entry into adulthood, a larger entropy. The song itself: more blood for more lambs. *The Class of Miss Macmichael* (1978) introduces Oliver Reed's repressive Headmaster Sutton with a flat chorus of "Onward Christian Soldiers"—appropriate behavior for a hysterical, moralizing boob, a kind of male Mrs. Trefoile figure, and yet another unambiguous villain to boot.

On the notion of morality and moralizing, no one was ever going to mistake *Georgy Girl* (1966) as a monument to traditional morality. Indeed, though the film was a commercial success, truly the only major one in the whole of Narizzano's career, it was assailed as racy and something of an offense against decency upon its original release. Yet the film does moralize in its way. Building out the idea of shame and self-flagellation, *Georgy Girl* prompts us to consider the walls we build between life's beautiful people and ourselves. Narizzano is there to tell us that we do build them ourselves;

Lynn Redgrave's Georgy in *Georgy Girl* peering through a crack in a literal partition between her life's 'beautiful people' and herself. This is a key point-of-view shot in the film.

the beautiful people don't need to build them for us. Taking responsibility is learning to settle for what you think you deserve, or what you've been conditioned to think you deserve. To find pleasure in the pain of that coming to terms. When you're a gay man like Narizzano, no matter how much culture progresses, you never lose sight of what that means. Narizzano's characters are outsiders, specifically ones who revel in a life to which they've acquiesced, as it's known to both fall short and provide inadvertent benefits, what one might call fringe benefits. His characters habitually become either battered nurturers or forever entrapped reprobates inured to any and all indignities.

Georgy Girl is somehow the peppiest, most upbeat picture in which cruelty comes naturally to nearly every character. Everything is punitive, and what Narizzano chronicles is the true "killing of Sister George," if you will—or at least an attempted spiritual murder. There are no real positive reinforcements for Georgy—the recurring characters in her existence are all down on her, despite her good nature. She's a breath of fresh air for James Mason's Mr. Leamington, but he's got some patently strange designs himself, in offering up a contract outlining her role as mistress, with all perks and privileges delineated in print. But while the film's ending may very well be cynical, it's not misanthropic—a tough balancing act. There is some twisty cheer in this cynicism. As Georgy hitches her wagon to eternity, the Seekers supply their own commentary in the cheeky new verses that conclude their chart-topping song: "Who needs a perfect lover when you're a mother at heart? / That's all you wanted right from the start. / Well, didn't you?" Some might argue that *Georgy Girl* is Narizzano's most known and recognized picture, his main claim to having made an undisputed classic, because of the song. Yes and no. Reducing its virtues to the song conveniently overlooks the film's Oscar nominations for Lynn Redgrave and James Mason, its National Board of Review honors, as well as the Berlin Film Festival directing award it won for Narizzano himself.

To recap the story, Georgy is the homely girl living with Meredith (Charlotte Rampling), an icy, heartless bitch who is a glamorous but unwholesome projection of the era's Swinging London. Georgy dallies with Meredith's manic boyfriend Joss (Alan Bates) while fending off the attentions of middle-aged millionaire Mr. Leamington, who desires her as mistress under exclusive contract. Meredith gives birth to an unwanted child who she neglects and scorns with a rancor unbecoming of any warm-blooded specimen, which ignites Georgy's naturally maternal instinct.

In *Georgy Girl's* third act, an infant is abandoned by her birth mother, and confiscated from her eager would-be adoptive mother, not unlike the Bette Davis character in Irving Rapper's *Now, Voyager* (1942), a not too dissimilar story, from yet another gay director, about another mistreated young woman who stumbles into motherhood, warmly and tenderly raising someone else's child, as a means of righting the wrong done to her. The endings of both films are also not traditional happy endings. This famous line could be Georgy's whole outlook from the ending of her movie forward. Georgy doesn't ask for the moon, the baby is enough. She "has the stars." Irving Rapper and Silvio Narizzano

Jules et Jim reversed, *Georgy Girl* is decidedly not. Georgy can only be but a fixture in the hip world of her swinging roomies.

certainly are not respectively the social realist that a Ken Loach is. Theirs is a cockeyed, enhanced realism, in contrast to Loach's contemporary BBC drama *Cathy Come Home* (1966), which made a pointed statement in its bitter indictment of how social services prey on destitute mothers. The social worker threat is present in *Georgy Girl*, but this is simply to remind us what our very able title lady is up against, in spite of her pluck, and the resources at her disposal. And, well, let's put it this way: there's no quasi-royal wedding in the wings in a Ken Loach case study.

Perhaps people could see themselves in Georgy, or project themselves onto her. Narizzano had never given the audience a more sympathetic surrogate, and never again would he. He threw them a bone and gave them an appealing avatar, peripherally looped in to the countercultural currents without getting swept up in its implicitly soul-crushing mandates. Narizzano does moralize against Meredith, and ultimately instructs us in what to think of Joss, especially as he makes his pathetic exit from the film.

The film's editor, John Bloom, remembers Narizzano's strategy for directing Alan Bates' performance. "Anything that was off-key, Silvio loved. And as such, the film is always off-key. The performances are pretty manic and over-the-top. But that's how Silvio wanted it. And there's a consistency in everyone's style, which works so wonderfully well. And ultimately, when there's a shift in gear toward the end of the film, with Joss and Georgy on the boat to Greenwich, it's very moving. And somehow it wouldn't have been moving if the rest of the film hadn't been

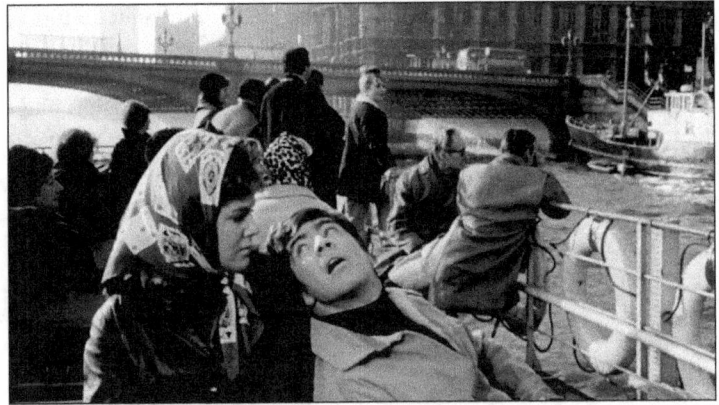

Alan Bates' Joss is revealed for who is really is, on a boat trip to Greenwich toward the end of *Georgy Girl*.

over-the-top." Joss, though he tries to endear himself throughout the runtime, never acquits himself. In one scene, Joss calls Georgy a freak because of her overriding need to save people. None of Narizzano's films are love stories, but a taste of being wanted or deemed important, even in a soi-disant context, as in the case of Mrs. Trefoile in *Die! Die! My Darling*, Treasure Evans in *The Sky is Falling*, and Headmaster Sutton in *The Class of Miss MacMichael*, invites folly—sometimes bloody folly—and disaster. With Georgy's case alone, it invites a shot at happiness, even with the caveats.

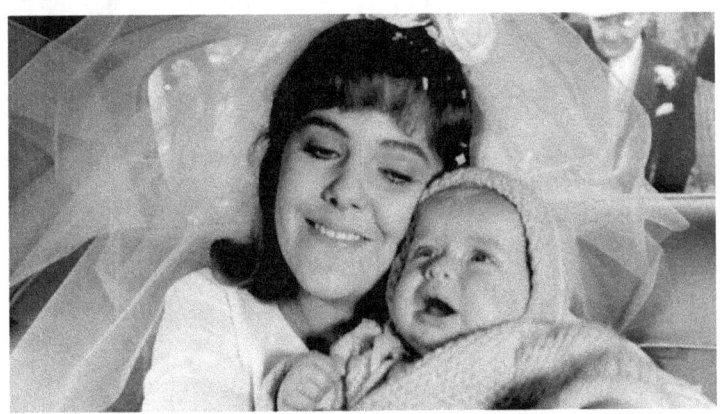

Bittersweet endings for us, but Georgy herself doesn't seem to mind. She's another in a line of mistreated movie women who raise someone else's child to emotionally right the wrongs done to them.

Narizzano's follow-up, *Blue* (1968), is a distinct left turn when one considers that it immediately follows a British New Wave megahit like *Georgy Girl*. One might even say it's a bit of a non-sequitur. Terence Stamp is indeed a curious coup of emergency casting, replacing Robert Redford after he pulled out at the eleventh hour. But he has a strange, insouciant, sexually ambiguous quality that likely endeared Narizzano enough that he undoubtedly came to prefer Stamp to someone more logical or expected (though critics of the era, and even today, malign the film for what they perceive as fatal miscasting). Stamp was a sturdy remnant from Narizzano's background in British cinema, a fresh, multi-purpose reminder of his own pedigree. And if you truly come to know Narizzano, you know there could have been no one for him but Stamp, save for maybe a young Dirk Bogarde.

On that note, *Blue* is point-blank the most homoerotic and queer-coded classic Western since Roy Ward Baker's British oater *The Singer Not the Song* (1961), which starred Bogarde, memorably clad in skintight leather pants. And when I use the term "classic Western," I am referring to those made before the emergence of the revisionist Western later into the Seventies. Both *Blue* and *The Singer Not the Song* are lambasted in often near-sighted ways, and I have a sense that for many, it's an objection to that very queer-coding. Historically, the critics who ripped apart *Blue* in 1968 preferred their Westerns and action-oriented pictures uber-masculine and stripped of sly sexual signals and a certain breed of... we'll say sensitivity. Or they liked it in certain vaguely satirical, winking contexts, as in Howard Hawks' *Red River* (1948).

Blue is of a different breed altogether. For instance, having our title hero kiss a man square on the lips before killing him in cold blood, as Stamp does in this opening, probably got under the skin of these classicist detractors. It was enough so that they could dismiss the whole affair as "pretentious" and "ponderous," and support their argument by pointing to other elements, like the twangy Manos Hadjidakis music score. What were Terence "Sergeant Troy" Stamp and the *Never on Sunday* guy doing in an American Western? With that audacious artistic choice alone, Narizzano was, again, looking for any means to broaden a genre perhaps overly familiar to movie audiences, considering the glut of Westerns then on the market. His fellow Anglo-Canux Sidney J. Furie and Ted Kotcheff proved that Canadians abroad making Westerns yielded some offbeat results. Furie with the visually radical *The Appaloosa* (1966), and Kotcheff with the geographically radical *Billy Two Hats* (1973), set on the American plains but shot in Israel. The anomalies of *Blue* drove its most truculent critics to madness and invective.

Blue is Narizzano's only movie shot in anamorphic wide-screen, and his framing and staging make the most of his new canvas size. Narizzano's camera ogles his very beautiful leading man... and yes, once again, "beautiful" is the word, as opposed to handsome or strapping, echoing the exaltation of the dead son's male beauty in *Die! Die! My Darling*. This is Terence Stamp in his *Toby Dammit* period, framed as the consummate picture of male beauty... and Narizzano wants you to see what he sees, without focusing so obsessively and snarkily on his muddled, peculiar, admittedly anomalous accent, which critics indeed tended to zero in on with poison-penned glee. Veteran cinematographer Stanley Cortez often ground production to a halt with his perfectionism, but he captures some of the most striking CinemaScope day-for-night work this side of James Wong Howe. Though there is a painterly elegance omnipresent throughout the film's starkly iconographic visuals, the story isn't terribly complex.

Narizzano and cinematographer Stanley Cortez's
expressive lighting and painterly compositions.

Doorway shot or not, *Blue* is no John Ford Western, and its own take on masculinity is in deep conflict with classic Western models.

In terms of story, Stamp is the eponymous Azul, the adopted white son of Mexican bandito Ortega, played by Ricardo Montalban. With Ortega's violent gang, Azul routinely raids peaceful Texas settler colonies until, one day, he defects. Wounded in the bedlam of a raid after rescuing the young Joanne from being raped by his adoptive brother, Azul is nursed back to health by Joanna and her father Doc Morton, played by Karl Malden. The Canadian Joanna Pettet had also become a Swinging London luminary, so *Blue* is very much the Swinging London Western, an honorable distinction in my book.

Like Georgy, who reinvents herself as wife, mother (of someone else's baby, mind you), and as kept woman, Blue also reinvents himself, once a killer, now a martyr for the innocent, torn between two lands and two worlds, just as Georgy is torn between the safe, the stuffy, and the traditional, as embodied by Mr. Leamington and her parents, and the hip, progressive sphere of existence as embodied in the pad she inhabits with Meredith and Joss. In the latter, she can only be but a fixture. Yet neither George nor Blue are totally at home in either of their choices. Their duality forever roars lion-like. It could be argued that the bandito "Azul" persona is homosexual, while the made-over, more civilized "Blue" persona attempts to be (or pass as) heterosexual. Though Narizzano was tearing himself away from the illusion of being "straight" immediately following his 1966 divorce from a woman, it was still daring and even dangerous to live as "out" in 1968. In this sense, Narizzano's own personal dilemma is reflected in the film he loved the most.

Blue attempts to forge a new path forward for himself, away from human cruelty, that engine that propels the Narizzano-verse, but dies dramatically in realizing either or any destiny. Narizzano himself said in an interview, "And finally, in the middle of the river, he's trapped between the two sides. He cannot go back to Mexico, and if he went back to America, what could he do? He couldn't become a peaceful farmer with them now that the blood is in his nostrils again, probably forever. I don't think that the end is pessimistic, for death is a kind of escape; he welcomes it, he walks into freedom. Isn't that what young people are doing today? They are choosing deaths of different kinds." This is about on par with, and very close to, Narizzano's heart: a man wrestling with identity, as he himself had always done, positing death as a viable way out of a cycle of confusion and disarray. The interviewer reflects this back at him, telling him how very nihilistic this sounds. He never bothers to deny it. No optimist, he. It's almost an epithet. This is not a Western built on mythopoetic construction and deconstruction, common to Ford and his generation of sagebrush bards. *Blue* is something tailored more for the roiling youth movement of its day, and to its director's pathologies.

Terence Stamp is a very different Western hero in *Blue*, the only Swinging London American oater.

Stamp winds up the classic Narizzano protagonist, in a river of
uncertainty between two conflicting identities on either side.
Blue is the ultimate film of Narizzano's identity poetics.

Blue is also unique for having hosted a second so-called
"piggyback movie" shot simultaneously on and around its set,
likewise under Narizzano and producer Judd Bernard's Kettledrum Films banner. The never-theatrically-released but thankfully
now available *Fade-In* (1968/73), directed by Jud Taylor, stars
Barbara Loden as one of *Blue*'s film editors, who falls in love with
Burt Reynolds, a local cowboy hired as a production assistant.
Sparks fly for them on location, and in one scene, Loden teaches
Reynolds a film editing concept known as the Kuleshov effect,
using Narizzano's own raw footage. Terence Stamp makes a quick
cameo in *Fade-In* and behind-the-scenes footage is sampled liber-
ally. There's nothing quite like this double feature in the whole of
cinema history.

Evidently, Paramount first thought that *Blue* was the beginning of a beautiful friendship with Narizzano. Robert Evans
announced a second Narizzano project in early 1967, well before
cameras had even rolled on their first partnership; the studio
purchased movie rights for an adaptation of Don Asher's novel
The Piano Sport, the story of a music conservatory graduate who
ventures to San Francisco intent on living a bohemian life, only to
find himself stuck between two spheres of existence, like almost
every Narizzano protagonist. But *Blue*'s critical and commercial
failure, perhaps the biggest disappointment of Narizzano's creative
life, put that follow-up into turnaround. In insisting that he could
never top it, he made its defeat, and his own defeat, all the harder
to bear.

Returning to England with Win Wells, he started and promptly
departed the production of *The Man Who Had Power Over*

Women (1970) over artistic differences. If we're to believe replacement director John Krish, "He was rewriting the script with his boyfriend and it was becoming gayer and gayer, page by page, line by line. The studio wasn't happy and he was thrown off the film." There you have it: Fired for a gay sensibility. Editor Thom Noble recalls, "The rewrites were Win's, and Silvio walked when they were not accepted. His replacement was the least likely person to be handed such a project. There are so many not-so-wonderful stories behind making that film." Narizzano quickly rebounded, however, finding a more appropriate vehicle for his personal and artistic disposition, adapting a hit Joe Orton play to the screen for British Lion, in what would provide another hard left turn in a career now accustomed to the type of reinvention his own characters had routinely undergone.

Loot (1970) is a gay fantasia, awash in big, bold, swirling, psychedelic colors, not to mention editing trickery, oppressive but perverted religion, and most importantly, capital H Homosexuality, this time unconcealed without shame or winking coyness—all in a comedic context for once, and of course pitch black at that. Got a big heist scene? Why not have our two crooks burgle the booty totally in the buff, giving the other a kiss on the tuchus for good measure? This zany, refreshingly sex-positive adaptation is a bizarre little artifact, one that abjectly failed to satisfy fans of the play upon which it was based. There's credence to that, because *Loot* is about 30% Orton, 70% Narizzano. Call it an aesthetic, I guess.

What emerges is a colorful piece of camp, a lollapalooza of larceny, complete with, by now, easy-to-discern directorial touches. Once again, it's a parade of people out only for his or herself. Narizzano also experiments sonically, taking the narrational element of the *Georgy Girl* title tune, to approach something like a Greek chorus with Keith Mansfield's sometimes expository song verses.

The critical establishment was split. The nays called it "a sad example of the process of literary castration" and bemoaned that "all that is left is a caricature of the original." The yays dubbed it "*The Italian Job* for the queens, by the queens." Who could have said it better? My favorite is this dismissmal from *Time* magazine: "*Loot* is a fey demolition derby, resembling an unlikely hybrid of the Marx Brothers, Agatha Christie, and a training film for the Mattachine Society. Narizzano has directed the bad taste in bad taste." That sounds to me personally like a resounding recommendation, despite obviously not being the critic's intentions. Today, the film

With *Loot*, Narizzano no longer needed to hide any of his (very) gay material. Subtext became text in one aggressive swoop.

has its devotees, a kind of mini-cult. I think at the very least, most everyone, even detractors, will recognize that Lee Remick is demonstrably having a jolly good time, as a duplicitous nurse with a Marilyn Monroe bouffant and a jumbo crucifix dangling around her ample mammaries. Purely in terms of mise en scène, the hotel set is a chef's kiss of production design. I personally consider the film a quick stop at the amusement park on the road to electroshock therapy treatments. In other words, a little pleasurable excursion before arriving at two outrageously harrowing self-reckonings, as seen in *Redneck* (1973) and *The Sky is Falling* (1975). One online film critic called *Redneck* and *The Sky is Falling* paired together, "poisonous little morsels."

There's always at least one performer in a Narizzano film who is guided by their director to a scenery-chewing performance. In *Die! Die! My Darling*, it's Tallulah. In *Georgy Girl*, it's Alan Bates. And in *Loot*, it's Richard Attenborough as a bellicose inspector, or rather the caricature of a bellicose inspector (a campy compound), complete with Hitler moustache. Many saw Narizzano's love of playing-for-the-cheap-seats performance histrionics as a mistake, rather than choice or style. To me, I just know I'm in Narizzanoland, and I happily get swept with the tide. He directs with an eye toward, and a flair for, grand opera, bold burlesque, and drag performance level camp. Everything is a little bigger, a little overdone, sometimes tastefully, other times not so tastefully at all. What price tawdry?

No one gets to calm down or take a breath in *Redneck*, a.k.a. *Senza Ragione*, which translates from Italian as "Without Reason" — an apt description of various bloodthirsty but seemingly motiveless atrocities enacted at the hands of Memphis, a psychotic career criminal played with unchecked wackadoo delirium by Telly Savalas. Savalas goes berserk in this picture — he presents as a total fucking madman who overcranks every line reading and chews every last shred of scenery, but I'll be goddamned if it isn't fun to watch him.

The picture starts as what appears a very typical Italian Euro-crime flick, opening with a heist and a chase sequence. Two tough hombres, the coarse, crass, sadistic Memphis and the shrewd but animalistic Mosquito, execute a jewel heist, and when they commander a vehicle in the ensuing chase, they realize only later that there is a 12-year-old kid in the backseat. They make a sprint

Loot is a chef's kiss of production design and mise en scene, as demonstrated by its central hotel set.

for the Italian countryside, but it hardly matters where because Savalas swallows every landscape whole. This is no policier or *Bonnie and Clyde* crime-spree picaresque. Predictably, in Narizzano's hands, it morphs into something else: a *very* queer deconstruction of masculinity. And whereas *Georgy Girl* managed to be cynical but not misanthropic, *Redneck* goes all in on the misanthropy, and it's out to convince you that that misanthropy is delicious in its lean 88 minutes.

The film's thematic centerpiece is a scene that little Mark Lester shares with Franco Nero. In this case, it's not merely Narizzano's camera that ogles the buck naked Franco shaving in the mirror, but also young Mark Lester, who not just observes but actively leers at his dastardly custodian's sculpted bod, his timid words halting and smitten. After Franco exits for a rendezvous with the well-monied lady giving them shelter, Lester disrobes and emulates what he just witnessed. In Lester's moment of mimickry, an act of sexual idol worship that not so coyly broaches homoeroticism, the film expands. His spiritual and sexual communion is spoiled by a brutish intruder, as Telly barrels in through the chamber window. But the film asks, what kind of man can or does one become, who models that for us, and when? And what dimension exists, including sexual, in the boundary between model and subject... once again, between life's beautiful people and ourselves? And what if one's model is a creature of unadulterated, world-worn, survival-minded machismo? Film historian David Del Valle observes, "He's making a comment on coming-of-age, because when you're coming of age around that, you're not going to have a childhood. It makes you wonder if Narizzano had a childhood himself. Maybe his childhood was interrupted." *Redneck* is rite of passage as Stokholm Syndrome.

Truly Mark Lester had come a long way from his boyhood in the Oscar-winning *Oliver! Redneck* might be the most twisted coming-of-age film ever made, next to perhaps David Greene's *I Start Counting* (1969). It's a young boy's awakening on multiple fronts, and we leave him at the end as we left the ill-fated Blue, torn between two worlds, two existences, on the precipice, a step away from death. Blue dies accepting his fate. The character in *Redneck* will be reborn. But how? That's up for us to debate. What we've got is an unabating blitzkrieg of insanity that mixes tones so erratically and schizophrenically that many accused it of not knowing what it wanted to be. In his case, I would argue that there is merit in the schizophrenia. The pace of these shifts is breathless.

In this sequence, Redneck reveals Franco Nero, and reveals itself as not just another Poliziotteschi or Euro-crime potboiler. It is here, with little Mark Lester's gaze and mimicry, that the film expands.

Redneck is way, way "out there"—that's the best descriptor one could walk away with. I mean, what else can one say about a film where Telly Savalas is accidentally castrated by a camper hitch as he frivolously drowns the family of five inside said camper? He spends the rest of the movie with a bloodied crotch. Narizzano's designs don't keep a stranglehold on the course of the story, but they do make for incredulous reaction.

Like *The Sky is Falling* (1975), the Narizzano picture that immediately followed it, *Redneck* was born of the wicked pen of Win Wells. These two films exemplify Narizzano at his nastiest and gnarliest... and most mean-spirited. But also at his most unflinchingly introspective and self-effacing. I liken *Redneck* to Eugene O'Neill writing a squalid potboiler as performed by the most flamboyant drag queens. And I liken *The Sky is Falling* to Eugene O'Neill writing a Grand Guignol Manson Family drive-in exploitation flick in European exile as performed by strung-out drag queens. These two films are the electroshock therapy alluded to in the earlier metaphor. Cruelty is not merely the human engine in these two films, it's their basic currency: a symphony of sleaze and renewal.

The Sky is Falling, originally slated to star Rita Hayworth, Rod Taylor, and Terence Stamp, later released on video in the U.S. as *Bloodbath*, follows a group of boozy, jaded, embittered, and wholly pathetic expats without a prayer, mostly Americans and Brits, holed up in exile in the primitive, superstitious, sunbaked Spanish village of Mojacar, where Narizzano and Win Wells had a second home and spent many of their years together. A proto-cult of young, beautiful, mysterious interlopers—one might even call them temptationists, as in a posse of tempters and temptresses— arrive and prey on the individual weaknesses and desires of this shambolic group, teeing them up to knock them off one by one.

All the expats in *The Sky is Falling* are splinterings of Narizzano himself. In Carroll Baker's Treasure Evans, a character which channels her role in *The Carpetbaggers*, there's the has-been Hollywood starlet à la *Sunset Boulevard*, who is awaiting her grand comeback call, much like Narizzano no doubt awaited career resurrection after *Georgy Girl* offered him the world and *Blue* took it all away. In Dennis Hopper's Chicken, there's the self-hating artist and libertine haunted by the past's most embedded demons. In Richard Todd's Terence, there's the stiff-upper-lip Brit who both can't be bothered anymore, yet also can't get started. And in Win Wells' Allen a.k.a. Alice, there's the runty, very outré homosexual desperate

Narizzano's broken and depraved ex-pats are systematically picked off
by the pretty temptationists in *The Sky is Falling*.

for any warm body ready, willing and able enough to redefine love
at its most capricious. They are all Silvio Narizzano, the many
parts, aspects, and angles of the director, in ways almost too intimate to have shared with an audience. This project was something
like a step beyond exorcism, opening with a John Donne verse,
"But I do nothing upon myself, and yet I am mine own execu-
tioner," which sounds more like a confession than an epigraph.

It's unwise to frame these two Win Wells-scripted mea-
maxima-culpas as well-festooned pity parties, even when audiences mostly detested the results. Joseph Losey's *Boom!* (1967),
adapted from Tennessee Williams' *The Milk Train Doesn't Stop
Here Anymore*, might be *The Sky is Falling*'s closest cinematic relation. The film operates on symbols more than direct narrative cues,

laden with, but also predicated on, dense, diffuse imagery that asks the audience to do more heavy lifting than on average. The images that hit hardest are, for instance, of the strung-out Dennis Hopper with a real heroin syringe protruding from his arm. Hopper was as unleashed as ever during his post-*Last Movie* (1971) European exile, at his most tortured, frenzied, and deeply addicted, just a stop or two away from his spinning-out on *Mad Dog Morgan* (1976). Playing a sadomasochist was not a big ask, likely not even given another moment's thought, especially at this idle, fraught, loudly self-destructive juncture of his career.

And of course, there is also the unjust desserts of Win Wells' dolled-up gay layabout, impaled up the ass by a live bull horn. Generously, one could interpret this as something like the genital-mutilation-by-broken-glass in Bergman's *Cries and Whispers* (1972), reframed as mortal wound. It can be experienced either as the ugliest fit of self-abnegating onscreen violence imaginable for a long-suffering, even diffident gay director, or simply as a grisly but necessary scene that indexes on a pervasive, savage method of brute humiliation tragically familiar in gay-bashing incidents and gay-related murders, a fear rampant among gay men at the time, long before, and long after. Normally this would be performed with an inanimate or blunt object, but in the film's unceasing onslaught of symbolic imagery, the bull symbolizes virility and manliness as aggression—the deadly default power

The rape of the bull sequence from *The Sky is Falling* is likely the most disturbing sequence in all of Narizzano's cinema. The scene's victim is its own screenwriter Win Wells, Narizzano's longtime partner.

There is far more male flesh on display than female in *The Sky is Falling*.
Narizzano's is the gay male gaze epitomized.

of the heterosexual man, the sexual power elite, over the perceived fairy or sissy. Either way, once again, cruelty.

No one is acquitted, no one is saved. Treasure Evans' comeback call never comes, with the phone left floating off its hook in her pool. Each sybaritic transaction hastens the characters' demise. *The Sky is Falling*'s opening pre-titles sequence welcomes, or prompts us, to consider the sin of the transactional. One could read various abstract or ambiguous sequences in various ways, but it's the village location photography that lends the texture and the local color such an experimental narrative work requires. The village is a living space, which is to say a space that lives—quite the evocation of hell through the prism of an escapee's heaven or haven, both hobbled and sustained by ritual and sacrifice. And once again, there's the Narizzano trope of the partition between the beautiful people and the forever exiled outsider class, with the expats and the visiting temptationists who ritually put them out of their misery. All the staples, the same refrain, different verses.

The Sky is Falling found itself stuck in the Spanish censor board's movie jail when it failed to clear hurdles on frontal nudity, homosexuality, drug use, fornication, and "depicting peasants in a bad light." Narizzano told reporters years later, "The movie is sitting in a vault somewhere because I broke all the rules." After a single public screening that Narizzano and his producer Andres Vicente Gomez were able to finagle, *The Sky is Falling* didn't emerge until thirteen years later, only on a muddy video transfer under a new title. Alas, even if the censors didn't imprison and impound the elements, it's unlikely Narizzano would have had an easier time circulating the film. The film is one of the most intimate looks in the mirror ever committed to celluloid. A new digital scan of the original 35mm elements, transferred in 2023, reveals a visual dynamism that had gone altogether unappreciated since its aborted release.

Following this good, bad, and ugly diptych of death and depravity, Narizzano switched gears altogether, inaugurating what I call his Trilogy of Pedagogy, which consists of the Canadian-made *Why Shoot the Teacher?* (1977), the British-made *The Class of Miss Macmichael* (1978), and the American-made *Choices* (1981), all films about schools, teachers and their young charges. Film historian Nathaniel Thompson observes, "It makes sense that he would eventually make films about the educational system, because being a Canadian who relocated to Britain and then living around the world, he's seeing how these institutions are set up and how they produce citizens. Everyone who's around you is a part of that school system, and you notice how it differs from country to country."

The first of them, starring Bud Cort as a young college graduate given the reins to an isolated little schoolhouse on the desolate Saskatchewan prairie, is a Canadian filmmaker's first and only Canadian film, shot in rural Alberta and set at the height of the Great Depression. Based on a book of the same name by Max Braithwaite, who ironically bears the same surname of *To Sir With Love* author E. R. Brathwaite, *Why Shoot the Teacher?* delivered a thumping commercial triumph for Canada's nascent homegrown cinema box office, an early milestone success for its own national product. Who's cruel this time? Well, it's the bitterly bone-chilling, unforgiving landscape itself, as well as some of the folksy, indifferent, hard-nosed, headstrong, and often downright hostile parents of the kids with whom the teacher has been entrusted. This is Narizzano's quiet return to his most charming and disarming, the better angels of his nature, if you will—a return to the bygone Silvio of *Georgy Girl*. As a result, he saw his best reviews and audience reception since *Georgy Girl* as well.

Why Shoot the Teacher? is a viable competitor for Narizzano's most genuinely good-natured and unassuming movie. But there's still a seasoning of darkness as we study, in one sequence, Cort's face as he almost begrudgingly learns to administer discipline. As in all Narizzano films, a perceived act of cruelty is met measure for measure. It's another punitive world. As the UCLA critic of the day

Why Shoot the Teacher?

sharply observed, "the country folks in the movie prove unwilling to accept newcomers into lives hardened by depression." Sounds pretty familiar, doesn't it?—as much a personal read on the director himself as it is a take on his film. Of course, romance once again, as it presents itself in the form of Samantha Eggar, can only ever be tentative. As one critic noted, *Why Shoot the Teacher?* is reminiscent of a more upbeat *Wake in Fright*, also about a beleaguered man working an outpost at an isolated schoolhouse, the comparison all the more apropos as *Wake in Fright*'s director Ted Kotcheff, mentioned earlier as a Narizzano accolyte, is listed in the closing credits as a production consultant.

The Class of Miss Macmichael feels almost like a comic opera, played for both goofy high notes and pathos, complete with an over-the-top Oliver Reed playing Headmaster Sutton for farce and broad humor, in such a manner such that he comes off like the love child of Tallulah Bankhead's Bible-thumping Mrs. Trefoile and Richard Attenborough's Inspector Truscott in *Loot*, another in a line of Narizzano's shamelessly hamming, hemming and hawing authority figures. But as we learned earlier from *Georgy Girl* editor John Bloom, the juxtaposition of normally modulated and over-modulated is a performance effect, a kind of dramatic synthesis, that Narizzano actively seeks. And in the final movement, it's the

In each movie, Narizzano routinely over-modulates one of the performances to over-the-top levels. The juxtaposition between "normies" and often grotesquely depicted authority figures is a trademark throughout, and no more so than in *The Class of Miss Macmichael*, with Oliver Reed going for broke in his portrayal of a cartoonish headmaster.

virtuous, plucky, eponymous heroine, Glenda Jackson, at the very height of her powers as a leading lady, who most profoundly explodes. The well-adjusted but bottled-up normie buckles under pressure from the fanatic tyrant, a villain of authority who is played to excess. As such, it's yet another burlesque.

Whereas *Why Shoot the Teacher?*'s humor is sly, *The Class of Miss Macmichael* sometimes cacophonously leans into the outrageous. In both cases, our protagonists wage furious *and* curious battles with bureaucracy and authority. In the latter film, the battles more resemble zero-sum games with a banana peel tossed into the picture for good measure. Narizzano did strongly protest when one critic in particular accused his film of leaning too hard into farce at the expense of verisimilitude, writing in response to *Daily Variety*'s pan, "Whatever one's view of the teachers that Sandy Hutson, author of the original autobiographical novel *The Class of Miss Macmichael*, met, the headmaster she fought, the kids she taught, the incidents she experienced, they are real and did happen. I feel you have misread the picture and would ask you to reconsider its intentions." That he took the time to write and submit such a thing for publication suggests a true belief and investment in his material and his craft, not fitting the constitution of a director who simply took the money with apathy and ran. He and Glenda Jackson did see the film as a rousing rebuke of an educational system run amok, and the travails of one teacher through every daily indignity, any and all triumphs few and far between.

Choices, a plodding Afterschool Special-adjacent American drama of a hearing-impaired high-school football star who gets booted off his team, opens on an unusual credit: "A Rami Alon Film" — Alon being the film's producer and screenwriter. So much for directorial auteurism here, by the film's own admission. It's quite probable that *Choices* had Narizzano jobbing, pulling down a paycheck, I'd assume in the midst of Win Wells' treatment for cancer. As such, it is his most anonymous film, and his weakest, now known mostly for marking Demi Moore's motion picture debut. But thematically, it does tie in perfectly with *Why Shoot the Teacher?* and *The Class of Miss Macmichael*, in that they are all about bureaucratic authority figures who impede the education, well-being, and/or development of the young. There's not much data to confirm any suspicion, but in speaking with lead actor Paul Carafotes, a number of things were brought to light, about Narizzano the man and the nature of his involvement. Carafotes attests that all on-set creative decisions were Narizzano's and Narizzano's alone. He also based his interpretation of the John Carluccio character on the "sweet, very sensitive" Narizzano himself.

Around the time he directed *Choices*, he told an interviewer, "I don't see any connection between my films, although there may be something to what the man in *Films and Filming*, I don't remember his name, said: that all my characters are in search of themselves, in search of an identity that they're happy with. Georgy can be seen as a girl coming to accept that she's a square; in *Blue*, the central character is trying to discover where his true loyalties lie." Was Silvio Narizzano acutely attracted to characters with identity crises because he was in search of himself, amid all the self-loathing? Which of those *Sky is Falling* splinter characters is the most him? In *Choices*, these ideas are present in the film's very title. Carafotes is torn in multiple directions: as violin prodigy and as football star, as aesthete and as jock, as model son and as rebel about to fall in with the wrong crowd. How does this character elect to pluck his strings, in a manner of speaking… or who plucks them? The film may lack the teeth of his others, but there might be something else there.

Throughout the decade, Narizzano's television work had continued unabated, in both series episodic and teleplay forms. He managed to rack up critical good will for two of these dramas in particular. *Poet Game* (1971), a co-production of KCET-TV Los Angeles and the BBC, from a play by Anthony Terpiloff, stars Anthony Hopkins as Hugh Saunders, an alcoholic poet in the Dylan Thomas mold, self-destructively spiraling toward his fortieth birthday, on an inexorable collision course with early spiritual death. In the ten years since *Twenty-Four Hours in a Woman's Life*, Narizzano hadn't lost his taste or inclination for space-defining opening shots staged in stylish, fluid (and florid) longhand. His severe compositions also flex visual muscles outside the normal contours of the era's wholly studio-bound productions. The character Hugh Saunders is yet another exemplar of cruelty and crisis, and he is surrounded by others who respond too often in proportion. It's another punitive "Narizzanian" world. Long-suffering wife Billie Whitelaw likewise turns to the bottle, which juices her up for every bitter confrontation. Long-disapproving dying father Cyril Cusack arrives unannounced and tortures Hugh with some last embittered stares. American mistress Susan Clark plays nurse and caretaker, defiant of her woebegone lover's familial commitments. In the broader context, one understands what the director saw in this material.

Anthony Hopkins in *Poet Game.*

Trevor Howard and Celia Johnson in *Staying On.*

A Granada TV adaptation of William Inge's *Come Back, Little Sheba*, starring Laurence Olivier, Joanne Woodward, and Carrie Fisher, produced for the anthology series "Laurence Olivier Presents," gave us a faithful read on material first adapted to the screen by Paramount Pictures back in 1952. When Narizzano's tele-remake premiered on New Year's Eve 1977, it reminded viewers of his virtuosity directing intelligent television drama.

What I count as his last two films are television productions that actually work in the dimension of cinema. Both films' characters grapple with death, loss, grief, change, and learning to cope. His last effort, *Young Shoulders* (1984), is especially brilliant, singular, and extraordinary. *Staying On* (1980), shot on location in India, finds an elderly British couple, Tusker and Lucie Smalley, who elect to stay behind in the small town of Pankot after the British Empire has fallen. These double exiles aren't the wretched heretics that the expats in *The Sky is Falling* were. These are people just doing their damnedest to weather change, to navigate a shift in their very existence. He's a doddering, petulant retired colonel, a born martinet. She's a chatty, wistful romantic who feels stuck, beholden to her craggy husband's whims. You might read it as a love story, in its way—a love story sans outward affection. But in applying the imported framework of Giuseppe di Lampedusa's beloved novel *Il Gattopardo*, Tusker and Lucie haven't yet realized that, in order for things to stay the same, they must change. Once again, we have two more Narizzano characters torn between places, two homes, two identities. *Staying On* had its world premiere at the BFI London Film Festival before its bow on television.

Young Shoulders provides the perfect distillation and apotheosis of Narizzano's prevailing thematics, approaching his overall personal best without question or hesitation. Though Narizzano was crestfallen in failing to first pitch the project as a theatrical feature, discovering he could only get it produced as a BBC "Play for Today," he's as overtly cinematic here as he's ever been at any point in any film, thus I count it as one of his main releases, right on the same pile with *Georgy Girl* and *Blue*. And I'll again note that a number of "Play for Today" telefilms, chiefly many by Mike Leigh, Alan Clarke, and Ken Loach, received arthouse theatrical premieres in the United States. Likewise, Rainer Werner Fassbinder when his work crossed the pond. *Young Shoulders* would have been a prime candidate for such an honor.

The material itself harks back to the earlier question: Where do you channel grief when you can't forgive yourself for what you've lost, or what you feel like you've lost? We feel the gravity of this question in *Die! Die! My Darling*, *Blue*, *Redneck*, *The Sky is Falling*, and others, and its implications were magnified by Narizzano's own struggles with depression. Paul is an alienated teenager increasingly at odds with his feuding parents, and all the more since his younger sister perished with her classmates in a survivorless plane crash. When he unwillingly accompanies them to the crash site in Portugal for a memorial service, a potentially fraught trip becomes a twisted rite of passage—twisted as Narizzano, by now, best knew how to render and present it.

In one key sequence in particular, sex and death become entangled in a context both erotic and aquatic. The father of one of the crash victims, a loutish lush looking to anesthetize himself on a bender of booze and broads, takes our flustered, withdrawn young hero to a seedy Lisbon nightclub. A stripper strongly resembling Dutch actress Renee Soutendijk performs a sexually provocative dance of horny gyrations with a wax shark. Narizzano's meticulous cutting repeats multiple times the camera move pushing in on young Paul, establishing a rhythmic pattern that brushes against the curves and sensual bumping and grinding of the aqua-woman on stage—a voluptuous minx who unlocks further confusion and epiphany. The camera movements themselves simulate sexual thrusting. Grief gives way to a consummately surreal, and wholly necessary, orgasmic release, giving fresh meaning to the term la petite mort.

The key nightclub sequence from Narizzano's masterpiece
Young Shoulders, set diegetically to Pink Floyd's "The Great Gig in the Sky."

Silvio Narizzano threw fascinating curve balls. I might be mixing my baseball metaphors here, but he was a bit of a cinematic screwball-pitcher, adept at naturally occurring surrealist sequences. These might seem incongruous and unwelcome in other directors' hands. If you've tracked Narizzano's trajectory to this, his swan song, everything adds up quite tidily, because one immediately notices how our director actively shoots *Young Shoulders* as cinema, in crisp, clear cinematic language, with all its scope, all its weight, and all its impact. This isn't just another little something for television. In its style and milieu, Fassbinder's cinema classics for German television certainly leap to mind, purely in terms of their visual, literary, and sexual sophistication. The approach, the staging, the shots, the cutting patterns, the experimentality, all bespeak something more ambitious, meant for consideration beyond the constraints of the small screen.

While the character of Paul is unambiguously heterosexual, without even a whiff of homosexual panic, Narizzano nevertheless shoots him adoringly, not far afield from how Jerzy Skolimowski shoots John Moulder-Brown in *Deep End* (1970), which, it just so happens, was another film produced by Kettledrum Films, with which Narizzano was then involved. Andrew Groves, who bears a ballpark resemblance to Moulder-Brown in *Deep End*, is ideally cast, the very picture of youth, chiseled bare chest in the dawn's half-light like a Rembrandt in the film's first scene, billowing curtains opening a portal of memory and regret, as a cascade of steel and glass. We know instantly there's no going back to the way things were. In the wake of calamitous loss, you wander the streets in a stupor wondering who's a ghost, and for a split second, you realize maybe everyone thinks you're the ghost.

All the more extraordinary is that this film was Narizzano's tool for coping with the untimely death of Win Wells, who departed just before cameras rolled, at age 50. *Young Shoulders* can be seen as almost like a therapy. This is a film about what happens when there is a hole in one's life, and how it can consume the person in question. And consume Narizzano it did. One senses he would have dedicated the film to Wells if the BBC had permitted it, and if Narizzano were less innately private. Whatever comfort or elixir the film provided in that regard was fleeting, though. In perhaps a consummate testament to great pain fostering great art, he went out on a clear artistic high, but a personal low.

Narizzano took one more TV assignment, on the Agatha Christie mystery *The Body in the Library* (1984), before retiring,

Andrew Groves as Paul in *Young Shoulders.*

becoming a hermetic biblical scholar, a man completely shut off. He finally learned to exorcise his demons the more classical way. But did he love himself as much? Could he? We'll likely never know. Even when he did awful things to his characters, even the ones who most resembled him, it's as if he felt that he could let himself off the hook just a little more. His filmography is a living document of therapeutic self-hatred, and art was as good a vessel as many queer people in general could get in a less enlightened world.

It's easy to assume that Narizzano could never be accepted as a popular director because the sadness was so palpable. But more often than not, the richest works are never the most digestible works. My position is that, if Narizzano ain't an auteur, then nobody is an auteur. If you'll allow me, "Hey there, Silvio, truly feel I know you very well. Do I wish that you had gone to work on many more films? Of course I do! Hey there, Silvio, there's so much of you in all those scenes. Maybe put them on the screens, and oh what a change there'd be. The world would see a new Silvio!" Or rather, maybe the world would see Silvio anew. I'll spare you further verses, but Silvio Narizzano is a director whose films almost must be experienced in the broader context of a career and a trajectory, as that is when they most open themselves up. One sees that through his work, he could shed the dowdy feathers and fly, a little bit.

Silvio Narizzano.

Theatrical Feature Films: *Die! Die! My Darling* (1965, a.k.a. *Fanatic*), *Georgy Girl* (1966), *Blue* (1968), *Loot* (1970), *Redneck* (1973, a.k.a. *Senza Ragione*), *The Sky is Falling* (1975, a.k.a. *Bloodbath, Las flores del vicio*), *Why Shoot the Teacher?* (1977), *The Class of Miss Macmichael* (1978), *Final Assignment* (1980, quit, replaced by Paul Almond), *Staying On* (1980), *Choices* (1981), *Young Shoulders* (1984)

Other Notable Works: *Thunder on Sycamore Street* (1957), *A Memory of Two Mondays* (1959), *Shadow of a Pale Horse* (1959), *Twenty-Four Hours in a Woman's Life* (1961), *Fade-In* (1968/73, as producer), *Pal* (1971), *Poet Game* (1971), *The Public's Right to Know* (1974), *The Cafeteria* (1974, for "BBC2 Playhouse"), *Come Back, Little Sheba* (1977, for "Laurence Olivier Presents"), *The Body in the Library* (1984, "Miss Marple")

4. Pictures From the Precipice
The Harvey Hart Vision
(with a Peek Into Norman Jewison)

This is the first publication of this essay, written especially for this volume.

If we Canadians can produce quality pictures inexpensively, we should be able to make them pay for themselves by distributing them in art theaters of the United States and Britain. It would be a great help if the Canadian government would subsidize Canadian films, the way the governments of Britain, France, Italy, and Israel do.

Harvey Hart, *Toronto Globe and Mail*
February 1963

Next to Sidney Furie and Norman Jewison, Harvey Hart is the only other Canadian director formally profiled in Andrew Sarris' *The American Cinema*, filed in the "Oddities, One-Shots and Newcomers" chapter. Sarris writes, "Harvey Hart and his Canadian colleagues—Jewison, Furie, Narizzano, Hiller, et al.— seem stronger on technique than personality. Nonetheless Hart's direction of *Bus Riley's Back in Town* almost transcended the egregiousness of William Inge's maudlin memories of the Middle West."

As you might predict, I beg to differ with Mr. Sarris on his contention that Canadians are stronger on technique than personality, and I would daresay that some of those Canadians he names are stronger on personality than many of those he prized. But of course, "eye of the beholder," subjectivity, yada yada.

Hart is thematically invested in pockets of society as they attempt to form something resembling community, at least in the form of robust enclaves. Norman Jewison is attracted to community as it is formed in the mainstream of society, often with an eye towards social justice, seasoned with his own brand of salt-of-the-earth ethnics; think of the sleepy New England village in

The Russians Are Coming! The Russians Are Coming!, the roiling southern hamlet in *In the Heat of the Night*, the heimish shtetl in *Fiddler of the Roof*, the rust-belt "bohunk" berg of *F.I.S.T.*, the tight-knit Brooklyn Italian neighborhood in *Moonstruck*, etc. Curiously, the Toronto-born Jewison feels the most outwardly "American" or Americanized of any of the Canadians in his generation. Harvey Hart's films are more recognizably Canadian in character and temper, with his lens consistently trained on unharmonious clusters of individuals as they forge much more shambling synergistic homes. Thus, the idea of community drives both directors, but different types of communities, with different angles on them.

Consider the newly disillusioned strangers to their own home town in *Bus Riley's Back in Town* (1965), the beachfront bohemian burnouts in *The Sweet Ride* (1968), the stormy quasi-society of prison homosexuals in *Fortune and Men's Eyes* (1971), the counterculturalist "rustic runaways" from civilization in *Mahoney's Last Stand* (1972), the fractured city of lapsed Catholics and decadent satanists in *The Pyx* (1973), the rodeo dynasties in *Goldenrod* (1976), and the brawny weapons collectors and gun enthusiasts in *Shoot* (1976). Hart routinely captures fragile—at best, tentative—collectives on the brink of realizing social cohesion.

As the classic joke goes, "What's the difference between Canada and yogurt? Yogurt actually has a culture." For a filmmaker hailing from a country that, for so long, awkwardly tortured itself over a twentieth-century heritage of always asking "Where and what is our culture?" this agitated quest for togetherness (be it ever so humble) is unmistakable in the work of Harvey Hart, who tailored scripts to his own vision, sometimes to the chagrin of his writers. (Be it noted that William Inge, who disowned the screen version of *Bus Riley's Back in Town* and took a pseudonym, did so not because of any such revision by Hart, but because of Universal's meddling, especially on Ann-Margret's scenes.)

Hart had well situated himself as a helmer for "Alfred Hitchcock Presents" (with teleplays by distinguished scribes like Leigh Brackett and James Bridges) before getting hired on *Bus Riley's Back in Town*, a film that cosmetically feels like a Universal picture down to the bone, with the studio's special brand of gloss. At his best, Hart always either knows where the shot is, or can suss out a smart vantage point for much, or part, or sometimes all (i.e. a "one-er"), of a scene. In *Bus Riley*, he toys consistently throughout with wide-angle lenses and conspicuous Y-axis placements, establishing

Hart's high-angle and low-angle camera placement is of the essence in *Bus Riley's Back in Town*. His Y-axis placement always lends a scene enhanced gravity. This is a cut above average Universal Studios product of its time.

a coherent formal syntax of high-angle or low-angle compositions that stealthily code the proceedings. The width of the lenses
diminishes the Michael Parks title character in size, as if he is swallowed up by the home town that has essentially disinherited him.
But it's in Hart's 'Scope films, in particular, where he experiments
most boldly. *The Sweet Ride*, with its relentless experimentation
in chiaroscuro, canted frames, bold shadow (with pronounced use
of fall-off and silhouette), and especially reflections—in mirrors,
windows, and other frames-within-frames—is a feast for the eye
when seen in its proper aspect ratio. However, seeing *The Sweet
Ride* in proper form remains tragically rare because of scarcity of
elements—no readily available home video copies preserve its screen
dimensions. As of this writing, there are only sketchy bootlegs.

There is one particular scene in *The Sweet Ride*, a compulsory
wild Sixties party with "acid-test" colors in patterns swirling every
which way, where Hart's stylistic audacity and visual imagination
is most pronounced. In three complementary shots, a heated argument presented in silhouette on one side of the frame is juxtaposed
with a Keystone Cops one-reeler projected onto a wall on the other
side of the frame, in a kind of glass-shard formation. When Michael
Sarazzin and Tony Franciosa enter the established composition to
stand in front of the film-projection, they simultaneously loom over
and mimic the original silhouetted figures. As Sarrazin and Franciosa leave frame, a silent-movie intertitle reads, "Oh, look, we're
headed off the cliff!" It's not merely the decoupage that is fine-tuned
in a scene such as this, but also the humor, the dramatic gravity, and
the graphic chutzpah that enhances what might have been something far more pedestrian in the hands of another. A clever sequence
of shots like this not only sets a scene, but sets the larger "scene,"
lending more weight to the narrative arc as it's arc-ing, in a manner
simultaneously funny and sobering.

In John Gregory Dunne's book *The Studio*, he recounts
long-in-the-tooth producer Joe Pasternak inspecting the rushes of
The Sweet Ride and bemoaning Harvey Hart's reliance on wide
shots. "This guy's in love with long shots. What's he got against
close-ups?" The editor informed Pasternak, "I told Harvey that
[he should get a close-up of Tony Franciosa]. He said he didn't
want one." Though the film does not lack for close-ups when
warranted, Hart (like any skilled director) uses them as punctuation in moments that require impact, as in his third act. Beyond
that, though, like many shrewd talents wary of post-production
studio tampering, he knew instinctively to "edit in camera" as much

No average beach movie, this. *The Sweet Ride* goes darker, literally and figuratively, playing with shadow, chiaroscuro, and reflection in pivotal dramatic moments.

The party sequence in *The Sweet Ride* has Hart using his screen dimensions to the fullest. The movie projection on the left acts as a counterpoint to the drama on the right, with Franciosa and Sarrazin entering frame for proportional mirroring.

as possible. "Coverage" opened up windows of opportunity for meddling hands. [See also the chapter on Irving Rapper, re: producer Hal Wallis' similar complaint.]

As in the party staging described above, and throughout, close-ups are superfluous because of how Hart often divides his anamorphic-size compositions in ways that defy the traditional need for facial proximity and, more generally, basic coverage. André Bazin might have responded to Hart's staging quite appreciatively, had he seen it. The human eye can have its own way and elect to concentrate on what it wishes to, within the expanse of Hart's frames here.

"My father had a special love for his cinematographers," says Bethelene Hart, the filmmaker's daughter. "He was a really private guy, and was quiet when it came to talking about his work, but he took pride in the type of images he created with his cameramen. He loved working things out with them."

In no other picture was his zeal for vivid imagery more on display than in *Fortune and Men's Eyes*. This 1971 film version of John Herbert's controversial 1967 play is alternatingly brutal, and (strangely and unexpectedly) sometimes tender, notably in the later scenes between Smitty and Mona, and the ones leading up to the Queenie character's prison Christmas pageant, with the prison "community" getting in on the act. The film didn't win itself many favors, but did find a fan in Canadian gay cinema auteur Bruce La Bruce, who writes that it "stands up today as a groundbreaking film about homosexual desire, criminality, and domination and submission in the gay world. (The prison setting is almost incidental: it could have as easily been set in any gay bar or sauna of the time.) As a document of queer life before assimilation, it deserves to be included in the pantheon of pioneering queer cinema."

In his extended appreciation, La Bruce showcases one of the film's key sequences: Rocky's rape (or, more specifically, "deflowering") of Smitty in the shower room. He describes it thus: "The brilliant shot of the shirtless and buff Rocky walking backwards *away* from Smitty as he turns on the sink faucets one by one, to drown out Smitty's cries for help, and the subsequent tracking shot of the faucets going *toward* the shower as Smitty is being raped, ending with the characters in the frame after the violation is over, is much more powerful and effective than any graphic treatment of the act would be. It's pure cinema, pornographic and artistic in equal measure."

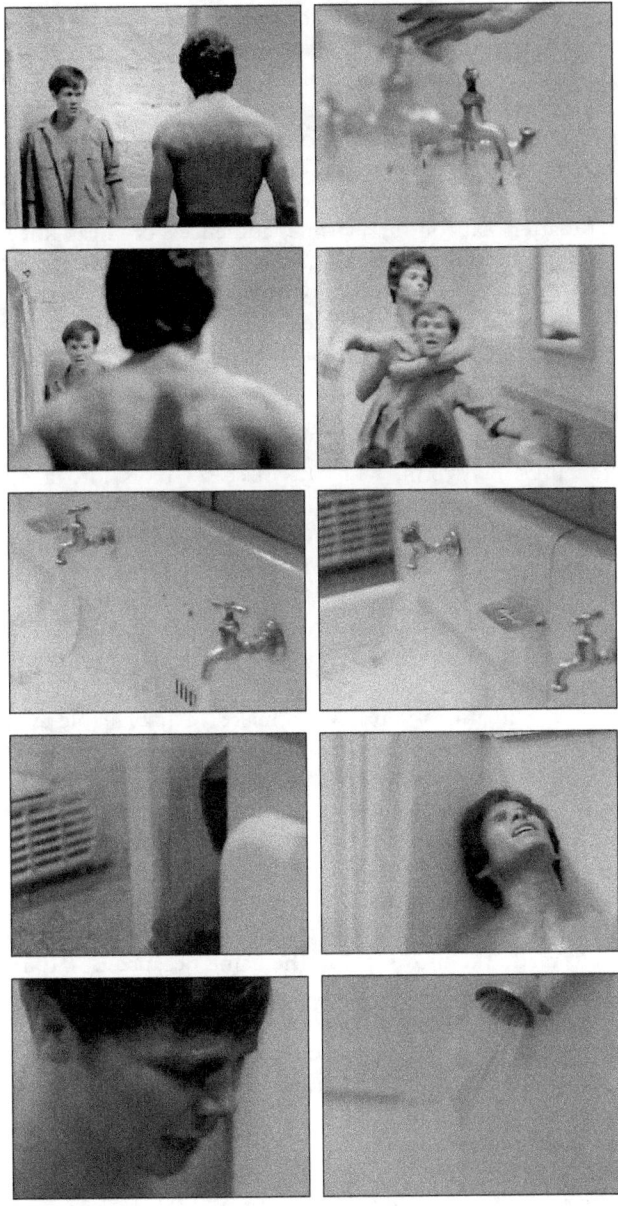

The shower rape sequence (left to right) in *Fortune and Men's Eyes* is a *pièce de résistance* in Hart's filmography, a perfect confluence of image, editing, sound, and camera movement.

Indeed, the shower rape in *Fortune and Men's Eyes* is a purely cinematic—and shockingly elegant—way of presenting a grisly act of sexual domination and brute sexual violence. This is Hart's doing, unquestionably. Another treacherous prospect, a savage gang bang scene, shows just enough for the sake of unflinching realism, but is fairly discrete, shot handheld from afar in an almost observational documentary style. This is precisely the type of subject matter that routinely primes audiences for cheap knee-jerk exploitation; La Bruce is correct in claiming that MGM treated the finished product quite unceremoniously as B picture rather than prestige project, but many of Hart's choices belie any such reflex, and thus have aged well. Let it be said that the studio ad campaign was antediluvian in its homophobia by comparison ("What goes on in prison is a crime!").

Production on *Fortune and Men's Eyes* started under debuting director Jules Schwerin, who was fired 24 days into a 40-day schedule. Hart was brought in to reshoot 90% of the scenes, adding a full 42 days to production (costing an added $175,000). Schwerin's rushes appeared too stagey to producer Lester Persky, who went on the record saying, "We kept hoping he would improve. The problem was his style of directing—a static camera not pertinent to today's filmmaking. It was too boring and too phony. We supported him as long as we could, and then finally couldn't. These are artistic evaluations you have to make." All available evidence suggests Schwerin was slavishly faithful to source material that even Sal Mineo, who famously directed his own stage production of it, saw fit to revise. John Herbert denied Mineo screen adaptation rights and privileges for the perceived insolence.

The producers and MGM execs gathered for a secret Montreal meeting at which the decision was made to fire Schwerin. Persky recalled, "All we did was screen the footage and let them evaluate it." They made the move late in the game because of late rushes and, for some time at least, the difficulty of finding a replacement director. An anonymous source also provided *Variety* with an account of the indecisive Schwerin's directorial weaknesses and inefficiency: "[He] would sit around and discuss things with his players and crew. Everybody was free to offer comment and suggest how a scene should be played. That was Schwerin's style, but the resulting footage didn't support his style." When Hart took the reins, Persky told the press that a "good bit of new material" had been written at Hart's behest. "In some cases we've gone back to earlier drafts that nobody but Schwerin had seen."

In a post-premiere interview, Herbert expressed his still unyielding loyalty to Schwerin, due to Schwerin's hardline allegiance to Herbert's undoctored play as the foundation for his own shooting script. Hart's attitude toward the "holy writ" of Herbert's original of course differed, as did his approach to staging action. I can personally see how he tailored the material to fit within the contours of favored themes. Schwerin later attested that only five truncated selections from his original footage were used in the final cut (mainly an early mess-hall fight between Zooey Hall and Lazaro Perez); everything else Hart rewrote, restaged, and reshot. Schwerin, for his part, never directed another film. It was his first and last effort.

The result proved effective. Hart was so happy with his work that he even toured a bit with the film as it opened nationwide. *Fortune and Men's Eyes* is Hart's masterpiece, and one of his most important works in auteurist terms, next to *The Pyx* (1973). From a purely structural perspective, *The Pyx*, which stars Karen Black and Christopher Plummer, is a marvel. Black's widower, Stephen Eckelberry, who happens to be a friend of mine, is an advocate for the film, stating, "At the time of its release, there were plenty of films that used flashback structure, but *The Pyx* was more than that. This was two separate timelines unfolding simultaneously at the same locations, offset by time itself. So that interplay keeps the interest and suspense alive. The detective follows the ghost of Karen's character, who will come to life for a moment then die again." Eckelberry has long dreamed of emulating this structure for a new film project of his own.

Putatively tied to Hart's early occult thriller *Dark Intruder* (1965), *The Pyx* is a dual odyssey, a two-hander in which the "two" in question never interact—an odd but bold "ne'er the twain shall meet" construction. One only "meets" the other as a corpse. The narrative is as bifurcated as the city it depicts, rolling on two tracks simultaneously: the lead-up to the crime, and its later investigation. The victim's spiritual arc skillfully mirrors that of the detective investigating her demise. Montreal as Catholic city, one literally overshadowed by an electric crucifix high atop Mt. Royal in the film's opening shot, is introduced with Black singing her own composition of "Song of Solomon," an opening epigraph in the same vein as Galt MacDermot's "Fortune and Men's Eyes" tune (fashioned from a Shakespeare sonnet) in Hart's previous film.

Hart's biggest staple, the vying for, but reckoning with the ultimate lack of, social cohesion is also personified by the Anglophone detectives and their Francophone counterparts talking past each other as they sort out the clues and case details. Amid these complicating constructs are clear binaries lain out: saints and sinners, the sacred and the profane, faith and nihilism, guilt and freedom (the debate-worthy final line, uttered by the Satanist culprit, is "You've set me free"). The third act mostly concerns itself with how sainthood is bestowed, as grace ceaselessly beset by impurity, and by an all-corrupting evil. John Boorman probes strikingly similar themes in *The Heretic* (1977), sometimes in similar ways (though *The Pyx* has far more poise and self-discipline, without question).

Visually, there is Hart's use of negative space, with unstable compositions that favor extreme screen left or extreme screen right configurations, along with shallow focus (long lenses are paramount in Hart's arsenal here), and a bronze color palate with periodic bursts of vibrant primary color. It is blue that becomes the most piercing color punctuation. Much has been made of Hart's deliberate pacing. The film's subjective excursions into memory take their time to unfold, especially a complex sequence involving a horseback reverie—a languid, slow-motion rhapsody on lost innocence—but these allow *The Pyx* to surface not merely as horror outing, but as almost Freudian inquest into degradation, with Karen Black ably meeting every moment. As already intimated, we're also left with a mirror, via Black, into Plummer's spiritually constipated detective at the precipice. The lapsed Catholics, propelled by untenable guilt, are Hart's spirit animals; what we get is a bit of character forensics. The satanists and assorted "fallen people" constantly challenge the perplexed souls to replace God, or their concept of God, with the deification of the self, and its darkest compunctions. Will they be cornered into playing God, and thus, through such grave sin, consummating their final fall from grace? And is such a God complex all that is left for individuals lost in a social fabric that fails to properly cohere?

Mahoney's Last Stand (1972) and *Goldenrod* (1976) are of a piece: Hart's chronicles of the Canadian Midwest, of rugged individualists carving out simplified lives divorced from the modern mainstream. The respective protagonists in both films, Alexis Kanner as Leroy Mahoney and Tony Lo Bianco as Jesse Gifford, might not be actively searching for interdependence or synergy, but they fall into it. Both principals try, at various points, to shake loose from the shackles of this interdependence, but they are inextricably bound to the social contracts of the micro-universes they have come to inhabit. Mahoney may relish the idea of complete

Harvey Hart uses both shallow focus and edge-of-frame placement of Karen Black as a stylistic choice in *The Pyx*.

Mahoney's Last Stand.

isolation à la Walden Pond, but he can't get it and finds himself stuck with a scrappy cohort, while Gifford struggles in his transition from rodeo king to crippled, full-time family-man farmer. Both vie for the simple life as a means of, for once and for all—or in some meager form, at least—achieving and (most importantly) sustaining the long unattainable.

Mahoney's Last Stand, which started its convoluted journey to the screen as *Mahoney's Estate* in 1971, is a collaboration with its star and screenwriter Alexis Kanner, a peculiar but endearing screen presence who later directed the daring, dynamic *Kings and Desperate Men* (1981), one of this author's favorite films of all time. Kanner's two works as creative force behind-the-scenes have very little in common stylistically or materially; *Kings...* is an almost experimental drama—a veritable audiovisual blitzkrieg (fascinating or flimsy, depending on who one asks). [Kanner and *Kings...* is covered in depth in Chapter 7.]

A beautiful, almost self-contained sequence near the finale of *Mahoney's Last Stand* is the site of one of Hart's greatest cinematic coups. When our protagonist finally gets his long-desired taste of solitude, heightened foley sound underscores setups of a fully nude Mahoney wandering around his property. We are treated to a veritable concerto of endlessly dripping water, the scrubbing of skin in an exterior tin bathtub, the rhythmic scraping of hard stone, the clucking of chickens, our hero's melodically aimless whistling, a straight-edge razor chafing a face, and of course the insistent deadness of ambient noise ("field tone" as opposed to room tone). It is the perfect ASMR-enhanced distillation of what feels like transcendental meditation in film form, uniquely rendered and lyrically—even poetically—lensed.

Goldenrod shares a kind of kinship with Paul Lynch's *The Hard Part Begins* (1973), not merely due to the casting of Donnelly Rhodes, but by virtue of milieu. In both, there is migration through the Canadian hinterland in search of rickety promise. There were other Canadian indie features of the Seventies that set up camp in the rural Canadian Midwest, with its quaint, quiet, provincial-beyond-compare podunk towns. Films such as *Paperback Hero* (1973, shot in Saskatchewan), *Who Has Seen the Wind* (1977, likewise Saskatchewan), *Why Shoot the Teacher?* (1977, shot on the Alberta plains), and tangentially *The Rowdyman* (1972, shot in small-town Newfoundland), all immortalized these parochial boon-towns and were some of the earliest works to do so.

Hart won Best Director at the Canadian Film Awards for his work on *Goldenrod*, which was ultimately pulled from its brief theatrical run in Ontario after CBS proffered a lucrative deal to broadcast it as a telefilm. It remains one of Hart's most warmly regarded pictures, by both critics and (at least) the original audience. Sadly, like the equally solid *Mahoney's Last Stand*, it's not often seen or screened today.

Shoot (1976) is one of the more curious entries in the *Deliverance* sweepstakes, with a basic setup that echoes forward to Walter Hill's brilliant Vietnam parable *Southern Comfort* (1981). It opens on a perversely sensual title sequence, with Cliff Robertson caressing, stroking, and groping his rifles, in preparation for a hunting expedition with his toxically masculine, armed-to-the-teeth friends. The presentation of weapons as fetish objects and, as in this opening, sex toys of a kind, literalizes violence as orgasm. This as a broadly North American complex is indeed our deadliest idée fixe, and it's at the root of *Shoot* as text.

While *Southern Comfort*'s initial inciting confrontation concerns military arrogance and basic etiquette (or lack thereof), *Shoot*'s inciting confrontation is knowingly otherworldly and unreal. There's a strange, I daresay Lacanian moment, a chilling silence that follows the spoken realization ("They look just like us") about their ad hoc adversaries. This off-kilter moment is an extension of the Lacanian mirror phase, interrupted by the Lacanian Real. The random, thoughtless violence breaks the pregnant pause in which Hart infuses a sense of the surreal. Some critics lambasted the film, and this scene in particular, for what they obtusely saw as its absurdity, and its "unrealistic" execution. *Shoot* was realized amid a glut of "bring the war home" movies that capitalized on Vietnam as gaping, infected open wound, registering public discontent with America's quintessentially unpopular involvement. But beyond this tentative subgenre, *Shoot* follows characters egregiously reduced to their animal selves (again, at least vaguely Lacanian ideas are at play here).

In *Shoot*, as in Hart's earlier *The Sweet Ride*, any sense of collective equanimity frays and completely disintegrates in the final act, reducing a core constituency to a last man standing, or every man newly for himself. As Vincent Canby summed it up in his original review of *The Sweet Ride*, "Jacqueline Bisset goes home to her family in Santa Barbara after being raped and beaten, Michael Sarrazin abandons his surfer life to take a dead-end job in a hardware store, and Tony Franciosa suddenly realizes the emptiness of his life." The film's Malibu haven becomes a paradise lost, a unit dissolved in a vat of "acid"—all that's left are an aging hipster, an empty house, and the equally empty threats of Franciosa's reactionary, gun-totin', hippie-hatin' neighbor (a kind of macabre running gag in the film, with a character who wouldn't look out of place in *Shoot*). And predictably, the gang in *Shoot* doesn't fare any better.

Tony LoBianco and Donald Pleasence in *Goldenrod.*

The gun nuts of *Shoot.*

An abandoned Harvey Hart project called *The Mad Trapper*, shut down just two weeks into shooting in 1978, owing to insurmountable money problems. One anonymous crew member recalls, "It was a good script and there was a lot of momentum built up. The producer, a rookie, just didn't realize what he was getting into. The cast was being trained to operate rifles, and some people were paid in full, while others received per diem only for the first week. Then there was nothing the second week. It was pretty shoddy." *The Mad Trapper* was to star Len Cariou, Leslie Nielsen, and Oliver Reed in the title role, as a cunning, resourceful fur-trapper hunted by the RCMP (that's "Mounties" to you non-Canadians). The same true story, of fugitive Albert Johnson ("The Mad Trapper of Rat River"), had been related in a previous film, Tay Garnett's *Challenge to Be Free* (1975), then later on again in Peter Hunt's *Death Hunt* (1981), with Charles Bronson playing the role. Not long afterward, something similar befell yet another Hart project, *The Swamp Fox*, which shut down three months into preproduction for much the same reason. These two misbegotten affairs offered proof that, though the Canadian film industry was making strides and getting its proverbial sea legs, things were still tough all over. Early on in Hart's short-lived Hollywood career, studio production notes for *Bus Riley's Back in Town* mention right up front his desire for a robust Canadian film industry, for a then startling lack of one. Hart remained a committed "hometown boy," and in seeing his dream more or less realized, he also became a repeat victim of that nascent industry's volatility.

Hart's final theatrical feature outings, two idiosyncratic though wholly anemic romances, *The High Country* (1981) and *Utilities* (1983), are inferior in every way when taking into account the director's extraordinary run from *Bus Riley's Back in Town* through *Shoot*. *Utilities* is especially a bizarre excursion, a romantic comedy predicated on the irresistible storytelling allure of... gas and electric bills. The film makes very little logical sense, rather like a basement-dwelling reprobate's angry manifesto. Its deadliest appellation, however, is "unfunny comedy." Both pictures positively reek of "quickie tax shelter" raison d'être and hardly give any kind of positive impression of the people involved. In general, non-genre oriented Canadian tax shelter movies very seldom get coverage, though there is a reason for that. Two by other directors that leap to mind are the inane, forgettable, but patently strange (in classic Canadian style) comedies *Nothing Personal* (1980) and *Middle Age Crazy* (1980). For all its many faults, one thing that should be noted about *Utilities* is that, out of any of Hart's ensembles, its characters come the closest to actualizing community and social cohesion; its "little people" join forces to declare war on the heartless corporations heating and powering their homes.

The High Country's gorgeous (but all too occasional) Alberta and British Columbia vistas speak better than anything in its clunky script, which comes complete with a grotesquely "playful" (and painfully misguided) attempted rape sequence, of a mentally handicapped young woman, no less. As produced by the low-budget genre specialist Crown International Pictures, the film casts Timothy Bottoms and Linda Purl as an unlikely pair on the lam, thrown together by hackneyed circumstance. It's difficult to gauge the true impact of Hart's original wide 2.35:1 panoramas when the only iteration made available since its hushed release is a pan-and-scan mutilation. Around this time, Hart's sensitive telefilm *Like Normal People* (1979) made more out of a romantic storyline between not just one but two mentally handicapped characters. What *The High Country* did, and does, however, is cement him as a director of rural tales, or at least ones comfortably removed from big, bustling city spaces. It also adds another notch to a "murderers' row" of Hart-ian misfits from unsavory pockets of society, a lineup that includes predators, prisoners, wastoids, Hell's Angels, hookers, satanists, gun nuts, and, now with *The High Country*, fugitives.

His post-movie-career telefilm productions (chiefly his acclaimed *East of Eden* miniseries and *Beverly Hills Madam*), while compelling and occasionally expressive, more effectively fit the definition "workmanlike," at least relative to his theatrical feature film output. None of these are really style pieces, as constrained by the limitations of the television format. His final credit, *Passion and Paradise* (1989), tells the same essential story as Nicolas Roeg's *Eureka* (1983), of the 1943 Caribbean murder of Sir Harry Oakes. As a counterpoint to the militant stylism of Roeg, it streamlines the narrative, presenting the history in far more linear fashion. (Let it be briefly noted that Hart's 1967 theatrical feature *Sullivan's Empire* was an unaired pilot for a proposed adventure series, as it was Universal's habit around this time to re-package and book their television product into theaters.)

But diving back further on the timeline—to the very beginning, in fact—Hart's direction of *The Apprenticeship of Duddy Kravitz* in 1960 as a TV play adapted by Mordechai Richler himself, as well as his treatment of *Sun in My Eyes*, based on the memoir of a survivor in Nazi-occupied Poland (and likely the first time that Canadian television ever dealt with the Holocaust), in many ways set him apart from his other CBC comrades. Kotcheff's taste in television material proved most eclectic, with Furie kept busy on shows like "Hudson's Bay," while Narizzano departed for London early to pioneer Granada TV. Hart's early contributions to the format are noteworthy as an expression of a Jewish voice directing Jewish material. His Jewish background, however, is not widely known or reported. The son of immigrants respectively from Wales and Leeds, England, he changed his name from Applebaum on the advice of actor Lorne Greene, who warned him he would never get work as a director with the name "Harvey Applebaum." He selected "Hart" as a tribute to both playwright Moss Hart, and Hart House at the University of Toronto.

Producer Victor Solnicki, with whom Hart had developed multiple projects, stated in one of Hart's obituaries that he "was the proudest of his work during the golden years of CBC-TV drama." His directorial voice, however, truly emerged when he graduated to the big screen. Hart's unrealized dream project, an adaptation of Philip Roth's first novel *Letting Go*, speaks again to his prevailing thematic, in telling the story of a young man attending college

A torn $100 bill: the same scene from Mordechai Richler's
The Apprenticeship of Duddy Kravitz, as staged in both Harvey Hart's
TV version and Ted Kotcheff's later film version.

upon returning home from the Korean War, looking for community and finding some whiff of it in a tenuous relationship with a young married couple, as well as various complicated women who enter his orbit. "My father worked with Roth for years on that project, and it was disappointing they couldn't make headway with it," Hart's daughter Bethelene remembers. In 1963, he did get to direct two short adaptations of Roth at the CBC, one of which was a chapter from *Letting Go* (titled "Paul Loves Libby") narrated on-screen by Roth himself. Both of these productions were executive produced by Daryl Duke (also profiled in this book), the later director of *Payday* (1973) and *The Silent Partner* (1978). If he had succeeded in getting the full cinema version made, it would have been the first big screen Roth adaptation, just predating *Goodbye, Columbus* (1969).

Two other pet projects of his likewise never got off the ground. The first of these was *Tisha*, based on a true story and hatched in the late Seventies to star Sally Field. It was to follow an adventure-seeking Alaska woman who journeys into the wilderness to run a ramshackle schoolhouse near a remote gold-mining settlement called Chicken. One can imagine that the title character, in true Hart-ian fashion, would have been emotionally invested in community formation in this backwater outpost. The other pet project, *Waves*, a comedy about the early days of radio, which surfaced around 1980, likewise never got off the ground, as Hart further resigned himself (lucratively) to TV directing, where expressions of his longings and preoccupations were muted, if they were even present at all.

In *The American Vein*, Christopher Wicking and Tise Vahimagi's 1979 survey book on directors volleying between television and film, they refer to Hart as "another member of American TV's Canadian contingent who has been adding his creative flavor to the prolific Hollywood blender, having steadily worked his way through some fairly notable small screen stories." They count him among the "top echelon of directors for telefeatures," yet also offer an odd caveat: "While Hart's uneasy fusion of style and content persists, his shows demonstrate that when the heart is in the right place, uneasiness can become an oddly disturbing virtue."

As with Sidney J. Furie until only recently, the biggest challenge to a wider reappraisal of Harvey Hart is the non-availability of quality film-scans and proper means of experiencing the currently hidden charms of his filmography. Specifically *The Sweet Ride*, *Mahoney's Last Stand*, *The Pyx*, and *Shoot* lack acceptable transfers with which one could reappraise Hart, either for basic quality of craftsmanship or for specific signatures. As of this writing, Disney's pitiful and downright disastrous stewardship of the Fox library ensures that a quality widescreen transfer of *The Sweet Ride* is not forthcoming (in point of fact, unlikely to ever happen). Rights issues with both the John Herbert and Galt MacDermott estates currently complicate a Warner Archive re-issue of *Fortune and Men's Eyes*. But enterprising scavengers can scrounge workable bootlegs out there in the wilderness to confirm or refute what I've written here.

I would squirm if relegating Hart to any journeyman pile, whatever the qualifier. His flourishes are just too distinct. With his bevy of television credits, separating out the theatrical features can be an onerous task. Even without the additional legwork of identifying the artistic trademarks within, the sheer density has perhaps clouded the pursuit. His artistic disposition is not terribly difficult to discern after spending any reasonable amount of time with the collected films; the work does bear a distinct signature.

As Bethelene Hart listened to my theories around her father's feature film work, her eyes lit up. "What you're saying makes so much sense, because I always think of those kitchen table scenes in *Bus Riley's Back in Town*. My dad's heart was in those scenes. If

Harvey Hart.

An excerpt from the novel
LETTING GO

Novelist Philip Roth's first onscreen credit came via a Hart production. Filming the full novel of *Letting Go* was Hart's dream project, but the CBC let him do only excerpts from his script for TV.

you really watch the film carefully, there's so much warmth there, with the families and the joking around and the sense of community. And that type of kibbitzing, that was 100% Harvey. You just see him having rehearsed with the cast to get there, and it shows. I just see his fingerprints all over those scenes in that film especially."

In many ways, it is the filmography of Ted Kotcheff that answers to the filmography of Harvey Hart. When community (or attempts at forming community) falters, what is left but to look to get out, or climb as to transcend the traps and the vicious cycles? In a whole other way, Silvio Narizzano's filmography works in response to both Hart and Kotcheff, with his torn-between-identities and torn-between-worlds refrain. If one is afforded the privilege of busting out, one longs for that which one left or lost. In this realization alone lie the (perhaps not so ineffable after all) identifiers of what makes a filmmaker resolutely Canadian—and these three Canadians in particular. They each chart interconnected steps in a process. Hart might have been the most overtly Canadian among this pack, because he is the one who stayed in Canada the longest, and never stopped trying to make a go of it there, something that is reflected in his characters as much as in his own personal constitution. Ironically, the all-American Bus Riley, whom I count as Hart's central avatar, is a very Canadian hero in this way. William Inge's restless creation as manifested in Hart's film version could have easily been transplanted to some similar Nowheres-berg in Ontario or Newfoundland or British Columbia.

Collectively, Kotcheff, Narizzano, and Hart form an exquisite symphony of the dispossessed. They are everything I love about Canadian filmmakers.

Theatrical Feature Films: *Bus Riley's Back in Town* (1965), *Dark Intruder* (1965), *Sullivan's Empire* (1967), *The Sweet Ride* (1968), *Fortune and Men's Eyes* (1971), *Mahoney's Last Stand* (1972/76, a.k.a. *Mahoney's Estate*), *The Pyx* (1973), *Shoot* (1976), *Goldenrod* (1976), *The Mad Trapper* (1978, unfinished), *The High Country* (1981), *Utilities* (1983)

Other Notable Works: "The Apprenticeship of Duddy Kravitz" (1960, CBC-TV), "Sun in My Eyes" (1960, CBC-TV), "The Dybbuk" (1961, CBC-TV), "The Luck of Ginger Coffey" (1961, CBC-TV), "Paul Loves Libby" (1963, CBC-TV), "Terror at Northfield" (1963, for "Alfred Hitchcock Presents"), "Lonely Place" (1964, for "Alfred Hitchcock Presents"), "Death Scene" (1965, for "Alfred Hitchcock Presents"), "Power of Attorney" (1965, for "Alfred Hitchcock Presents"), *Panic on the 5:22* (1974), *The Prince of Central Park* (1977), *The City* (1977), *Like Normal People* (1979), *East of Eden* (1981, miniseries), *Beverly Hills Madam* (1986), *Passion and Paradise* (1989)

5. Kinkaphonic Kino-Eye
The George Kaczender Vision

This is the first publication of this essay, written especially for this volume.

There is a documentary about Canadian cinema entitled *Weird Sex and Snow Shoes* (2004)—and the George Kaczender filmography fits neatly within such an aptly named Canadian canon, it's plain to see. In the Canadian series "On Screen," which produced an episode covering the making and release of Kaczender's *In Praise of Older Women* (1978), filmmaker David Weaver offers up a workable rationale: "There's always the sort of accusation that Canadian movies are full of weird sex. We don't have a lot of the things that studio pictures rely on to attract attention. We don't have the marketing machine, we don't have the big stars, we don't have the incredibly groundbreaking visual effects that a lot of the Hollywood films have, but what we do have is, we have sex." Kaczender lived this in his work, as a motto or mantra. He is proof that a director's work need not be unassailable—and might even be critically reviled—yet in auteurist terms still cohere better than others more answerable to qualitative appraisal. I have a certain affection for Kaczender because he's loud and proud of being unabashedly kinky in his way (and thus very much himself, it would seem). In terms of this kink as a cinematic "virtue" all its own, he is a proto-Cronenberg.

In Praise of Older Women, a major cause célèbre of the early Toronto Festival of Festivals which grossed $20 million on a $1.5 million budget (a major progression in the history of the Canadian box office), isn't what you'd call a "good" movie, per se, but you can trace its DNA later to the very naughty, bawdy-by-design, and (again) kinky shenanigans in his wild and woolly *Your Ticket is No Longer Valid* (1982), one of the strangest and most perverse fetish and sexual roleplay movies that you will find outside of a video store porn section. Sourced from a Romain Gary novel and right in line with Gary works like the saucy, X-rated *Birds in Peru* (1968), it stars Richard Harris as a tycoon with a limp johnson, who indulges in impotence kink involving... gypsy cuckoldry. (Huh?! Wuh?! Ehh, I won't elaborate too much here, but for now, it's the best way to describe the central premise.)

Or observe the opening of *Agency* (1980), with its deodorant commercial staged in a fleshy, leathery S&M nightclub. Also, generally, one can behold *Agency*'s overall treatment of subliminal messaging in the advertising industry as an unfailing "sex sells" formula for profit and hegemony. For all his faults, he's a filmmaker I learned to love, and any reservations I have vis-à-vis quality strangely benefit the experiential aspect of his work. It's paradoxically campy non-camp, or non-camp camp. In Sarris-ian language, Kaczender was a "lightly likable" oddball, whether or not you appreciate the experiences he *thrusts* before you, wink wink. He lets his predilections and proclivities all hang out in a way that rendered more prominent heterosexual masters the subject of rigorous study, for excavating the roots of fetish.

This is all in there from the very outset. Kaczender's early short film *The Game* (1968), about a teenage lothario and gigolo-in-the-making, foreshadows the ladykiller hijinks in later Kaczender films, most notably *In Praise of Older Women*.

I got to know Kaczender a bit towards the end of his life, thanks to my friendship with Karen Black, who worked with him twice, loved him, and kept in touch through the years. (Karen was that way with a few of her directors, most notably Ivan Passer, whom I also met through her.) George was a Hungarian gentleman who was the Canadian bard of arty pulp. This expressed itself sometimes as high-end trash.

His debut feature *Don't Let the Angels Fall* (1968) was Canada's first ever official entry at the Cannes Film Festival, and certainly comes the closest in Kaczender's filmography to an unqualified artistic success. I would go further and call it a full-on masterpiece. Backed by the National Film Board of Canada, *Don't Let the Angels Fall* is one of Canadian cinema's most effective portraits of suburban alienation, with its evocative portrait of a family in crisis. Pauline Kael famously referred to the sumptuous but laconic soirée sequences in beloved Antonioni, Resnais, and Fellini films as the "come-dressed-as-the-sick-soul-of-Europe-parties," so we might declare Kaczender's debut feature a "sick-soul-of-Canada" movie, with its stark depiction of a politically unstable "Quiet Revolution"-era Montreal looming inexorably toward a reckoning in the approaching October 1970 crisis (during which Pierre Trudeau invoked a version of martial law).

Kaczender's *Agency* conspicuously opens on a
TV deodorant commercial set in an S&M disco nightclub.

Arthur Hill plays a middle-aged securities advisor distracted by vivid memories of a business-trip fling, while contending day to day with a hapless wife, a politically radicalized college-student elder son (who is himself infatuated with a Francophone nightclub chanteuse), and a nihilist 13-year-old son in the throes of early spiritual death. Everyone in the film's central, superficially well-to-do family is looking for escape, meaning, or release. In his juxtaposition of unresting sexual desire (mirrored in both father and eldest son) and nihilism, Kaczender taps into a searing specificity, vis-à-vis an agitated Montreal suburban culture in denial, where the social protections its inhabitants have been conditioned to expect stand on the verge of collapse. They can no longer seal themselves off from a larger world. In an early scene, a bathroom stall door is flung open and Kaczender zooms into a piece of wall graffiti: "Pray for Sex!" Even in this relatively restrained first film, sex is deemed liberation, in a short-lived sense at the very least. Sex makes the world go round.

The cutting patterns in *Don't Let the Angels Fall* are very Nouvelle Vague-inflected and very "Roeg-ian," though the film prefigures "Nic Roeg the director" by a year or two. Roeg the cinematographer, however, had shot Richard Lester's *Petulia* (1968), which integrates similar modern, avant-garde editing patterns. In Kaczender's film, a downbeat conversation between husband and wife will be laced with a few frames of Hill with his mistress. Or the scene of the young nihilist son reading a somber poem to his middle-school class suddenly splices in a wide-angle shot of the boy reading the poem to a large, barren, empty room.

Kaczender's follow-up came four years later with *U-Turn* (1973), released by the Cinerama Corporation in the United States as *The Girl in Blue*. The film was inspired by a scene in *Citizen Kane*, when Everett Sloane's character, Mr. Bernstein, rhapsodizes

Don't Let the Angels Fall.

a girl he once spotted only for a moment, and fancied, at a ferry crossing. Kaczender took that as a foundational concept and built a narrative around the search for such a girl. Occasionally, one can sense echoes of Eric Rohmer, especially *Claire's Knee* (1971) in *U-Turn*, in terms of approach if not success. While it's certainly not as beguiling as his debut, Kaczender continues here in building an elemental thematic dissertation on erotic obsession, one that culminates in the ne plus ultra of Kaczenderian idiosyncrasy, *Your Ticket is No Longer Valid*, unquestionably the kinkiest treatise on all the things at the center of the filmmaker's gravity.

Especially fascinating is to immediately note the involvement of editor Ralph Rosenblum (*Annie Hall*, *The Producers*) in the opening credits of *Your Ticket is No Longer Valid*. Rosenblum had turned to directing around the time he lent cutting-room assistance to Kaczender. *Acting Out* (1980), an X-rated documentary hybrid portrait of everyday people and their filthiest, most far-out sexual fantasies, was his first ride on the, a-hem, hobby horse. When I spoke to him, Kaczender did not recall exactly the cause or source of Rosenblum's involvement on *Your Ticket is No Longer Valid*, but it's not hard to imagine Kaczender having seen *Acting Out* and thinking Rosenblum the right type of open mind to cut his picture.

I honestly cannot tell you, dear reader, if *Your Ticket is No Longer Valid* is a film one can actually "like"—it is just that much of an oddity. Film historian Nathaniel Thompson rightly calls it "truly deranged" in the course of his review of another Kaczender film. I can say, definitively, that *Your Ticket is No Longer Valid* feels extremely personal, and I know based on my own conversations with Kaczender, that he felt it his most important work, the locus of his voice as a filmmaker next to *Don't Let the Angels Fall*. With its carnivorous sex scenes and unabashed (and almost even refreshing) shamelessness, *Your Ticket is No Longer Valid* is an impossible object, a projection in both senses of the word, a stupefying portrait of a filmmaker completely unchained. One might potentially see it as derivative of a segment in Woody Allen's *Everything You Always Wanted to Know About Sex, But Were Afraid to Ask* (1972), namely a new take on "What's my perversion?," but of course played 100% straight and earnest, venturing deeper into the weeds of erotic fixation. (Ironically, *Everything You Always Wanted...* is the one Woody Allen film of the era that Ralph Rosenblum did not edit.)

As in *Don't Let the Angels Fall*, flash cuts and bold, disjointed, often startling interjections are key to the editorial language in *Your Ticket is No Longer Valid*. In many bold sequences, this is pushed to further extremes than in previous work. Even at the very height of a disturbing ending, we fade out on a Jackson Pollock-esque barrage of staccato bursts of color and movement that index on associations from earlier in the runtime, as if it has ultimately become an avant-garde work.

Richard Harris, who was passionate about the project and spoke of it wistfully in the years following its spotty release, told the press at the time that there was a 150-minute version which was cut by nearly an hour, leaving us with what we have now. The original Romain Gary novel was heralded for its mesmerizing free-associative structure. It shifts seamlessly between the character's present-tense stream-of-consciousness and the memories that get triggered in the course of this interior monologue, allowing two scenes to sometimes play simultaneously. Time gets meshed, with streams running concurrently. This is a framework that the film sheds for a purely linear progression. One wonders if the lost longer cut structurally hewed closer to the source, but in evidence are the helter-skelter editing patterns that suggest Harris' interiority manifested in montage.

In his denouement, as in Silvio Narizzano, Kaczender affords more literal heft to the term "la petite mort." If it's a "cheesecake" melodrama (i.e. something approaching softcore), it's one with

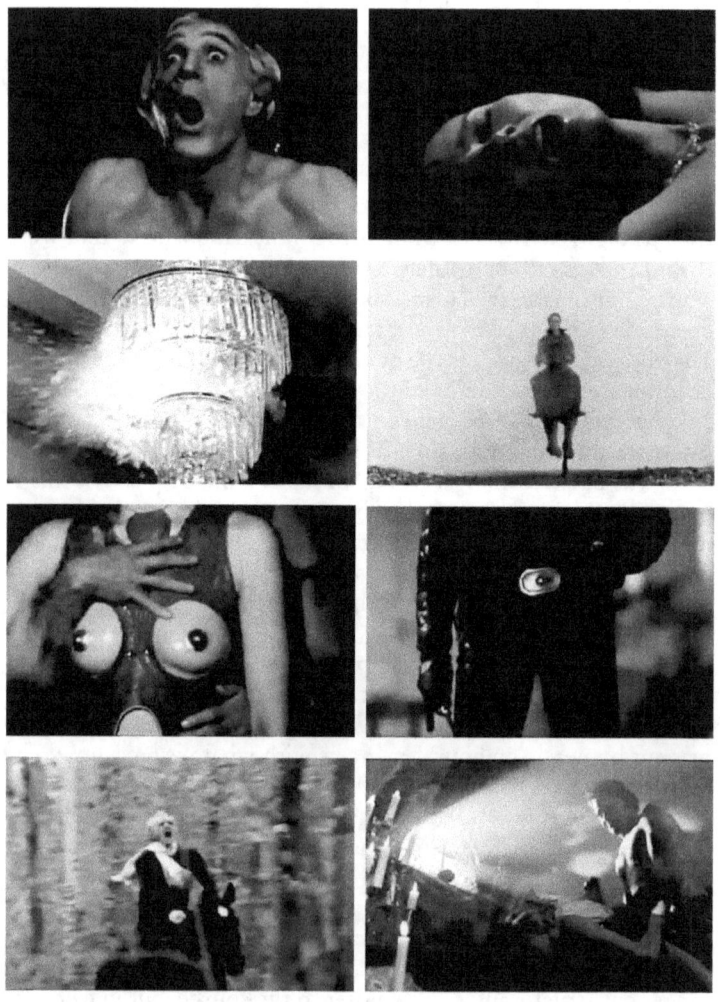

Above (left to right): The frenetic flash cuts at the end of
Your Ticket is No Longer Valid, during its deadly finale orgasm,
give the term "climax" added heft.

ambition, and some sense of grand cinematic design. The presence of both Jeanne Moreau and George Peppard, the former a high-end madam who is Harris' passport to the wonderland of his sexual fantasy, and the latter his coarse, crass mirror image in middle-age malaise, are both ambassadors of a kind. Each gets a showpiece scene, most crucially the gleefully sexist Peppard character who colorfully recounts "falling out of" a Danish model. All this stops in no way short of rendering the whole affair an uninhibited phantasmagoria of "filth," an admittedly puritanical term used ironically here. The best one could say is that... it *is* an experience. You've either been warned, or tantalized.

Smack dab in the middle of Kaczender's patently strange career is the boudoir picaresque *In Praise of Older Women*, adapted from a novel by Stephen Vizinczey. One could see its sexual odyssey as a horny prelude to *Ticket*. It's a more commercial proposition than *Ticket*, however: a young man's sexual awakening as he fucks his way through a parade of lovers, most of whom are women in a certain age range (as played by Susan Strasberg, Helen Shaver, Marilyn Lightstone, Alexandra Stewart, and of course, Karen Black). Where is Joan Collins when you need her? *The New York Times*' Janet Maslin reached an orgasm of invective in her review, writing that "its sex scenes are so close to slapstick that they're funnier than the screenplay, which is full of howlers." Kaczender's lack of inhibition during the sex scenes sometimes does manifest in bedroom excess, a steady drumbeat of scene-by-scene earth-shattering orgasms that viewers were to potentially measure their own against (and they were likely to leave feeling in want of better). All this echoes back to the far more restrained *Don't Let the Angels Fall*, which suggested sex as freedom, most memorably in the scene featuring the "Pray for Sex" graffiti.

Sex as freedom is Kaczender's admittedly simplistic but no less sincere filmic philosophy. Like Vizinczey's novel, the film of *In Praise of Older Women* does depict the pivotal 1956 Hungarian Revolution, which altered the course of Kaczender's own life. The studly hero Andras Vayda (played by Tom Berenger in an early formative role) emigrates to Montreal to continue his ribald escapades. In this respect, the film becomes almost as much a Bildungsroman for its adapter as it is for the original author. Two of Kaczender's closest collaborators, producer Robert Lantos and cinematographer Miklós Lente (who shot four of his seven features, plus at least one short), were likewise Hungarian refugees of 1956. Philip Kaufman likewise explored sex as a means of transcending political

In Praise of Older Women.

reality in his adaptation of Milan Kundera's *The Unbearable Lightness of Being* (1988), but of course does so far more successfully (and more tastefully) than Kaczender in *In Praise of Older Women*. The latter pulpifies a more delicate source text, in a way that misses "slam-dunk" satirical opportunities (for example, Vizinczey's cutting observations about gender and class in Montreal get completely jettisoned). This pulpiness gets extended to Kaczender's follow-up, *Agency* (1980), a Canadian mega-production of its time, starring Robert Mitchum, Lee Majors, and Valerie Perrine.

Paul Gottlieb, who adapted *In Praise of Older Women* into a screenplay, had written the novel of *Agency*, a thriller set in the advertising industry, which was, in turn, adapted into a screenplay by Noel Hynd. It's a soggy film that fails in its stated purpose as a thriller, because Kaczender doesn't seem to understand the thriller form, thus it comes off like a high-end telefilm. That's not to say it's without certain charms, however. While the aping of Seventies conspiracy thriller tropes of the Alan J. Pakula variety is fumbled on a formal level, the actual conspiracy at the heart of the plot is quaint within the modern context, lending the movie a kind of time-capsule or novelty quality today. The notion of subliminal political propaganda (via print ads, and commercials for products like chocolate milk and deodorant) is now "so forty years ago" in the age of modern propaganda outlets and news media that operate with wanton impunity.

Co-star Saul Rubinek remembers of Robert Mitchum: "He was a big score for the production, but he thought the *Agency* script was pretty lousy. This was clearly just a big paycheck for him. One day, I saw him leafing through it and writing 'NAR' at the top of many of the pages. When I asked him what 'NAR' meant, he told me it stood for, 'No Acting Required.' He said that I was the only part in the script that was anywhere near fully written, and that I was the only one who was going to get to do any real acting." Indeed, Rubinek was the only member of the cast nominated for a Genie Award.

Kaczender worked outside Canada on only one of his films, the British-French coproduction *Chanel Solitaire* (1981), a well-heeled, all-star biopic of Coco Chanel, with Timothy Dalton, Rutger Hauer, Brigitte Fossey, Karen Black (once again), and Marie-France Pisier in the title role. In terms of opulent, old-fashioned biopics, one could certainly do worse. With its $1 million costume budget and its high-key melodrama, *Chanel Solitaire* is movie-candy for a class of queer and gay male audience. But with Kaczender's trademark pulp, *Chanel Solitaire* falters as biopic. It proves nearly as worthless vis-à-vis as any piece of Forties biographical fiction, à la *Rhapsody in Blue* (1945) or *Night and Day* (1946). The latter two, however, at least focus on the artistic processes of their subjects. In expending much of its runtime on Chanel's various love affairs, *Chanel Solitaire* overlooks its real raison d'être: telling the story of a visionary lady who built a fashion empire. Moments of camp liven things up, and the foundational epic splendor of the production carries more forgiving viewers through many lulls in scripting, but these so-called "charms," inadvertent or otherwise, can only do so much. On Kaczender's part, the whole affair feels half-hearted. The movie tanked, both critically and commercially.

The rest of his career is a bit spotty, including a misbegotten video thriller called *Prettykill* (1987), involving a serial killer targeting prostitutes. But though Kaczender in the thick of his career might be deemed a purveyor of very adult schlock, his style and material feels very consistent, and one with which you can develop a relationship as a viewer, even while weighing sometimes significant flaws. What remains clear, however, is evidence of his budding mastery early on in *Don't Let the Angels Fall*, and in some of his early short subjects. There is a twisted apotheosis in the outrageous *Your Ticket is No Longer Valid* that will intrigue or repel, or maybe both. Kaczender might not have been one of Canada's greatest directors, but within the work is the spunk of a definable personality, one that is easy to pick up on. And hell, I like that… and I like him.

Theatrical Feature Films: *Don't Let the Angels Fall* (1968), *U-Turn* (1973, a.k.a. *The Girl in Blue*), *In Praise of Older Women* (1978), *Agency* (1980), *Chanel Solitaire* (1981), *Your Ticket is No Longer Valid* (1982), *Prettykill* (1987, a.k.a. *Tomorrow's a Killer*)

Other Notable Works: *You're No Good* (1965, short), *A Seduction in Travis County* (1991), *Christmas on Division Street* (1991), *Jonathan, the Boy Nobody Wanted* (1992), *Where Are My Children?* (1994), *Indiscretion of an American Wife* (1998)

6. The Pirate of the Canadabbean
The Allan Moyle Vision
(with a Peek Into Miloš Forman)

This is the first publication of this essay, written especially for this volume.

It somehow makes sense to first define Miloš Forman's thematic focus and artistic pulse, in order to situate Allan Moyle's as its offshoot and as its giddily punk-rock bastard child. Forman, as a refugee from communist Czechoslovakia, hung his hat as an artist on the idea of revolt, at least as far as his American work is concerned. In *Taking Off* (1971), a film one could imagine Moyle also having made, musically inclined Village kids butt heads with their frumpy, forbidding parents. In *One Flew Over the Cuckoo's Nest* (1975), Jack Nicholson leads a ragtag cohort of lunatics in a revolution against an oppressive sanitarium staff under the command of Louise Fletcher's tyrannical Nurse Ratched. (Forman, for his part, asserted that in his origin country, "Communism was our Big Nurse.") *Hair* (1979), with its scraggly hippies, is about revolt and revolution against the establishment in the most straightforward manner possible. In *Ragtime* (1981), Colehouse Walker, Jr. first revolts against a posse of brazenly racist volunteer firefighters, then against racially unenlightened society as a whole. *Amadeus* (1984) sees Mozart rebelling against the musical rulemakers and dogmatists under Emperor Joseph II, while Salieri rebels against God himself for rendering him talentless. And of course, *The People vs. Larry Flynt* (1997) is nothing if not the portrait of a dyed-in-the-wool rebel and agent provocateur.

Allan "Bozo" Moyle is easily linked to ideas about revolution and subversion that Forman brought to the screen—however, Moyle is more laser-focused on the act of revolt as cultural phenomenon. He sees even a moment of revolutionary spirit as casus belli, as the root of cultural groundswell. The groundswells in the respective pictures, especially *Times Square* (1980), *Pump Up the Volume* (1990), *Empire Records* (1995), and *New Waterford*

Girl (1999), emerge as cutting-edge lifestyles by final fade-out. Liberation is only gradually recognized as birthright. His heroes are never caricatures, no matter how broadly they are drawn. They emerge as revolutionary heroes, the voice of their respective generations, sometimes by accident. Like Scorsese, Moyle is a king of the needle-drop, and he's a specialist in idol-making moments within a certain mode of pop cinema. For example: In *Times Square*, there is Robin Johnson's performance of "Damn Dog," and the angry siren-song duet "Your Daughter is One." In *Pump Up the Volume*, there is the fugitive Christian Slater's blasting of "Hello, Dad, I'm in Jail" from a mobile broadcast jeep, and his Leonard Cohen pirate-radio segues. In *Empire Records*, there is the finale rooftop concert set to Coyote Shivers' "SugarHigh" and The Cranberries' "Liar"—a kind of GenX hard-rock Andy Hardy show.

Moyle fits even the most rigid definition(s) of the term "auteur" in that he, by and large, conceives his own stories, exercises control over the writing of his scripts, and makes films that speak to a clearly delineated (and easy to express) sensibility—a way of seeing. *Times Square* originated from a diary Moyle found in a second-hand couch, while *Pump Up the Volume* originated from his unpublished novel. He is essentially Miloš Forman crossed-pollinated with Allan Arkush (*Rock 'n' Roll High School*, *Get Crazy*), with a very Canadian artistic license all his own. His alienated teenage folk heroes are in mutiny against provinicalism, this being a staunchly Canadian state of being in the Moyle context. In fact, an explicitly Canadian brand of provincialism is given a targeted roasting in his sleeper *New Waterford Girl* (1999).

It's not just that the provocative-by-default Moyle is invested in the idea of "cool"—it's a flamboyance of cool. Moyle's very existence on the scene prompts the question, what if Holden Caulfield grew up, became an apostle of Lenny Bruce, listened to The Ramones, Richard Hell, and The Pixies, then became a pop filmmaker? Of course Salinger would have never afforded Holden that much in his novel, but in another Caulfieldian sense, newly minted coolness is how one transcends the phony, the prefab, or the corrupted. Moyle might be the closest that modern cinema comes to a truly Salingeresque author, turned on and tuned into a Vanta-black "How to Talk Dirty and Influence People" ethic. There is an irascible, come-out-and-play, middle-fingered temperament at work here. In the Moyle-verse, a protest campaign of TV's dropped off rooftops is a cri de coeur, a black trash-bag "blouse" is high-fashion punk chic, and detonating school supplies stuffed in a microwave signifies a rebel yell from a suburbia (or other bourgeois habitat) deep in denial. His is another cinema of transgression (outside of how Nick Zedd and his movement defined it).

His characters get to ask the "questions that matter," such as, "It's 10:00, do you care where your parents are?" Or, if you want droll: "Wasn't Marshall McLuhan the guy who started the Sex Pistols?"

While reigning Eighties "teenmeister" John Hughes is fun enough and nostalgic enough, I've always said that *Pump Up the Volume* is the film Hughes would have made if he'd had the guts. For one, Moyle's teenage alienation has muscle, and the courage of its convictions. The action never stops at rap sessions. Jonathan Rosenbaum was the most effusive, proclaiming it "probably the best radical youth movie since *Over the Edge* (1979), thanks to an excellent script and cast, and a driving, rebellious soundtrack of about a dozen pop and rock singles by everyone from Leonard Cohen to Liquid Jesus." He even went as far as to describe it as "a clarion call for freedom and collective action both hopeful and energizing, it qualifies as a generational statement as *Rebel Without a Cause* did in the '50s, but without the defeatism and masochism. Not to be missed."

Technically, *Montreal Main* (1974), credited to Frank Vitale, was a collective, some might say communal, effort of independent cinema, and could be considered Moyle's debut. On a personal note, *Montreal Main* inspired me during a demoralizing downturn, when I was considering leaving the film industry in the early

Christian Slater as pirate radio agent provocateur and folk hero in Moyle's masterpiece *Pump Up the Volume.*

2010s. It was the ingenuity and the energy of it that I found intoxicating—the overall feeling that it had been made from scratch, wholly on a lark one afternoon as the creators were just sitting around idling the hours. For the record, that's not how it was made at all, but there is a delightfully impromptu feel baked into its construction. In terms of camera language, moments of documentary vérité are counterbalanced by an almost Hitchcockian fastidiousness (as in the scene when the masked Frank first meets Johnny). But its insight into the fabric of life as lived by these characters, named for the actors playing them (e.g. Frank Vitale plays Frank, Stephen Lack plays Steve, Allan Moyle plays "Bozo," his actual nickname), stirred me into action, giving me a special shot in the arm. Ultimately, it inspired a feature film I wound up directing around that time.

Vitale's sensibility draws a boundary between two classes of people: the eccentric denizens that haunt the seedy boho district of Boulevard Saint-Laurent, and a hip, progressive but sheltered middle-class family in the Montreal suburbs. As the former invades the spaces of the latter, and an intense "platonic romance" between a grown layabout artist (played by Vitale himself) and the family's teenage son slowly develops, the geographical, social, and even moral boundaries that the city itself reinforces begin to dissolve. Amid this exceedingly polite (oh Canada!) clash of civilizations, no one seems to notice that the controversially young object of desire comes of age and experiences his first jolt of existential crisis. *Montreal Main* is one of the most extraordinary Canadian films of its time, and one of my personal favorite films of any time or country. It is a fresh iteration of *Death in Venice* for a still thriving Canadian counterculture, with more than a few things to say about what it means to be Canadian.

After seeing *Montreal Main* in 2010, it took quite a few more years for me to track down Moyle's formal (i.e. credited) directorial debut *The Rubber Gun* (1977), which was restored and re-released in 2025 by Canadian International Pictures. But upon seeing it around 2014, I relished it as a sassy little rejoinder to my beloved *Montreal Main,* featuring many if not most of the same faces, including Stephen Lack, Peter Brawley, Pam Marchant, and Moyle himself. Other aspects mirror its predecessor too. The cast members once again play characters named for themselves. A quirky, grungy, guerrilla energy gets reborn in *The Rubber Gun,* dropped into a new and only vaguely related context. An ingratiating queerness, one that is simultaneously casual yet overriding, is again on display. Specifically, there is an all-too-brief stop inside a drag club, along with various catty one-liners on either end of that sequence. Everything reunites to fuel an only slightly more plot-driven film. This time, Moyle plays Bozo as a McGill sociology student writing his thesis on a commune of artists-turned-addicts. In first boasting to his thesis advisor, "This particular group has been vitalized by drug use," Bozo eventually comes to witness the fabric of the group fray and nearly disintegrate. The loquacious grand poobah of the commune, Lack, lobs any number of barbs for a growing number of pickles, but for once, it signals nothing but impotence.

Megaproducer Robert Stigwood bankrolled Moyle's sophomore outing as director, the marvelous *Times Square* (1980). While this was not an altogether happy experience for Moyle, resulting in an editorial overhaul of his original cut, *Times Square* is something of a masterpiece of its kind, and the locus of Moyle's auteurship. There's Tim Curry as the "shit-stirring" Grand Instigator disc-jockey Johnny LaGuardia (a radio voice-of-dissent presence that echoes forward to Moyle's next film *Pump Up the Volume*), there's the dynamic teenage duo "The Sleez Sisters" consisting of a sheltered, repressed girl taken under the wing of a more streetwise counterpart (a dynamic that echoes forward to *New Waterford Girl*), and there's the nascent youth movement that springs from their collective efforts (the common outcome in nearly every Moyle film).

Times Square's screenwriter, Jacob Brackman, a onetime *Newsweek* and *New Yorker* journalist, had previously worked with Bob Rafelson on *The King of Marvin Gardens* (1972). As an equally accomplished pop lyricist, Brackman was in many ways an ideal scribe for Moyle's original concept, because he could uniquely fuse gritty street realism with a visceral rock 'n' roll ethic, without getting mired in the traps set by earlier "streetwise cinema." One of the key casualties of Stigwood's post-production tinkering was the lesbian love story component as more fully developed between the two principals. It is a pity that audiences lost a full ten years of Moyle movies, as he retreated from directing following Stigwood's ill treatment. The Eighties were an especially ripe primetime for youthful insurgence of the kind Moyle came to regularly ignite on screen after the decade finally concluded.

Perhaps, however, it took a full ten years for a youthquake masterpiece like *Pump Up the Volume* (1990) to fully percolate. Perhaps something as comparably subversive could have only been a Johnny-come-lately affair, after a decade of teen-driven

Dynamic young female duos, one the liberator and the other
the liberated, are at the heart of *Times Square* (above) and
New Waterford Girl (below).

product had effectively primed the target audience. Though *Fast Times at Ridgemont High* and John Hughes whet the popular appetite, *Pump Up the Volume* is a primordial howl that opens point blank and wholly without euphemism: a throaty, sardonic disembodied voice on pirate radio asks us, "Do you get the feeling that everything in America is completely fucked up? Do you know that feeling, that the whole country is one inch away from saying, 'That's it! Forget it!' Think about it, everything is polluted, the environment, the government, the schools, you name it."

Perhaps, ironically, it took a Canadian to package and (more importantly) deliver such an unflinchingly blunt opening salvo about the country to his/its south. I hesitated on the possessive term in the previous sentence because one could ask, is Moyle speaking as a Canadian outsider on behalf of Canada here? We soon learn that we've landed in a mixtape culture Arizona. The exchange of tangible recordings becomes a language all its own, a code only understood by the alienated teenage interlocutors. This motif is not merely the bid at quaintness or nostalgia we may recognize it to be when watching it today. It's the cultural currency, as rudimentary as a handshake. Much is made of "world-building" in modern screenwriting parlance, but this film actually does it. Moyle's own influences, the presiding spirits in many of his films, loom large in the film world that gets built here. Leonard Cohen's "Everybody Knows" is the sound that fires the first "warning shot" on every "Hard Harry" radio show. Cohen, a poet that some glibly call Canada's answer to Dylan, is perhaps the most pronounced accent mark of any of these. It's a flag raised early in the runtime, as if to indicate the director's own lineage.

The reverence for Lenny Bruce is made explicit in the form of the book that the Christian Slater character Mark checks out from the library. The stew of all of these influences is enough to foment an uprising—a wholesale rejection of complacency and complicity. Clad in a pair of Clark Kent-esque specs, as to avoid detection, the ghostly-by-day and spirited-by-night Mark becomes something of an unseen superhero to a high school in the throes of a corrupt regime almost reminiscent of the type of comic book villainy inherent in the reference. Slater's character is a werewolf of the airwaves; when the moon comes out, he's a feral titan of self-expression, an angel of antagonism, but by day, he's a cowering, awkward kid frightened of his own budding power. At the end, his final gesture before being carted off by the authorities is to remove his glasses and advise his crowd of adoring teenage fans to "Talk hard!"

Pump Up the Volume is a refreshingly fearless polemic, precision-engineered as entertainment. It is a big yawping *j'accuse* directed at power and authority, from the bowels of a suspiciously quiet suburbia, with its special strain of lah-di-dah provincialism that this Canadian filmmaker knew all too well. We shouldn't be in any way indignant or dismissive of John Hughes because he couldn't deliver such a decisive uppercut right on middle-class America's kisser. John Hughes, after all, wasn't Canadian. Set a

Canadian loose, abroad in America and armed with a camera, he'll show you how to throw down.

Touchstone Pictures wooed Moyle to direct *The Gun in Betty Lou's Handbag* (1992), a likably buoyant comic fable that is nothing if not flawed, but clearly spoke to Moyle's burgeoning interest in defiance as an art form. It sees another young repressed female milquetoast get—and quickly redeem—a ticket to live large, not at all unlike the heroines in *Times Square* and *New Waterford Girl*. In the broader context of the movies surrounding it, it's a cute, featherweight time-filler at its best. Bracketing that, one can discern a noble attempt at a *Desperately Seeking Susan* (1985) style feminist crime romp. Both, after all, are centered on sheltered suburban housewives who get a welcome but perilous taste of excitement. Had Susan Seidelman been unable to direct *Desperately Seeking Susan* (though of course thankfully, she was), one suspects that such material fits perfectly within Moyle's wheelhouse. It's a pity that his shot at a similar script didn't yield better results... or at least more commercially successful ones. In its early stretches, the film's camera language and tone do tend to sometimes echo that of fellow Canadian Patricia Rozema's *I've Heard the Mermaids Singing* (1988), a formative, "quirk-forward" work of Canadian pluck that was making the rounds at the time of its production.

Moyle's effortless hipness peeks its head out here and there, but cannot sustain (one assumes because of studio interference, at least in part). I will note a favorite funny moment in *The Gun in Betty Lou's Handbag* as reflecting Moyle's hand and sensibility beyond the shadow of a doubt, despite whatever level of studio interference: in rummaging through a collection of cassette tapes for incriminating evidence, the title character quips, "Look at this! Barry Manilow, Debby Boone, Paul Anka in Vegas! This guy deserved to be shot." This is a line that could and would have appeared in any other Moyle picture, before or after. Critic and scholar Adrian Martin observes, "It is almost a miracle that [Moyle] has been able to infuse such life into the standard elements of virtually every Touchstone Pictures production—lifestyle and fashion jokes, cute animals, bloodless violence, reassuring romance, and a touristic touch of local colour."

Empire Records (1995) is a proto *High Fidelity* (and superior to it in every conceivable way, in this author's opinion), though it doesn't quite have the teeth—let alone the bite—that *Times Square* and *Pump Up the Volume* have. The Moyle voice, however, is unmistakable. Though the film is upbeat on the whole,

Empire Records.

it is pierced with some pained punctuations that lend it further weight, especially in the scene of a mock funeral that becomes grounds for some agonized confessionals reminiscent of the ones that propelled *Pump Up the Volume*. The scene culminates in the "interred" Robin Tunney character Debra tearfully relating that she "felt invisible." One can readily imagine a Hubert Humphrey High student calling into Hard Harry's show with such an admission. The film does not reinvent the wheel with its basic story—the collective quest to save an independent record shop from a corporate takeover—but it works on a wavelength similar to Michael Schultz's *Car Wash* (1976): wringing unexpected pathos from another pell-mell ensemble. Our heroes, this time a posse, are a familiar breed of ever crafty, self-styled, amiable but angsty edgelords or misfits. Rory Cochrane is our impish, unflappably sardonic ringleader, cast in the mold of Christian Slater. It's one of the more enchanting entries in the "slacker musical" subgenre, and introduced "Rex Manning Day" into the vernacular, at least among a considerable-enough cohort of GenXers and elder millennials.

Moyle's last masterwork, *New Waterford Girl*, is shot and set on Cape Breton Island. What could have been a reductive inverse of *Times Square*—à la, a new dynamic female duo's misadventures subverting a bucolic, narrow-minded Nova Scotia community—is imbued with local color to a degree that surprises even those expecting some perceptible manner of it. The trappings are clear: uniformed boys lined up in hockey gear, townsfolk crossing themselves at the slightest provocation, the pronounced Maritime accents, the all-embracing belief in the everyday divine, the off-the-wall impunity of lines like "Class is over, go eat some halibut."

Weirdsville.

New Waterford Girl is the closest I've ever seen a male film-maker get to achieving a female gaze, a rare merit that exceeds the objective primacy of female protagonists in his oeuvre. In other words, it's (again) a "way of seeing" that compounds the basic narrative arrangement. Moyle's sensitivity to this gaze reigns supreme. The performances of Liane Balaban and Tara Spencer-Nairn are simply terrific, with all the cockeyed chemistry of Trini Alvarado and Robin Johnson in *Times Square*. The success of the pairing, in conjunction with the film's loopy compassion for the larger ensemble cast, culminates in an emotionally fulfilling denouement that expresses part of what propels Moyle authorship, the stuff that his movies were always about: the promises of a big wide world beyond the natural limits of our hermetically sealed environments—promises only sealed and kept if one delivers on provocation, and sometimes just by merely thinking bigger. Moyle's protagonists are the ones who have turned the provocation into a kind of art, however shambling the art is.

His other pictures, especially *Weirdsville* (2007), are good in isolated moments, but do not live up to the promise of those early titles. They altogether lack the "fire and music" of Moyle's more formative works. The biggest success of *Weirdsville* are the stoner one-liners, redolent of a *Bill and Ted* or *Cheech and Chong* vintage. The weakened impact of these later works might be explained by the fact that Moyle was exceptionally understanding (as a boomer, no less) of how to interpret specific GenX needs and desires. Lest he were doing a period film in which he could recapture such period-specific rat-a-tat-tat, Moyle seems far better suited to the times during which he was producing his best work. This is not to limit him, but strictly to define the contours of his comfort zone.

Allan Moyle as screen presence resembles something like Alexis Kanner's long-lost younger brother. His stony, offbeat sprezzatura occasionally punctuated by a wild-eyed, insouciant grin, is on sometimes frightening display in *Montreal Main*, especially in one crucial crack-up scene. He also appeared in Leonard Yakir's *The Mourning Suit* (1974), a Canadian curiosity that I got the rare opportunity to see, in which he plays a musician who falls into a fraught relationship with an old Orthodox Jewish tailor as he mourns the "death" of a son who married a Gentile. This role is miles away from his characterizations in *Montreal Main* creator Frank Vitale's *East End Hustle* (1976, which he co-wrote), in which he plays a call girl's boyfriend, and perhaps most importantly Richard Benner's queer Canadian landmark *Outrageous!* (1977), in which he plays a paranoid schizophrenic.

Allan Moyle might be considered a cult director by definition. *Times Square* and *Empire Records* especially were sizeable flops before they were reclaimed by now-loyal cults that warmly embraced them when they appeared later on television and video. By virtue of five titles, *The Rubber Gun*, *Times Square*, *Pump Up the Volume*, *Empire Records*, and *New Waterford Girl*, he is one of the Canadian filmmakers I have long loved the most. He's an artist unafraid of his roots, and in most respects proud of them, but he's also not afraid to shake the stems that grow out from them. If shaking turns into breaking, it's mostly out of passion rather than desire for wanton destruction. The Moyle tremors that do the shaking are youthquakes, and that is the essence of his cinema. Indexing on one of *Times Square*'s working titles, he's got the shakes.

Theatrical Feature Films: *The Rubber Gun* (1977), *Times Square* (1980), *Pump Up the Volume* (1990), *The Gun in Betty Lou's Handbag* (1992), *Empire Records* (1995), *New Waterford Girl* (1999), *Jailbait* (2000), *Xchange* (2000), *Say Nothing* (2001), *Weirdsville* (2007)

Other Notable Works: *Montreal Main* (1974, uncredited as director, but principal contributor), *Man in the Mirror: The Michael Jackson Story* (2004, documentary)

7. 49th Parallel of the Mind
Lindsay Shonteff, Daryl Duke, and others

These short essays were written especially for this volume.

Dime Cinema-ist: The Lindsay Shonteff Vision

Lindsay Shonteff is, for me, still a subject for further study. I'm not the "expert" on Shonteff that I am on other members of his "Class of 1950-something Ontario," namely Furie, Kotcheff, Narizzano, and Hart. But I would have felt remiss if I hadn't included him at all in this volume, and within this chapter. It's hard, at the moment, to give him something close to equal due next to the others, all of whom have been extensively profiled herein. The lack of availability of Shonteff's work frustrates those who might pursue something close to a full study or treatise, though that is gradually changing. Various video releases of *Devil Doll* (1964), along with the British Film Institute's disc edition of *Permissive* (1970) and a very small handful of others, provide one with at least a starter kit. A film I would argue is one of Shonteff's most important pictures, the kink-bizarro Jack the Ripper-inspired horror thriller *Night After Night After Night* (1969), directed under the pseudonym Lewis J. Force, is still languishing in the archives, only having previously surfaced on now-ancient VHS transfers.

Shonteff was very much Sidney J. Furie's charge—one might even go as far as to say his protégé. Shonteff's hiring on *Devil Doll* (1964) had everything to do with Furie's lack of personal availability and his recommendation of Shonteff as a stand-in. This was a friendly favor to a fellow Canadian newly arrived to England. Shonteff, for his part, had directed only one self-funded feature prior to this British debut, that being a catchpenny Canadian Western called *The Hired Gun* (1961), shot in Kleinburg, Ontario, starring a cast of predominantly non-professionals (excepting Don Borisenko). *Devil Doll*, a successor to the more famous Michael Redgrave segment "The Ventriloquist's Dummy" in *Dead of Night* (1944), retains the ability to provoke acute unease using the various smoke-and-mirrors tools and stylistic accoutrements that only the cinema provides. Shonteff knows when to hold on a shot in *Devil Doll*, and it was enough that it got him contracted to a number of projects in the year that immediately followed. These, of course, were pulpy exploitation films bearing such lurid titles as *Curse of the Voodoo* (1965) and *The 2nd Best Secret Agent in the World* (1965). In contrast, *Run With the Wind* (1966), about the girlfriend of a boxer who is wooed by a caddish folk singer, is a now seemingly lost bid at more mainstream appeal. Though it offered Shonteff less niche respectability, the final result failed to register, it would appear. He returned to directing grindhouse items like *The Million Eyes of Sumuru* (1967) in short order.

Shonteff's skills as filmmaker became (and likely, were always) very niche. Among the aforementioned class of Canadian filmmakers, he attained the least in the way of traditional success. No Hollywood studios wound up doing business with him. Stories circulated about how Columbia Pictures had proffered a contract, but the argumentative Shonteff had bones to pick with the terms, tanking the entire deal. On a personal note, I remember Sidney Furie telling me something at lunch many years ago, along the lines of, "I don't think Lindsay wanted that type of success. He liked making his genre stuff with more freedom than a major studio would have ever allowed. It was just enough that he had to deal with independent money men, sometimes sketchy guys, who didn't care about things like final cut as long as the movies supplied enough sex and violence, the stuff they could easily sell." If I'm indeed remembering Furie's take correctly, it provides an insight into the way things mostly went for Lindsay Shonteff throughout his life and career. And it's why many of his pictures have fallen between the cracks. Ownership in such instances would spur all manner of problems on prospective re-releases of such titles. In that sense, he's Canadian cinema history's "lost man." All the more unfortunate it is that none of these "creative safety measures" prevented Shonteff taking a number of pseudonyms throughout his career, presumably after losing creative control of certain productions. By the time he perhaps realized that the business operated much the same way outside the majors, the ship had sailed.

I would argue that *Permissive*, a salient peek into the subculture of rock groupies, is one of the better pictures that bears his name, though many of his editing choices are puzzling, especially desultory jump cuts that flash forward to important things revealed later on. Though these sometimes spoil the progression of the story, it is quite possible that Shonteff was experimenting with a type of montage increasingly common in popular counterculture cinema outings, especially *Easy Rider* (1969). The acting by an unseasoned cast is more than occasionally ropy, as it was for many of the Shonteff pictures that succeeded it.

Anticipating Stanley Kubrick's shooting of his Vietnam epic *Full Metal Jacket* (1987) at the East London Gas Works, Shonteff shot *How Sleep the Brave* (1981), a Vietnam saga all his own, entirely in Berkshire, England. Of course, because Shonteff's budget was paltry in comparison to Kubrick's, his results are not nearly as convincing. The strings do show, so to speak. That is not to say that *How Sleep the Brave* is without virtue. Shot with a band of American expats, the film does attempt something of a serious statement about the Vietnam quagmire while indexing heavily on the classic war films that Shonteff loves, all the tired tropes included. It is clumsy, but in its best moments, it feels like it owns its own awkward mojo. Backhanded compliment? If you write about Shonteff from this perspective, this is a wavelength on which you must operate.

the middle of all this, he makes *The Yes Girls* (1972), a strangely Corman-esque low-budget sex movie... about the making of a low-budget sex movie. Though it could certainly do with more of it, the film does pack a satirical punch, ending with our protagonist, a wet-behind-the-ears (and in other places) ingenue freshly escaped from an institution for delinquent girls, scoring a big fat Hollywood deal. One can easily sense Shonteff making fun of it all. We can almost hear his voice instructing, "It's all a big fat joke—not just this movie, but life as we know it." To randomly invoke *The Boys in the Band*, "Life's a goddamn laugh riot!"

So... this has been your little peek into the life and career of Lindsay Shonteff: no hit, no raging success, no laurels or awards, no first or last hurrah. We are left with the portrait of a working director who had some semblance of a brand: horror quickies, scrappy neo-noirs, and spy flicks (mostly all Bond knockoffs). It's not so far-fetched that one day we will see a complete box-set topped off with a career retrospective documentary along the lines of what Severin did for schlock auteur Al Adamson. But until then, Shonteff's body of work is left to the most adventurous cinema spelunkers. As a Canadian, Shonteff had a compulsory taste for the anarchic and the cockeyed, and if you ask me, that's more than enough. For many of the same reasons I like George Kaczender, I also like Lindsday Shonteff.

Theatrical Feature Films: *The Hired Gun* (1961, a.k.a. *The Last Gunfighter*), *Devil Doll* (1964), *Curse of the Voodoo* (1965, a.k.a. *Curse of Simba*), *The 2nd Best Secret Agent in the World* (1965), *Run With the Wind* (1966), *The Million Eyes of Sumuru* (1967), *Night After Night After Night* (1969), *Permissive* (1970), *Clegg* (1970), *The Yes Girls* (1971, a.k.a. *Take Some Girls*), *The Fast Kill* (1972), *Big Zapper* (1973), *The Swordsman* (1975), *Spy Story* (1976), *No. 1 of the Secret Service* (1977), *Undercover Lover* (1979), *How Sleep the Brave* (1982), *The Killing Edge* (1984), *Lipstick and Blood* (1984), *Number One Gun* (1990), *The Running Gun* (1992), *Ice Cold in Phoenix* (2004), *Angels, Devils and Men* (2009)

○ ○ ○

A Silent Partner: The Daryl Duke Vision
(with a Peek into Peter Yates)

Daryl Duke is a case in abject frustration. On the strength of *Payday* (1972) and *The Silent Partner* (1978), Duke should have had a glorious, blazing, barnstorming feature film career. Instead, he only made four movies. A fifth, *Griffin & Phoenix* (1976), first ran as a telefilm but was released theatrically in some territories. The studios should have been beating down his door, but as we have come to expect, that's too often not how the business works. I have personally had run-ins and relationships with people who have worked with Duke, the most crucial one being Elliott Gould, the lead in *The Silent Partner*. He and the others attest to Duke's intelligence, his impeccable on-set constitution, and his value as an overlooked talent. Gould remains duly proud of his work on *The Silent Partner*, and Rip Torn went literal decades telling as many as he could that *Payday* was likely his best performance.

So what happened? I believe much of it has to do with the fact that his first two films, masterpieces of their kind, failed to secure good distribution. *Payday* was the first film produced by Saul Zaentz, before he built an empire producing Oscar darlings like *One Flew Over the Cuckoo's Nest*, *Amadeus*, and *The English Patient*. Shot and released concurrently with Paul Lynch's *The Hard Part Begins* (1973), another chronicle of a traveling second- or third-string country music performer playing the circuit, *Payday* is one of the most sublime slice-of-life pictures to come out of its decade. As the portrait of an unrepentant libertine who, as critic Peter Hanson eloquently writes, "mows down everyone who stands between him and glory or self-destruction, whichever

Payday.

comes first," it announced the arrival on the scene of a reckonable directing talent. Duke does not sacrifice star magnetism on the altar of character appeal. Torn is never less than dazzling as a morally repulsive rascal who believes his own hype and nurses an addiction to chaos (or as Pauline Kael described him, "a goaty, rancidly unromantic third-rate Johnny Cash"). Duke commits Torn's performance to the cinematic permanent record with no small measure of balance, grace, and dignity, and this is no small feat considering the turpitude on display. His work in *Paycheck* is a testament to Ted Kotcheff's favorite Chekhovian aphorism, "I'm not the judge of my characters, I'm their best witness."

The original 1973 reviews of the film were ecstatic. *The New York Times* called it a "brilliant" and "clear-eyed study of people whose lives are linked to the road," and later named it one of *The Best 1000 Films Ever Made*. The notoriously difficult-to-please Pauline Kael recommended it as "an acrid, hard-boiled melodrama with a feel for authentic characters," though she lamented that it "didn't get the distribution it deserved." Indeed, the Cinerama Corporation's lackluster distribution arm did no service to the film, even with all its ample qualities. They failed to weaponize the solid notices and good press to corral more people into theaters. This was, after all, early in the career of Zaentz as movie producer (after he had scored some measure of music industry success with Fantasy Records, his biggest act being Creedence Clearwater Revival). He did not yet have the wherewithal or acumen to circulate the film more effectively himself, let alone parlay producerly street credit for a more major distributor. *Payday* withered and languished for years, showing up occasionally on the revival circuit to a modicum of renewed attention before it was given a new lease on life with a 2008 Warner Home Video release.

Curtis Hanson's nifty scripting of *The Silent Partner* plays a vital role in its success, all the more so because he originally had designs on directing it himself. But Duke's execution of Hanson's script is certainly not nothing. It is a film of moving parts and pieces that coalesce around exquisite moments of tension and buildup. It can't be frittered off as mere disposable potboiler considering the way that Duke guides the ship. The bank sequences are a Hitchcockian marvel of shot syntax and airtight montage. In my time with Elliott Gould, he spoke in great depth about his friendship with Hitchcock during the master's final years. Gould would beat the drum for *The Silent Partner* in Hitchcock's presence, and when Hitchcock finally got around to seeing the picture, he was nothing but complimentary. The historical record indicates that Duke left the project over creative differences, leaving Hanson to finish the inserts and pickup shots, then tend to post-production chores. Whomever had the final say, the resulting film is enormously impressive. The sheer brutality of some of the scenes is startling — the infamous "fish tank sequence" especially oozes shock value. The film's sharper edges fearlessly announce themselves. This is not at all the labor of a wilting lily, but someone with the tough-as-nails tenacity of the man who had already proven himself with the hard-hitting *Payday*. Janet Maslin wrote in *The New York Times*, "Just as he did with *Payday*, Mr. Duke has put together a dense, quirky, uncommonly interesting movie, this time with a high quotient of suspense." If Duke has a signature in these two first pictures, it's an uncompromising toughness, an unflinching eye, and a mettle that is unsparing. These two are patently thick-skinned motion pictures.

Again, *The Silent Partner* suffered from poor — and even disastrous — distribution (or lack thereof). As the first feature produced by Carolco Pictures, *The Silent Partner* suffered in a way akin to Saul Zaentz's then-unschooled stewardship of *Payday*, so much so that the two films' releases were almost mirrors of each other. The Saul Zaentz Company and Carolco were both outfits that later

The Silent Partner.

became giants, but struggled early on learning the industry ropes. Both films were celluloid guinea pigs for their backers—casualties of their early growing pains in the biz. In spite of critical raves, Duke's superior crackerjack thriller went largely unnoticed on its initial run, dying a tragic box-office death. Television airings and video releases provided a new lease on life, just as they had for *Payday*. Among cinephiles today, a question persists about Duke: "How did the system at large let him get away?"

Taking into account the jagged glory of the Duke features discussed so far, what is there to make of *Griffin & Phoenix* (1976), the tearjerker telefilm that garnered so much acclaim and goodwill that it was eventually given a theatrical presentation (a rare honor, especially for a non-Universal product)? Some territories *only* got it as a theatrical feature film (under the alternate title *Today is Forever*, with a bit of nudity added). A special title card opened the American release under its proper original title: "On its first national exhibition, its impact on the American public was so great that the decision was made to bring this extraordinary experience of love and death to the cinema world." Writer John Hill's spec script, which he later novelized, long prefigures *The Fault in Our Stars* (2014) in its story of two terminally ill lovers or companions who cling to each other as they emotionally navigate however much time they have left to live. This is a peek at Duke's softer, sensitive side, but the hard edge comes out as his cinematic exercise in "melete thanatou," the classic philosophical practice of meditating on death as to prepare oneself. At the end of *Griffin*

& *Phoenix*, a hand-scrawled monument to the characters' love for each other is painted over, the world having already forgotten them. All the tender efforts to stave off the inevitable, and even the traces left behind quickly evaporate. The film was remade in 2006 with Dermot Mulroney and Amanda Peet.

But what else do *Payday*, *Griffin & Phoenix*, and *The Silent Partner* have in common, if anything? It's admittedly difficult to draw a throughline. Having not seen his seldom shown or discussed *Hard Feelings* (1981), I cannot speak to any of its potential associations. That film is scarce even on "gray market" back channels. But if Duke kept on, he could have become Canada's answer to Peter Yates. To explain, Yates is a challenging director to discuss in relation to auteurship. In my distaste and near disgust for the word "journeyman," Yates was an artist of some distinction in commercial cinema who conspicuously wore the cloak of journeyman. Beyond his being a genre chameleon, there is little else to thread together titles as disparate as *Bullitt* (1968) and *Breaking Away* (1979), or *The Friends of Eddie Coyle* (1973) and *Krull* (1983). What style there is, is covert. Thus, making an auteur claim for Yates might come off as a willful act, but one could make an argument that Yates is attracted to stories about men caught up in systems that they had no say in designing, and with which they have grown increasingly uncomfortable. British critic Brad Stevens once posited to me that "Yates' *One-Way Pendulum* (1964) is about a man who attempts to rebuild the Old Bailey in his living room, and this seems to provide a template for much of Yates' later work, which involves consciously 'rebuilding' other films. *For Pete's Sake* is *What's Up Doc?*, *The Deep* is *Jaws*, *Breaking Away* is *Rocky*, *Mother, Jugs & Speed* is *M*A*S*H*, *Krull* is *Star Wars*, etc."

This is a keen observation, yet few if any would argue with the out-there-on-its-own greatness of *Eddie Coyle* or *The Dresser* (1983), nor would they put up a fuss about such classification for *Payday* or *The Silent Partner*.

Payday is the portrait of a morally dubious specimen in much the way that Yates' *The Friends of Eddie Coyle* is. *The Silent Partner* is a thriller that keeps time like a good Swiss watch, similar to the way that Yates' *Robbery* (1967) does. Likewise, one can imagine Yates having had a go at *Tai-Pan* (1986), a lumbering James Clavell adaptation that started its journey to the screen decades before Duke wound up realizing it, having already passed through the clutches of directors as diverse as Michael Anderson, John Guillermin, and Richard Fleischer. Under the producership of Dino de Laurentiis, Duke's translation is lacking in distinction. The best thing about the film is Maurice Jarre's rousing epic score, along the stylistic lines of the music he provided for David Lean (in particular, the *Tai-Pan* soundtrack cue titled "Love and Typhoon" could have graced any big Lean set-piece).

Duke, as evidenced by his work on three pictures, had preternatural abilities with the cinematic form that do not escape modern film enthusiasts who have the privilege of generous access and retrospect. He is proof positive that a director can be consummately skilled in any number of ways, and in any number of genres, yet be overlooked and shafted by virtue of poor circulation.

Theatrical Feature Films: *Payday* (1972), *Griffin & Phoenix* (1976, a.k.a. *Today is Forever*), *The Silent Partner* (1978), *Hard Feelings* (1981), *Tai-Pan* (1986)

Other Notable Works: *I Heard the Owl Call My Name* (1973), *The President's Plane is Missing* (1973), *A Cry for Help* (1975), *The Thorn Birds* (1983, miniseries), *When We Were Young* (1989), *Fatal Memories* (1992)

○ ○ ○

Working the Angles:
The John Trent and George Bloomfield Visions

The careers of John Trent and George Bloomfield are unremarkable overall, though I would argue that their respective best works are both 1970 counterculture dramas named for their hapless heroes: Trent's *Homer* and Bloomfield's *Jenny*, both of which were bankrolled by second-tier American studios (National General Pictures and ABC Circle Pictures). The latter film in particular is one for which I have tremendous affection. Marlo Thomas, a few years after her tenure on "That Girl," is surprisingly affecting as an otherwise typical girl-next-door type who gets knocked up on a date at the drive-in (which is screening a revival of *A Place in the Sun*, no less). Fresh-faced Alan Alda is a filmmaker and film editor who is desperate to dodge the Vietnam draft as his number comes up. They enter a marriage of convenience. It is also fascinating that Bloomfield and Trent followed up these gentle, Americanized "state of the union"-type dramas with, for lack of a better way of putting it, sadism sagas involving psychopaths who hold unwilling parties under siege. Sour followed sweet.

In *Jenny*, though, Bloomfield is attempting something "bigger" than what he's able to fully deliver on, but it's almost too easy to admire the ambition. There are even times when the film aims high and hits its mark. The bullseyes are not in hefty supply, but they are there to be debated. The overall deliberate pacing makes them somewhat easy to assess midstream. The baby that arrives at the end is born a symbol, and the final image is surprisingly affecting. The film's strenuous arthouse rigors, with its frenetically edited fantasy montages, have led us to a final image that plays at length, as it slowly fades to white. If nothing else, it's one of the better counterculture-adjacent box-office non-successes of its time. As original *New York Times* reviewer Roger Greenspun argues, "*Jenny* is a very old-fashioned film, gently accumulating the paraphernalia of a certain opportune modernism. All the movie memories are intellectual properties of a sort that you may discard if you wish to sigh over the sad-happy story of a girl and her guy and her baby. But it isn't so easy to make old-fashioned movies now, and the values and lifestyles the film plays with, keep playing with it in return—so that *Jenny* often stumbles into (and alas, out of) a better kind of movie than it has any right to be."

Jenny does effectively capture draft anxiety and the creeping redefinition of the traditional family unit. British director Waris Hussein was doing something similar overseas with *A Touch of Love* (1969), about a single, independent mother-to-be. Meanwhile, as was reflexive at the time, the film lightly skewers deluded elders, as exemplified by Vincent Gardenia's character. Playing Jenny's toothmaker father ("Jenny tells me you make teeth—I've always been very interested in teeth"), Gardenia is depicted as a kind of John Bircher type who believes the Nazis should have marched as victors on Russia to eradicate communism early on, to the baffled Alda character's polite dismay.

With Bloomfield and *Jenny*, it's the n-teenth case of a Canadian who has ventured to the dominant country to his south for his feature debut. Personally, I generally have a jones for the American cinema of 1967–1980 (be it genre pic, experimental, auteur piece, programmer, counterculture flick, you name it), but I would argue that the 1969–70 season had a flavor all its own; one might call it a "spirit of despair." The fire of contemporary youth activism and free love was woven into even the "square" pictures of those two years. The spirit was so downbeat and corrosive, it dissolved every other pretense at normalcy and business-as-usual, like a miracle solvent. Veiling this is a haze of calamitous loss, the unabating sting of fresh wounds in the wake of RFK and MLK's respective slayings. The films boil over with a realization that all roads, scenic or dull, curving or stretching straight out toward the horizon, lead to disillusionment. Hollywood doesn't dare touch such doldrums anymore. By the time the Eighties rolled around, it was deemed that unadulterated escapism offered some way out.

Jenny, generally panned upon its 1970 release, has this "spirit of despair," and Bloomfield's Canadian eye is acute in his observation of it. John Trent's *Homer*, a vaguely more Canadian picture in nature, has a taste of it too, though it is not as delicate or subtle as *Jenny*. *Homer* is earnest, certainly, but never achieves anything closer to high art (as *Jenny* does), nor does it seem to aspire to. Subtlety was never John Trent's forte. His best known and most popular picture, *Sunday in the Country* (1974) starring Ernest Borgnine, is one in a slew of vigilante "nasties" that popped up in the wake of *Straw Dogs* (1971), immediately before the more grotesque *Death Wish* (1974) and its sequels entered the cultural bloodstream.

Shot in Schomberg, outside Toronto, *Homer* opens with some obvious and by then overly familiar generation-gap conceits—the classic "I'm not gonna cut my hair!" is thrown in for good measure. American director Hall Bartlett evoked such a dynamic more poetically in his *Changes* (1969), just to address how the era's tired zeitgeisty tropes got better mileage elsewhere. In *Homer*'s story of an 18-year-old proto-hippie farm kid who yearns to escape and become a musician, it's the soundtrack that is most extraordinary here: Buffalo Springfield, Led Zeppelin, Cream, The Byrds, and The Steve Miller Band. In fact, *Homer* marks the first time that a Led Zeppelin song (namely "How Many More Times") appeared in a movie. As a result, the film has never been officially reissued, on video or otherwise. A YouTube copy exists with the offending tracks wholly muted out.

The brutality in Trent's *Sunday in the Country* is more or less mirrored in George Bloomfield's *To Kill a Clown* (1972), which recasts Alan Alda. This time, he's a crazed Vietnam vet who, with his two vicious Dobermans, holds a young couple hostage at a beach house. It's certainly interesting to see Alda play against type, as a damaged and potentially homicidal martinet, but the film is another artifact in an unpleasant canon of violent programmers that pitched returning war veterans as ticking time bombs. When that film likewise flopped, Bloomfield turned to *Child Under a Leaf* (1974), a dour soap opera starring Dyan Cannon as a Montreal housewife who has borne her lover's child. As in *Jenny*, there's a baby born a symbol and "pregnant with meaning," but also, the often intriguing arthouse rigors of *Jenny* are cranked up to overdrive here. The only endorsements *Child Under a Leaf* received were from Rex Reed (for what that's worth) and, curiously, Danny Peary (in his *Guide for the Film Fanatic*). Otherwise, the film was savaged in no uncertain terms. Martin Knelman writes in his Canadian cinema book *This is Where We Came In*, "Everything about Dyan Cannon's character tells us she's spoiled, shallow, and ruthless, yet we're supposed to weep for her."

With its reductive, tinkling, sometimes bossa-nova Francis Lai score, *Child Under a Leaf* is an odd coda to a kind of unofficial trilogy of Bloomfieldian bleakness. It's a digestible enough melodrama replete with the period's finest in shag furnishings—perfect for those with either a Dyan Cannon fetish (she's not too shabby overall), or a taste for Seventies-style romantic histrionics, but little else. Bloomfield's career peaked with the respected Canadian historical epic *Riel* (1979), starring Christopher Plummer, Leslie Nielsen, and William Shatner. It was produced as a miniseries by none other than John Trent, before a shortened, streamlined version played theatrically in other territories.

On the flipside of this joint study, Trent's anemic comedies— *It Seemed Like a Good Idea at the Time* (1975), *Find the Lady* (1976), and *Middle Age Crazy* (1980)—fail to assure viewers that Trent is anything more than an unabashed mediocrity in the director's chair. He was perspicacious enough, however, to recognize John Candy (who co-stars as "Kopek" in both *Good Idea* and *Lady*) as a marketable comedic talent years before others did. The best thing in any of those three is a cheeky animated title sequence in *It Seemed Like a Good Idea at the Time*, with the voice of star Anthony Newley ribbing the names as they appear onscreen. Above all, Trent was historically important as a producer with an executive position (next to David Perlmutter) at Quadrant Films, which sponsored works by Bob Clark, David Cronenberg, and Ivan Reitman. (Quadrant also produced George Bloomfield's final theatrical films, the dreadful *Nothing Personal* and *Double Negative*.)

What remains—well, at least in the case of Bloomfield—is the early promise of *Jenny*. His is a case of high hopes dashed by a grand pretense that faltered as often as (or arguably more than) it paid artistic dividends. Trent, though lacking much of any voice or taste as an actual artist (i.e. director), wound up playing a crucial role in the development of Canada's best upcoming talent. All without saying that many make a viable argument that *Sunday in the Country* is a masterpiece of its kind, as sick and stomach-churning as it gets. Trent and Bloomfield's intertwining careers microcosmically chart an arc for the Canadian film industry during the time they were both working. There were many talented fellow-countryman directors who didn't get the second or third shots in the director's chair that they did. While Trent perished in a car accident in 1983 at the age of 48, Bloomfield retired from features into a lucrative television career before dying in 2011.

John Trent's Theatrical Feature Films: *The Bushbaby* (1970), *The Heart Farm* (1970, a.k.a. *The Man Who Wanted to Live Forever*), *Homer* (1970), *Sunday in the Country* (1974), *It Seemed Like a Good Idea at the Time* (1975), *Find the Lady* (1976), *Crossbar* (1979), *Middle Age Crazy* (1980), *Best Revenge* (1984)

George Bloomfield's Theatrical Feature Films: *Jenny* (1970), *To Kill a Clown* (1972), *Child Under a Leaf* (1974), *Riel* (1979), *Nothing Personal* (1980), *Double Negative* (1980)

○ ○ ○

Winning Hearts on Losers' Sleeves:
The Paul Lynch and Les Rose Visions
(with a Peek into Peter Pearson)

> There is a town in north Ontario, / With dream comfort memory to spare, / And in my mind I still need a place to go, / All my changes were there. / Blue, blue windows behind the stars, / Yellow moon on the rise, / Big birds flying across the sky, / Throwing shadows on our eyes. / Leave us / Helpless, helpless, helpless, helpless.

> Neil Young, Canadian songwriter, "Helpless"

Donald Shebib's *Goin' Down the Road* became such an instant Canadian classic that it cut the pattern for the "cinema of losers" that followed in its wake. Paul Lynch with *The Hard Part Begins* (1973) and Les Rose with *Three Card Monte* (1978) were just two of the filmmakers who capitalized on this emerging custom-made national subgenre: chronicles of predominately male nobodies going nowhere—hemmed-in dreamers of a die-hard vintage, down on their luck but too naïve, polite, or bored to fully implode. Martin Knelman writes of Lynch's film, "It manages to catch the feeling of the nowhere towns that all seem the same, and to create from the subject of their stifling boredom a movie that is the opposite of stifling and boring."

Both *The Hard Part Begins* and *Three Card Monte* were made for just less than $100,000.

Lynch has been a close personal friend of mine going on fifteen years, and I knew him personally before I got more closely acquainted with his film work, thus it is hard to be completely objective. While Vancouverite Daryl Duke mounted his on-the-road-again country music joyride *Payday* (1973) in Alabama more or less concurrently with Lynch's similar *The Hard Part Begins*, it was Lynch who shot and set his movie in their native Canada. Lynch's is a wonderfully earthy picture, with a lead character that is, in essentially every way, far more gentlemanly than the one in the Daryl Duke counterpart—in country music terms, more Porter Wagoner and less Johnny Paycheck. Knelman continues, "If there were justice in show business, this movie would do something good for the career of Paul Lynch, the director." Lynch did wind up climbing the ladder of success, however onerous the journey proved to be. To invent a word for the occasion, the ascent was contortionary (as to say, the Canadian film industry put him in some cumbersome and precarious positions, until he scored his first major commercial hit in a lucrative genre seven years later).

Rose's funky little career sprint was no less arduous. Personally, I happened upon both *Three Card Monte* (1978) and *Isaac Littlefeathers* (1984) by chance, while browsing physical media; I was attracted to the unusual title of the latter and the wonky video box of the former. Rose's passion projects are nowhere near the greatest works to ever come out of Canada, but nor did Rose intend them to be. They're refreshingly unpretentious and come right from the heart, never more or less than what they present themselves to be. And above all other considerations, at least there's the unassuming charm of something very Canadian on-screen at all times. These are purebred pictures. *Three Card Monte* plays like a slightly more R-rated and Canuck-ified *Paper Moon*, complete with nifty truisms like "You slide a lot further on bullshit than you can on sand." In terms of style, there is not terribly much, though an opening scherzo of ricocheting pool balls is a dazzling coup of cutting. Moose Jaw, Saskatchewan-native Richard Gabourie, who won the Canadian Film Award for Best Actor in this role, stars as a peripatetic flim-flammer named Busher who teams up with a 13-year-old runaway. Of course, in the case of *Three Card Monte*, we're talking Canada, where happy endings are as much in short supply as poutine at a health-food café.

Canada's nonpareil record for such stories guaranteed tragic trajectories and a vast preponderance of bummer endings. In *Three Card Monte*, a thieves' highway of hitchhikers, scammers, boozers, card-sharps, and a general class of itinerant sad sack, reaches its terminus when our remorseless hero cannot take an off-ramp when it's offered. Quite tragically, he suffers the consequences, because to make his way in the world any other way would be to merely admit another kind of defeat. Only a constant hustle dangles any promise of manumission. The cost for one's salvation is surrender, one that is unacceptable.

In the case of the hero as played by Donnelly Rhodes in *The Hard Part Begins*, the cycles keep cycling, with no passport to the stars in the offing. It all boils down to who's got the upper hand, who's afforded the leg-up, whose noses are left to the grindstone, and if those toilers can ever get a foothold. One can live impractically in hope, or one can pay piecemeal for such delusion on a lifetime layaway plan, under which you have to keep putting your dreams away for another day. Thus is—or at least was—life in the Great North, at least as these movies instruct us.

Lynch's sophomore feature, *Blood & Guts* (1978), does for wrestlers what his freshman film did for honky-tonkers. If John Badham (covered later in this book) is America's "subculture specialist," then Lynch started out as the Canadian equivalent. On the Canuxploitation database of reviews, this wrestling circuit odyssey is designated the "last in the line of Canadian loser films," and in this last outing, there is at least a nonbinding but implicitly understood code of ethics that our characters live by. This is the type of robust community that Harvey Hart's characters longed to fully realize. As a newcomer is absorbed into their midst, the wrestlers are just generous enough, but are vigilant and protective of what they've built. Writer John Hunter, who brilliantly scripted *The Hard Part Begins*, returns here, and his presence is often felt. Film scholar Joseph McBride is credited as co-writer, and I know he still feels somewhat bitter about the production, including toward Lynch and his producers (including Quadrant Films' David Perlmutter).

From one form of pugilism we go to another, with the boxing-focused *Isaac Littlefeathers* (1984), Rose's barely released final feature. A part-Native (half-Cree, half-Métis) boy is adopted by a Jewish shopkeeper (Lou Jacobi), raised as a Jew, and groomed as an up-and-coming prize fighter. Rose had been steadily developing the project since 1976, but was unable to secure funding for it, even in the tax-shelter ecosystem following the successful release of *Three Card Monte*. Following some scattered screenings, it did at last find a home on the CBC, and then cable. *Isaac Littlefeathers* is the type of film that only Canada can produce. One might get the sense that it's contrived, but it's Western Canada flavor and its warmhearted-to-a-fault disposition make for a winning cocktail.

Lynch and Rose found themselves "doing their time" on pictures that better fed the bottom line. Lynch, for one, after the success of *Halloween* (1978), was encouraged to pitch horror. He concocted *Prom Night* (1980), a slasher hit inspired from a billboard Lynch saw on Sunset Blvd, starring newly annointed scream queen Jamie Lee Curtis fresh off the Carpenter classic. Lynch's work continued apace with the moody but gnarly *Humongous* (1982), a still-stylish outing replete with split diopter shots and bluesy accent lighting; it became a slasher cult item during its run on cable. Betwixt *Monte* and *Isaac*, Rose got another shot at a passion project for the CBC "For the Record" series of films (akin to "Play for Today" in England): *Maintain the Right* (1980), about one man facing down political corruption at the Royal Canadian Mounted Police. Gerald Pratley complimented the film's moral dilemma as "well thought-out." Beyond that, there was a limp, quickly dismissed unofficial follow-up to *Monte*, *Title Shot* (1979), which cast *Monte*'s Gabourie alongside Tony Curtis. The pitiful *Gas* (1981), the awful tax-shelter comedy to end all awful tax-shelter comedies, was nevertheless picked up by Paramount for distribution. (*Gas* would make a torturous but ideal double bill with Harvey Hart's equally feeble *Utilities*—what was it with tax-shelter comedies and service-provider indignation?)

Actor Saul Rubinek once rued the early period at the Canadian Film Development Corporation (later Telefilm Canada), stating, "It's a shell game, and that shell game is art, commerce, and nationalism. And as soon as you make it art, they say, 'Ahh, but it's not commercial.' Then you make it commercial, and they say, 'Yes, but it's not Canadian! Or French-Canadian!' And as soon as you make it Canadian, they say, 'But it's not art or it's not commercial.' And you get shifted around by these bureaucrats until you die." And therein lies the struggles Lynch and Rose faced in trying to craft simple human stories about the types of strivers we recognize in everyday life—the prickly pleasures in tales of the puckishly picayune.

Paul Lynch, for one, happily made due as a Canadian industry filmmaker, carving out a niche for himself as a director-for-hire, after his first few very personal feature-film forays chronicling subcultures that intrigued him. He eventually proved comfortable hopping genre at a fairly regular clip, later making his home in episodic television. I personally wish he'd given us a few more peeks into concealed little worlds that subsist on their own rules and self-definitions. His *Cross Country* (1983), likewise written by John Hunter, had some hints of that too. Les Rose wasn't quite so lucky. After the travails of *Isaac Littlefeathers*, he basically retired.

Peter Pearson was a fellow traveler of theirs, having directed *The Best Damn Fiddler from Calabogie to Kaladar* (1969), one of the great median-length works of Canadian film history and in general. With that prize-winning journey into the Canadian sticks, and his proper feature debut *Paperback Hero* (1973), Pearson similarly taps into the vagaries of small-town life. The two Pearson films, in concert with the kindred efforts of Les Rose and Paul Lynch, build loserly shadow-plays driven by the escape fantasies of semi-educated seekers and two-bit backwater dreamers. In the case of *Paperback Hero*, the lead's vibrant fantasy life has been fueled by classically American myth and its cultural machinery (e.g. Westerns, dime novels)—again, the sense that the medicine for melancholy, hardship, and ennui waited for these dead-enders "down in the States." Pearson directed only one more feature, a failed comedy called *Only God Knows* (1974), before packing it in as movie director. He ruffled some feathers with a series of politically charged shows for the CBC, include four for their "For the Record" series (most notably *The Insurance Man from Ingersoll*), only to then essentially retire to fill positions in the nascent cinema bureaucracy, first as president of the Director's Guild of Canada, then as executive director of Telefilm Canada.

Some people are born to juggle. Give them three balls, they'll get the trick down in ten minutes or less. Lynch succeeded because his need to be on a set and in the zone was unconquerable. Once in a while, another gem would come along, and he'd quietly take it on, without basically any fanfare. He's Canadian, after all—so… fanfare? Who needs it? Others find juggling impossible. Les Rose couldn't hack the pressures, but we're left with at least three lovely, delightfully human films of his that are worth tracking down.

Paul Lynch's Theatrical Feature Films: *The Hard Part Begins* (1973), *Blood & Guts* (1978), *Prom Night* (1980), *Humongous* (1982), *Cross Country* (1983), *Flying* (1986, a.k.a. *Dream to Believe*), *Bullies* (1986), *Blindside* (1987)

Les Rose's Theatrical Feature Films: *Three Card Monte* (1978), *Title Shot* (1979), *Maintain the Right* (1980), *Hog Wild* (1980), *Gas* (1981), *The Life and Times of Edwin Alonzo Boyd* (1982), *Isaac Littlefeathers* (1984)

Peter Pearson's Theatrical Feature Films: *The Best Damn Fiddler from Calabogie to Kaladar* (1969), *Paperback Hero* (1973), *Only God Knows* (1974), *The Insurance Man from Ingersoll* (1976), *Bananas from Sunny Quebec* (1993)

○ ○ ○

The One-and-Dones:
Alexis Kanner, Patrick Loubert and Gordon Sheppard

Journalist Robert Fulford once remarked that "a generation of English-speaking Canadians grew up believing that the smartest among them would eventually 'graduate' from Canada," because "real things happened elsewhere." While it's true that Canadian restlessness feeds into the power of Canadian film art (to whatever degree), Canada did lose many of its best and brightest talents to Britain and Hollywood. It also failed to nurture some of its more "way out there" homebody talents—filmmaker oddballs who, in spite of everything, chose to stick around. In the Seventies, as Canada continued colonizing its cinematic wilderness, it fostered a great many distinctive voices, many of whom have already been profiled in this book. While some of these talents later ripened to enjoy long, rewarding, sometimes highly profitable careers, others withered after their first time out. In most cases, they were unable to fund follow-up endeavors when their debuts were deemed much too odd and "niche" for public consumption. And the system at that point was much too fragile to support perceived upstarts who, for all intents and purposes, failed their "test runs."

The three I have in mind here are nothing if not "oddities"— that's the most appropriate word. Unfortunately, as far-out as they dared to play, no one at the time seemed even remotely ready for their stylistic audacity.

Alexis Kanner's *Kings and Desperate Men* (1981) is one of my favorite films. Shot in the winter of 1977 in Montreal, it was released sporadically throughout the decade that followed. Merely describing the mechanics of plot does such a radically experimental narrative film no justice. It is a frenzied audiovisual phantasmagoria, a free-for-all of schizoid sound editing and sometimes nearly avant-garde cutting patterns. Patrick McGoohan plays an urbane talk radio host held hostage in his loft studio by crusading terrorists who wish to broadcast an on-air retrial for a man they've deemed wrongfully convicted, with the listening audience to act as phone-in jury. Kanner himself co-stars as the foppish terrorist ringleader. As the "trial" progresses, disembodied voices, echoes and distortions, Christmas hymns, fragmentary street scenes, religious imagery, and portraits of random broadcast listeners, underscore the furious battle of wits and wills between captor and captive. Kanner's depiction of a frozen Montreal brands images on the brain that are indelible.

Director Ronald Neame became a fierce advocate, telling the press, "Alexis has had great difficulty marketing it because of its uniqueness. A film like this has got to be nursed, and here in America, there are very few places in which to nurse it." Neame took care to recommend the film to the late, great Arthur Knight, and it in turn became such a favorite of his that he screened it multiple times for his classes at USC. He wrote in *The Hollywood Reporter*, "Style is the essence of *Kings and Desperate Men.* Kanner's script is rich in ironies and sophisticated verbal parries, all of which the urbane McGoohan plays to the hilt. But if the verbal bouts are often dizzying, Kanner's camera moves and editing are even more so—almost perverse in their laconic, elliptic avoidance of the obvious. [...] For all the flash and flair of his technique, Kanner has not stinted on the intellectual excitement of a battle of wills. It's fascinating to watch, and every bit as compelling to listen to."

Before I became further acquainted with cast member Andrea Marcovicci, I interviewed her about her not-too-happy time on the production. Those on set had jokingly retitled it *Kings and Desperate Crew.* Her account—of two avowed alcoholics (McGoohan and Kanner) having a boozy, drinking-buddy field day while the script supervisor devolved into daily cold-sweat panics—is harrowing. No one had an easy time keeping director and star under control, to the point that, when Marcovicci was told she was wrapped, she hurled an ashtray at McGoohan's head in disgust as revenge. Though I consider

Kings and Desperate Men.

the completed film at least something approaching genius, it was bedlam to make. This contributed to Kanner being denied a second go in the director's chair, as much as any other factor. Kanner managed to corral a great deal of press attention by casting Canadian First Lady Margaret Trudeau in the role of McGoohan's wife. The part isn't necessarily one you would call "juicy," but her very presence lends the film further weight as a piece of Canadian history.

Years later, Kanner unsuccessfully attempted to sue the creators of *Die Hard* (1988) for stealing their concept from *Kings and Desperate Men*. He spent the rest of his days attending fan events for "The Prisoner," the much beloved cult show on which he co-starred with McGoohan. Kanner's opus, his one film as director, never did clear the necessary hurdles, though he never stopped beating the drum for it. I've seen *Kings and Desperate Men* I don't know how many times, so often I can now quote all the dialogue. I have also had the privilege of screening it to two separate audiences, and it spurred lively conversation. It's so purely cinematic, and it seems that most have limited frame of reference for how artfully scattershot it plays. It writes its own audiovisual grammar in a way that likely scared off future investors, just as much as Kanner's reputed behavior on set did.

Kanner told *Screen International* in 1985, "My long-term ambition is to live like John Huston, make the odd picture, appear for somebody else in the odd picture to make a few bob to pay the bills, and then go to [La] Scala, Milan, to direct *Rigoletto* or something. But I guess you have to live a long time and do a lot of work to become John Huston." Kanner never realized that ambition, but his one movie is worthy of reappraisal today. The boldness of its montage and its madhouse soundscape may well have been ahead of its time. As of this writing, it has not had a video release since 1989, when it premiered on a poorly color-timed VHS.

Gordon Sheppard's *Eliza's Horoscope* (1975) is the second of my three one-and-done oddities. In his *A Century of Canadian Cinema*, Gerald Pratley notes, "When this film was shot in the summer of 1970, Warner Bros. withdrew when the film's budget exceeded the original estimate. Work proceeded in stops and starts for the next four years, requiring the use of three directors of photography." He brands the film "heavily allegorical and densely symbolic."

The Oxford-educated Sheppard began his career with the CBC in 1960, as a writer and interviewer on public affairs programs such as "The Lively Arts." It was after leaving government service that he began work on *Eliza's Horoscope*. Of its impetus, Sheppard once wrote, "It began in a coffee bar on Bishop Street in Montreal in the spring of 1967, when I overheard two female university students discussing their romantic activities with men in terms of astrological signs. I was surprised. Of course I'd heard of astrology and horoscopes, but it never occurred to me that people would take astrology so seriously as to take amatory decisions based on people's signs. But in the spiritual disarray of that era, I soon saw that this made sense. In Quebec, which was in the throes of the Quiet Revolution, the Catholic Church was losing the powerful hold it had long held over French-Canadians; and in the Western world in general, people were in a quandary as to what faith to embrace to try and make sense of life. People were trying different paths, from Buddhism to Hare Krishna sects to the Moonies, not to mention the spaced-out spiritual visions of Timothy Leary and LSD. I realized that astrology was another alternative, though it was one which I personally found hard to credit for a number of reasons."

Sheppard cast Elizabeth Moorman, whom Sheppard met at the Playboy Mansion when trying to lure Hugh Hefner into financing the project. Her title character, a Pisces, learns from an astrologer that she will marry a rich and handsome Aries she will meet in the next ten days. Just as she sets out to make the prediction come true, she meets fledgling terrorist Tommy (brash, young Tommy Lee Jones), an angry half-Cree activist involved in the Red Power movement, who is dead set on blowing up one of the city's bridges. Also involved in Eliza's life is her boarding house roommate Lila, an old music hall performer, now a bar waitress, who tries to woo Eliza away from astrology and into an embrace of Catholicism.

In many ways, *Eliza's Horoscope* may have alienated audiences even more than *Kings and Desperate Men*. The only "star power" it boasted was Lila Kedrova, who had won an Oscar for her supporting role in *Zorba the Greek* in 1965. Québécois filmmaking legend Michel Brault is credited as one of the film's three cinematographers, next to Paul Van Der Linden (the "eyes" of *Kings and Desperate Men*) and Jean Boffety (an Altman and Lelouch favorite). That it has by now popped up on multiple bargain-bin video labels ensures it has circulated far better than either of the other two films profiled in this section.

Despite his travails over the course of nearly five years, Sheppard's budget rounded out to $1.6 million when all was said and done—perfectly on par with lower-bracket Hollywood studio product of its time. Though *Eliza's Horoscope* was never reviewed far and wide, there is today a wide swath of internet reviews from average viewers, most of whom are confused and sometimes downright flummoxed by its freaky-deaky eccentricities and unabashed esotericism. Considering that production commenced in the summer of 1970, its inextricably Sixties tone and tenor had likely aged like milk by the time Sheppard finally made good on delivery. A breed of tripped-out, acid-flyer midnight audience never got the chance to claim it for themselves. It was never allowed to become more than a passé artifact that slipped between the cracks. Sheppard's editorial rhythms do successfully ape those of, for instance, Resnais (at least in a watered-down, dime-store sense), and this alone makes it worth pursuit by intrepid cine-adventurists. Gerald Pratley was cautiously complimentary, calling it "ambitious, thought-provoking, and obscure," rightly deducing that "[its] promise eluded producers."

Animator Patrick Loubert's live-action *125 Rooms of Comfort* (1974) is the third of the oddities. Loubert stitches together an odd patchwork of characters, which ably answers to the ones offered up by our other two one-and-doners. The story is deceptively simple, but full of... well, deceptions. Heir Billie Joyce (Tim Henry) becomes half-owner of the seedy Grand Central Hotel in downtown St. Thomas, Ontario (the real landmark establishment where it was filmed). He is a former rock musician finishing a stint at a mental institution, due to an unexplained penchant for committing aimless acts of violence, and an inability to conform with off-stage standards of behavior. He is not interested in refurbishing his newly acquired property, but rather in selling his portion. When Billie visits the hotel in order to complete the sale to Oscar Kidd, an entrepreneur from the United States, he discovers that the co-owner Jim obviously has a sub rosa agenda of his own. He also learns that several employees of the Grand Central are counting on him for assistance in retaining their jobs, because of Jim's chicanery. From there, things get... weird. Billie starts galavanting around the halls decked out in formal female attire, hair, and makeup. In one sequence, he is chased by a group of men from a hotel-catered stag party. He becomes involved with a range of capital-C characters, including Leo, an itinerant third-rate lounge comedian, and Oscar Kidd's dipso wife (the great Jackie Burroughs, whom I call the "Meryl Streep of Canada"), who offers her body to Billie.

125 Rooms of Comfort.

Loubert's animation background comes in handy in the striking opening title sequence (rotoscope, one assumes). While Frank Tashlin parlayed his skill as animator working in live action with bold, brash comedies and comic mashups on themes of consumerism, fame and media consumption, Loubert parlays his own here with an overall outsider's sense of the unreal, or the paranoid schizophrenic. Tashlin is the boisterous American, while Loubert is the polite but oh-so-weird, "roll me over, lay me down, and do it again" Canadian. He is intent on staging his scenes with surreal, distorted camera movement and placements, which is apparent from the film's first five minutes.

Whether or not one enjoys or in any way appreciates this is dependent on personal constitution. Like *Eliza's Horoscope* and *Kings and Desperate Men*, this is a "specialty item," the type that in most cases "you have to send away for." Maybe it comes back in a plain brown wrapper—not for sexual explicitness, but for all manner of other gleeful perversions. Gerald Pratley calls it a "likable little film" but does not lavish too much praise. The film never surfaced anywhere outside of Canada—it was homegrown and home-kept, still languishing in off-label, long-out-of-print VHS purgatory (although some spelunker has cared enough to upload it to YouTube in its entirety). Loubert licked his wounds and returned to his "comfort rooms" of short-form animation. Later on, he was hired as executive story writer/editor on major animated features such as *Rock & Rule* (1983) and *Babar: The Movie* (1989).

If these pictures were produced closer to today, an A24-type company might have come along to swoop them up. Certain markets now have a taste for strange and "out there" cinematic conjures. Their custom-tailored type of "strange" became fashionable in more progressive-minded pockets with the advent of, for instance, David Lynch. One can imagine Lynch tuning into the bizarre frequencies on which these one-and-doners were transmitted. As for myself, I love each of them, especially *Kings*, which I deem a masterpiece. There were plenty of other Canadian filmmakers who gave us debuts of some distinction, yet never got their foothold with a second opportunity. I'm thinking mainly of Sylvia Spring's *Madeleine Is...* (1971), Leonard Yakir's *The Mourning Suit* (1975), Clarke Mackey's *The Only Thing You Know* (1971), Martin Defalco's *Cold Journey* (1975), and David Acomba's *Slipstream* (1973), among others. In each, there is the brazen impetuosity of "commercial prospects be damned, I'm making this for me because... who knows if I'll get to do this again?" That, on its own, is something quite extraordinary.

8. A Bridge Between Two Nights
Toward a Canadian Sensibility on Film

Published on my now defunct ConFluence-Film Blog in 2010, when my keen interest in Canadian cinema was first developing.

C'est ce pont que je construis
De ma nuit jusqu'à ta nuit
Pour traverser la rivière
Froide obscure de l'ennui
Voilà dans le pays à faire.

It is that I build this bridge
From my night to your night
To cross the river
The cold, dark stillness
Here in the country to be realized.

Gilles Vigneault, (b. 1928)
Québécois poet, "Il me reste un pays"

As someone born and raised in the United States, and as one who enjoys a hearty intake of books and films, I often encounter discussions of the "great American novel" and the "great American movie." One ultimately begins to question the litmus test by which an exalted status like either of these honors gets determined. Needless to say, though, it is always most every American writer or filmmaker's goal. But to what extent does the word "American" really play into said great work's identity? What does a work's national identity even mean, and does the same standard hold if one goes, say, north or south of the vast forty-eight state expanse?

Keeping that in mind, the concept of a national cinema is a curious one, and, one might say, a troubling abstraction. For natives of any given flag, "national cinema" remains shrouded in a veritable crazy-quilt of convolutions and conflicting agendas, all of which claim ties to nationalism. Also often stitched into this crazy-quilt are loaded distortions and subversions. Nonetheless, many tend to hold the position that a film should not just merely serve in representing a land, its society, and its general sensibilities, but should instead fully embody and *be* them. Of course, shifting political climates, power structures, and perspectives on history and popular memory enter into the equation when national cinema is discussed openly. Other fascinating cases like Balkan cinema— and what is breezily defined in rather generic and limiting terms as "third world cinema" or "regional cinema"—are worth considering in this light as well. The key question that is often asked vis-à-vis the national cinema criterion is, "It's good, but is it really a [fill-in-the-homeland] film?" Undue pressures are thus placed on filmmakers to deliver Cinema for Motherland. Some heavyweights of film theory and cinema studies, especially hardened auteurists, have even gone as far as to claim that the existence of a national cinema is totally apocryphal.

Marshall McLuhan once said that "Canada is the only country in the world that knows how to live without an identity." In large part due to the works of documentarian, National Film Board founder, and wartime Film Commissioner John Grierson and, slightly later, animator Norman McLaren, the Canadian film industry was truly born, although there were certainly lesser-known progenitors of the country's cinema working prior to them (these men are documented in the 1974 documentary *Dreamland: A History of Early Canadian Movies 1895–1939* directed by Donald Brittain). However, until the Seventies, it was never a nation with a solid foundation in terms of its film industry; it should be noted that it was also around this time that Michael Snow's landmark, structuralist experimental epics began to emerge. By this time, the Film Board's base had moved from Ottawa to Montreal at a time of political unrest within the "two solitudes of Québéc."

Although Canada had a fine background in documentary cinema, it was without a doubt overwhelmingly gratifying for Canada's non-entity of a film industry when trailblazing independent fiction films such as Claude Jutra's *A tout prendre* (1963), Larry Kent's *The Bitter Ash* (1963), and David Secter's *Winter Kept Us Warm* (1964) surfaced with little or no financial assistance from official production sources in Canada. Most everything else of substance (and of lengthier run-time) then carried a signature, National Film Board of Canada imprimatur. Even prior to the titles named above, feature films like Sidney J. Furie's double-bill of *A Dangerous Age* (1957) and *A Cool Sound from Hell* (1959), William Davidson's *Now That April's Here* (1958), and René

Bonnière's *Amanita Pestilens* (1963, produced by famous Ottawa film personality Budge Crawley and featuring a young Genevieve Bujold) seemed to vanish from sight, remaining largely unseen even today.

When the Canadian Film Development Corporation (CFDC) was established in 1967 to stimulate a fully functional, financially sound film industry in Canada with the help of millions of dollars of government funding, the paradigm began to shift. It was under its auspices that directors like David Cronenberg and Ivan Reitman rose to later prominence. The production company Cinépix often worked in cooperation with the CFDC. Attentions centered largely on works intent on establishing a late-to-arrive Canadian identity in the cinema, and this yielded rather compelling results. This, it is important to note, was all under the aegis of the government. Heads of production were answerable to the Canadian Parliament.

There is not a great volume of works formally written on the subject of the early Canadian film industry. However, I continue to observe how the Canadian films I digest are all so profoundly and intensely personal, and in an altogether different way than most other works of international cinema when considering country of origin. One can easily assess the reasons for Canada's astounding brand of personal cinema. For one, the late-to-arrive Canadian film industry sowed its identity with the help of novice, passionate directors at a time when equipage was becoming more portable and when the American film industry was itself entering a bold period of personal filmmaking due to shifting audience interest.

One of the things I find fascinating is that each province of Canada has exactitudes in terms of cinematic stamp and sensibility. One can distinguish, for example, a Québéc film from a British Columbian or an Ontario film, with little to no effort. In the case of Québéc, unrest was in full bloom amongst Québécois at the outset of Canada's film revolution, during which time the long-ruling Québéc leader Maurice Duplessis (whose ultra-conservative reign was known by many as La Grande Noirceur, or "The Great Blackness") died in office, setting the stage for the struggle towards a new rule, one that favored a balanced, pluralist socio-political climate. This era, which covers a turbulent span of six years in Québéc, is known as the Quiet Revolution.

On a personal note, the overall, international canon of regional low-budget independent cinema is rightly beloved because viewers associate the given films with authentic voices expressing something essential about life in seldom-considered pockets of the world. This idea is often embodied in Canadian films of this time, but this did not come without its confounding obstacles. I find it appropriate, and of use, to profile two beloved pioneers in the development of the Canadian cinema art: one Francophone (who later made some English-language films), the other Anglophone.

○ ○ ○

Patrie intime de ma foi,
Dans une immuable assurance,
Je veux vivre encore avec toi,
Jusqu'au soir de mon espérance.

Intimate homeland of my faith,
In an enduring assurance,
I still live with you
Until the evening of my hope.

Charles-Nérée Beauchemin (1850–1929)
Québécois poet, "Patrie intime"

Claude Jutra: The Archaeologist Poet

Note: I remind you, dear reader, that with this having been originally written in 2010, it predates the scandal that forever tarnished Jutra's legacy. I will be discussing the films themselves, and the filmmaker behind them on those terms, rather than his personal life or recent ignominy. He remains, in spite of everything, one of my most treasured filmmakers.

It could be said that Claude Jutra is Canada's Orson Welles. I do not lightly make this claim, nor do I make such a bold comparison to merely raise eyebrows. The analogy is not only apt because Jutra directed what is often officially recognized as the best film ever produced in Canada, *Mon Oncle Antoine* (1971), or because his follow-up film, *Kamouraska* (1973), was an ambitious epic that wound up emasculated by its producers, much like Welles' follow-up to *Citizen Kane*, *The Magnificent Ambersons*, but also because Jutra struggled greatly towards the end of his life in producing work that he could call his own, striving to exist within the rapidly evolving world of filmmaking in both English and French Canada—and as we all know, Welles' final decades were spent hustling for money to realize his sundry projects throughout

Kamouraska.

decades when American cinema was shaken to its core. Like Welles, Jutra would shoot bits and pieces of film when he could scrounge up money. He would travel, mostly to other parts of Canada, to get funding for projects, and would take acting gigs in the films of others, much like how Welles globe-trotted to secure completion funds, taking often thankless parts in dozens of movies. Jutra's heart was buried deeply in Québéc and his finest works were made for Québécois.

By the time he was exiled to English Canada in the late Seventies, he had resigned himself to making television films for the Canadian Broadcasting Corporation (1976's *Ada* and 1977's *Dreamspeaker*, to name the two most widely known). He immediately followed his brief television tenure by directing two compromised English-language features, particularly *Surfacing* (1980), an ill-fated but nonetheless fascinating adaptation of Margaret Atwood's popular novel. The other, *By Design* (1982), a comedy heartily championed by Pauline Kael, followed two lesbian fashion designers in their quest to have babies. He ended his career with one last Francophone masterpiece in Québéc, *La dame en coleurs* (1985), but is known to have lamented, "Sometimes I wonder, why are things easier for me in English Canada and so difficult in Québéc? Then I remember the answer: Everything is more difficult for everybody in Québéc.

Jutra had launched his career in cinema with a series of NFB-funded short films and documentaries (including the award-winning *A Chairy Tale*, co-directed with Norm McLaren) and completed his first feature film, the groundbreaking *A tout prendre* (1963). *A tout prendre*, seen now, fits more into the Nouvelle Vague movement than even some bona-fide French New Wave films. While Jutra obviously owes much to those works, the film stands on its own two—very Canadian, very Québécois—feet. By the time Jutra made his second feature, *Wow* (1970), which remains his most overtly political work, he was already something of a legend in Montreal. However, he was attacked throughout his career for what was perceived as political neglect. His disinclination to make cinema that would more directly and confrontationally jostle Québec out of its complacency rankled contemporary critics.

Jutra could, however, hardly be called apolitical. He was an ardent separatist who refused the Order of Canada, supported the Québec sovereignty movement (which supported Québec's right to exist independently of Canada) and demonstrated against Duplessis during the revolution. He hailed from a liberal upper-class Montreal family who also vehemently opposed Duplessis' backwards policies. However, Jutra's cinematic politics were carefully revealed from a controlled distance.

Martin Knelman, in *This is Where We Came In: The Career and Character of Canadian Film*, writes that "when Jutra tries to be overtly political, whether onscreen or off, you feel it's a violation of something deep within his nature." In the same breath, Knelman continues, "Jutra's work isn't political in the same narrow, didactic terms as, say, Arcand's *Rejeanne Padovanni* or Michel Brault's *Les ordres*; yet maybe Jutra is political in a deeper way." This could not be any more true. Jim Leach, in his book *Claude Jutra: Filmmaker*, notices that "Realizing that no form is ideologically pure, [Jutra] chose to work within existing forms, with the result that his films were rarely perceived as formally or politically innovative."

Though the politics of Jutra's masterpieces, *Mon Oncle Antoine* and *Kamouraska*, failed to register in the cold light of day, he ventures to contextualize the current by depositing his stories in the safety of history. In the early Seventies, more topical films by the likes of Denys Arcand, Gilles Carle and Jean Pierre Lefebvre (who was identified by one critic in 1962 as "the Canadian incarnation of Godard") offered a stark contrast to Jutra's. *Mon Oncle Antoine* is often designated as a "coming-of-age" film, but it is

Mon Oncle Antoine.

decidedly more the snapshot of a time and place (much more so than most coming-of-age films, which focus on a single character rooted in time-place trappings by chance rather than by design). Some naysayers of its day felt that its so-called "nostalgia" was ill-wrought. Its nostalgia does stir one's desire to actively participate in the film, to climb into the screen as to absorb oneself in its gray but warm Christmas cheer, but this element is never made to be too precious nor does it obstruct our understanding of Jutra's political views. He's cueing us into the fact that current strife is rooted in the strife of past and popular memory. The very specific depiction of the Anglophone characters plays an outsized role here.

Mon Oncle Antoine follows twenty-four hours in the life of a teenage boy named Benoît living in Black Lake, an asbestos mining town circa 1940. *Kamouraska*, at least in its 1983 director's cut, is a gorgeous-lensed three-hour period melodrama based on a bestselling 1970 Canadian novel by Anne Hébert, set in a frozen Québéc town of the 1830s and starring Geneviève Bujold, who plays a woman who has plotted with her lover to murder her husband. It's kind of a frosty, sweeping nineteenth-century version of *The Postman Always Rings Twice. Mon Oncle Antoine*'s primary location Black Lake was a key locale during the Quiet Revolution, and seemed to stand as a microcosm for the mistreatment of the working class under the Duplessis reign. *Kamouraska* is based on the real-life 1839 murder of Louis-Pascal-Achille Taché, and the story of the fictionalized events surrounding this crime can be taken as an allegory for the complicit of Quebec. And that allegory is ripe: a French woman enlists an English doctor to murder her husband, born of Québec nobility. These films are piercing assessments of a nation in denial of its past, in disgrace over its present, and in doubt over its future.

What one must consider is, at this time in Québec, to be political in one's cinema was the equivalent of being "national." I find *Mon Oncle Antoine* to not only be one of the best films, Canadian or otherwise, I have ever seen, but also one of the most intensely political films, even though its political statements are camouflaged within an all-encompassing tableau of life in Black Lake, with a narrative that is intent on revealing larger and more revealing truths, rather than limiting itself to then-pressing topicalities; its ending is the young lead character's realization that things cannot continue in the muted manner to which the town has become accustomed. Benoît, for the first time, has learned to judge what he sees within his insulated, sleepy and dissipated world, and he is awakened to a harsh reality about the warped rhythm of routine that comes with life in Black Lake. The working-class nativity scene he spies upon, which mirrors the earlier general-store window display in the town, is a gateway. Much like the end of Truffaut's *400 Blows* (it should be noted that Jutra and Truffaut were friends), the film freeze-frames on Benoît peering through the window at this "twisted nativity," the dead teenage son of a miner is the focal point, sans a manger.

Earlier in the film, the townspeople quietly but grimly accept the meager Christmas gifts thrown by the oppressive English-speaking mine-owner in a manner that suggests throwing swill to hogs. This all happens without so much as an expression of discontent from the miners and their families, who watch silently and guardedly as the boss passes through town in a sleigh, haughtily puffing his pipe. They are clearly torn, simultaneously aware that any Christmas offering, even a pathetic trifle, is acceptable to the children who depend on it. It is Benoît who indulges in the only act of dissent. At another point in the film, Duplessis is explicitly mentioned, albeit in graffiti on the wall of a public john.

As a presiding spirit over the film, we get not just Jutra the director but Jutra the actor, playing the role of Fernand, the bookkeeper of the general store owned by Benoît's aunt and uncle. Pauline Kael compared his presence in the film to that of Jean Renoir in his *The Rules of the Game* (*La régle du jeu*), writing, "While you are watching the movie, you realize that the spirit behind the movie is also present in the movie, in the performance of the director." The comparison is apt because Jutra the actor is certainly a presiding spirit.

In the scene when Benoît catches red-handed Fernand and his aunt following an illicit tryst, Jutra allows himself to be the target of his protagonist's judgment. The non-professional actor Jacques Gagnon, who plays Benoît, gets the film's finest bit of nonverbal acting, all with his eyes and almost totally without dialogue. On Jutra's part as the director, I see it as an exquisite admission of personal guilt and complicity. We have a boy at the coming-of-age precipice, discovering how to judge and how to weigh the burdens of his reality. The film's director wills himself into a just prosecution in the precarious "courtroom" of a hallway outside a bedroom of assignation, as if to say, "Everyone in Québec at this time in some way contributes to the tensions and problems like those depicted in the film, either by direct action or by complacency." There is a boldness in this staging and the arrangement of the film's action that is thrilling. This is indeed a call to action.

Le pauvre québécois,
Découragé, saigné à froid,
Gagna son toit par le châssis
Et s'y pendit.

The poor Québécois,
Discouraged, bled cold,
Its roof by the frame gained
And hung itself there.

Felix LeClerc (1914–88)
Québécois songwriter, "La québécois"

The success of *Mon Oncle Antoine* abroad and in English Canada did not bode well for Jutra in the aftermath of political turmoil in Québec. Around the time Jutra was shooting *Mon Oncle Antoine* in Black Lake, Québec had found itself in the throes of the 1970 October Crisis, a series of events triggered by the twin kidnappings of government officials by members of the Front de libération du Québec, which had detonated a total of 95 bombs between the years of 1963 and 1970. The October Crisis was one of the few times in Canadian history when a form of martial law (the War Measures Act) came into effect, and civil liberties violations became a fact of life. The Canadian military arrested and detained 497 individuals without bail—all but 62 of them later released without charge.

Jutra found himself in the embarrassing position of being English Canada's favorite French-Canadian filmmaker. However, if *Mon Oncle Antoine* elicited suspicions of a wayward political aversion in Jutra's work, then his follow-up, *Kamouraska*, did nothing but confirm his artistic recalcitrance and inflexibility. What they got was an opulent literary adaptation, the likes of which were not at all common in Canadian cinema. Although critic John Hofsess made the claim that *Kamouraska* is apolitical, he added that the film "couldn't have been made anywhere in Canada except Québéc" and that its "psychic roots" are deeply embedded there. Jutra is known to have said in the wake of *Kamouraska*'s original failure, "For us, a hundred years ago is prehistory. It is before everything."

I first saw *Kamouraska* on VHS in its full 174-minute director's cut, reassembled by Jutra in 1983 for a television broadcast, a full decade after the film's Canadian and French premieres. The original theatrical version ran a truncated 124 minutes. *Kamouraska*, which was co-produced (with Québéc's Carle-Lamy Productions) by Parc Film in France, functions in very much the same way as *Mon Oncle Antoine* with its delicate, poetical implications and, from my perspective, an obvious reading of the film is an allegorical one. Elisabeth Tassy (Bujold, in what is sometimes regarded as her best screen performance) is the belle of the convent. When, after only a few short-lived weeks of marital bliss, her husband (the Lord Squire of Kamouraska) reveals himself to be a "live-in rapist" slob of overwhelming ill manner, Elisabeth takes as a lover a rugged American-born doctor named George Nelson (Richard Jordan).

Martin Knelman was one of the film's key defenders, even at a time when that position was rather unpopular. Bujold won the Best Actress award at the Canadian Film Awards that year, but the film managed to just slip away in a manner that was almost unprecedented, despite its high profile and the exalted status it held as a major production (the most expensive Canadian production in history up to that time). In comparison, I can only think of Michael Cimino's later *Heaven's Gate* (1980) to compare. That similarly epic film's own history, its withdrawal from theaters, its recut, its disappearing act and its re-emergence in full-ish glory, are extremely analogous to *Kamouraska*.

The film marked the end of an era for Jutra, who discontinued his longtime working relationship with cinematographer Michel Brault (a filmmaker in his own right, responsible for the Canadian masterpieces *Pour la suite du monde* and *Les ordres*) after shooting wrapped. Reasons for the termination were unknown even to Brault, but his work on *Kamouraska* is textbook beautiful soft-lighting. Most of Jutra's and Brault's compositions appear to the eye as paintings. Also important to note is that, in a political move, Bujold declined her award for Best Actress at the Canadian Film Awards, claiming that she was standing by Jutra and his crew when they opposed the unification of Quebec.

Jutra's previously mentioned 1980 feature *Surfacing* could have been brilliant, considering *Surfacing* author Margaret Atwood's similarly delicate "poetically political" touch and her feminist perspective on Canadian national identity. Considering Atwood's stance, one must also keep in mind that *Kamouraska* revealed Jutra's gifts for entering a female psyche. The mind boggles to think what the film might have been had Jutra been allowed to revise the script to his liking before it was locked for shooting. Jutra was brought in to replace another director and most of the elements of preproduction were already well in play.

Unfortunately, at the time, the Canadian film industry was beginning to show signs of buckling and bowing to trends. The now dreaded "tax-shelter" items were pandering shamelessly to American film marketing demands, so *Kamouraska* became a victim of a tampering blitzkrieg that limited its scope and its identity as a Canadian film, with all the fascinating, rich "baggage" that carries. As it is, Jutra enters the Northern wilderness world unassumingly, without looking to recklessly define it. Though more certainly should have been done to further realize the land itself as a character in the story, the film still has flashes of brilliance that are all too intermittent.

> Une autre vie est là pour nous,
> Ouverte à toute âme fidèle:
> Bien tard, hélas! à deux genoux,
> Je rêve d'elle!

> Another life is there for us,
> Open to any faithful soul:
> Although late, alas! on two knees,
> I dream of it!

> Louis-Honore Fréchette (1839–1908)
> Québécois poet, songwriter, "Le rêve de la vie"

Jutra's life did not end happily. The victim of early-onset Alzheimer's Disease, he committed suicide by jumping into the St. Lawrence River in late 1986, only to be found five months later when the river thawed, with a sign around his neck reading, *"Je suis Claude Jutra"* ("I am Claude Jutra"). It was with that chilling, tragic farewell that Canada and Québéc lost one of its most distinguished (and one of its most frustrated) artists, a little more than a year after his aforementioned American analog, Orson Welles, shuffled off himself. Jutra's impact on the national cinema, or what there was and is of one, cannot be underestimated. Few if any can undermine the value and enduring impact of his masterpiece *Mon Oncle Antoine*. Jim Leach, in *Claude Jutra: Filmmaker*, writes, "Jutra's problems were hardly unique in the history of Canadian cinema, but this only made it easier to think that his 'sad fade-out' was less a personal response to a medical condition than a symptom of a cultural condition."

Theatrical Feature Films: *Les mains nettes* (1957), *A tout prendre* (1963), *Wow* (1970), *Mon Oncle Antoine* (1971), *Kamouraska* (1973), *Pour le meilleur et pour le pire* (1975), *Surfacing* (1981), *By Design* (1982), *La dame en couleurs* (1985)

Other Notable Work: *A Chairy Tale* (1957, short), *La lutte* (1961, short), *Rouli-roulant* (1967, short), *Ada* (1976), *Dreamspeaker* (1976), *The Wordsmith* (1978), *Seer Was Here* (1978)

o o o

Donald Shebib: The Margins Aren't Nowhere

No study of English Canadian cinema is complete without Donald Shebib, who scored a critical and commercial knockout in 1970 with his micro-budget independent film *Goin' Down the Road*, and it is a work that still remains canonical in the annals of Canuck cinema. It is difficult to think of other Canadian works that sit quite as high in the canon as this landmark drama, shot on 16mm with never more than four people on crew, financed with a $19,000 CFDC grant and the director's personal savings. Its reputation is comparable even to that of *Mon Oncle Antoine*, which is apt because it embodies the Ontario/Maritimer identity in Canada the way *Antoine* embodies the Québéc identity. Shebib, however, never scored another success to even nearly equal that of his first feature.

Goin' Down the Road.

A few critics of its time made a point of branding it the Canadian *Midnight Cowboy* (1969), a grossly obvious parallel—but upon closer inspection, it's not a judicious one. Paul Bradley and Doug McGrath star as Maritimer buddies Joey and Pete, who pack it up and cruise into Toronto in the 1960 Chevy version of a "wing and a prayer." The story, of course, sounds perfectly familiar: two hometown blokes in search of a better life, but who are instead relegated to thankless positions in big-city society.

There is a 1972 television interview with Shebib from *The Pierre Burton Show* included on my DVD of *Goin' Down the Road*, in which the filmmaker unabashedly admits to being "turned off" by the act of reading. He claims to have been largely television-educated, though his knowledge of pre-Forties classic films is clearly encyclopedic and his general grasp of world history is impressive. Even though the screenplay of *Goin' Down the Road* is credited to William Fruet (who would pen Shebib's follow-up film *Rip-Off* (1972), then make his directorial debut with the excellent *Wedding in White*), one senses that the salt-of-the-earth qualities of Pete and Joey are a direct result of Shebib's direction, which colors brightly within Fruet's outline drawing. Texan-American independent filmmaker Eagle Pennell would hone a similar approach in his

American independent dramas *The Whole Shootin' Match* (1977) and *Last Night at the Alamo* (1983). *The Whole Shootin' Match*, in particular, can be thought of as *Goin' Down the Road*'s brash, scrappier American cousin. Both are ultra-low rent buddy films that never pander to expectations of what buddy films are and/or should be, as both try to tap into the more hidden rhythms of day-to-day living.

The performances in Shebib's grand debut possess a snappy level of folksy, gloriously unpretentious, down-to-earth repartee (even though these guys would undoubtedly hear the word "repartee" and think it's just some candy-ass French word). Knelman writes, "[the characters] are forced to exist as freaks in a [Toronto] ghetto culture for displaced Maritimers" where they "cannot blend into the background." We empathize so much with them that, amazingly enough, we can almost condone when the two go on the run from a petty crime that ends in violence. The film itself is about indignity, suffered by "backwater folks" on the fringes of Canada's Americanizing cities. We watch how the boys, with only $26 to their name, are reduced to working in a bottling factory upon their decidedly un-triumphant arrival. Plans have fallen through and the dream is drying up fast. Whereas Joey observes that they made more money in the bottle factory than they ever did in their Nova Scotia home, that is not enough to reassure Pete's hardening cynicism. They find their only true solace in the buxom French-Canadian secretary of the factory-owner, who provocatively struts her way past the charmingly primitive working stiffs, as if they were cracker-barrel cavemen.

Interestingly, Shebib's *Rip-Off* looks at the flipside. As Knelman puts it, that follow-up film is about people who have "the social advantages that Pete and Joey were victimized for their lack of," who "can't live up to what the media says their lives should be." Neil Young's famous line "Everybody knows this is nowhere" is something resembling a core expression in Shebib's first two features. Responses to *Rip-Off* were somewhat hushed, though Shebib innately understood that Canada had its discontents on both sides of the proverbial coin. He continued to duly highlight this grand chagrin in later work (including 1973's *Between Friends*, 1976's *Second Wind*, and 1981's *Heartaches*). *Goin' Down the Road* also spawned a number of later films about other quixotic figures in small, hidden-away Canadian hamlets (*The Rowdyman*, *The Hart Part Begins*, and *Paperback Hero* among them)—all with dreams of mobility, in all that word's connotations. For Jim Leach, this group (or school) of films explored "the tension between American dreams and Canadian reality."

Shebib directed a sequel to *Goin' Down the Road* forty years after the original, entitled *Down the Road Again* (2011). Though I have never seen the film, I do recall the late Telluride Film Festival director Tom Luddy describing it as a major disappointment. The true spiritual follow-up to the triumph of Shebib's glorious debut is the female flipside of the story, *Heartaches* (1981), starring Canadian-born Margot Kidder and Annie Potts, as two who meet on a bus to Toronto, get an apartment together there, and go to work at a mattress factory. As in Bill Fruet's excellent *Wedding in White* (1972), which Shebib wrote, pregnancy with an illegitimate child is a key story element, or the essential predicament.

Whereas Claude Jutra operated within the scope of history with great freedom, a filmmaker like Donald Shebib operated within the cage of cold modernity with similar and like-minded freedom. What is astounding to realize is that there is certainly reciprocity between the two artists' filmographies. Both provide clear, penetrating evocations of a Canada in flux.

Theatrical Feature Films: *Goin' Down the Road* (1970), *Rip-Off* (1972), *Between Friends* (1973), *Second Wind* (1976), *Fish Hawk* (1979), *Heartaches* (1981), *Running Brave* (1983), *The Climb* (1986), *The Ascent* (1994), *Down the Road Again* (2011), *Nightalk* (2022)

○ ○ ○

Conclusion: A Cute, Acute Awareness

Yes, as you've no doubt put together by now, I am that strange American with the strongest of proclivities toward Canadian art and Canadian cinema, specifically Canadian independent cinema. I often prefer it over even my own country's analog. In my multi-decade study of Canadian film, I've of course encountered and befriended a number of filmmakers and performers from that... how to say this right... quietly dynamic country up north, and I've had some robust conversations with them. One of these individuals even became my best friend and mentor. This is someone who grew up in 1940s and '50 Toronto, and he explained to me what he called the national inferiority complex that was instilled in him from an early age. Friends of his were known to ask, 'If you're so good, why aren't you down in the States?' Down in the States! It felt like we were never good enough." That's what he remembers. What a way to be set up for life! But what lies underneath Canadian independent films is the one thing that perhaps intrigues me the most: you get the sense that the filmmakers believe that they better put their most intensely personal, intimate selves into these pictures, because maybe, just maybe, they won't get to do this again. And the conditions of the film ecosystem in Canada early on did stack the cards against them. At the heart of Canadian cinema is a beautiful desperation. Every filmmaker's face belongs to a cockeyed and cocksure mosaic distinguished by streaks of color you never knew existed.

> She loved to talk about art things. Like, whose work shows talent, and whose doesn't. And whose work shows acute awareness. Like, at first, I thought she meant like a cute face. And whose work came from half-lives half-lived. Isn't that great? Half-lives, half-lived."
>
> Polly (Sheila McCarthy)
> in *I've Heard the Mermaids Singing*

The ending of Patricia Rozema's formative Canadian classic *I've Heard the Mermaids Singing* (1987) that speaks to the historic plight of Canadian filmmakers, and Canadian artists in general. The lead character Polly has been ignored, underestimated, even spurned, throughout the runtime. Her art comes from a very real, very personal place, and yet it's summarily dismissed as trite. "The trite made flesh," to quote the specific condemnation. Maybe, on some level, she feels she must ape the style of others in order to be successful. "Am I even smart enough to imitate something successfully?" she might ask herself in classic self-abasing fashion. Yet, as the final sequence reveals to us, like all her counterparts she contains multitudes. She's got power, she has a unique way of looking at reality—and at dreams—and she has something to show us, more than has been acknowledged by the assumed connoisseurs, arbiters, critics, and experts. This is a world that few get to see outside Polly's dominion. She is the consummate, quintessential Canadian artist. Like those who turn their cameras on her, she sings a heart-shattering song on a wavelength of sound that few get to access, outside of mermaids.

Martin Knelman wrote in 1977: "That there were almost no Canadian movies coming out didn't seem as odd at the time as it does in retrospect. The Otherness of culture was something taken for granted by anyone who had grown up in Canada. In school we memorized poems about the English countryside and read plays about faraway kings. We were reading American magazines, listening to American radio, watching American TV, and buying American name brands. Why should we not have accepted Hollywood fantasies as our own? When educated moviegoers found an alternative to Hollywood, it wasn't a breakthrough for Canadian movies. When Canadians started going to tiny arthouses to see Fellini and Bergman, we were still following American taste. It didn't seem to occur to anyone that we could or should provide our own alternative."

Knelman's frank language here speaks to a prevalent frustration. America and Hollywood built the exhibition apparatus and owned the chains and controlled the reins. The National Film Board of Canada backed groundbreaking shorts and documentaries, from the likes of NFB founder John Grierson, Norm McLaren, Arthur Lipsett, Michel Brault, Donald Brittain, and others. Canadian feature-length narratives were rarefied.

Winter Kept Us Warm (1964), directed by David Secter, was shot on the shortest of shoestrings at the University of Toronto. Though it received a $750 grant from the university's student union, that was after the film was declined production grants from the Canada Council, the Ontario Arts Council, and the National Film Board. Talk about a tough room, even for a film that eventually achieved landmark status. And prior to that, when Sidney J. Furie completed his two independent dramas, he couldn't get them shown anywhere in Canada. Things were mostly quiet. Too quiet.

The backers of Don Owen's *Nobody Waved Good-bye* (1965), including the brass at the NFB, were shocked when the film scored both critically and financially. Classic reaction, in the context of what I'm discussing. The film had a low-budget swagger and, occasionally, what you might call a documentary aesthetic, rubbed off from Owen's NFB training, but it was a crossover hit that spurred many to ponder if Canadian cinema was sustainable. Columbia Pictures picked up the film for distribution, after all. Maybe anything *was* possible for the world's quietest cinema ecosystem.

It took another five years for those dreams to fully re-emerge and this time, take flight with Donald Shebib's *Goin' Down the Road* (1970). There are also two extraordinary films by women: Sylvia Spring's *Madeleine Is...* (1971) which is often recognized as the first Canadian narrative fiction feature directed by a woman, and experimental icon Joyce Wieland's *The Far Shore* (1976).

In 1975, Canada ushered in the tax-shelter era, and this saw a major rise in genre productions, largely slasher horror and teen sex comedies, à la *Meatballs* and *Porky's*. Newly emergent Canadian auteurs got the fuzzy end of the lollipop, upstaged by Hollywood (specifically, "imitation Hollywood") once again. The type of uniquely Canadian character-driven dramas pioneered by Shebib, Owen and others, took a back seat. Strike that: they were stashed in the trunk, without any chance to breathe.

So, let's fast forward a few years. We arrive at 1987; Patricia Rozema delivers *I've Heard the Mermaids Singing* to the Cannes Film Festival Director's Fortnight, where it opens to a standing ovation. After winning the Prix de la Jeunesse, it's picked up by the fledgling Miramax and performs extraordinarily well on the arthouse market. It's what might very well even be considered a crossover hit. The film, one of the few to get funding from the government's feature film fund, $350,000 to be exact, immediately goes into profit.

Most consequential in retrospect is that Patricia Rozema emerged as a key architect of the Toronto New Wave, which was both a community and a movement, boasting the talents of Don McKellar, Bruce McDonald, Peter Mettler, and Atom Egoyan. It was a community insofar as they all worked on each other's films, in varying capacities. Rozema, who is of course unique among this crowd for being the only female, once said, "I think in the creation of *Mermaids*, I did see it in political terms. I thought of the underdog. Canada is not a superpower by any means. It's very quietly, comfortably democratic, but it's plagued by a sense of inferiority. We're not a type-A personality nation."

Rozema captures something quintessential about Canadian artists in *I've Heard the Mermaids Singing*. In one fantasy sequence, Polly scales the side of a skyscraper wearing a maple-leaf tossle cap. The corporatists inside the building, including one played in a special cameo by Rozema herself, can't make sense of what she's doing, or why. The grand charade appears useless by its very nature. The central metaphor is that Canadian artists scale a literal perimeter, that being the United States border, a world power-player, a behemoth, a towering corporate monolith. Polly becomes unstuck to the glass and falls. Rather than plummeting to the ground with a horrible splat, she ecstatically takes flight over the city. The phantom lady over Toronto, if you will. A bit of a nod in that line; I invoke Jacques Rivette's *Céline and Julie Go Boating*, one of the greatest movies about storytelling, because

Polly's artistic eye, her artistic awareness, the way she sees the world, might first appear cute, but she is a driven storyteller and a rapt spectator all in one. She is acutely a seer who, while not fluent in the risible "curator-ese" that the object of her affection (and the person she most emulates) speaks—another flashing metaphor, here—her inner life is no less discerning.

From *I've Heard the Mermaids Singing*, a satirical bit involving an art critic and gallery owner discussing a painting hung before them:

CRITIC: The lack of resolution of his themes almost add to a vaguely literal internal transformation of his subject.

GALLERY OWNER: It's an external transformation.

CRITIC: Internal.

GALLERY OWNER: External, look at the lemon!

CRITIC: What about the fork?

GALLERY OWNER: Oh, the fork is irrelevant!

CRITIC: You might be right.

In "The Love Song of J. Alfred Prufrock," T. S. Eliot repeats the couplet, "In the room the women come and go / Talking of Michelangelo." Rozema's film takes its title from a line in the same poem: "I have heard the mermaids singing, each to each. / I do not think that they will sing to me." It is in the Canadian character to doubt one will hear the mermaids' song. It's the humility of the national character that elevates the art, in my opinion. The 49th parallel of the mind pays dividends, and the artists who reside there prove to us that… it's always the quiet ones.

Afterword: I feel at this juncture that, with this Canadian section, I've overlooked a number of other great early Canadian film artists, mainly Larry Kent, Don Owen, Paul Almond, Julian Roffman, Mort Ransen, and Robin Spry. This is grist for the mill for a potential volume two. Though this book is deliberately focused mostly on English-language works, I would also like to cover many of the great French-Canadian filmmakers at a future time. Suffice to say, the country's cinema is dynamic in every way, and deserves far more fresh history and criticism than what I've provided herein. It's the beginning, not the end.

PART TWO
THE AMERICANS

9. The Necessary Performance
The Irving Rapper Vision

This is an extended and enhanced version of the intro chapter to my upcoming book Now, Irving Rapper, *which is also the basis for a documentary of the same title.*

My little gypsy! Now we can live! Now we can live!

Leonardo (Michel Ray) in *The Brave One*

The final scene of Irving Rapper's *Now, Voyager* (1942) has been emulated, imitated, parodied, and generally memorialized to the hilt—such that it has become an indelible part of our shared cinematic heritage. Bette Davis, Paul Henreid, two lit cigarettes, two sensuous, longing stares, one classic line ("Let's not ask for the moon, we have the stars"). Rapper even poked fun at himself during the opening of his *The Voice of the Turtle* (1947); its opening shot glimpses an anonymous extra self-consciously lighting two cigarettes beside his smirking date.

As the *New York Times* obituary read, "Some directors are remembered for a distinctive voice, some for exploring specific genres, others for long associations with a stable of favorite actors. Mr. Rapper is best known for a single scene." Through the decades, it increasingly became habit to reduce Rapper's entire career to this single moment of glory. However, Bertrand Tavernier and Jean-Pierre Coursodon revered Rapper's broader aesthetics across multiple films in their text *50 ans de cinéma américain*: "It is in his aesthetic ambitions that Rapper seems the most exacting, whether it is a question of the particularly sleek image, the decorations and accessories of the mise en scène, and the spectacular camera movements." On the latter count, they parenthetically attribute a quotation to Rapper himself: "I had a rule: keep the camera moving all the time, in the most fluid way possible."

Despite this late commendation, Rapper himself is largely ignored by auteurist film scholars and historians, his contribution

Now, Voyager.

to cinema undermined by indifference, limp conformity, and short-sighted dogmatism. Andrew Sarris' formative *The American Cinema* neglects to give him so much as an entry, even among the "bush leaguers" Sarris deems marginally identifiable. (Incidentally, Rapper's *Washington Post* obituary notes, "Sarris said in an interview that Mr. Rapper's Broadway background and work as a dialogue coach in his earliest days in Hollywood are evident in his skill with actors.")

Some obtusely explain away Rapper's signatures by branding him a functionary purveyor of glossy studio house style (specifically Warner Bros.), or a mere thankless cog in various "star as auteur" enterprises (specifically in the case of his Bette Davis pictures). Because Rapper led the era's Warner Bros. directors in studio suspensions, for refusing to "job" on favored studio projects that failed to rouse his passions or speak to his affinities, Bogart is known to have quipped, "Skippy, any more suspensions and you'll be holding up the San Francisco Bay Bridge." The rebellious Rapper's taste and personal standards may have often deprived him of paychecks, but his selectivity speaks to an overall personality and focus, through which one can clearly map his cinematic authorship.

Being both gay and Jewish in an era when it was difficult to be either, let alone both, Irving Rapper was acutely aware of what it meant to play a part and "pass." For fear of the law and guaranteed pariah status, queer artists desperately strived to code as straight and hence "normal," while Jews attempted to code as Gentile for want of broader social and cultural acceptance. These ideas are extensions on the notion of performing; Rapper's characters consistently "play parts," as it were, compelled to do so—sometimes quite onerously—by both circumstance and design. It is life as theater, or as opera. This conceit reaches its apotheosis in his penultimate film, the astonishingly sympathetic and progressive *The Christine Jorgensen Story* (1970), in which the title character first struggles to "pass" as a man, especially during her time in the military. Upon submitting to gender-affirming surgery, she then must "pass" as the woman she is, in a Fifties society with neither sympathy nor frame of reference for such surgical remedy (or for queer identity in general).

In Rapper's *Forever Female* (1953), aging Broadway star Ginger Rogers refuses to acknowledge she is too old to play a role written for an ingénue. As the beleaguered playwright and producers rework the show to meet her needs, and her desire for self-conception, the ruse becomes another instance of a Rapper heroine "passing"—in this case, the performance of a performance. Affixed to the deceptions, affectations, and appeals are conflicting notions of public and private life, the reciprocity of both, and how private hungers disrupt or otherwise alter public illusion(s). [Anthony Harvey, another gay male director covered later in this book, traffics in the same public vs. private themes himself.] Rapper's predilection for society's shape-shifters, and his "converts," lie at the heart of his worldview as an artist.

A third-act speech in *Forever Female* expresses something pivotal about the type of "necessary performance" familiar to many an Irving Rapper character:

Why hide out? So that I can relax and put on weight. Let my hair go, be as sloppy and as carefree as I like, so that I can put behind me, for a while at least, the dieting and the massaging and the hair-dyeing in the beauty parlor and all the other little tortures that my profession and my vanity inflict upon me. In short, so that for two heavenly months out of the year, I can be my age. Why can't I be my own age? You ask an actress to give up being 29 when you're an

Rapper situates William Holden as something like a living caricature drawing in the Sardi's opening of *Forever Female*. As he spies on the table of Ginger Rogers, he blends in with the aid of Rapper's visual humor.

older and wiser playwright, and you write a play for a woman of 34. Or 35. Or even 40... you will find that the actress will come to you and say, "Why does she have to be 34 or 35 or even 40? Why can't she be 29?" It's such a wonderful age. Can you blame us for lingering and lingering and lingering and then finally having to be dragged through? And it is not only in the theater. Look at the audience sometime. It's full of 29s.

In *Now, Voyager*, the newly liberated Charlotte Vale is forever playing roles and, in some sense, "passing," especially as she finds her footing in the world, at long last. In one key scene, she punctuates her liberation by throwing down the gauntlet for her disapproving mother's dubious "benefit." Pronouncing that she is no longer afraid of life, she essentially performs this new, refined version of herself to a very unreceptive and embittered audience. The declarative "tour-de-force" is so effective that it literally kills her mother. (As a film scholar friend cheekily put it, "That scene on its own, the act of killing your mother by being fabulous, is very gay and very Jewish.") In the film's final act, Charlotte also plays the role of attentive surrogate mother, the kind of maternal figure that her own severe, intransigent mother could never be for her. The object of her care and trust: a homely, emotionally damaged girl very reminiscent of her younger self—another Rapper role-play. As Tavernier and Coursodon remark, "Rarely does a film play as deliberately as *Now, Voyager* on the process of identification, relying so much on the concept of fulfillment and of revenge, by interweaving it closely with a respect for the established order."

By its very title, *Deception* (1946) speaks to its own hyper-relevance in the Irving Rapper oeuvre. Davis' character, Christine Radcliffe, a onetime concert pianist, weaves a web of unchecked pretense and duplicity that ensnares two volatile artists and enshrines her own magisterial projections of feminine power. The picture kicks into gear when Christine, pleading financial embarrassment, takes Paul Henreid's character Karel back to her apartment, only to have him castigate her for its extravagance. The rest of the narrative plays on levels of subterfuge. The interpersonal gambits reflect the sound and fury of the tempestuous symphonies that underscore them—and even inform them. In one key scene, one of the best in Rapper's oeuvre, Claude Rains' character makes a grand show of ordering an extravagant dinner as an attentive wait staff dotes on him. Sitting helpless across from Rains are a visibly

Rapper pre-visualized many of his scenes. He doodled many ideas for shots on the opposing pages of his script. When he photographed Gladys Cooper from behind, with her hand on the bedpost as she listens to her rebelling daughter talking offscreen, the scene becomes far richer than if it had been staged with traditional coverage.

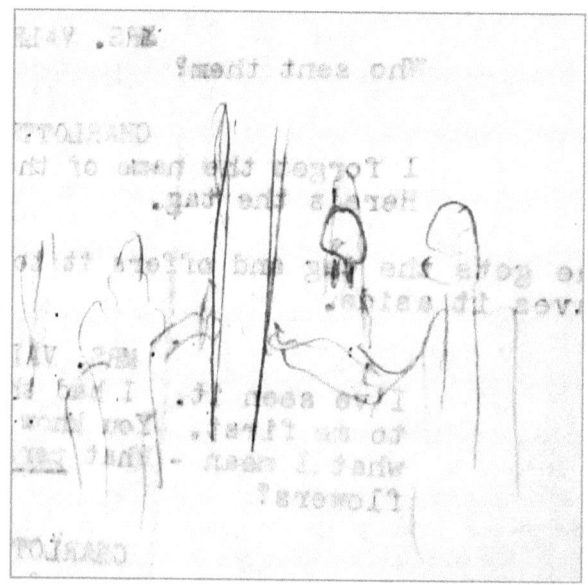

flummoxed Davis and Henreid. It is a performance par excellence, within the context of both the character in the scene itself, and Rains' contribution to both it and the larger film. Truly, no other director would have dared let an unflappable Rains upstage Davis in such a manner, and with such style. (When the cast finished the first table read of the script, Bette Davis said, as dryly as only she could, "That's quite a part you've got there, Claudie!")

Rapper stages for spatial distance with wide lenses, evoking the era's revolutionary deep focus photography à la Gregg Toland (courtesy here of cinematographer Ernest Haller). The sets are lavish prosceniums in which he choreographs his deceivers like a field general strategizes a special—and potentially perilous—maneuver. Space is part of Rapper's stylistic currency, such that producer Hal Wallis vocally lamented Rapper's tendency to "edit in camera." By avoiding more traditional scene coverage whenever possible, and by favoring precise, dynamic, and unalterable single-shot staging, Rapper limited an editor's ability to redirect or refocus his scenes after the fact. While Wallis respected this same tendency in Busby Berkeley, Rapper's taste for the same frustrated him.

For his part, Rapper once remarked, "I didn't preplan quite in the sense that Hitchcock does. I'd plot out the opening and closing of a sequence, and its highest dramatic point only. I'd sometimes begin with fully detailed plans and sketches." Wallis' biographer Bernard F. Dick notes in *Now, Voyager* that, "When Charlotte makes her first appearance, the camera tracks her, showing nothing but her unattractive shoes. Thus, when Charlotte is finally seen, her frumpy appearance has already been anticipated by her footwear. An editor could add nothing to the shot, since Rapper did not cut until Charlotte entered the parlor." The author also cites another sustained shot in the same film: Gladys Cooper's hand on a bedpost, as Bette Davis speaks to her from offscreen. Rapper's personal copy of the *Now, Voyager* script, housed at the Margaret Herrick Library in Beverly Hills, comes complete with a primitive "storyboard" sketch that Rapper drew on the back of the scene's page. He had pre-visualized the scene in a wholly untraditional way for a Forties Hollywood studio picture. Wallis' memos, housed in USC's Warner Bros. archives, express annoyance at Rapper's experimentation, but the proof, as they say, is in the pudding.

These ideas and visual flourishes are especially suffused into later films like *Another Man's Poison* (1951) and *Marjorie Morningstar* (1958). In the former, pulp novelist Janet Frobisher (Davis

The dinner scene from *Deception*, a showpiece for Claude Rains.

again) presides over a delirious round of skullduggery: a violent fugitive impersonates the husband she has just murdered, ironically mirroring the potboiler machinations of her spicy bestsellers. A burgeoning thematic trend line is not difficult to discern here. (It is noteworthy that the 1956 B noir thriller *Strange Intruder*, which Rapper admitted that he directed because he "needed the work," also involves a twisted masquerade that ends in macabre fashion.) Once again, Rapper stages Davis and the supporting players for optical width, fluid mobility, chiaroscuro lighting accents, and an almost geometric design precision that is striking in contrast to other similar pictures of the era. It suffered reputationally, because it was ceaselessly compared with *All About Eve* (1950), released the previous year. The looming archways and harsh contours of the film's primary set, the Frobisher estate, provide Rapper with an ideal arena for treachery.

In the finale of *Marjorie Morningstar* (1958), the eponymous wannabe actress heroine experiences a "theatricalized" personal revelation, with public and private briefly enmeshed. She is momentarily a spectator standing outside the reality she has known and accepted throughout. It is a fresh peek into a familiar world that now appears pathetically small; this stacked "scene" that unspools seemingly for her benefit reveals the social delusion

Rapper introduces Bette Davis' character in *Now, Voyager* with a shot of her ugly orthopedic shoes. Only later do we first see her face. These visual conceits and clever, impactful accent marks occasionally drove producer Hal Wallis to madness.

Rapper shoots the apartment set of *Deception* in geometric patterns.
He even sets up outside the space through a window at a pivotal moment
before a fraught musical performance.

that both comprises and fuels that world. Theater itself stands in for life, revealing a bittersweet truth. Marjorie, with new line of sight, is liberated from the perpetual burden of "passing"—as the good daughter, as the "nice Jewish girl," as the dutiful and self-abnegating lover to a tortured narcissist-cum-artiste, and as a performer herself. This ending is hence quite different from Herman Wouk's novel, and much more in line with the "Rapper-verse." *Marjorie Morningstar* is the last major studio project over which Rapper had at least reasonable creative control. Though most American critics maligned it, many European critics later ran cover for it, including Christian Viviani in *Positif*. Rapper's troubled follow-up, *The Miracle* (1959), about a very literal (and supernatural) shapeshifting—a saintly masquerade—was beset with all manner of untenable challenges (though distinguished French critic Henri Agel and filmmaker Yves Boisset were adamant defenders).

The struggle of coming out from under the burden of performing is writ large in the finale of *The Brave One* (1956), the story of a Mexican child who saves a bull calf named Gitano and raises it as his own, only to find their friendship threatened by a fated public confrontation with a famous matador. When Gitano does "perform" at length, with agility and uncommon nobility, a coliseum of rapt spectators comes to clamor for his pardon ("Indulto!") just as the matador raises his dagger. When this rare concession is granted, our young protagonist jumps the barrier and runs into the ring to embrace Gitano. In tearfully assuring his beloved, newly sprung companion, "Now we can live! Now we can live!," a Rapper ideal is exemplified. As other Rapper characters eventually come out from under the burden of performing or "passing" or "coding," so can they fully live. In his book *Behind the Screen: How Gays and Lesbians Shaped Hollywood*, author William J. Mann speculates how the lifelong loner Rapper could have identified with the child protagonist in *The Brave One*, as a "boy not like the others." That boy finds solace in a relationship no one else really understands. No wonder it was his favorite among his own pictures.

Though he rarely directed genre, at least in the explicit sense his onetime collaborator and professed mentor Michael Curtiz had, Rapper's command of craft and his personal style elevated the Hollywood melodrama to aesthetic heights that only Douglas Sirk and Vincente Minnelli later achieved in Technicolor the following decade. (Tavernier and Coursodon open their study of Rapper with a parallel to three fellow Warner melodramatists: Jean Negulesco, Vincent Sherman, and Curtis Bernhardt. Their readings of these directors suggest that, even within the constraints of the studio system, each revealed distinct directorial signatures that exceeded mere "house

The ceaseless performance of Rapper's characters, on and off the stage, is laid bare at the end of *Marjorie Morningstar*, with Natalie Wood observing Gene Kelly and his entourage from afar, finally seeing it all for what it is.

When the industry welcomed CinemaScope into its filmmaking toolbox, Rapper made excellent use of it in *The Brave One*, his favorite of his own pictures. Jack Cardiff was his cinematographer on the film.

style." Of the four, however, it was Rapper who received the most sustained consideration in their text.) When Rapper did finally make the leap to color himself, with the sublime *The Brave One* (1956, shot by the legendary Jack Cardiff) and the unjustly dismissed *Marjorie Morningstar*, he rounded out a foundation of performance integrity that he had established and reinforced well before the Actor's Studio gospel was coherently codified. His training as a dialogue director in some of the top Warner pictures of the Thirties came in handy.

Novelist Steve Erickson attempts to distill the nature of Irving Rapper's authorship in his novel *Zeroville*:

"We also are sponsoring a retrospective, as…" he pauses, "…as an unofficial tangent, you might say, to the official festival, a retrospective of one of your great American auteurs. Well, actually he is British, but he made all of his films in America. Irving Rapper."

"Irving Rapper?"

"You know of Monsieur Irving Rapper?" Cooper Léon asks.

"*Now, Voyager.*"

Relief floods Cooper Léon's face. "Of course I was certain a scholar of film such as yourself would know of Irving Rapper. Cinema's great poet of la femme dérangée. As you say, *Now, Voyager. Deception. The Glass Menagerie. Marjorie Morningstar.* Would you care for another?" He points at Vikar's vodka tonic.

Zeroville is a sort of "loser odyssey" through the Hollywood of the late Sixties. Cineastes and cinephiles are its principal characters, and this is neither the first nor the last time Irving Rapper is mentioned. To whatever extent Rapper was the "poet of *la femme dérangée*" (the disturbed woman), Bette Davis' roles in Rapper's films showcased her acuity for playing tortured, scheming, or demented women. The crowning exploitation of her uncanny skill came in Robert Aldrich's trendsetting box office sensation *What Ever Happened to Baby Jane?* (1962), produced at Warner Bros. when Rapper had exiled himself to Europe to helm a pair of leaden Biblical epics that played the B movie circuit in the United States (1961's *Joseph and His Brethren* and 1962's *Pontius Pilate*).

Baby Jane's success was blown up into a curious subgenre invariably known as "Hag-sploitation" or "Grand Dame Guignol." Arguably, antecedent traces of Rapper can be detected in Aldrich's film, in terms of Davis' especially fearless performance. It's more difficult to make a similar case for Davis' other Warner weepie/"women's picture" stalwarts like Curtis Bernhardt or Vincent Sherman, who directed her in vehicles wherein she played characters more resigned, often more saintly, less fractured and fractious—furthermore, women more comfortable in their own skin, with no need for the type of elaborate deceits that Rapper's scripts furnished. Illusion, delusion, and theater need not soothe or beguile the heroines in the Davis films directed by these others.

Many still fault Gene Kelly's miscasting in *Marjorie Morningstar*, but the *Time Out Film Guide* posits, 'The switchback from arrogance to vulnerability feels open and authentic in a way Kelly rarely displayed in his musical work, making it easily his most underrated performance.

Joseph L. Mankiewicz's *All About Eve*, however, certainly operates more on the pre-established Rapper-Davis wavelength (the conniving Eve Harrington's attempted theft of Margo Channing's identity and mystique would have certainly appetized Rapper).

Rapper cross-stitches elements of grand opera (especially Puccini) into his pictures, and this is often interpreted as camp by some critics. Opera is itself a kind of atavistic presence in *Now, Voyager*, *Deception*, and *Another Man's Poison* (with Davis as diva, or indeed prima donna), and part of the joy and intrigue in Rapper's work is witnessing the operatics synthesize with the more subtle rhythms of the acting, i.e. the aforementioned performance integrity that presaged the prevalence of Actor's Studio methodology. A propensity for both would stymie most other filmmakers, but Rapper turned the fusion into a personal style and an artistic voice that distinguished him from other resident soaper specialists. Along these lines, Tavernier and Coursodon observe, "This aestheticism, both extravagant and refined, is perfectly in symbiosis with the artificiality of certain subjects that it transcends, making this artificiality the driving force, the secret spring that will impose the various emotions, either directly or in response."

Comparing him to George Cukor in his focus, approach, and constitution, the Turner Classic Movies mini-biography of Rapper notes that he "gained a reputation as a director of 'women's pictures.'" It continues: "If Rapper was clearly capable (and willing, perhaps, if necessary) to extrude the formal needs of genre (sometimes to the heights and ferocity of Huston, Wellman or Vidor), he seemed perfectly able to concede to what seemed to be a brilliant anticipation of what was necessary for these performance trends - as if he was setting a stage for them (yet, perhaps just didn't have the secret ingredient to get them like those that knew Stanislavsky), this is something about which to marvel."

In Pauline Kael's flag-planting essay "Circles and Squares," which famously countered Sarris' *politique des auteurs* doctrine, she recalled that "my friends and I would keep an eye out for the Robert Siodmak films and avoid Irving Rapper films (except when they starred Bette Davis whom we wanted to see even in bad movies)." Kael's tastes were curious and often unpredictable, but indeed, here she does presume the factors and aspects that bind his work, even though in her case they provoke distaste (which, nonetheless, is more than the neglectful void that Sarris afforded Rapper in his own most formative text). Kael's taste generally skewed toward a more strident, "manly" brand of cinema that the decidedly more genteel Rapper was never keen to provide (and furthermore, she was also no stranger to accusations of homophobia).

It was by hitching himself to the starpower of Bette Davis that Rapper staked his claim as a film director. As mentioned, this followed his tenure as "dialogue director" for Michael Curtiz, William Dieterle, and Anatole Litvak, all of whom had difficulties with the English language. They would direct the floor, Rapper would deal with the actors. As Rapper himself attested, "There were no specified duties. What happened [was] the talkies came in and the movie world split in two. They invited or asked as many stage directors as they could get to come out [to Hollywood]... and the movie directors would tend to the movie part and the dialogue director was supposed to coach the actors and listen to the dialogue." For directors with sub-optimal command of English, namely Curtiz and Dieterle, Rapper's role of dialogue director proved most handy. On *The Charge of the Light Brigade* (1936) with Errol Flynn, Rapper claimed, "Mike Curtiz's English was so bad he was afraid some Americanisms might slip into the script. Mike's Hungarian accent got thicker with the years, but his forte was composition of shots. The way he could move so quickly would be for a dialogue director to rehearse the cast in their dressing rooms as Mike was arranging the cameras and lighting on the stages." By this token, Rapper was the key directorial force behind the performance calibration on such classics as *The Life of*

The eponymous sequence in *Rhapsody in Blue* presented a challenge to Rapper, who sustains 12 minutes of screentime with visual dynamism that manages to make the playing of music more tactile and immediate than it has ever felt on a movie screen.

Emile Zola (1937), *The Adventures of Robin Hood* (1938), *Juarez* (1939), *All This and Heaven Too* (1940), and *High Sierra* (1941). Curtiz, for one, came to trust Rapper and his instinct for acting unconditionally.

The arc of Rapper's directing career spans his debut with the Warners B soaper *Shining Victory* (1941), all the way to his rather bizarre swan song, *Born Again* (1978), a biopic on Nixon apparatchik Charles Colson's evangelical Christian conversion (the vicissitudes of conversion generally being a secondary theme in Rapper's cinema, as in *One Foot in Heaven, Now, Voyager, The Corn is Green*, and *The Christine Jorgensen Story*). His career is not lacking in occasional strange detours, failed experiments, and studio interference (which is most noteworthy in relation to his *Anna Lucasta* and his adaptation of *The Glass Menagerie*), but the poetry in passages like the "religiously" cinephilic nickelodeon sequence in *One Foot in Heaven* (1941), the toad race in *The Adventures of Mark Twain* (1943), the visually expressionist title number in *Rhapsody in Blue* (1945), the staircase confrontation in *Deception* (1946), the delightfully cheeky opening of *Forever Female* (1953), the extended bull-fight finale of *The Brave One* (1956), the depictions of Catskills resort life in *Marjorie Morningstar* (1958), and many other presences, seem at times as vivid, indelible, and immediate as the famous *Now, Voyager* finale with which he has been routinely eulogized.

On a personal note, my own interest in Irving Rapper developed soon after my longtime friend, Midwestern filmmaker and film instructor Sunrise Tippeconnie, first planted the seed. I was instantly drawn to the director's staging aesthetic, his finesse with the mobile camera, his conscientious design, and his operatic flair. Upon further research of his gay and Jewish identity (the latter of which is quite extraordinarily center-staged in *Marjorie Morningstar*, with its bar mitzvah and Passover seder sequences, well before it was "kosher" in mainstream movies), I formed a spiritual kinship and committed to him as a subject, as someone who is myself gay and Jewish (and someone who has strived to "pass" at one time or another, either implicitly or with concerted effort).

Because of the lack heretofore of serious scholarly consideration, the allure of a more intensive study of Rapper proved irresistible. In their beloved 1969 book *The Celluloid Muse: Hollywood Directors Speak*, Charles Higham and Joel Greenberg admire Rapper's "unacknowledged technical skill" and "his tremendous flair for the cinema," while also stating, "Like so many Hollywood

Marjorie Morningstar is the rare studio film of its era to not only depict
outwardly Jewish characters, but to get all the little details astonishingly
correct, as in this early bar mitzvah sequence.

talents, he has been put firmly—and one hopes only temporarily—
on the shelf by the newest generation." My hope, as a relatively
young film scholar, is to pick him back off that shelf in the twenty-first century and lay the groundwork for an Irving Rapper
resurgence, or at least re-examination.

If John Ford's Irish Catholicism directly informed his favored
themes of tradition, ritual, and patriotism, if Orson Welles' orotund
presence (and sharp mind) assured his command of Shakespearean
pageant, and if the exiled Jules Dassin's acceptance in Greece as
"first generation Greek" informed his later Dionysian frolics,
Rapper might be the only filmmaker of his era whose work is fully
informed by his gay Jewish identity. He's one of the rare early
directors with an unabashedly queer sensibility (perhaps *the* most,
with the great Mitchell Leisen right next to him). It's no wonder
that *Now, Voyager*, a 2007 inductee into the prestigious National
Film Registry, still famously connects so strongly with gay male
audiences. Bette Davis biographer Ed Sikov observes, "*Now,
Voyager* suggests a gay man's quest for self-acceptance as much as
it explicitly tells of an independent, free-thinking woman's emergence from a state of self-loathing and sexual inhibition." As I will
attempt to prove in this text, his other works (if better known and
more circulated) would elicit the same admiration in that sector,
and well beyond.

Irving Rapper.

Theatrical Feature Films: *Shining Victory* (1941), *One Foot in Heaven* (1941), *Now, Voyager* (1942), *The Gay Sisters* (1943), *The Adventures of Mark Twain* (1943), *The Corn is Green* (1944), *Rhapsody in Blue* (1945), *Deception* (1946), *The Voice of the Turtle* (1947), *Anna Lucasta* (1949), *The Glass Menagerie* (1950), *Another Man's Poison* (1951), *Bad for Each Other* (1953), *Forever Female* (1953), *Strange Intruder* (1956), *The Brave One* (1956), *Marjorie Morningstar* (1958), *The Miracle* (1959), *Joseph and His Brethren* (1961), *Pontius Pilate* (1962), *The Christine Jorgensen Story* (1970), *Born Again* (1978)

10. Fresh Lost Worlds
The Joan Micklin Silver Vision

This is the expanded version of a piece published on the Criterion Collection "Daily," under the title "Between the Lines of Joan Micklin Silver," on February 25, 2025.

> Before I could turn around, my youth was gone.
> Let's chase our youth with horse and carriage.
> When I finally catch it under a bridge,
> Where the pigeons once rested.
> I beg the years, "Please come back!"
> Even if for a short while.
> "No, no, we cannot go back.
> When we were with you,
> You should not have embarrassed us."
>
> An old Yiddish lullaby

In the F. Scott Fitzgerald novel *This Side of Paradise,* the woebegone Amory Blaine defines a sentimental person as someone who "thinks things will last" and a romantic person as one with "desperate confidence that they won't." Through the prism of that profundity, *Hester Street* (1975) and a number of Joan Micklin Silver's subsequent films can be seen as constructing a tragicomic reality wherein those two threads—the comedy of the romantic person, and the tragedy of the sentimental person—are not merely entwined but skillfully braided. All the more fitting, then, that Micklin Silver immediately followed her feature film debut, *Hester Street* (1975), with *Bernice Bobs Her Hair* (1976), an adaptation of one of Fitzgerald's short stories.

Fitzgerald's insight can be applied as something like a navigational tool in tracing Micklin Silver's trajectory, with the contrast between the sentimental and the romantic most clearly distilled in her masterpiece *Chilly Scenes of Winter* (1979). Her later Jewish-American classic *Crossing Delancey* (1988) catches its heroine

Between the Lines.

Isabelle (Amy Irving) ensnared in a battle of milieus. Is she the sophisticated Upper West Side doyenne of a prestigious literary salon, or is she prey for the Lower East Side's quasi-shtetl of matchmakers and pickle-pushers? Micklin Silver's work encompasses thematic perennial: characters bound up in a perpetual tug-of-war between past and present realities—tradition and modernity, expectation and outcome, the settled and the unsettled, culture and counterculture.

Micklin Silver's sophomore feature, *Between the Lines* (1977), an ensemble comedy about deradicalization (or a process of deradicalization), fleshed out the Fitzgerald framework that would be even more fully realized in *Chilly Scenes of Winter*. For most of the runtime, the staff at an alternative, independent Boston free press, the *Back Bay Mainline,* collectively believes that, somehow, their neverland lives and routines will last, even as the threat of big bad corporate takeover looms. The metaphorical warm memory of a wild, drunken night out that extends—well past any point of practicality—into the wee hours of the morning finally transitions into protracted hangover.

Between the Lines and *Chilly Scenes of Winter* reflect a condition prevalent among many at the time: the wary acceptance of a new, likely less idealistic era. With the final nails driven into the coffin, the Sixties fighting spirit is left in a tattered funeral shroud. Yet, to its credit, the film is never really cynical. Of *Between the Lines*, Micklin Silver once expressed, "I wanted to deal with the confusion and indecision that the characters are feeling. They keep saying that they are interested in working out their great ideals, but they're really busy with their personal lives. And suddenly, the paper is sold out from under them." Vincent Canby, in his astute *New York Times* review, observes that the film is about "growing up after you've already grown up." The film's motley crew hear — and, in some cases, emit — the culminating whimper after a decade of "bang" (in all its literal and figurative meanings). They were sold a bill of perishable goods for which payment is now due.

In one crucial scene, Michael (Stephen Collins), the self-appointed chronicler of his generation, celebrates securing a publishing contract. At a local watering hole, he describes his book as "about all of us, about the life and times of our entire generation, in and out of the fire." His words trample those of disenchanted girlfriend Laura (Gwen Welles), who dares to put the pitch more bluntly and succinctly: "It's about the end of the Sixties." A woman, once again in a Micklin Silver film, cuts through delusions and self-absorbed babble, much as another Laura does in the director's next film, *Chilly Scenes of Winter.* A few scenes later, the Gwen Welles Laura's discovery of a trove of protest rally photographs in the apartment of forlorn and lovelorn journalist Harry (John Heard) suggests a wistfulness for something already lost ("We were dangerous then, sowing the seeds of dissent").

Similarly, when Lynn (Jill Eikenberry) quits her job in protest at the finale, she becomes another Micklin Silver female who cuts through empty manners and polite euphemism when submissive men attempt to interpret for her. After Jeff Goldblum's Max interjects on her behalf, to soften her acrimony toward their new boss, Lynn indignantly claps back, "No, that's not what I'm saying! Boy, we really stick together, don't we? We want to work for the *Mainline,* not some communications empire. You don't have to learn my name, because I quit." The film's women are the only ones with the wherewithal to truly tell it like it is — in other words, the true keepers of the revolutionary spirit, and the last with any esprit de corps. The men are, on the whole, a rather impotent contingent relative to their distaff counterparts. If unable to document for posterity the hallowed recent past, or package it for their own advancement, they fold. For example, Harry can only fantasize about defying authority when it really counts most. (In a momentary wish-fulfillment break from reality after his unceremonious firing, he leaps onto the new corporate overlord's desk and fires a plastic dart at his head.)

In *Chilly Scenes of Winter,* Peter Riegert's character, Sam, inadvertently defines the epithet *we-could-haves* for Sixties radicals. As his friend Charles (John Heard) is getting ready for a date, Sam scoffs at a suggestion by Charles' younger sister that he buy new clothes, joking, "What do you want from a child her age? She never even went to Woodstock!" Charles, at first puzzled, replies, "Neither did we." Sam pauses in a way that indicates that his explanation so obviously speaks for itself: "We could have." Charles can only concede. In the Sixties, a romantic notion meant the orchestration of a fashionably scrappy but pyrrhic-victorious revolution, or changing the world in some sense, however vaguely. In the Seventies, lonely Charles' romantic notion is to change his own world by rescuing his beloved Laura (Mary Beth Hurt) from a neglectful husband. He also endeavors to save her from what he sees as her own low (she would say realistic) self-image. "I do not have a lousy opinion of myself," she argues. "I have a realistic opinion of myself. You have this exalted view of me and I hate it!"

Both *Between the Lines* and *Chilly Scenes of Winter* are very "zeitgeisty" films, specifically made for, and suited to, the time in which they were produced. That said, they are not mere artifacts. John Heard as performer is an appealing, effective, and affecting avatar in both: a scrupulously bottled-up, weltschmerz-y embodiment of generational angst, one who set the standard for what was fast becoming a prevailing Micklin Silver male archetype. This archetype manifests again later in *Finnegan Begin Again* (1985), with Robert Preston, and in *Crossing Delancey,* with Peter Riegert. These are all restless figures living less for the now than for a romanticized then. Their life rhythms hinge on comforting haunts,

Chilly Scenes of Winter.

Crossing Delancey.

ingrained habits, and moribund ideals. The anomalous, the passé, and the obsolete are their security blankets. Riegert's Sam the Pickle Man's personal constitution involves going to shul for morning prayers, acquainting himself with and even patronizing the most provincial neighborhood businesses (including Sylvia Miles' yenta matchmaker), and... well, he sells pickles right out of the barrel... for a living. In all these ways and more, he lives in a world similar to the one inhabited by the staff at the *Mainline* in *Between the Lines.* For these Micklin Silver men, the pulse of an old world, whether from one, ten, or a hundred years ago, still beats in symphonic palpitation. [Jeremy Paul Kagan could be considered a male thematic counterpart to Joan Micklin Silver. See appendix.]

Micklin Silver's time-afflicted heroes individually make a trial-by-fire conversion from the Fitzgerald-defined sentimentality—in this case a form of denial—to become apostates, orphans, and martyrs of a kind. As more change is foisted upon them, their "desperate confidence" about things not lasting becomes conspicuous. She stated in an interview, "When things are very sad, I can always see a funny thing in them. And when things are funny, I still see a sad thing in them. I've always thought that was a little bit Jewish and a little bit female. It's a point of view, where I see material maybe a little differently." This perspective, which propels all her films, lends further specificity to her authorship.

Few filmmakers contemporary to Micklin Silver, besides perhaps only Woody Allen and Elaine May, gave voice to an unapologetically Jewish-American sensibility. There are also traces of this in the work of Paul Mazursky, especially in his depiction of Jewish wives and mothers. May, who along with Micklin Silver was among just a handful of female directors working in Hollywood at the time, imbues *A New Leaf* (1971), *The Heartbreak Kid* (1972), and *Mikey and Nicky* (1976) with a similar streak of uproarious, often dark, often outrageous, and — most importantly — often tastefully cruel humor. (Admittedly, at certain specific points, not so tastefully too.) In *The Heartbreak Kid,* newlywed Charles Grodin crafts, connives, and contrives various schemes to ditch his schlumpy new wife on their honeymoon, until he finally succeeds in one painful — but painfully funny — sequence at a seafood restaurant. In *Hester Street,* the would-be tragedy of the Steven Keats character Jake's caddish behavior toward the very old-world wife he's trying to ditch, and later in *Chilly Scenes of Winter,* Charles' ultimately unrequited infatuation with Laura, are grounded in a curious, just-short-of-caustic, but nevertheless humane humor. In all cases, distressing situations that might be played straight and thus tragically in other hands ingeniously become the stuff of distinctly Jewish comedy in the hands of May and Micklin Silver.

Micklin Silver once ever-so-slightly resisted my making the assertion that all her films had a Jewish voice, especially in discussions of what I consider her masterpiece, *Chilly Scenes of Winter,* which features no outwardly Jewish characters, and *Between the Lines,* which features only one (Jeff Goldblum) out of the large ensemble. Goldblum's Yiddish-inflected lecture to a woman's college journalism class is especially memorable in this regard. I retorted, "It's not out of place for a rabbi to make a joke or a humorous aside at a funeral, and for the funeral-goers to at least chuckle. Charles, Gentile or not, is a handsome schlemiel in whose misery we unexpectedly find laughs, to keep from crying. Crying from what? Most of all, from recognition." She understood the point. She had long explained it as a more all-encompassing human comedy, but recognized it was infused with, or filtered through, her own cultural sensibility.

The word "pilpul" is one of the few from the Talmudic lexicon to have been adopted and appropriated into English dictionaries. Literally meaning "pepper," pilpul is defined in Merrian-Webster as "hairsplitting critical analysis; casuistic argumentation especially among Jewish scholars on Talmudic subjects; rabbinical dialectic." As Jewish study occurs in at least groups of two "chevrutot" ("study partners") who argue the differing positions, so the pilpul

A Jewish ritual divorce sends living embodiments of old world
and new world on their separate paths in *Hester Street.*

exists in Micklin Silver's work in a metaphorical sense. In *Hester
Street*, that Gitl uses her modulated new-world street-smarts to
sustain her old world preferences speaks to Mr Bernstein's final
piece of Talmudic logic, when debating what to sell in the store
that he and Gitl intend to open. "We mustn't be too quick to say
this or that," Mr. Bernstein proclaims, just as the shot's movement
freezes and the final still frame fades.

The most obvious—and perhaps the most amusing—example
of rabbinic compromise, invoked by pilpul, involves the muzuzah,
the parchment that hangs in the doorways of Jewish homes. Rashi,
perhaps the most prominent Torah scholar, taught that the mezuzah
should be placed vertically in the doorway. However, Rabbeinu
Tam, Rashi's grandson and another in a line of prominent scholars,
taught contrarily that the mezuzah should be placed horizontally.
So, the Shulchan Aruch (Code of Jewish Law) teaches that, to
fulfill the commandment of mezuzah in the best way possible, one
should respect both opinions by placing mezuzot on a 45-degree
slant. Thus, Gitl's acculturation, a classically Jewish one, hangs
at that same awkward, but comfortable, slant. Furthermore, she
leverages her equanimity and innate wisdom to negotiate having
it both ways. Though her husband has rushed to assimilate, she
refuses to. Rather, she adapts in another way altogether, using a
new-world system against itself. Her Americanization is the horse
of a different color.

Finnegan Begin Again.

Micklin Silver's other characters thus must learn to slant, or slouch, toward new ways and new realities: the Mainline staff in *Between the Lines*, Charles in *Chilly Scenes of Winter*, Isabel in *Crossing Delancey*, Robert Preston's title character in *Finnegan Begin Again*, and the crisis family in her underseen but charming A *Fish in the Bathtub* (1998). *Finnegan Begin Again* is a film that is seldom discussed in studies of Micklin Silver. It is premised on a (mostly) platonic friendship between a woman drowning in a midlife romantic crisis and an irrepressibly cheerful advice columnist well past his prime. The latter character lives in a packrat paradise, the filet of a decaying neighborhood in Richmond. In the most literal terms, he is not permitted to let go of his past — "the old ways" — because he lives among its artifacts, at his ailing wife's behest. In dutifully taking care of her, he finds solace in an increasingly complex friendship that, at the very least, gets him out of his disheveled house of humdrum. In one scene, Preston offers a prescription from which the film draws its title, one that could treat countless characters in Micklin Silver's artistic universe: "That's just the way it is. Something ends, and we begin again, and again, and again. It's about the only thing we can be sure of."

The later features — *Loverboy* (1989) and *Stepkids* (1991), which was released under the cumbersome studio-mandated title *Big Girls Don't Cry... They Get Even* — are disappointing, to say the least, especially because they surrender the thematic throughline Micklin Silver had steadily (and carefully) constructed in her first six features in addition to multiple short films. Nowhere is there even a hint of personality in *Loverboy*, an almost ludicrous

Old-world Gitl (Carol Kane) first enters the *treifineh medina* (the un-kosher world) in *Hester Street.*

left turn into saucy sitcom territory. It's an exceedingly typical Eighties teen sex comedy with a soupcon of atrocious gay panic jokes, and a barrage of rowdy slapstick set pieces. Most of the way through, it's almost impossible to fathom how the film bears her name. *Stepkids* has at least some aspiration to something beyond throwaway—the cast and the basic setup dangle occasional pleasures, especially when the principal character is a fairly well-written, canny and quick-to-the-punch teenage girl.

A film for HBO, *A Private Matter* (1992), stars Sissy Spacek as Sherri Finkbine, a historically real children's television host in parochial 1950s Arizona, who sought a medically recommended abortion and reaped the whirlwind of public controversy and condemnation. The film is sympathetic to average women in their struggle for equal rights and bodily autonomy—individuals who never desired the spotlight guaranteed by such public scrutiny, but were distressingly hurled into it. In the morass of unwanted attention, women like Finkbine are cast as modern, rational, forward-thinking torchbearers in a sea of shrill, moralizing zealots and puritans. Once again, there is a dialectic of old world vs. new world. Beyond that, the film is a searing indictment of how society rushes to condemn women with the strength and wherewithal to defy oppressive patriarchal strictures and thus determine the course of their own lives (just as many other Joan Micklin Silver heroines had, in the films leading up to this one).

I met Joan by the strangest and most cosmic of coincidences, on a gray December morning in what was (most appropriately) a

A Private Matter.

Manhattan chilly scene of winter. The night before, I had attended a 35mm screening of *Chilly Scenes of Winter* at IFC Center and had intended to propose a book project to her at the venue: the first to ever cover her life and career. She was swarmed by adoring fans and friends after her Q&A (with star Mary Beth Hurt and producers Griffin Dunne and Amy Robinson also present) so the moment was not opportune.

In asking around for an email address that might connect me with Joan, I was given a phone number instead—one that its provider wasn't sure still worked. That Sunday morning, the streets were strangely desolate walking past Bloomingdale's on my way to catch the subway. I tend to get nervous on the phone, especially with cold calls to strangers, so I was rehearsing what I might say to Joan if she picked up. I also strategized what to say if someone else picked up. It was just at this very moment of composing and rehearsing this script that Joan herself turned the corner, strolling directly toward me. It was as if I, or my intensity of purpose, had conjured her. I couldn't believe my luck—and even weirder was that it seemed we were the only people on this normally busy New York street, with nary even a car whizzing past. In approaching her, I stuttered, attempting to explain myself and my proposition. In a rush herself, she rattled off an email address and told me to message her. That's how it all began. When I later asked her why she offered up her email address so easily to a perfect stranger, she simply replied, "I don't know, but somehow I just trusted you, I guess"—the beginning of a beautiful friendship.

Over lengthy sessions in her parlor and chats over breakfast in her kitchen (usually English muffins and soup), we started the process of getting her on the record. All these years later, I treasure the time I spent with her, including the day the two of us laughed ourselves silly when she impersonated Otto Preminger. (Ironically, after Preminger abruptly fired Joan as screenwriter on his 1971 film *Such Good Friends*, it was Elaine May who pseudonymously delivered his final shooting script.)

Throughout multiple conversations, Joan made her personal stakes in her choices of material abundantly clear. One particular recording I made reflects this: "I wanted to make films that meant something to my family—which is why I made *Hester Street*—and to my generation. Perhaps because I'm a woman, I felt I had another way of saying that and doing that, one that people maybe hadn't seen before, so I was determined." The filmmakers we cherish, we cherish because they show us "new ways of seeing." While that is certainly true of Joan Micklin Silver, her films also reveal new ways of understanding what we've lost to the past—whether the recent past or the distant past—both individually and collectively. And most remarkably, she dares show us how that can be funny.

Author Daniel Kremer with Joan Micklin Silver
in her New York apartment, spring of 2015.

Joan Micklin Silver, author Daniel Kremer, and Carol Kane
at a New York Jewish Museum event, winter 2016.

Theatrical Feature Films: *Hester Street* (1975), *Bernice Bobs Her Hair* (1976), *Between the Lines* (1977), *Chilly Scenes of Winter* (1979, a.k.a *Head Over Heels*), *Finnegan Begin Again* (1985), *Crossing Delancey* (1988), *Loverboy* (1989), *Stepkids* (1991, a.k.a. *Big Girls Don't Cry, They Get Even*), *A Private Matter* (1992), *A Fish in the Bathtub* (1998)

Other Notable Works: *The Immigrant Experience: The Long, Long Journey* (1972, short), *The Fur Coat Club* (1973, short), *The Case of the Elevator Duck* (1974, short), *How to Be a Perfect Person in Just 3 Days* (1984), *Prison Stories: Women on the Inside* (1991, segment: "Parole Board"), *In the Presence of Mine Enemies* (1997), *Invisible Child* (1999), *Charms for the Easy Life* (2002)

11. Survival Scars
The Franklin J. Schaffner Vision

This is the adjusted and revised script for a video essay featured on the Islands in the Stream *Blu-ray release from Imprint Films in 2022.*

> I've always thought he was a tremendously gifted picture director. I can't make any criticism of him. I mean, there's nothing that I think he can't do. He's one of the best we have.
>
> George Roy Hill

An Oscar-winning filmmaker directed John F. Kennedy's "Cuban Missile Crisis" speech and his name was Franklin J. Schaffner. In fact, Franklin J. Schaffner directed most of Kennedy's televised speeches, inspiring Jackie Kennedy to call him "the best director in the world." Andrew Sarris noted that a prominent French critic once described Schaffner as a Henry James character come to life. "Quiet, elegant, subtle." *Los Angeles Times* critic Kevin Thomas remarked that Schaffner "looks and speaks more like a college professor than a top Hollywood director." He was "perhaps the quietest director in the film industry." In *American Cinematographer* magazine, Jerry Goldsmith called him "probably the most musical director I've ever worked for." But today, Schaffner is seldom discussed in any context, even at the mention of his most critically and commercially successful titles. They'll remember the films, but never the director.

In his now classic book, *Adventures in the Screen Trade*, screenwriter William Goldman observes that no one mastered the CinemaScope frame better than David Lean, Richard Attenborough, and Franklin J. Schaffner. That Schaffner began his career as an image maker on the small screen in live television drama, alongside the likes of John Frankenheimer, Sidney Lumet and Arthur Penn, is significant. Erwin Kim, astoundingly Schaffner's one and only biographer, writes in his 1985 book, "Curtiz was the Warner

Bros. house director in the golden age of cinema; Schaffner was the CBS house director in the golden age of television."

His preternatural skill with panorama didn't get a working-out until 1963, when he made his big screen debut in monochrome with the William Inge adaptation *The Stripper* (from the play *A Loss of Roses*), one of only two movies he made with a female protagonist. His follow-up, *The Best Man* (1964), penned by Gore Vidal, was and still is rightly recognized as one of the finest American political dramas ever made (and I contend it is his best film). Though Vidal's stamp of screenwriting authorship is clear from the film's cutting, incisive dialogue, for which his satirical spear was sharper than ever, Schaffner's interest is rooted in "men of their moment"—U.S. Presidential contenders—tub-thumping, clout-chasing, and image-building for the "ways and means" of making (and lastingly impacting) history. Beyond that, as such stentorian-voiced "men of the moment," they work to cast longer shadows that stretch beyond their mere single moment in time. In that much, they are the first in a line of Schaffnerian "men out of their own time," an idea I will flesh out further in this study.

Kim argues that "Schaffner has come to be regarded as a specialist in the big-look pictures. But this does not suggest the range, the richness, and the subtlety that can be found in his body of work. No matter the size, shape, or subject matter of his films, the intimacy of theater and the immediacy of television course through Schaffner's body of work." In his estimation, Franklin J. Schaffner was "the director with a historian's touch." Manny Farber coined the term "uppercase filmmaking," which is similar to the meaning of "big-look picture" here (and dear Mr. Schaffner, God bless him, was the hard opposite of Farber's "termite artist").

Papillon.

Franklin J. Schaffner was a far more visually expressive director than acknowledged. He's remembered for "big-look" pictures, with massive crowd shots and epic vistas, but as evidenced in these moments from *Patton* (top), *Nicholas and Alexandra* (below) and *Papillon* (left), there was more to his work than just that. *Patton*'s opening is now iconic in American cinema history; Schaffner himself demanded that the concept for this opening be brought back from an early draft of the script.

These days, he's known mostly for the awards named after him, at the American Film Institute and the Director's Guild of America. Both institutions have their Franklin J. Schaffner Awards for excellence in directing, but seldom is he discussed as a distinctive artist, despite his 1971 Academy Award win for Best Director in a decade that also awarded auteurs as distinctive as Bob Fosse, William Friedkin, and his own *Patton* screenwriter Francis Ford Coppola.

What is the Schaffner sensibility, and is there one? One immediately takes notice of the grandeur of his productions, along with his outsized but brooding heroes. But he shares these characteristics with a number of other directors, and their work. Here's the catch, though: Schaffner was not the brawny Americanist that a John Ford or a John Sturges was. *Patton* may open with the title character poised against a gigantic American flag, but not for the purpose of patriotic spectacle. As in *The Best Man*, whatever American ambivalence is in Schaffner's works' bloodstream isn't a poison but a vitamin. It isn't that the typical Schaffner hero is merely a rebel, a loner, or an outsider. That's much too general. Schaffner men are a particularly stubborn brand of rugged individualist, emphasis on rugged. They seek comfort not in approval or commendation, but in the charm and assurance of personal distance, and in a kind of noble solipsism. Or maybe more specifically, a mostly benign solipsism they *feel* as ennobling, even when they are family men. As we encounter in *Nicholas and Alexandra* (1971), *Islands in the Stream* (1977), and *Welcome Home* (1989), there's always part of them that even those closest to our hero (or heroes) cannot touch or even approach. In the case of Czar Nicholas, he takes his entire family down with him, in what is a *pièce de résistance* sequence in Schaffner's overall cinema: the bravura finale that stages the execution of the Romanovs as a prelude of absolute, terrible silence, with only a nearby clock ticking down toward a percussive requiem of gunfire. All that's left of them before the end titles are blood stains on a textured basement wall.

Willa Cather once wrote, "The heart of another is a dark forest, always, no matter how close it has been to one's own." These Schaffner men can never allow themselves to be fully known. That would violate an unspoken code of survival. They are men out of their own time. Vincent Canby observes in a 1971 review, "Someone in *Nicholas and Alexandra* describes Russia as an eighteenth-century country in a twentieth-century world, which may well prompt a few theses about the director's hang-up with people

The Best Man.

and things outside of their own times." Schaffner, on his love of historical films, responded, "I guess I'm really fascinated by the study of giants with feet of clay rather than ordinary people with heads of clay."

There's always something deeply and demonstrably wounded about the quixotic and obsessive Schaffner hero. They are somehow always dispossessed. Schaffner may be the easiest to define in auteurist times among his Golden Age of Television contemporaries, thematically and visually. In what is arguably Schaffner's most famous film, *Planet of the Apes* (1968), Charlton Heston plays the astronaut Taylor as a fierce, prideful solipsist primed for any mode of existence away from the obscene, violent folly of humans on Earth. He volunteers himself to a mission for which the consequences are not defined or even conjectural. He will, at long last, be permitted to retreat into himself entirely, without contrition, regret, or excuse. When his spacecraft crash-lands in foreign territory, his two compatriots fret, while Taylor is immediately at peace with the fact that he is stuck on a strange planet in a time unknown, a literal man out of his own time. He is precisely where he wants to be, light years from the hustle-bustle rat race, far from any madding crowd.

Islands in the Stream.

In a twist ending that has become baked into the wider culture, Taylor gets more than he bargained for in his own story of *Planet of the Apes*. At the end, he again goes off alone, disconnecting himself from another mad society, another type of hellscape, another madding crowd, only to meet the now infamous grim revelation in one of the grimmest of all famous movie endings.

These ideas sit not far from the Schaffner-Heston film that preceded *Planet of the Apes*. *The War Lord* (1965) is the work that most coherently inaugurates Schaffner the auteur. Heston plays a viceroy, a master of all he surveys, who has conquered a Druid village to enforce the rule of his faraway liege. But can someone sway his monomaniacal professional constitution, and can forces and temptations bring him out of himself? He soon finds his authority tested by local resistance, the rapt attentions of a pagan maiden, and growing fissures within his own garrison. What begins as a tale of military might gradually turns into a study of the limits of power, the fragility of loyalty, and the personal costs of conquest. *The War Lord* surprised critics of the time. Considering the grandiosity of its spectacle-promising title, the film was praised for how introspective it was, and how it effectively belied the "epic" stereotype. In a manner similar to General Patton later on, Heston's character, Chrysagon, becomes trapped by his own command, and like Taylor in *Planet of the Apes*, he hobbles off on horseback at the finale as one man against a wider, wearier world.

It's said that no man is an island, but how about a whole country? George Patton is another kind of warlord altogether, a man who is America itself. It's not just that he's a walking symbol — he is a living embodiment. In the iconic opening sequence, he is almost an abstraction, and the camera never averts its gaze. We never see Patton's audience. It's all him. One might argue the character is a monument to patriotic self-abnegation, but in Schaffner's hands we get the portrait of a man obsessed, willfully trapped inside his inflated self. Victory mustn't be merely America's, but his own. His personal triumph is a win for the old red, white and blue, and by extension, the world as he sees it. Is he a visionary tactician, a reactionary brute, or a Don Quixote? Of course, the answer is all three. He is thematically a blood relative to Heston's Taylor, and in more than one way, a mission is not merely something to execute; it's a maneuver to affix oneself to permanence, a bid for an ideal state of being, an ease of self-definition from which certainty of self flows forward, body and mind as gilded prison. As one French critic noted, Patton doesn't evolve. The events, the politics, and the tactics all change around him.

In *Papillon* (1973), Shaffner vaguely alludes to the Steve McQueen title character's past before his incarceration in the film. Often, in fantasies that our hero cannot grasp, let alone hold onto, he sees a future of the dead. Otherwise, he's rootless — another disconnected loner, another rugged individualist, emphasis again on rugged, with one objective: escape. His alliance and tenuous friendship with the Dustin Hoffman character, counterfeiter Louis Dega, is an unanticipated byproduct of that primary pursuit. There's always the informal arrangement, the understanding that puts the amity into perspective. Papillon is the most literal, solitary man, stuck in solitary confinement through a substantial portion of the 150-minute runtime. But Papillon's repeated mantra is a defiant rebel yell, "I'm still here, you bastards!" This from a man, several times an inch away from death, who can only be enough for

Sphinx.

himself. Ultimately, his struggle lies in choosing either going it alone or sticking it out. In a life with Dega, he is of course destined to a fate not totally unlike Taylor's in *Planet of the Apes*, in this case literally cast adrift. Captured, escaped, captured, escaped, in a perpetual loop of existence. To co-opt a Leonard Cohen line, "The frontiers are his prison," and like Patton, he likely never truly changes or evolves. The circumstances change around him. This flies in the face of a lot of dogma about storytelling.

Islands in the Stream (1977) follows a wounded artist living alone and trapped inside himself. With a quiet but sometimes conspicuous desperation, he seeks some form of connection with the only individuals who can offer it to him: his three young sons. But as with everything in the Shaffner sphere or the "Shaffner-verse," nothing lasts forever. George C. Scott's character, Thomas Hudson, bids a customarily stony but fraught farewell to that which temporarily anchored him, only to lose them to distance (in this case, for once, the non-charm of distance). Two additional tragedies happen in the wake of the visit, and with this, he can no longer even grant his rummy buddy Eddie, played by David Hemmings, the benefit of any doubt. Schaffner's earlier film *The Double Man* (1967), sees Yul Brynner as a cold, almost emotionless widower who steps into an espionage trap while attending his son's funeral. Both Brynner and Scott, in their respective Schaffner films, seek to alleviate post-traumatic existential dread with a specific mission that is all-encompassing—an existential make or break, pursued not simply to execute, but to maneuver oneself towards permanence.

Both Dave Kehr and Bertrand Tavernier recognized *Islands in the Stream* as Schaffner's one true personal film. To me, there are certainly more than one.

Schaffner is a maker of epics, but not in the manner of a Lean or a Cimino. I once told someone that Michael Cimino must render all material big and epic because he just can't help himself. He takes a cop thriller like *Year of the Dragon* (1985) and gives us a detour to mainland China as sweeping, painterly, and extravagant as any DeMille set piece. Rather, Schaffner's epic backdrops are simply present without over-asserting or overexerting themselves. As with John Ford, momentous history is a literal backdrop in many of Schaffner's frames, while our foreground traffics in character and intimacy. In one scene of *Nicholas and Alexandra*, the typically retreated-inside-himself Czar Nicholas, here envisioned as a consummate Schaffner character, is unpersuadable prior to making a cataclysmic strategic decision, one that triggers many seismic historical ruptures, with the big-picture macro complementing the interpersonal micro. As Bertrand Tavernier and Jean-Pierre Coursodon note in their massive tome *50 Years of American Cinema*, "Schaffner will never lose sight of the intimacy in the long shots, and he does not crush the characters under the spectacle."

Schaffner himself said, "There is a temptation, I suppose, to turn your cameras on the more dramatic battle or crowd scenes, but you cannot lose sight of the individuals with whom the audience is emotionally involved."

The Boys from Brazil (1978) likewise gives us two insulated men on similar life-defining missions, with crashing trajectories, not just cross purposes but cross lives. Nothing could be closer to the Schaffner vision, even when standing on moral principle at the film's end, as Laurence Olivier's character forbids the killing of a child to preempt a potential second Holocaust.

The War Lord.

In the early Eighties, Schaffner directed two consecutive critical and commercial flops: *Sphinx* (1981) and *Yes, Giorgio* (1982), both of which were, on paper, commercial propositions that digressed from their director's established favorite themes. Schaffner himself went on the record saying, "We no longer know where the audience is, who the audience is, or what the audience wants."

What is still in evidence in *Sphinx* is the compulsory widescreen visual splendor, his usual breathtaking command of compositional width and panoramic sweep. The main issue is that the whole affair has the perfunctory feel of a lavish but hopelessly half-hearted white flannel saga, with trashy beach-read potboiler trimmings (courtesy of the source novel by bestselling author Robin Cook). The overall feeling one gets watching it, is that Schaffner had a real swell time losing himself in researching Egyptology, with many a late night spent poring over dense history texts. Knowing his history buff nature, it's easy to imagine him cheerfully saturating himself in a world of pyramids, papyrus, mummies, hieroglyphics, and cartouches. This, however, doesn't translate to the screen in the form of a compelling narrative. No great big screen "page-turner," this. And nothing is improved by the charisma vacuum of lead Leslie Anne Down (though Frank Langella picks up some slack, with an "edge of camp" turn in brownface). It is most noteworthy, though, as only one of only two Schaffner films with female protagonists. An attempted rape scene is handled with both muscle and delicacy, two paradoxical sides of the Schaffnerian artistic persona.

All that can be said of *Yes, Giorgio* is that it's a hideously soppy romance poorly performed by a cast headed up by a buffoonish Pavarotti. Its best aspect is the pleasant John Williams-scored love ballad "If We Were in Love," which is wistfully orchestrated by Williams during the closing credits. One could potentially labor over a thesis that the Pavarotti character is another Schaffnerian "man out of time" in the sense that the kind of romance and chivalry he unctuously perpetuates is dead—but, in his hands, it is cloddishly resuscitated.

Schaffner would come home, in a manner of speaking, with *Lionheart* (1987) and *Welcome Home* (1989). The first, an epic of the medieval Children's Crusade, was co-produced by Francis Coppola but wound up getting compromised by budget cuts and a botched release. Jerry Goldsmith's score contributes a feeling of size and scale all its own, elevating its weaker stretches. Goldsmith had not worked on either *Sphinx* or *Yes, Giorgio*, so his reunion with Schaffner on *Lionheart* was a welcome one that their fans and admirers eagerly anticipated. Also returning are many of the director's most deeply embedded auteurist hallmarks. It is routine, on the whole, for a figure like that of a knight errant to be referred to as "timeless," in common parlance, but in the Schaffnerian sense, this becomes literalized, as in another addled hero somehow existing outside of his own time. An introspective crusader—a true believer in the mold of Patton, Papillon, and the politicians in *The Best Man*, albeit this time younger—is bound by knightly ideas of honor and chivalry. As the brutal exigencies of medieval reality continually undermine him, duty dictates that he nevertheless rise to the occasion. *Lionheart* could have well been titled *Son of the War Lord*, or *War Lord, Jr.*, recalling Schaffner's 1965 picture (and not merely because of similar trappings).

His final picture, *Welcome Home*, starring Kris Kristofferson as a presumed dead P.O.W. who makes a surprise return to find his life in America usurped, is a ripe note on which to end a career. The character's scars aren't even survival scars. They are scars *on* his survival. Kristofferson's character, Jake, is the inverse of George C. Scott's General Patton, a beaten-down veteran to whom guts and glory now mean little. As one infantryman in *Patton* put it, "His glory, our guts." Kristofferson's character is a victim of gravity, very "out of time, baby" as the Rolling Stones would have it, therefore perfectly Schaffnerian. When he died in July of 1989 at the age of 69, he was still president of the Directors Guild of America. Months later, *Welcome Home* was released posthumously.

If Schaffner had ended his career on *The Boys from Brazil*, after only ten features, it's quite possible he would be generally remembered better, and studied by the scholarly class. Scholars and historians are known sometimes to be as unkind as critics if a director ends his filmography on four consecutive perceived misfires. Schaffner biographer Erwin Kim capably illustrates how his subject selected his scripts based on a largely crowd-pleasing repertoire of favored themes, all of which fell under a single umbrella. In Kim's words, "There might be a single element that catches his fancy, a sequence, or a 'moment on the screen that may be fifteen seconds long, which is really what the French love to call the coup de cinéma.'" He also stresses that he was "monomaniacal, working on no more than one project at a time."

In creating a "character sketch" of Schaffner, Kim observes, "Schaffner does nothing to attract attention to himself, but it is obvious he is in charge." He was referring to his demeanor on set, but he could have very well been referring to his ostensibly stealthy but wholly perceptible—and even assertive—directorial signatures. One even sees it in his direction of John F. Kennedy during the Cuban Missile Crisis television addresses. That JFK and the crisis about which he warned the country was real didn't render these ideas any less applicable or resonant. By some measure, he can be seen as Schaffner's ultimate quiet man, directed as timeless hero at a moment of truth—at an all-time historical inflection point. His fiction work almost cosmically bears this out, as if it were a preordained course of natural events that he followed the path he did. It's the scars that don't show which always make up the kind of figures that intrigued Franklin J. Schaffner, as filmmaker, as craftsman, as artist, as auteur, and as a man.

Theatrical Feature Films: *The Stripper* (1963), *The Best Man* (1964), *The War Lord* (1965), *The Double Man* (1967), *Planet of the Apes* (1968), *Patton* (1970), *Nicholas and Alexandra* (1971), *Papillon* (1973), *Islands in the Stream* (1977), *The Boys from Brazil* (1978), *Sphinx* (1981), *Yes, Giorgio* (1982), *Lionheart* (1987), *Welcome Home* (1989)

Other Notable Works: "12 Angry Men" (1954), "The Caine Mutiny Court Martial" (1955), *A Tour of the White House* (1962). Schaffner's television resumé is the most extensive and wideranging of any of the directors profiled in this text. Too many credits to list properly.

12. Ammo for Shooting Clouds
The John G. Avildsen Vision

This is the adjusted and revised script for a video essay featured on the Save the Tiger *Blu-ray release from Imprint Films in 2022. This piece tends to concentrate on and favor Avildsen's pre-*Rocky *career, as a New York-based independent filmmaker.*

> I want that girl in a Cole Porter song. I want to see Lena Horne at the Cotton Club, hear Billie Holiday sing fine and mellow… walk in that kind of rain that never washes perfume away. I want to be in love with something. Anything. Just the idea. A dog, a cat. Anything. Just something.
>
> Jack Lemmon as Harry Stoner
> in *Save the Tiger*

These days, cinephiles know director John G. Avildsen as the king of the underdogs. There's even a feature documentary about him by that name. And the subtitle of the only critical study text of him falls right in line with that designation. *The Films of John G. Avildsen: Rocky, The Karate Kid, and Other Underdogs*, by Larry Powell and Tom Garrett. But few seem to discuss Avildsen as a chronicler of the counterculture, because that was the niche he carved out *before* he trained his camera on the much beloved Philadelphia pugilist known as The Italian Stallion. He and Sylvester Stallone set the 1976 box office ablaze with *Rocky*. And with that success, Avildsen's atoms reconfigured and his focus shifted.

In his Oscar speech, he said, "I guess what *Rocky* did was give a lot of people hope, and there was never a better feeling than doing that." The film used a timeless formula, that of a streetwise but book-dumb ham-and-egger, with heart—so classic an American narrative template that it reached parody status by the time *Rocky* sprawled out into a cash-cow franchise that's still growing. So synonymous with underdog heroes did Avildsen become that most audiences seemed to altogether forget the eight (and a half) features he made before the crowd-pleasing game-changer that set him on his path to Oscar and pop culture glory. What are those eight and a half? There's the now lost *Turn on to Love* (1969), *Guess What We Learned in School Today* (1970), *Joe* (1970), *Okay, Bill* (1971; also known as *Sweet Dreams*), *Cry Uncle* (1971), *The Stoolie* (1972), *Save the Tiger* (1973), about half of the comedy anthology *Foreplay* (1974), and *W.W. and the Dixie Dancekings* (1975).

The one early one they might remember is his sleeper hit *Joe* (1970). In terms of genre classification, one hardly knows what to call it, really. Parts of it are quite funny... but a comedy? No, I would say not. Parts of it are horrific... but... well, maybe it's a counterculture horror film, of a kind. The lifelong liberal Avildsen goes slumming, you might say, with two white male bigots, separated by economic class but aligned in too many other ways. The first, Compton, is an affluent executive with an overdosed hippie daughter, and the other, Joe Curran, is a rough-around-every-edge, gun-crazy, blue-collar factory machinist with some hefty culture war grievances. Their ostensibly unlikely friendship commences with an ugly drunken racist diatribe at a downscale pub presided over by a stoic Irish bartender, albeit one with a ceiling for Joe's wretched ranting. When they reconvene to celebrate Compton's murder of his daughter's drug dealer boyfriend, it becomes a real "boys' night out." Of course, as you'd expect, they bond over common hatreds. At one point, Joe expresses a macabre nostalgia for his war years.

> JOE: Listen, no one's gonna blame you for killin' him. A guy like that, with your daughter. Look, there are plenty of people with kids, you'd be a hero! The guy was selling dope, right? So now he can't make dope fiends out of people anymore, can he?
>
> BILL: Yeah, that's right. God knows how many kids he hooked. Maybe that's why I get this—I've had it a couple of times later—the feeling of... pleasure? Satisfaction.
>
> JOE: Yeah yeah, like in the war! You remember how you felt in the war sometimes? After you killed a few of them? You feel bad and you feel good at the same time.

It's enthused, maybe even a bit misty-eyed, so much so that when Joe later picks off a houseful of hippies without so much as batting an eye, we're not terribly surprised, though there is an extra twist that I won't broach herein.

Let's flash forward to *Save the Tiger*, the picture Avildsen would make three years later. Jack Lemmon's Harry Stoner character is no bigot and certainly no bloodthirsty culture warrior, but he shares Joe's wistfulness over his years in the war. We're to believe that these were better times, when the world generally made sense: heroes and villains clearly defined, sanctity shielded from cynicism, national pride never condescended. That's all gone now, a blighted golden past. And now, none of it makes sense to him anymore, his values overshadowed by a world of people out for themselves, and it boils over in one key sequence:

HARRY STONER: Son of a bitch, don't sell America to me! I used to get goosebumps every time I looked at that flag. When I was a kid sitting alone in a room with a radio, if they ever played the national anthem, I stood up all alone in the room. I stood at attention. Don't sell me America! Now they're making jockstraps out of the flag. Maybe it's terrific. Maybe it's healthy, I don't know. But I do know there are no more rules.

PHIL: It stinks, Harry.

His exchanges with a hippie hitchhiker girl also magnify every generational disparity.

HARRY STONER: How old are you?

MYRA: Twenty.

HARRY STONER: (smirking) Nobody's twenty!

MYRA: Groovy suit.

HARRY STONER: Thank you.

MYRA: Do you want to ball?

HARRY STONER: It's awfully nice of you to offer, but I'm a little behind schedule.

Lemmon's Harry and Peter Boyle's Joe might not be underdogs as traditionally defined in the Avildsen-verse, but they're united by a tendency that is today a popular meme: "old man yells at clouds." Joe, for one, doesn't just yell; he brandishes a rifle and shoots at those clouds, without even aiming. These are aging relics from a defunct America, now on the outside looking in, with frustration, contempt, confusion, rancor, and in Joe's case, bloodlust. Time has passed them by, and neither accepts it gracefully, although their respective so-called gracelessness manifests... quite differently.

Jack Lemmon won an Oscar as Harry Stoner in *Save the Tiger.*

Avildsen looks at the brewing counterculture from another posture than that of his peers. *Easy Rider*, and all the films that emulated *Easy Rider*, were free-flowing accounts of liberated characters wholly unconcerned with the disdain or bewilderment of skeptics outside their spheres of existence and influence. Not so with Avildsen. In his naughty sex comedy *Guess What We Learned in School Today?* (1970), for instance, the sexual revolution comes to a small, conservative, well-to-do suburb. Uptight parents oppose the progressive sex education their kids are receiving, labeling such influence a communist plot. Sound familiar, American readers? This kind of thing, after all, still catches headlines today. Once again, the counterculture is blasted through an unlikely prism. These are yet more affronted outsiders, in this instance, a gang of repressed fuddy-duds who wage a culture war of their own. Would you call them anti-heroes? Even that is dicey, because Avildsen cheekily wants them to lose the fight, which would mean liberation for all parties. And of course much of the satirical impact of Avildsen's work here stems from the fact that, uhh… methinks the "ladies" doth protest too much. Translation: These fuming fogies are fucking freaky, in private. It's an outrageous skewering of the right wing in a way that only Avildsen could stage it. A spoonful of sugar makes the medicine go down, indeed. Or in this case, a spoonful of sexy.

Avildsen returned to X and sex with 1971's *Cry Uncle*, a bit of a raunchy underground classic in some circles. A raunch noir, if you like. Allen Garfield plays a randy private eye and kind of what you might call serial copulator. He's on the trail of a murderer, but the plot isn't important, unless you're the type who judges pornography for verisimilitude and narrative structure. No, I wouldn't call *Cry Uncle* pornographic, though I do retroactively wish I had a nickel for every proverbial pearl that was clutched among folks who didn't know what they were in for, during its initial run. The prurience is the point. Let's just say it earned its X way back when. The actor, Garfield, and the character he plays, Detective Jake Masters, are

THE GREAT AMERICAN OBSESSION
GETS LAID TO REST.

PLAYBOY MAGAZINE
says: "'Guess What We Learned
In School Today' Is tops in its class
of recent comedies drawn from
the hotbeds of sexual revolution."

"Guess
What
We Learned
In School
Today?"

Dennis Friedland and Christopher C. Dewey present a Cannon Production starring Richard Carballo
Devin Goldenberg · Zachary Haines · Jane MacLeod · Yvonne McCall · Rosella Olson introducing Diane Moore
Original musical score by Harper MacKay Written by Eugene Price Produced by David Gil Directed by John G. Avildsen
Color by Deluxe® · A Cannon Release Distributed by Craddock Films, Inc. [R]

certainly no Adonis figures. Our protagonist is corpulent, hairy, sweaty, and schlubby, but that doesn't stop him from shtupping everything in sight, including a corpse. Nor does it prevent him from having his way with a willing parade of femmes, both fatale and banal. In what is nothing short of a consummate depiction of body-positivity, we often find him in states of undress, eternally ready for a screw. And Avildsen isn't out to make any of it look pretty. But the funny bone is connect'd to the jawbone here, that's the world of the Lord, and our filmmaker hopes to tickle one and strain the other. (There might be another bone he attempts to tickle as well.)

So where and how does *Cry Uncle* fit within what was previously established in discussing the counterculture pulse in both *Joe* and *Save the Tiger*? Well, one might say that Avildsen sees comic potential in cross-pollinating Joe's gruff construction with the kind of sexually liberated youths whose loose morality and taste for anarchy Joe detests. Ditto that of the girl hitchhiker in *Save the Tiger*. He took Joe's body type and coarse disposition, filled it out with a constitution similar to that of Joe's human targets, topped it with a hearty spoonful of sleaze, and wound up with Jake Masters in *Cry Uncle*. Is Jake a social outcast like the other Avildsen characters we've covered so far? Maybe, maybe not, but he sure doesn't give a flying fuck. It is perhaps this devil-may-care swagger that rendered the film a low-level hit in the nascent midnight movie scene at the time of release. It remains a gleefully uncouth rhapsody of lowbrow.

Avildsen's follow-up was comparably more tame. Following the "offense against decency" that *Cry Uncle* was, what wouldn't be, you're probably asking. His comedy *The Stoolie* (1972), starring none other than standup czar Jackie Mason, is the earliest blueprint for Avildsen's later chronicles of the underdog. It gingerly hinted at what would become a predilection. We have a schemer-dreamer police informant named Roger who absconds with $7,500 of police decoy money. He's the type of guy that Jackie Mason himself would call a fonzanoon ("a guy who farts in the bathtub and bites the bubbles"). As you might expect, he lives large on the stolen money, high on the hog in Miami, where he tries to attract a mate, with predictably wavering results—though he does wind up kindling a little romance, with the scandalously overlooked actress Marcia Jean Kurtz, a performer you might call a ubiquitous but unheralded "salty siren" of a long lost New York cinema.

The Stoolie was a "little" film, produced and shepherded by its star, but it scored some respectable reviews in its day, even if it didn't do much of any business. It has advocates today, many of whom express how they eventually found themselves rooting for Jackie Mason's rumpled schlemiel. *The Stoolie,* in that regard, belongs more to mainline Avildsen. But like Joe, Harry, Jake, and even Rocky, he's yet another social outcast, of a particular Avildsen vintage. Only Roger and Rocky are keen on beating the odds, though. They are the direct inverse of Harry in *Save the Tiger,* who has effectively checked out. Nevertheless, by virtue of its gritty, thrifty look alone, *The Stoolie* still easily conforms with Avildsen's other early pre-*Rocky* pictures.

There is yet one more in this lot to discuss in this context. *Okay, Bill!* (1971) is a downright rarity these days, much like Avildsen's debut, *Turn on to Love* (1969). It's never had a video release and film prints are so scarce that it seems no one has screened it since its original release. Avildsen himself posted clips from the film on his YouTube account, but that's the most anyone has seen of it in over fifty years. It does seem to fit right in with our subject though. Per the IMDb's synopsis, it's "the story of a young, successful stockbroker who zips off on his motorcycle to Greenwich Village, to venture into the hippie counterculture world." Other synopses suggest that he ditches his conservative existence to run wild

Jack Masters (Allen Garfield) on the case and in the mood in *Cry Uncle!*

Jackie Mason in *The Stoolie.*

with an eccentric fashion photographer and his colorful entourage. Based on the works surrounding it, I suspect there is unrest, a sense that the protagonist cannot fully enter this subculture, as much as he tries—that he remains on the outside looking in, but I can't confirm because I haven't seen the whole movie. Maybe one day, fingers crossed.

Turn on to Love's synopsis isn't dissimilar: a bored housewife starts hanging out in Greenwich Village and gets involved with pot-smoking hippies and an Italian filmmaker. Sense a pattern here? It's all squares getting it on with the dropouts. That one intrigues mostly because it's a rare female protagonist for Avildsen. (Pretty please, cinema gods?)

The Burt Reynolds vehicle *W.W. and the Dixie Dancekings* (1975) directly preceded *Rocky*. I'm a bit hard-pressed to find a common thread in that film regarding the themes we're discussing, but it's an endearing piece of light entertainment with, at best, an underdog subtheme. Avildsen was set to direct *Serpico* (1973), but producer Marty Bregman replaced him with Sidney Lumet before cameras rolled. A cop with hippie aspirations, too weird for fellow cops, too much of a pig for fellow hippies. Outside looking in, double-time: Serpico would have been a perfect early Avildsen hero. Honestly, I would have rather seen Avildsen's result than Lumet's workable substitute.

SERPICO, ORIGINAL THEATRICAL TRAILER:
There are many sides to Serpico. A hero who was hated.

A loner who was loved. And to some people, the most dangerous man alive.

Avildsen opens and closes *Save the Tiger* on the Bunny Berrigan Big Band tune "I Can't Get Started." It's a dirge for the Harry Stoner character, and a kind of anthem for the other Avildsen characters in this early period. Each has schemes, some (but not all) have dreams, but when they take a good long look around at current realities, they simply can't get started. It's a tad cynical and a hell of a springboard for a guy who would go on to build his reputation as king of the underdogs. What we've got is a fascinating trajectory, from yelling or firing at clouds, to simply aiming for them. From can't get started to going the distance, conquering whatever odds at full speed. Normally idealism dies with age. For Avildsen, age and commercial success clearly proved to him that the little man can triumph and that dreams sometimes really do come true.

Theatrical Feature Films: *Turn On to Love* (1969), *Guess What We Learned in School Today?* (1970), *Joe* (1970), *Okay, Bill!* (1971), *Cry Uncle!* (1971), *The Stoolie* (1972), *Save the Tiger* (1973), *W.W. and the Dixie Dancekings* (1975), *Foreplay* (1975, segment: "Inaugural Ball"), *Rocky* (1976), *Slow Dancing in the Big City* (1978), *The Formula* (1980), *Neighbors* (1981), *Traveling Hopefully* (1982), *A Night in Heaven* (1983), *The Karate Kid* (1984), *The Karate Kid Part II* (1986), *Happy New Year* (1987), *For Keeps?* (1988), *Lean on Me* (1989), *The Karate Kid Part III* (1989), *Rocky V* (1990), *The Power of One* (1992), *8 Seconds* (1994), *Inferno* (1999)

13. Somebody Call the Tone Police
The Ivan Passer Vision
(with a Peek Into Jerry Schatzberg)

This is the first publication of this essay, written especially for this volume.

Passer is technically a European director who Americanized, having made one now-classic Czech feature before retreating to the United States in the wake of the Soviet invasion. He emigrated to America in 1969 with friend Miloš Forman, for whom he had written the Czech New Wave landmarks *Loves of a Blonde* (1965) and *The Fireman's Ball* (1967). Both of these preternatually gifted refugees made their American directing debuts shooting simultaneously in New York in 1971: Passer with *Born to Win* and Forman with his marvelous *Taking Off*. (Buck Henry would often relate how Forman's English was still a "work-in-progress" during the shooting of the latter.) Passer's American films, much like his buddy's, deal with very American subjects, and are remarkably consistent in their construction: two-bit characters pursue harebrained schemes to topple power structures and come out on top. As we watch these loners, pariahs, and oddballs hatch and then execute, the freakiest kind of human comedy is interwoven, with periodic punctuations of human horror. This sometimes results in a conscious tonal confusion that often puzzled and perturbed critics. But circumstance and reality tragically blow up in the characters' faces, always leaving both them and us with something remarkably melancholic and downbeat by final fade-out.

I got the chance to meet and speak with Ivan Passer, thanks to my friendship with Karen Black. I first saw *Born to Win* as a teenager, and watched it on repeat, because I quickly grew fascinated by the way it captured the New York City of its time. It is perhaps the quintessential Mayor John Lindsay "fun city" picture, which is to say, the grimiest, grittiest, gloomiest, smoggiest, shaggiest, dirtiest-low-down New York ever committed to celluloid. For years, it was available only on degraded bargain-bin tape and disk copies,

George Segal as J and Jay Fletcher as Billy Dynamite
in Passer's *Born to Win*.

sourced from a fuzzy, censored, poorly edited-for-TV print (excising three whole minutes from the runtime). I watched one such copy with Karen Black herself, when I was her houseguest for a month. She provided a running informal commentary about working on the film, during which she rhapsodized Ivan and described him as one of her favorite director collaborators. She also spoke of her great love for *Intimate Lighting* (1965), his deservedly vaunted debut. (To this day, I kick myself that I didn't record it, not that I had the means to, lacking a smartphone in 2008.)

Though *Born to Win*, about the daily exploits and misadventures of a silky-smooth but scrappy hipster hairdresser as he contends with a $100-a-day heroin habit, is grim on the page, Passer admitted that he kept on finding the humor in the material. Having evolved from a theater piece called *Scraping Bottom* by David Scott Milton, the film thrives on Passer's sometimes confounding tonal blend. One might call it a comical cross-stitch. When the film premiered at the New York Film Festival, critics were flummoxed. The reviews bear this out; Pauline Kael commented that maybe it was "the mixture of moods (comedy and horror)" that rattled people. She lamented that the "producers barely opened it," simply allowing it to escape. Roger Greenspun of the *New York Times* called it "a dreadful disappointment, not without its reasons, and not, I think, without honor." Looking at it now, especially in a spiffy (but still grainy and grungy) new Blu-ray transfer, it's easy to see how it was far ahead of the curve. And so was Ivan Passer himself, as a filmmaker.

This ostensible stylistic conflict, a kind of tonal and materialist dialectic, set a pace for the rest of Passer's quintessentially offbeat career. His follow-up *Law and Disorder* moves along briskly, peppered with broad, frenetic comic set pieces that suddenly—like a shock to the system—turn south. He hits us with, for instance, a genuinely upsetting overdose freakout scene involving one of the lead character's daughters. There are plenty of other dark turns along the way, which brush against potentially incongruous strains of absurdism and farce. Contrast the film's final fatal showdown with a wild and wacky earlier scene at a town hall meeting, featuring Allan Arbus as an eccentric sexual deviance expert. *Cutter's Way* is Passer's masterpiece, his ultimate saga of a moral crusade waged by people at the mercy—the very bitter end—of a rugged and rigged world. John Heard's embittered and volatile scalawag Cutter deputizes those around him in his attempts to get ahead of the bastards—or more profoundly, the bastard class. There's a contrast to be had here with the dotty, delightful *Intimate Lighting*; his American films are point-blank much darker (including his endings). His is a funny, absurd world fraught with the peril of tragic consequences wrought by the capricious actions of desperate, demonstrably pathetic strivers.

Passer's auteurist trajectory is in many ways similar to Jerry Schatzberg's. The latter launched himself into motion pictures from still photography with three distinctive features—*Puzzle of a Downfall Child* (1970), *The Panic in Needle Park* (1971), and the

John Heard, Jeff Bridges, and Lisa Eichhorn in *Cutter's Way*.

The irrepressible J (George Segal) cradled by Parm (Karen Black) in *Born to Win*.

Cannes Palme-winner *Scarecrow* (1973)—which definitively established his name and his authorship right from jump street. With his fourth feature, *Sweet Revenge* (1976), onward, he more or less got lost in a Hollywood wilderness, tackling projects too often beneath his talents. I will note, however, that though many of the films are not up to the high standard Schatzberg set early on, even a teen sex comedy like *No Small Affair* (1984) is clearly a cut above the rest of its asinine ilk. And this is also certainly not to say that, on the overall, the later Schatzberg works are altogether bereft of artistry or a signature (his 1989 comeback picture *Reunion* especially has its moments). It is simply that those first three made weighty promises about his future as one of America's premier directors—promises that were not quite kept.

While Passer might not have enjoyed Schatzberg's level of success (*Born to Win* and *Law and Disorder* in particular were released to incredulous reaction, and that's putting it generously), that similar three-film streak feels nothing short of momentous in comparison to what came after. Following *Cutter's Way* with the likes of *Creator* (1985) and *Haunted Summer* (1988), which were idiosyncratic in their respective ways, lacked the "fire and music" of the earlier work.

Andrei Konchalovsky's American films of the Eighties should also be invoked here. Both Passer and Konchalovsky—with their Eastern European and Russian sensibilities—affix a kind of "figurative fish-eye lens" to their American portraiture. They thematically and dramaturgically distort as to paradoxically clarify, overcranking reality as to help free the audience (especially the American audience) of delusion—as to see things clean and unencumbered. No longer are the surfaces of American life (and the myths created around them) denuded of meaning. Konchalovsky's *Shy People* (1987), about a feral bayou family, is especially keen to operate this way. In doing so, both filmmakers find unexpected humor amid the horror, as a foregone conclusion.

George Segal's J in *Born to Win* is strangely cheerful in buzzing, barreling, and boogying through each overcast day, each shenanigan, each cockamamie mission, each new literal shot in the arm. Throughout is his knowing, incorrigible grin, the oil that greases the next connivance. J, for all his faults, is a likable bloke, one we can recognize as having made some very sorry choices in life. Yet we still wish to see him live up to the eponymous "born to win" tattoo on his tracked-up arm. Even when there's a contract out on his head, J is indefatigable and immutable. He will keep squirreling, squirming, and contorting himself to win the day. He's got allies in the seediest corners of town, and his gift of the blarney is prodigious, almost supernatural, in its ability to (a) bail himself out, (b) ensnare others, and/or (c) ensnare himself further. John Heard's profligate Alex Cutter in *Cutter's Way* likewise has an uncanny power to sucker others into doing their all-too-literal damndest

George Segal and Jay Fletcher in *Born to Win*.

for a quixotically macabre (and strangely ideological) scheme that is doomed to fail... and worse. J and Cutter are birds of a feather in their restless machinations to come out on top—one is affable and almost benevolent in his thieving and hustling, while the other is odious, vitriolic, nevertheless witty, and out for blood at any cost.

It's the gnarliest of details that Passer tends to always get right. This is in the DNA of most of his films, and if you were to have asked Karen Black, who plays J's dippy, free-spirited girl-friend Parm, Passer was attuned to the needs of actors in carving out character detail that played into a larger framework, to make such shadings and accent marks not just known but, most impor-tantly, vivid. She related a story to me about the scene involving her own real-life cat, Nathan, who plays himself in the awkward tryst scene that follows Parm and J's larcenous meet-cute. Scripted was the relation of a punny rather than funny joke: "What has four legs and chases cats?" The punchline is "Mr. Katz and her lawyer." Karen, for her part, found the joke "very sad," whether in context or in general. Passer instructed that she incorporate that down-beat reaction into the scene, rather than laughing as written. Karen related to me that the soft-spoken Passer was a gentle soul who wanted the life to come out of collective work. As Bertrand Taver-nier, an avowed fan and proponent of Passer's, notes, "There is no condescension in the films of Ivan Passer. You always feel he is on the same level with his characters."

The attention to detail extends to mise en scene as well. In a second-act scene, in which Segal cloaks himself in a pink shag ladies nighty, the gaudy paisley wallpaper and chintzy furnishings—the most meretricious Seventies decor imaginable—almost too perfectly offsets the urban filth on display in the rest of the film. This only briefly glimpsed domain of power and privilege can't help but be the finest of sleazy fineries, a monument to bad taste. In another scene, a brief but haunting little tour through a secret alleyway peopled with strung-out junkies and transients, Passer's attention to grimy detail sees him taking to documenting American urban decay like a duck to water... or, more appropriately, like a pigeon to a Broadway gutter. With its unusual, off-kilter comedic bent, *Born to Win* both competed with and distinguished itself from a glut of drug and addict-themed dramas in its release year, including Schatzberg's *The Panic in Needle Park*, Stuart Hagmann's *Believe in Me* (1971), Floyd Mutrux's *Dusty and Sweets Magee* (1971), and Noel Black's *Jennifer on My Mind* (1971).

Fresh corpses acted upon by outside forces in the death scenes of
Born to Win (above) and *Cutter's Way* (below).

Passer also had a special flair for death scenes, often tainted
with irony... or with simultaneously muted but gobsmacking
gallows humor. In *Born to Win*, J's compadre Billy takes a hot-shot
(a narcotic injection tainted with battery acid) and promptly dies.
The obstructed doors of an elevator close repeatedly on the newly
deceased's elbows, simulating Billy's dying embrace of J played in
a cruel loop—a punishing playback. In *Cutter's Way*, Alex's delir-
iously angry but oddly exhilarated horseback gallop through a
well-heeled lawn party ends, once again, with the dead acted upon
by an outside force. Cutter's one and only hand, now lifeless, is
still poised on the grip as his friend Bone squeezes the trigger on
his behalf, firing a presumably fatal shot (we cut to black before

we see the result). In *Law and Disorder*, Ernest Bognine's Cy stays behind in a danger area, out of loyalty, only to be gunned down by a tenement sniper, like a dog in the street.

Pauline Kael was also an advocate of Passer's. In reviewing *Intimate Lighting*, she writes, "Passer is witty with tiny, match-flare-size details; he shows us lives that have become a negotiation of small irritants." This can be applied to other Passer pictures as well. Cutter erupts at the slightest provocation, at the most meager nuisances, metaphorically swatting flies with a bazooka. J in *Born to Win* never blinks or flinches, but is still miffed by a ceaseless stream of what he considers mere bad luck—this from a man who says he is "not addicted, just habituated." Each Passer protagonist negates one step in the five stages of grief (Anger, Denial, Bargaining, Depression, Acceptance). Cutter leaves out Acceptance—no way will that man ever let things lie, sleeping dogs or otherwise. J leaves out Depression—ever the cockeyed optimist with no reason to be. The ragtag citizens in *Law and Disorder* leave out Denial—they know full well the urban woes that plague them, and would never delude themselves into thinking that all is well in their city. The question is, what do they put in place of these "grief holes"? Their substitutional "medicine" is the stuff of both comedy and horror.

I believe a more apt title for Ivan Passer's *Law and Disorder* (1974) might have been *Citizen's Arrest*, as it follows the hijinks of a citizen's auxiliary police force guarding their apartment complex against a chaotic, crime-ridden New York. Passer recounts the seed of the idea: "I met a taxi driver who told me he was part of a vigilante group in Lower Manhattan, trying to protect the neighborhood against crime. I thought it was a great idea for a comedy." The end product is, of course, another prime Mayor Lindsay "fun city" entry; this is a sometimes even more unforgiving, "wild, wild West Side" Big Apple. The title *Law and Disorder* suggests a Benny Hill kind of affair (it was, in fact, also the title of an Ealing-style farce directed by Ealing vet Charles Crichton), while the gut-punch surprise moments of gravitas suggest something rather different. Passer lamented killing off one of his characters: "For some reason, I killed Ernie Borgnine's character in the film. It was a change of genre inside the film. The audience was laughing all the time, and suddenly this guy was killed and the audience was stunned. I learned you should never do that."

Perhaps that is the ruse though—Passer lures us in with innocuous titles like *Born to Win* (rather than the bummer original *Scraping Bottom*) and *Law and Disorder*, then contrives various

Ernest Borgnine and Carroll O'Connor and in *Law and Disorder*.

dramatic sneak punches right in the kisser to defy expectation. Even *Cutter's Way* is a more benign title than its original release moniker *Cutter and Bone* (renamed during its formative re-release because it was feared people might mistake it for a movie about surgeons). Passer recalls that United Artists execs imposed the title *Born to Win* on his film, but though there is a surface innocuousness and a kind of reflexive hope for the underdog, one leaves the experience of seeing the film reckoning with its sorrows.

Until I saw a 35mm print of *Law and Disorder* at New York's MoMA back in 2009, I had always confused it with Aram Avakian's *Cops and Robbers* (1973), with Cliff Gorman and Joseph Bologna. I was a Passer enthusiast even then, but the title blended in with a bunch of other pictures' titles, so it got lost in my neural recesses for a while. But that screening for a New York audience was informative, in that they responded quite acutely to the film. I place it on par with seeing *The Taking of Pelham One Two Three* (1974) with another New York audience; both Passer's film and that one revel in a kind of local insider's humor. However, in its day, Kael called the film "a painful failure, lumpish and crude," asserting that "Passer doesn't have the unconscious equipment for the look and feel of ordinary American life." She deduced that "he is trying to strike a compromise between his feelings and the demands of the American marketing system—and satisfying neither." The film does take big comedy swings, especially in scenes involving Karen Black as a mouthy, horny, and-ready-to-blow hairdresser-in-heat. As usual, Karen leapt into a knowingly over-the-top, guffaw-worthy character role with gleeful abandon, whether or not critics ruled that "it worked."

Russian director Eldar Ryazanov shares a specific kind of tragicomic sensibility with Ivan Passer. Ryazanov, most known for his beloved Russian classic *The Irony of Fate* (1975), revealed his aptitude for fearless, "big swing" tragicomedy reversals over the course of multiple Soviet classics of the Seventies and Eighties. He often allowed his highly kinetic comedy set pieces to play at length, as a means of letting the laughs steadily build as a kind of process. A dash of suspense only amplifies the laughs. We see that approach at play in the opening of *Law and Disorder*, with Passer holding his first two shots over extended periods; he likewise stages for comic suspense, first with a risibly elaborate TV theft, then with a gang of very efficient carjackers who strip Borgnine's Chevy Caprice in real time (in a matter of two minutes). In some sense, this is a brand of "humor-at-length" we might not be terribly used to in Western countries. [Ryazanov is surely worth further investigation, dear reader; I recommend the aforementioned *The Irony of Fate*, then *Office Romance* (1977), *A Railway Station for Two* (1982), then *Forgotten Tune for the Flute* (1987).]

On a personal level, I've always been skeptical of unspoken rules concerning tonal consistency, which is partly why I find Passer of special interest. While many would warn or admonish that such a gambit is a juggling act that requires keeping one's balls/objects well up in the air, I find "Passerian" tonal departures an intriguing means of knocking the audience off-balance. Many of the directors I cherish never relinquish even the vaguest sense of control to the audience. American audiences especially have a difficult if not impossible time handing that level of control over to a filmmaker; having a sure handle on the course of a film experience instills a sense of security, however limiting it may be. In most cases, surprises must be precision-engineered, or else the spears gets sharpened. Passer sees life itself as a constant, ever-evolving flow of day-to-day, hour-to-hour "tonal shifts." There's a very Czech brand of humor at hand here, with its topsy-turvy sense that "life's a goddamn laugh riot." Passer has us consider that our existence in this reality is, by its very nature, absurd—and he prods us to laugh in recognition, while breaking occasionally to confront, unimpaired, its inevitable tragedies.

Ace Up My Sleeve, a.k.a. Crime and Passion.

Bizarrely dropped into the middle of this loose trilogy of tonal melange are two European high-crime excursions, *Ace Up My Sleeve* (1976, a.k.a. *Crime and Passion*) and *Silver Bears* (1977). The former defies any quick and easy categorization. Again, we have the peremptory cons and tricks and schemes and chicaneries, but the Passerian blend in this case is one that worked for, quite frankly, no one. But though it is widely considered Passer's worst outing, *Ace Up My Sleeve* is such a strange whosy-whatsit of a film that is difficult to nail down, either for what it's doing or what it even *is* in any basic sense. I find it a somewhat amusing puzzle, beguiling by virtue of its askew presentation. No less than seven writers, including Passer himself, had a hand in the screenplay. Alan Trustman (*The Thomas Crown Affair*) and William Richert (the future director of *Winter Kills*, who had also collaborated with Passer on *Law and Disorder*) also did their time on it. Omar Sharif plays a business kingpin who gets sexually turned on by his own financial setbacks, as established in an early boardroom rendezvous. With mistress Karen Black, he hatches a plan for her to marry a wealthy industrialist, then divorce him for a sizable settlement, to cover for his malfeasance. If I were to explain how the film somehow transforms into a haunted house story in its last half, I'd be denying you, dear reader, the type of weird encounter with a movie that many live for, so I'll just suffice to leave that dangling.

Michael Caine, Louis Jourdan, and Cybill Shepherd in *Silver Bears*.

Though *Ace Up My Sleeve* was its original title, and Passer's preferred, for having premiered in most international territories as such (by a nose, over Sam Arkoff's AIP retitle *Crime and Passion*), other titles in other languages prove bizarre indeed. One translates as *Frankenstein's Haunted Castle*. The film is a pastiche: by turns, Harold Robbins (or Jackie Collins), and then James M. Cain, and then, improbably, Bill Castle. Its outer-spacey Vangelis score is putatively a misfit for the material, but considering the overall narrative dissonance, it may be operating on another level entirely. After all, consider some choice scenes: Omar Sharif's bath-time chorus of "She'll Be Comin' 'Round the Mountain" is interrupted when a heavy-set buxom woman lifts him baffled out of the tub (doing so by pressing his face flush up against her bare melon breast). Or, in another, Karen Black seduces Sam Bottoms by ravenously—and almost grotesquely—consuming a "prop" tangerine. As she retreats to his nether region for a round of fellatio, a suit of armor comes to ghostly life.

Even the most skilled of cinema decoders would find him or herself bewildered by *Ace Up My Sleeve*. Roger Ebert, in his review, called it "not only one of the silliest films ever made, but one of the most inexplicable." Vincent Canby echoed Ebert in the *New York Times*, calling it "a grossly disoriented and disorienting shaggy-dog of a movie that seems to have no point." In Passer, though, there is always a design: the high-stakes struggles for power, money, and surival always pave out some downright cuckoo detours. (Consider also George Segal's men's store jacket switcheroo in *Born to Win*.) With *Ace Up My Sleeve*, its co-screen-writer William Richert helped lay a blueprint—at least mood-wise —for not only his madball conspiracy thriller *Winter Kills* (1979) but especially his uneven comedy *The American Success Company* (1979), a multi-tonal fusion of perverse fairy-tale and wigged-out satire on capitalism shot in Munich.

While *Ace Up My Sleeve* set up camp in the Swiss Alps, *Silver Bears* (1977) is peripatetic in its hopping around from Vegas to Morocco to Switzerland to Italy. I have always described *Silver Bears* with a question: "What if Alan J. Pakula's nearly impene-trable banking thriller *Rollover* were a rollicking comedy?" I find its world-of-high-finance convolutions obscure and often inscru-table, but there is never any doubt that this is a Passer picture (his first and only shot in the 2.35:1 aspect ratio). That the film opens on withered male flesh, at a Turkish bath, may remind one of a "throw-away" scene from *Born to Win*: in a locker room, Passer holds on a shot well after Segal exits frame, as a similar older body-type drops his drawers (this elicited a big ol' weird audience chortle when I attended a public 35mm screening many years ago). Flabby or mangled (à la Cutter) flesh seems to be a refrain of sorts. The charm of *Silver Bears* is rooted in its screenplay by *Charade* scribe Peter Stone, and its high-end cast, including Michael Caine,

Passer directs a scene from *Haunted Summer.*

Cybill Shepherd, Louis Jourdan, David Warner, Martin Balsam, Tom Smothers, Stéphane Audran, Charles Gray, and a young Jay Leno. It feels like Passer's most expensive project—that cast, the globe-trotting vistas, and the high-concept plot-centrism, bespeak the not puny budget dollars at the production's disposal. Passer's staging for the 'Scope frame is solid enough that one wishes he would have dabbled more in the wide canvas size. Even if one loses track of the intricate story (an uber-refined, "lingoistic" heist flick), one can still delight in the scenery, the light and airy touch, and the players on display, who make hay of both. I'd rank it over the woefully opaque *Rollover*, I'll acknowledge that much.

To say that *Cutter's Way* was a change of pace from Passer's two previous expeditions into the high life is putting it lightly. Back to the world of losers and strivers he went, with gusto. With a poetic slow-motion image that just as slowly transitions from black and white into color, *Cutter's Way* opens on a hallucinatory note. As the credits roll, a lady in a white gown dances toward us in a brassy fiesta parade. So begins the masterpiece that Bertrand Tavernier calls "one of the greatest American films of the 1980s" and "the best film about post-Vietnam America, next to Karel Reisz's *Who'll Stop the Rain*." Jonathan Rosenbaum admitted to having seen the film "perhaps thirty times," claiming that it may be his favorite American film (period, yes). *Cutter's Way* is, needless to say, not without important admirers (and there are a great many of them to boot), but the film took decades to secure its foothold as a more widely known and respected work. Some say it requires multiple viewings to begin percolating. Danny Peary puts it thus: "It is a picture that demands several viewings to be judged fairly, simply because it takes that long to break bad viewing habits."

Of any of Passer's pictures, *Cutter's Way* is the leanest on comedy—at least the type of unfiltered, upper-case comedy which was Passer's stock in trade—though it is certainly not without a—a-hem—cutting humor. The story: Playboy Richard Bone witnesses the dumping of a corpse in a dark alley on a rainy night. When he fingers a wealthy oil tycoon named Cord as the criminal perpetrator, his renegade friend Alex Cutter, a crippled Vietnam veteran, lets his imagination run wild. Cutter hatches a scheme to corner then topple/ruin their suspect, a steely, insulated member of the power elite. When Cutter enlists the victim's sister Valerie in their fanciful plot, he becomes an obsessive Ahab in a symbolic quest for revenge against the shadowy, monied men who sent him off to the unjust war that mutilated and maimed him. At the mercy

The hypnotic opening shot of *Cutter's Way.*

of the whole endeavor is Cutter's long-suffering, depressive, alcoholic wife Mo.

Danny Peary marvels at the efficiency of *Cutter's Way*: "How quickly [Passer] manages to establish the cruelty of J.J. Cord, the snobbery of Cord's thick-skinned socialite wife, the opportunism of Valerie, the hurt that the woman in the hotel feels when Bone insults her sexual prowess, and the peculiar traits of Cutter, Bone, and Mo." Cutter spends a fair amount of the runtime inveighing against hypocrisy, going off half-cocked with racist diatribes, and self-indulgently sermonizing with unroyal indignation about the way the world should be. He's a cripple who uses his various disabilities to glean pity, only to parlay that into a ruthless domination he exerts both pitifully and pitilessly. Peary observes how Cutter "makes sure everyone suffers from his presence." It is not enough that Cutter pursues Cord with a vigor for justice, not even for the crime in question (which becomes almost a shaggy-dog case or red herring in the filmic context) but in a larger, more generalized sense. He must also sadistically spook the target as best he can, thus shamelessly tipping him off to his objective.

Passer's window into the material and the Cutter character is biographical. He speaks of how "the victims of violence infect other people," and cites his encounters with embittered, forever scarred, sometimes nihilist, and downright mean-spirited survivors of concentration camps, a class of people he knew growing up in Czechoslovakia. It's all a more intellectually robust take on "hurt people hurt people." Though the project was originally intended for

Intimate Lighting.

Robert Mulligan, then Mark Rydell, it's difficult to imagine Passer's filmography without it. While an adaptation of Newton Thornburg's novel *Cutter and Bone* might have comfortably nestled alongside a Mulligan noir like *The Nickel Ride* (1975), it truly lives and looms large in Passer's sometimes tentative career because it is thematically far more germane. A Rydell version of the novel I don't even want to consider. Passer's characters belong to a blithely careless fraternity with a specific purpose and constitution.

Nick Redman, in his audio commentary for *Cutter's Way*, makes a salient point: If *Cutter's Way* had been produced five years later, in the heart of Reagan's "morning in America" nationalistic ethos and amid the trend toward Rambo-esque action histrionics, we might have been subjected to tiresome foxhole flashbacks. Passer's inclination to leave us with Cutter as a hollowed-out shell, fueled only by blind rage and booze, might have been smothered, favoring manifestations of his war days which would have upstaged the main action to no advantage. There likely would have been a glint of patriotism thrown in, to temper the type of prevailing bitterness with which a yuppified Eighties audiences had lost patience. But at the tail end of the Seventies, the film manages to be authentically its director's own.

Cutter's Way is my pick for the best of 1981, and it would seem these days that time has finally caught up with it; it's more timely than ever in our current political era. Its politically populist prescience is stunning in the heart (read: the bowels) of this year of our lord 2025. And once again, the attention to detail, even in its smallest moments, is extraordinary. For instance, when Bone boats past a line of offshore oil platforms that tower over his craft, we perceive the presence of Cord and sense the shadow of unchecked power looming large over him in a way he hasn't yet acknowledged by that point in the story. Tavernier loved another such example: a pack of white horses crossing the street in front of Bone's car at the beginning. Such a touch, or flourish, offers us another narrative and visual "diacritical mark," out of many others—all of which are heightened by Jack Nitzsche's ethereally twangy music score. It is thus no wonder Rosenbaum claims to have run the film so many times. Something new emerges on every viewing.

His follow-up to his masterpiece, an all-out comedy called *Creator* (1985), is a strange, unlikely left turn more in the spirit of *Ace Up My Sleeve* and *Silver Bears*. Peter O'Toole stars as a scientist using university resources to clone his dead wife. Passer told me in one of our two conversations that he made *Creator* purely and simply because he was attracted to its mix of pathos and humor, but it's also likely that the grimness of *Cutter's Way* instilled in him the emotional need to do something just a bit less severe. (I can relate myself, in that, for instance, as a filmmaker, I've always immediately followed my black-and-white films with big, bold color films, as a palate cleanser.) He could never distance himself from the bright and buoyant, even when he paced, pierced, and/or peppered it with startling spasms of trauma-drama. I am at a loss for how to approach *Creator* as of this writing. I've made perfect sense of John Schlesinger's *Honky Tony Freeway* (1981), for instance, but it took years, and I have enjoyed that one far more in a basic experiential sense. *Creator* is rather a banal detour, because it's such a letdown after the brilliance of *Cutter's Way*, rather akin to the way one feels with the Archers, catching *Oh... Rosalinda!!* (1955) immediately after the triumph of *The Tales of Hoffman* (1951). (Incidentally, *Creator* is not without the occasional good line of dialogue; "An orgasm is the fun of creation," is a favorite.)

A couple years later, Passer joined an illustrious roster of first-tier directors at Cannon Films, when they opened up an arthouse wing to balance out the schlock that had become synonymous with their dubious (but no less entertaining) studio brand. (His "Cannon arthouse" directing comrades included Schatzberg, Konchalovsky, Godard, Mailer, Polanski, Zeffirelli, Frankenheimer, and Barbet

Schroeder, among others.) The result, *Haunted Summer* (1988), a period piece about Lord Byron and Mary Shelley spending a summer in a villa on Lake Geneva, was forced to compete with Ken Russell's *Gothic* (1986), which dealt with the same material. Neither wound up doing much for their respective makers, critically or commercially. *Haunted Summer* is effortlessly ravishing from a visual perspective, thanks to Giuseppe Rotunno's cinematography, but it ever so conspicuously lacks that something extra— something which even *Silver Bears* possessed. What's worse, that which is lacking most of all is Passer's marvelous perverse humor, cast aside in favor of a more earnest approach. As a result, despite certain perks, the effort feels passionless.

Fourth Story (1991) has clear, inarguable traces of Passer's penchant for uneven humor, as it is infused into neo-noir trappings in this particular case. It's unfortunately the last sign of life from the Passer school of auteurship. Critic Filipe Furtado writes, "The first half plays almost like a romantic comedy in noir clothes, while the second half is split between Freudian horror and absurdist comedy." He also notes the various silly coincidences in the course of the narrative, but concedes, "given that Passer never tries to be credible, that never matters much." *Fourth Story* is a film that knows and harps on its roots; in one scene, Mimi Rogers quips, "I guess I just expected somebody more like Humphrey Bogart,"

Intimate Lighting.

when she visits the office of private investigator Mark Harmon. Later, Passer mocks any number of noir tropes and conventions, as in "Carry a gun? Are you kidding? I'm a P.I.!" The film is disposable in its way, but not at all lacking in personality. His HBO epic *Stalin* (1992) is perfectly workmanlike, but anonymous. This is likely because, in consciously divorcing himself from any overriding concern for aesthetics, Passer favors his inclination to purge any festering enmity toward the Communist ills that forever altered the course of his life. *Stalin* stands in his filmography as a filmic clearing of the political air, featuring Robert Duvall doing a yeoman job in the title role. [Passer's friend Miloš Forman's taste for messy but glorious rebellion is aired in a wholly other way, as covered in the Allan Moyle chapter of this book.]

So and so and so, I've been going on for pages about the American films, but have barely touched upon *Intimate Lighting*. Yes, I know, I know, dear reader. I'm not going to let you down now, but it simply occurred to me that *Intimate Lighting* would provide ideal material for a grand finale, the *fortissimo* coda to this Passer Pasacaglia. First of all, what more can one say than that his debut is pure genius? There is damn good reason Ivan Passer's arrival in America was so anticipated and hailed. *Intimate Lighting* is a constantly surprising film of generous spirit, a slice of life in the Soviet Bloc that taps into rhythms of existence that subsist on enticing key signatures played out in obscure time signatures. Underneath that is the concealed but no less present specter of oppression and cagedness, a feeling then all too common among people living east of the Berlin Wall. Its poignancy lies in the characters' regret over their lives' bitterest compromises. In likely its most important scene, two buddies get blotto on home-made brandy. They achieve a fleeting salvation from the burden of their disappointments the only way they know how, through a bottle that activates truth and honesty. When Dave Kehr writes that Passer has succeeded in a "genuine comedy of melancholy — a gray comedy," he is either wittingly or unwittingly remarking (like Kael earlier) on the broader expanse of its director's filmography. Even once Passer arrives in America, the films are born out of the lingering ache of displacement. This inevitably strikes some dissonant chords. In the United States, Passer would come to sing a song of the exile exclusively indexed on pleasures and pains that coexist in fragile equilibrium. This equilibrium is a film-by-film toy that tantalizes both filmmaker and audience.

In a late career interview, when asked to discuss the elements that connect or bind his work, Passer expressed his love for stories of male bonding and/or male friendship. Surely, this is the raw material of *Intimate Lighting*, but is also present with J and Billy Dynamite in *Born to Win*, Carroll O'Connor's Willie and Borgnine's Cy in *Law and Disorder*, and Cutter and Bone in *Cutter's Way*. He never leaves his characters in the lurch to be dismissed or judged; to do so would be facile, empty, and cheerless. Canadian Ted Kotcheff's Chekhovian mantra concerns being his characters' "best witness" rather than their judge. Passer goes further here to some degree. He is embedded among his characters, equipped with an acute understanding of their predicaments. In his time on the ground, he finds the humor in their tragedy, and the twisty, caustic contradictions in their oh-so-ostensible liberations and manumissions.

Theatrical Feature Films: *Intimate Lighting* (1965), *Born to Win* (1971), *Law and Disorder* (1974), *Ace Up My Sleeve* (1976, a.k.a. *Crime and Passion*), *Silver Bears* (1977), *Cutter's Way* (1981, a.k.a. *Cutter and Bone*), *Creator* (1985), *Haunted Summer* (1988), *Fourth Story* (1991), *Pretty Hattie's Baby* (1991, incomplete), *Stalin* (1992), *Nomad: The Warrior* (2006)

Other Notable Works: *A Boring Afternoon* (1964, short), *While Justice Sleeps* (1994), *Kidnapped* (1995), *The Wishing Tree* (1999), *Picnic* (2000)

14. The Regionalist
The Charles B. Pierce Vision

This piece ran in Filmmaker *magazine on April 17, 2017. I've revised and enhanced it for publication in this book. This piece will veer more into the biographical, as that is how the original published piece was constructed.*

Remembering her filmmaker father Charles B. Pierce, Dallas designer Amanda Squitiero first mentions the place he called home. "Arkansas claims him and he claimed Arkansas," she says, having recently marked the seventh anniversary of his passing.

Emerging regional filmmakers now see more opportunity than ever to achieve the most ambitious of visions on skid-row budgets. Now, one might strain to remember a time before the digital revolution, when pockets of independent filmmaking could exist outside of the New York and Hollywood ecosystems. In this regard, Pierce realized cinema as the art of the possible, which could exist and even thrive in a place like Arkansas. In that routinely undervalued zone between New York and L.A.—that vast expanse often pejoratively referred to as "flyover America"— Pierce directed thirteen feature films, the majority independently financed.

Today, Pierce is in part perhaps best known for writing the famous Dirty Harry line, "Go ahead, make my day" (based on his own father's catchphrase) for *Sudden Impact* (1983). As a writer-director, he is regarded by some as an anonymous purveyor of schlock and innocuous low-budget Westerns. It is easy to argue otherwise, however, when his output gains respect and admiration with each passing year, as more of his titles hit the video market. But cinephiles, historians, and film scholars are tragically quick to forget or write off Pierce as a trailblazer or icon of any stripe, despite his making independent film history with *The Legend of Boggy Creek* (1972), a $25 million-grossing golden goose, produced on a $160,000 budget. (Adjusted for 2017 inflation, it grossed $145 million.)

Pierce proved definitively that independent films could rake in dough. This ad for *The Legend of Boggy Creek* boasts of its box-office returns. Years later, it is acknowledged as a financial red-letter day in the history of indie film.

Educated cultists of the era branded him the George Romero of the South, but that's disingenuous in many ways. Pierce's most personal films reference canonical American motion picture classics with an unusual level of reverence and a sometimes surprising level of visual sophistication (evidenced especially in his early Westerns). *Winterhawk* (1975) and *Grayeagle* (1977), his two meditations on *The Searchers* (1956), both fit within the contours of the panoramic John Ford Westerns that open the American frontier epic to themes of tradition, family, chivalry, spirituality, and rugged individualism.

Pierce's flair for CinemaScope landscapes recalls Ford's but also Anthony Mann's in terms of sheer scale and depth. Background history is often literally framed through a foregrounded intimacy. While Ford's sensibility is informed by his Irish-Catholic upbringing, Pierce's equally humane sensibility flows mightily from his Arkansas Baptist heritage. "Amazing Grace" appears in many of Pierce's pictures as a key directorial trademark. "'Amazing Grace' is how dad let everyone know it was him behind the wheel," says his daughter Squitiero.

In the prime of his career, Pierce directed many alumni of the classic Ford pictures he cherished, including Slim Pickens, Jack Elam, Ben Johnson, Paul Fix, Jeanette Nolan, Woody Strode, Denver Pyle, "Iron Eyes" Cody, Leif Erickson, and Elisha Cook Jr. In *The Searchers*, Lana Wood played the ten-year-old incarnation of Natalie Wood's character; in *Grayeagle*, she essentially plays the Natalie Wood surrogate. Beyond these casting coups, there was a pertinent souvenir that Pierce most prized: a personal letter from John Wayne, applauding him for his efforts in keeping the dying (or at least transforming) Western genre alive. Pierce also prized the grandeur of the big screen; as Squitiero recalls, "You couldn't have given him a big enough canvas, or a wide enough one." Indeed, this is a rare proclivity for an independent of his era, and perhaps any era.

Early regional cinema is exemplified by pictures like Joseph L. Anderson's *Spring Night, Summer Night* (1967, southeast Ohio), Tobe Hooper's *Eggshells* (1969, Austin, Texas), Wendell Franklin's *The Bus is Coming* (1971, Cleveland, Ohio), Eagle Pennell's *The Whole Shootin' Match* (1978, Austin, Texas), Rob Nilsson and John Hanson's *Northern Lights* (1978, North Dakota), Victor Nuñez's *Gal Young 'Un* (1979, Central Florida), Penny Allen's *Paydirt* (1981, southern Oregon), and Horace B. Jenkins' *Cane River* (1982, Natchitoches Parish, Louisiana). In the able hands of these makers, some of whom were neophytes, it's easy to deem regional filmmaking a heroic act, without fear of hyperbole.

Today, regional cinema at its boldest is exemplified by directors like Paul Harrill (Knoxville, Tennessee). Harrill won the 2001 Sundance Film Festival Short Filmmaking Award for *Gina, An Actress, Age 29*. He recently directed his first feature-length drama, *Something Anything*, also shot in and around Tennessee. Says Harrill, "For me, the fundamental premise of regional filmmaking is this: Where a story happens matters. There is an integrity to shooting a film regionally, and it goes beyond landscape." He nevertheless concedes, "It can be challenging making regional films, even today. I'm in awe of filmmakers like Eagle Pennell, Penny Allen, Charles B. Pierce, and Jon Jost, who managed to produce important regional films well before the digital age."

Filmmaker Mark Thimijan recalls his tenure as Lincoln, Nebraska's filmmaker-in-residence: "I started out there in the Nineties around the time Alexander Payne shot *Citizen Ruth* (1996) in Lincoln and Omaha. I ventured to L.A., lived there for a couple years, came back to Lincoln, and found that I was this island. In my time, I was probably the only person in Lincoln with an itch to make films. There was just no one else doing what I wanted to do." Thimijan then set about shooting his first short film on 35mm. Where was the closest place to rent a 35mm motion picture camera? Minneapolis, Minnesota… over 400 miles away. Thimijan arranged to meet the rental house representative halfway, in Des Moines, Iowa. "It was kind of like an illicit drug deal, except that it was this beautiful machine, but I have to say that laying my hands on it still got me high. Locals thought I was crazy wanting to shoot 35mm on a such a project, but I was determined. Part of it was that I was still skeptical about digital technology at the time."

Thimijan sought the help of able hands (some of whom previously crewed on Alexander Payne's *About Schmidt*), cobbled together all the local talent he could find, and then delivered the exposed stock to Los Angeles for processing. *The Girl Who Could Run 600 Miles Per Hour* toured festivals in 2006 and 2007. Since then, Thimijan has shot two feature-length films digitally: *Barstool Cowboy* (2008) and *She Lives Her Life* (2016). The latter is a loose, Cornhusker State remake of the Godard classic *Vivre sa vie* (1962).

Many of the stories behind Charles B. Pierce's debut picture are not so dissimilar. It is here important to dispel the myth that Pierce enjoyed a tenure as a Hollywood set-dresser. Many bios, remembrances, and obituaries erroneously attest to this credential.

Charles B. Pierce as Mayor Chuckles,
hosting the local children's show *The Laffalot Club.*

"That was another Charles Pierce entirely," Squitiero clarifies. After a stint as a TV weatherman in Shreveport, Louisiana, Pierce gained notoriety as Mayor Chuckles, the star of the popular local children's television show "The Laffalot Club." With his knack for fine art, Pierce enhanced the Mayor Chuckles schtick by sprucing up and completing the drawings and paintings that the show's young guests would scribble while on air. (When Pierce became a film director, the handsome posters he commissioned from illustrator Ralph McQuarrie were central to his films' identity on the marketplace.)

His return to Arkansas came in 1971, inspired by a wave of chilling stories he heard firsthand about a sasquatch-like monster haunting the swamps and forests near the town of Fouke. In collecting eyewitness testimonies, he set out to craft a faux-documentary portrait of the fear and trembling that enveloped parts of that community. Pierce secured $160,000 in financing from Arkansas trucking company magnate L. W. "Buddy" Ledwell, for whom Pierce had done a visually striking, hit commercial that played throughout the Southwest. Between October 1971 and April 1972, with nine Texarkana high school kids moonlighting as

A sighting of the Fouke Monster in *The Legend of Boggy Creek*.

his crew, Pierce shot *The Legend of Boggy Creek* on a borrowed Techniscope-capable camera, acting as his own cinematographer.

Upon picture wrap, he drove the exposed film cans to a lab in Burbank, California, for processing. In editing, interviews were paced with staged dramatic sequences, and underscored by a number of original, homestyle folk tunes provided by composer Jaime Mendoza Nava, who would become one of Pierce's key collaborators.

The film made $55,000 in its first three weeks at the Perot Theatre in Texarkana. When *The Legend of Boggy Creek* expanded to other parts of the country, it eventually raked in its then-whopping $25 million in receipts, becoming the tenth highest grossing film of 1972. Its surprise success spawned a copycat cycle of "creature features" which dominated grindhouses and drive-ins throughout the Seventies. Its "mockumentary" style later influenced Daniel Myrick and Eduardo Sanchez in the creation of their indie blockbuster *The Blair Witch Project* (1999). Says Myrick, "We wanted to tap into the primal fear generated by the fact-or-fiction format like *The Legend of Boggy Creek*. It's certainly the one film that most inspired me."

Of *Boggy Creek*'s then-innovative approach to subverting the documentary form, Squitiero remembers, "He really did believe that the Fouke Monster existed, so he thought that the documentary form best suited it. I think he also knew it would be scarier if people had to consider the possible truth of everything." To elaborate on the motives behind Pierce's structural design, the on-camera interviews unfold much like folk stories, giving the film the rich, resonating impact of oral history. *Boggy Creek* is a cross-genre essay on collective memory and shared experience, specifically how they can unite and forever bind communities.

This gives the interspersed horror sequences an unexpected weight that Mendoza-Nava's suitably quaint (as in rudimentary as hell, but catchy) folk tunes help to accent. The notion of oral history and heritage would furnish Pierce with a sense of thematics that pervade his work.

Newly flush from the lucrative yield of his debut triumph, Pierce embarked on a much more personal, non-genre film with *Bootleggers* (1974), the story of two feuding families living in the Ozarks of the Twenties. Shot by then fledgling cinematographer Tak Fujimoto (*The Silence of the Lambs, Ferris Bueller's Day Off, The Sixth Sense*) in 2.35:1 widescreen, *Bootleggers* proved a financial disappointment to the ever hopeful, lovably quixotic Pierce, who, according to Squitiero, considered it one of the best pictures of his career.

"It's amazing to me that he just always made things happen," says Squitiero. "He was so skilled at scraping together a way to do things. He had a way to do anything. But he would laugh at himself because he couldn't go out and do a gangster film or a standard love story. He always felt he would fall on his face, because he would only deal with subjects that touched him—specifically, films where he felt he had something to say. He loved Westerns more than anything, and he loved horror films. Everything he did was personal. He still wanted to make films that he felt people would pay to see."

As to his process, she recalls, "If the budget required, he'd be the sound recordist, the gaffer, the grip, and an actor. He wanted as much artistic control as he could have, which is why he needed to be an independent. He also loved giving new people chances. Some of those same folks who are still in the industry got their start under my dad."

Pierce lit some fires under others, stirring them into action. His close childhood friend Harry Thomason and *Boggy Creek* co-screenwriter Earl E. Smith would go into Arkansas-based motion picture production for themselves. Smith directed the horror-Western hybrid *Wishbone Cutter* (1976, a.k.a. *The Shadow of Chikara*), starring Joe Don Baker and Sondra Locke. Thomason helmed five Arkansas films, including *Encounter With the Unknown* (1973), *The Great Lester Boggs* (1974), and *So Sad About Gloria* (1975), before taking up a career directing television ("Designing Woman," "Evening Shade"). Thomason also shot a short behind-the-scenes documentary on the set of *Winterhawk*.

The first in Pierce's series of Westerns, *Winterhawk* (1975), had its roots in a vision conjured by magic-hour light as it hit a distant figure in a lonely landscape. "He had a very strong feeling about *Winterhawk*," says Squitiero. "He used to drive a lot from Texarkana to L.A. and would race across the desert. One time, he stopped and saw an Indian standing beside a jeep looking off into the sunset. The way he described it, a hundred years disappeared, and the image became an Indian standing beside his horse. On the rest of the drive, he dreamed up a story of a proud, forgotten American Indian." He followed *Winterhawk* with a cycle of Native American-themed Westerns, including *Grayeagle* (1977), *Sacred Ground* (1983), and *Hawken's Breed* (1987). Though I'm not a John Ford acolyte myself, there is something endearingly guileless and innocent about Pierce's worshipfulness toward Ford. His ardor is contagious in its way, and almost inspires me to feel more warmth for the man myself. Almost. Pierce's touch is decidedly more benign, if obviously not as replete with the semiotic thrills proffered to the scholarly class by Ford's films. This does not reduce Pierce's mimicry to anything less passionate or personal. Generously, one can say that he speaks through Ford, using him as an outline, a jumping-off point to formulate and tailor his own voice. And he is touchingly sincere in doing so.

Another frontier epic, *The Winds of Autumn* (1976), follows a 12-year-old Quaker boy's lone search for vengeance and features Native Americans only peripherally. A picture to which Pierce felt close, it features more than a few passing nods to his favorite film of all, George Stevens' *Shane* (1953).

In 1976, Pierce rose to prominence again when he delivered another based-on-fact drive-in horror hit. *The Town That Dreaded Sundown* recounted Texarkana's most infamous cold case, that of the Phantom Killer, a brutal, hooded menace who terrorized the town just after World War II. Pierce's film prefigured the dawn of the slasher movie craze spurred by John Carpenter's *Halloween* (1978), as well as the onslaught of thrillers about serial killers. Though financially successful, the film opened up old wounds afresh in Texarkana. "During filming, he started getting death threats," says Squitiero. "It became such a problem that we moved to Texas for a long time as a result. My mother moved us into a fortress because she was worried about our safety. Things cooled down in Texarkana, enough so that the Little Rock Film Festival started giving their Charles B. Pierce Award for best film made in Arkansas."

Winterhawk (above) and *Grayeagle* (below) comprise a John Ford homage double feature, featuring many classic Ford players in the cast. These are sincere works made with love for Pierce's favorite director.

Due in part to the modest commercial success of *The Town That Dreaded Sundown* (which was remade in 2014), Samuel Z. Arkoff offered Pierce a three-picture deal at American International Pictures (AIP). Under this contact, he made *The Norseman* (1978), and *The Evictors* (1979). The former, a critically savaged box-office flop, starred Lee Majors as a Viking warrior, while the latter starred Vic Morrow and Jessica Harper (just after her starring turn in Dario Argento's masterwork *Suspiria*). *The Evictors*, shot in Louisiana and also based on alleged fact, completes a "trilogy of terror" that commenced with *The Legend of Boggy Creek*.

To Pierce's dying day, his AIP days stirred bitter memories. Squitiero recalls her father's rancor: "I remember him getting so frustrated that he would carry on and say, 'No one will ever tell me what I'm doing on my motion picture. It's my motion picture!' It was always a 'motion picture' with him, rarely a 'film' and certainly never a 'movie.' He hated the word 'movie.'"

The Town That Dreaded Sundown.

In the Eighties, Pierce suffered his career's biggest embarrassment, a failed sequel to *The Legend of Boggy Creek* that was later parodied on *Mystery Science Theater 3000*. Although he was hesitant, producers had been hungry for a sequel for well over a decade. He went on record with *Tulsa World* saying, "I really didn't want to do *Boggy Creek II*. I think it's probably my worst picture. This time, I spent almost as much time on the creature suit as I did on the film itself." The director also appears as lead actor in *Boggy Creek II: And the Legend Continues* (1984); in some of his previous films, he had popped up in colorful walk-on roles or supporting parts.

On *Hawken's Breed* (1987), which starred Peter Fonda, he was denied final cut. "*Hawken's Breed* was the product of a very unhappy joint financial venture," says Squitiero. "I think that experience frustrated him more than the problems he had on the AIP pictures. Really, he was happiest when he was completely independent. He became a bit of a recluse after *Hawken's Breed*. He wanted to slow down, so he spent his time fishing, painting, drawing, taking still photographs."

In the late Nineties, he returned briefly to his cinematic vocation with two video features, the wholesome family drama *Renfroe's Christmas* (1997) and the mountain-man saga *Chasing the Wind* (1998). Neither film saw wide release; *Chasing the Wind* has completely fallen out of circulation.

His final years, leading up to his 2010 death, were ones spent thinking and talking about the next film projects. One journalist, who enjoyed a telephone relationship with him towards the end, recalls: "He was a very sincere person, and always got to the meat of what he wanted to tell you, no BS. Despite what fate had handed him, he was not bitter... at least beyond what anyone who has ever

This sequence from *The Winds of Autumn*
is at the very heart of Charles B. Pierce as homespun artist.

worked in Hollywood is, by default. He had purchased an early HD video camera and was shooting beautiful nature footage for a project that never got completed. And he was considering doing a remake of *The Legend of Boggy Creek*."

Squitiero paints a portrait of her father: "He was colorful, perhaps the best raconteur who ever lived. No one could recount a story like he could. He'd paint a really clear, vivid picture in your mind. And the stories of the making of his films are often just as wild and action-packed as the films themselves. He had all the wonderment of a child." A particular tale of an out-of-control buffalo on the set of *Winterhawk* is a favorite of hers.

If a single sequence in one of Charles B. Pierce's films were to function as an X-ray of his artistic soul, the deeply touching runaway horse sequence in *The Winds of Autumn* best defines his unmistakable humanity. Twelve-year-old Quaker boy Joel (played by Pierce's own son, Chuck Pierce, Jr.) treks alone through the wilderness. As he begins to ascend a mountain on horseback, a snowfall begins to dust the landscape. When Joel briefly dismounts the horse, the animal gets spooked and runs off and leaves the boy freezing, hungry, and ever more desperate. He walks for miles through the cold, as the thickening frost and bitter winds beat against him. Suddenly, just ahead of him, an Indian wrapped in furs appears astride his own horse, clearly awaiting his arrival. Joel's runaway horse stands beside him. The boy is dumbstruck and relieved as the Indian leaves two rabbit carcasses on the horse's saddle and rides off. The boy leans into the animal's mane for a quick prayer of thanksgiving before wearily mounting him again to continue his trek. Here, Pierce's aptitude here for purely visual storytelling, realized shot-by-shot with the pacing of his edits, augments what would have naturally been an effective and affecting sequence merely as written on the page. The filmmaker's heart-on-sleeve quality, far from undercutting the material or muddying the waters with cheap sentimentality, becomes its chief expressive strength. There is no illusion at work—this is a window into Pierce's very soul, with intimations of a coherent worldview.

Despite his having been a longtime DGA member, Pierce's passing was not honored at the Oscar ceremony's annual "In Memoriam" tribute (in the same year Farrah Fawcett was likewise ignored). In Arkansas, June 16 was declared "Charles B. Pierce Day" by the two Texarkana mayors, Bob Brueggeman (of the Texas section) and Wayne Smith (of the Arkansas section). Today, director Jeff Nichols (*Take Shelter*, *Mud*, *Loving*) has picked up the mantle of Charles B. Pierce in regularly returning to make feature films in his native Arkansas.

So, how can an independent filmmaker of today follow the example of Charles B. Pierce, who often released more than one feature per year, in a region that lacked the infrastructure for such endeavors? The good news is that, today, with access to digital tools, making regional films of value is much easier to realize. In the mad dash to the East and West Coasts, it is perhaps easy to forget those stories that emerge from the perceived flyover "void" where the "purple mountain majesties" and "amber waves of grain" dwell.

Regional filmmakers have greater capability to build bridges of empathy, and to achieve the art of the possible, as Charles B. Pierce knew it. In the film world, people often most admire those who make "it" happen, whatever "it" happens to be. The purpose of this piece is not simply to draw deserved attention to a departed artist's neglected body of work, but also to claim his life as a testament to ingenuity and passion for the craft.

Theatrical Feature Films: *The Legend of Boggy Creek* (1972), *Bootleggers* (1974), *Winterhawk* (1975), *The Winds of Autumn* (1976), *The Town That Dreaded Sundown* (1976), *Grayeagle* (1977), *The Norseman* (1978), *The Evictors* (1979), *Sacred Ground* (1983), *Boggy Creek II: And the Legend Continues* (1985), *Hawken's Breed* (1988), *Renfroe's Christmas* (1997), *Chasing the Wind* (1999)

15. Uniquely American Maladies
The Larry Peerce Vision

This is the first publication of this essay, written especially for this volume.

Pierre Rissient and Fritz Lang were walking the Croisette after the 1964 Cannes premiere of Larry Peerce's debut *One Potato, Two Potato*, the year that Barbara Barrie won the festival's Best Actress award for her performance in its leading role. Rissient, who detested the film and deemed it hack work, confronted Lang, who professed to love it. "If I directed that film with that same material, I would have made the same film. You wouldn't have hated it then!" Rissient indignantly begged to differ, thinking his friend (and one of his most idolized film artists) obtuse or even senile for stooping to measure himself, and his genius, against the upstart Peerce.

Peerce did successfully launch his career with *One Potato, Two Potato*, but the contentious Rissient-Lang dispute presaged a filmography that, on the off chance it is ever seriously considered, stirs often ornery debate among those who find him either an intriguing anomaly with flashes of brilliance, or the consummate hack, at best a flash-in-the-pan nonentity-turned-competent journeyman. My own sense has always been that a director who gave us work like *The Incident* (1967), *Goodbye Columbus* (1969), the misunderstood *The Sporting Club* (1971), and something as backward (and even outright bananas) as his John Belushi biopic *Wired* (1989), should not be overlooked or wholly counted out. It takes a strange gift indeed to deliver a film as fascinatingly misguided and as "wired" as *Wired*, which plays like a Larry Buchanan biostravaganza with a budgetary steroidal injection. But that's much later… in fact, it was his final theatrical outing.

Let's lay the groundwork and consider the big picture.

It strikes me that Peerce tackles sicknesses and disconnects in American complexes and institutions. He builds, or contrives, microcosms through which one can better understand and parse the American ethos. At his best, he's an American director making

The ensemble cast of *The Incident.*

American films on American themes. Those thematics seem to revolve around the idea of destabilization, of a ritual, naturally inherited, or timeworn order. How his characters respond to that destabilization, and how the destabilizers recalibrate in response to that response, is consistently the source of the drama, at least across his formative first half-dozen pictures.

One Potato, Two Potato and *The Incident* are both in their respective ways incisive, hard-hitting essays on racism as a specifically American malady, with localized brands of it threatening a fabric that Peerce takes pains to establish in scrupulously constructed and often extended first acts, while *The Incident*, when paired with *Two-Minute Warning* (1976), offers a fragile mosaic (or, more accurately, a "mosaicized") America perched in the literal crosshairs. (Peter Bogdanovich's masterpiece *Targets* from 1968 would make a perfect third for a themed screening.) In both Peerce pictures, a cross-section of society is targeted and terrorized by a violent and/or homicidal entity. One was considered closer to "high art" while the other was derided as all-star junk. But they offer up the American melting pot as incubator for cruel, thoughtless, randomized violence, with a colorful collection of star-spangled sitting ducks. It's the "we're all hanging by a very precarious thread" idea.

Though *Goodbye, Columbus*, *The Sporting Club*, and *A Separate Peace* are variably faithful to their source texts (with some critics finding *A Separate Peace* too reverential, thus emotionally distant), they provide fertile ground for Peerce to probe the social codes—the "secret clubhouse handshakes," one might say—of the riche, both nouveau and classique—or rather, "new money" and "old money." *Goodbye, Columbus* and *The Sporting Club*—adapted from novels by Philip Roth and Thomas McGuane, respectively—are especially trenchant social satires ruminating on class, privilege, and upward mobility, respectively within Jewish and WASP circles. In *The Sporting Club*, characters almost literally throw cherry bombs into the pre-established order of the eponymous club, of the grand shadow hierarchy, of the ruling class, not to mention everything else in sight that might qualify wittingly or unwittingly as a symbol or a target. Like the earlier quip in my intro chapter, if there are sacred cows in sight, these characters love all-you-can-eat steak.

Departed British film critic Tom Milne observes about *Goodbye, Columbus*: "Self-effacingly directed by Peerce, the film stakes everything on minute observation of detail: the ghastly gusto of mealtimes in the parvenu dining room; the loose-limbed insolence in every movement made by the scion of the family; the worship of appearance rather than accomplishments in everything that is said and done. [...] The film is funnier than *The Graduate* (made a couple years earlier) and much less pretentious."

Goodbye, Columbus' subtext involves the indulgence and gluttony of the privileged and monied, on often vulgar display. Richard Benjamin's character, Neil, is a Nick Carroway-esque interloper, a have-not who "touches the garment" of the affluent Patimkin clan, only to retract and retreat in near repulsion when he finally breaches the brittle dynamic between Ali MacGraw's Brenda and her family's plenitude, thanks to an errant diaphragm.

Goodbye, Columbus.

All the elements described by Milne explode upon themselves in *The Sporting Club*, an abrasive and knowingly off-putting venture into confrontational misanthropy that unsurprisingly (and even understandably) resulted in commercial failure. As with Silvio Narizzano and his *The Sky is Falling*, Peerce's historical misfortune is that his most important picture from an auteurist standpoint is a coarse and divisive outrage-machine that never got out from under some strangely puritanical condemnations among a class that was, most curiously on this occasion, too easily offended.

As in the rest of his early pictures, Peerce holds an almost cartoonishly over-warped funhouse mirror up to deceptively over-polite societies, revealing grotesqueries in exclusive, hermetically sealed inner sanctums. The roundly massacred *The Sporting Club*, a passion project for which he stubbornly rejected plum job offers (as borne out by multiple text accounts and oral histories), gave rise to the notion that whatever moment(s) Peerce had enjoyed in the sun had decidedly passed, that whatever critical measures of grace—or any benefit of the doubt he was afforded—were left squandered. And he never really recovered what he'd lost in the film's almost ritual slaughter at the hands of fuming critics.

Let it be noted that veteran critic Stephen Farber stood against the current in publishing an impassioned *New York Times* rebuttal to its uniformly wretched notices, including from the paper that was publishing him. In a piece titled "Did They Give 'Sporting Club' a Sporting Chance?" he writes, "*The Sporting Club* doesn't aim to please. It's an assault on the audience, gleefully piling insult upon insult, outrage upon outrage—and some unsuspecting patrons might want to strike back. Ordinary bad movies stupefy an audience, but there's nothing ordinary about *The Sporting Club*. Even the people who hate it will have trouble shaking it off. Is it awful or is it great? Probably a little of both. It's a true original, an unstable mix of burlesque, satirical allegory, Gothic melodrama, high tragedy, with a little hint of musical comedy thrown in for good measure. With America settling into new apathy, Peerce's belligerence is more desperately needed. His film is rough and brutal, but it clears the air and opens up new possibilities for American movies."

By the time Peerce's controversial melodrama *Ash Wednesday* (1973) rolled into theaters, it cemented the worst impressions and pronouncements about his trajectory since early success, the critics sealing his fate with poison pens that were, this time, blotted with cyanide. *Ash Wednesday* follows a woman of considerable means,

The class consciousness of *The Incident* and *Goodbye, Columbus*
explodes upon itself in *The Sporting Club*.

played by Elizabeth Taylor (firmly in her bizarro period), who
receives extravagant—and graphically presented—plastic surgeries
in order to win back her philandering attorney husband (Henry
Fonda, in a glorified cameo). It was dismissed as a shallow, turgid
soap opera that showcased needlessly blood-and-guts facelift
sequences. Again, as with *Columbus* and *Sporting*, there is the
indulgence and gluttony of the privileged on full display, roasted in
sometimes unsparingly mean-spirited ways, all concealed beneath
a layer of gloss.

Elizabeth Taylor in *Ash Wednesday.*

Critic and historian Peter Hanson writes that *Ash Wednesday* features Taylor's most vain performance, because "after all, the real love story here isn't between Barbara (Taylor) and Mark (Fonda), but rather between Taylor and her own beauty." What many miss, however, is that the film's take on glamour is cynical, especially when seen in the broader context of the director's purview. Gay audiences who have stumbled onto the film have celebrated it, though because of its obscurity and scarcity, it's not the queer cult item that other Taylor pictures have since become. Its "lady survivor" spirit, and certain other encodings, appealed to a gay male contingent who might have caught the film during its pitifully short-lived run.

Though shot and set at an Italian winter resort, *Ash Wednesday* is still laced with Peerce's jaded Americanism, which can be traced back to an earlier film. In the short speech that Jack Klugman's character, Ben Patimkin, gives in *Goodbye, Columbus*, he explains that, "In the real world, you need a little *gonnif* [Yiddish for "thief" or "cheat"] in you." This is complemented later during the wedding scene, when Klugman's brother inveighs against his own unimpressive economic reality. "I've got more brains in my pinky than Ben has in his whole body," he tells Richard Benjamin's Neil. "Why is he at the top and me at the bottom?" A half-horrified Neil, who has made it his business to infiltrate the Patimkin family's trappings of privilege throughout a lusty summer, is left with the horrible gravity of a new realization—about how a uniquely American rat race impacts the family dynamic. As someone of lower-class status, this bleary encounter clearly weighs on him. The story of how a much longer version of this scene was controversially excised from Peerce's final cut is accounted in Ralph Rosenblum's book *When the Shooting Stops* (but Peerce does leave us with the essential point, for sharper impact).

Klugman's character, by his own admission, has gotten ahead in America—and hereby upstaged his "smarter" sibling—by a little all-American cheating. In *Ash Wednesday*, Liz Taylor is herself on a quest to cheat Father Time. Beyond any motivation to keep a husband, in an America obsessed with aesthetics, presentation, and feminine beauty untainted by age, she must likewise arouse an inner gonnif to "keep up appearances." It is fairly obvious how this conceit plays into *The Sporting Club* as well, with its generational spread of upright, respectable, WASP-y gonnifs. The haves and have-nots on the subway car in *The Incident* paint a picture as well. So many Peerce characters, foreground and background, are born cheaters—gonnifs in wonderlands.

Betwixt *The Sporting Club* and *Ash Wednesday* came Peerce's adaptation of John Knowles' novel *A Separate Peace* (1972), a text still read in many American high school English classes. The disruption of a world inhabited once again by the Anglo-Saxon WASP, the patrician class, in this case by the onset of World War II, is the conflict that centers Peerce's thematic signature here. *A Separate Peace*, however, is a far more basic affair than the films that came before it. It appears too much as if Peerce is playing it too safe and (ironically) vying for a bit of stability after the overwhelming failure of *The Sporting Club*. It didn't pay off, and the film flopped.

"When I came back from shooting *Ash Wednesday* in Europe, my career was over," Peerce told a journalist in 1978. In a later interview, he was honest in his appraisal: "*Ash Wednesday* is not a film I'm very proud of. It was a nine- or tenth-month experience that's a novel in itself, so... I won't go into that." After a costly run of three flops that all but promised Peerce a far less fortuitous remainder of the decade, he turned to schmaltz (though financially successful schmaltz) with his *Other Side of the Mountain* diptych (1975, 1978), a weepie saga of *Love Story*-inspired pap, based on the true story of skier Jill Kinmont. I will here note the irony, considering that Peerce opted to do *The Sporting Club* in lieu of *Love Story*, with the latter job going to Arthur Hiller. Though the first of the two *Mountain* films brought him back into the studios' good graces, it was an overall departure from an authorship that Peerce had quietly minted. He knew the story didn't really bear his stamp; he repeatedly declined producer Edward S. Feldman's offer to direct it, before being chewed out by his agent and accepting. Peerce is surely workmanlike in the watchable *The Other Side of the Mountain*, but gone are the edge and grit and hard-hitting swagger of his earlier outings. It was the ultimate lesson to its director that "soft" sells.

Around the time of the release of *The Other Side of the Mountain Part 2*, Peerce was interviewed in the *Los Angeles Times*, admitting that his career was on "shaky" ground and stating categorically that sentimental soapers and tearjerkers (what the author called "four-hankie pictures") were not *really* in his wheelhouse. "It's not me, and it will in no way occur in *Bell Jar*," he admonished, making a promise about his follow-up picture that he arguably failed to keep. The opening paragraph states that as he was about to depart on the film's promotional tour, he "seemed just as anxious to depart his professional past and get a fresh start."

But there is one way in which the *Mountain* saga does open Peerce's filmography to further discovery. Seen in the context of *Ash Wednesday* and the later works *The Bell Jar* (1979) and *Love Child* (1982), *The Other Side of the Mountain* works for Peerce within a classic earlier idiom, that of the Warner Bros. "women's picture" of the Forties, in which Bette Davis and Joan Crawford headlined melodramas that involve women's struggles with love, loss and sacrifice, and one can imagine Davis and Crawford assuming the roles in these Peerce pictures had they been made in that earlier era. Instead, we have Marilyn Hassett, an actress Peerce had discovered and then married, who carried *The Other Side of the Mountain* but fumbled the much more ambitious (and ill-advised) *The Bell Jar*, based on the Sylvia Plath novel that would have been unadaptable even in the hands of an unrivaled genius.

Peerce's consummately flawed, chutzpah-dik adaptation offered spear-sharpening critics more red meat. They took aim at a film version they felt was far too literal, one which was too blunted and "dulled-up" for the demands of the prized prose. Plath's book meant a great deal to a great many, so critics and audiences were always going to put the film up against every daunting yardstick.

Peerce's adaptation of Sylvia Plath's *The Bell Jar*.

Amy Madigan in *Love Child*.

It proved the adage: If you're adapting a major landmark novel, a treasured classic, you better bring the goods. Pervasive throughout the film, however, is a rather "square" take on feminism that was more redolent of those Davis and Crawford vehicles than Plath's novel.

The comedy spree *Why Would I Lie?* (1980) and the rock musical *Hard to Hold* (1984) proved more anonymous as Peerce outings. Farce was never the director's forte, and his background in directing musical documentaries such as *The Big T.N.T. Show* failed to enhance or give spark to *Hard to Hold*, a dreary Rick Springfield vehicle, which comes off like a rock 'n' roll version of Franklin Schaffner's dire Pavarotti romcom *Yes, Giorgio* (1982). *Hard to Hold* and *Why Would I Lie?* feel alien to Peerce. *Love Child* (1982) and *Wired* (1989) are his last two films of any true distinction.

In both *One Potato, Two Potato* and *Love Child* is a central defining premise: the birth of a child as the destabilizing event. Peerce is one of the few directors who consistently casts character life cycle events as a source of societal instability, and, as in *Two-Minute Warning*, the first 50-60 minutes of *Love Child* consist completely of set-up, with little in the way of aggressive plot development. Though the ending is facile telefilm triumphalism that lacks the poetry it could (and should) have had—and who's to say if the studio didn't impose its perfunctory exalt-the-underdog denouement?—there is still reason to grant Peerce a wink and a nod for his efforts, considering the cares he has taken to plant us into the film's environment in the most tactile way. As a point of comparison, *Two-Minute Warning* painstakingly works its way up to the sniper even being noticed, let alone addressed. It's all part of a careful design, not a mistake or an accident. Whereas the victims in Bogdanovich's *Targets* are anonymous (with its onscreen deaths no less horrific as a result), *Two-Minute Warning* devotes its first hour of its runtime to character sketches of the sitting-duck victims-in-waiting. One wonders what Guy Debord would have made of the spectators-as-prey narrative proposition in both, considering that Bogdanovich's film climaxes at a bloody drive-in screening of a crummy horror film, and Peerce's at a big, ratings-bonanza football game.

His final theatrical feature *Wired* is a case study in hubris, grave robbery foisted upon the public as entertainment, but that's not to say it's not fascinating, especially as an inquiry into Peerce's punctured purview. Good rule of thumb: Never inter a D.O.A. cinematic cadaver without a rolling autopsy! These autopsies should continue indefinitely when traces of misplaced personality are present. Its staggering misguidedness and its religious-fervor taste for irreverence is somehow intriguing, however. *Wired*'s anarchist energy may save it from being pat in the way that many earnest biopics inevitably are, but as critic Nathan Rabin eloquently put it, "As it staggers blearily from low to low, Peerce's abomination blurs fantasy and reality in ways that diminish both. Had the filmmakers succeeded, they would have reinvented the biopic by injecting it with a vast ocean of gallows humor, magic realism, and postmodern mindfuckery. The filmmakers took enormous chances, none of which paid off."

The film is, with total certainty, a ridiculously offensive, ass-over-teakettle turkey, so much so that one is left only to instantaneously agree that it's an insult to John Belushi's life, career, and legacy. Yes, no qualifiers, it's *that* offensive. But, by some counts, it is far more interesting to watch than an average failure, and in many ways, more interesting than certain calculated (and especially overcalculated) successes. Is this the result of something Peerce is doing? There's at least one madly inspired scene, with Belushi playing the devil for his soul on a *Blues Brothers* pinball machine. Regarding destabilization, one might argue that, like Larry Buchanan's bizarro forays into the biopic genre, *Wired* destabilizes a very staid form: the biopic itself. It's here, in this film alone, that the destabilization trope may be applied only externally. The best term I've seen applied, a kind of neologism, is "bio-fantasy."

Peerce also distorts his image with the use of the split diopter lens in *Goodbye, Columbus*, in a finale scene of bitter arguing.

Peerce bristled at a controversy of biographical discrepancy earlier on, with *The Other Side of the Mountain*, albeit in a less egregious fashion. Peerce related to a journalist once that Jill Kinmont "got very upset" after objecting to a line about pills in the film. "If anything, [that part of the film] makes her more human." At that point, he acknowledged that tiptoeing around sensitive material left him frustrated. He objected to feeling hamstrung in dealing with the more "abrasive moments" in the *Mountain* films, thus covering a deceased subject on *Wired* undoubtedly felt freeing. Of course, though, he was stuck with the anger and indignation of Belushi's surviving friends and family. It's plain to see he pushed that freedom too far in his theatrical swan song, in service to his zealous anti-drug message.

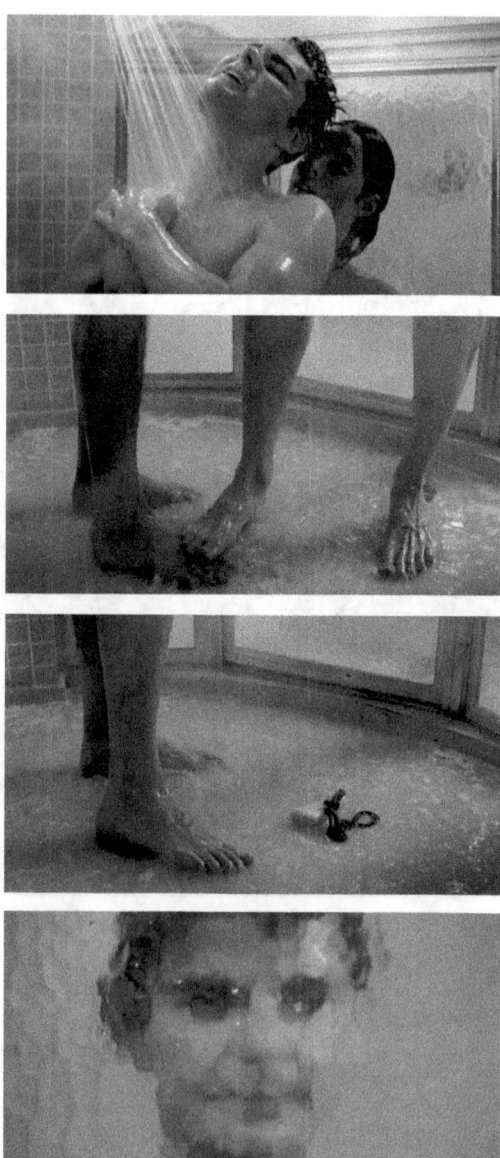

A conversation between legs and feet. Dropped soap and a face distorted through a frosted-glass shower door greet a disturbing revelation. Peerce's visual playfulness finds a gravitational pull in such a dramatic moment.

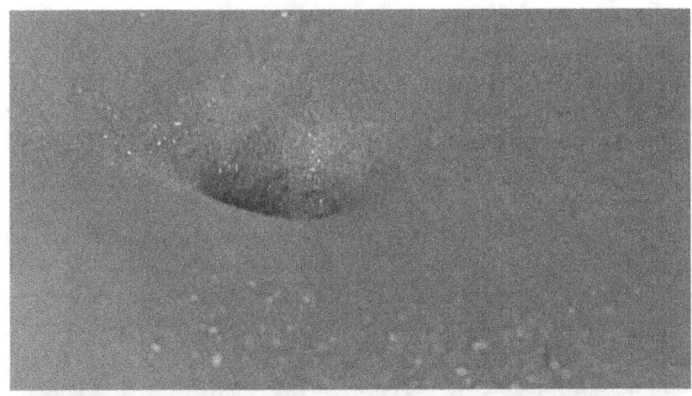

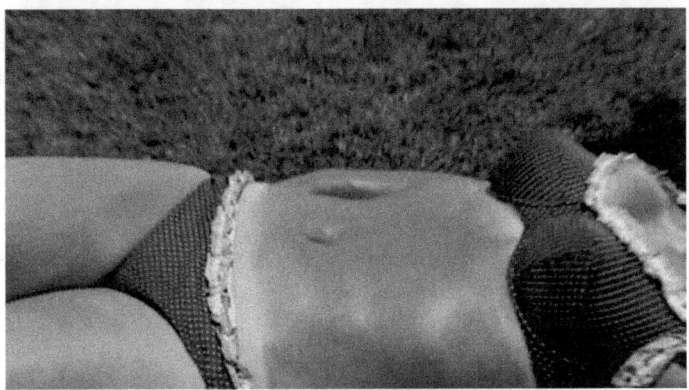

Peerce often opens his films on fragments and abstractions.
In *Goodbye, Columbus*, it's the undulating navel and belly of a bit player,
who takes us to a swimming pool where we meet our principals.

Visually, what is there to Larry Peerce? There are bold graphic matches, aggressive zooms, and radical rack focuses not quite on the order of Richard Rush tricksterism, but there is still more conspicuous sleight of hand than on average. Does it all cohere as definable style? Debatable. His camera language is more proactive than any "journeyman." Individual scenes deploy expressive use of lenses. One that especially leaps to mind is the final confrontation in *Goodbye, Columbus*, in which an unmet split diopter shot frames Richard Benjamin. He chastises the Ali MacGraw character with the bedroom set in the background utterly distorted by the split diopter. The composition keeps in sharp focus both him on the far right, and a dresser on the far left, while center frame is severely, and very conspicuously, blurred. The shot's payoff, when MacGraw finally enters Benjamin's frame, motivates its overall use, but the instability of the earlier piece of coverage sans MacGraw expressively lends to the scene a further unease, an "aggro" imbalance. In another sequence, dropped soap followed by a close-up of Benjamin through a frosted-glass shower door gives striking dramatic punctuation to a disturbing confession made to him by MacGraw.

But it is the zoom lens that is the most important tool in Peerce's arsenal. His are not tempered zoom shots. They are forceful, even zealous one might say. Yet they are not the lunging formal whip-zooms of the spaghettis or Italian policiers, which feel like bold pronouncements. Peerce zooms are largely accompanied with pans and other types of camera movement, self-narrating rather than motivated by character movement or choreography. Peerce often opens his films on pieces disconnected from a larger whole. For example, *Goodbye, Columbus* opens on total abstraction: the undulating tummy and navel of a nubile bikini-clad young lady (complete with a very Peerce-ian zoom-out). In *The Sporting Club*, there is dangling signage suspended from a crane and disconnected from its place atop an office building, followed by a woman's undulating upper body having mounted an unseen paramour, framed through the surrounding shelves. Hands, legs, eyes, shadows, and silhouettes open both *Ash Wednesday* and *Two-Minute Warning*. Marilyn Hassett's monologuing head is disembodied in darkness in *The Bell Jar*.

Peerce declined Charlton Heston's offer of the director's chair on *Gray Lady Down* (1976) because he felt he "couldn't say anything" with the material. "*Two-Minute Warning* was different. That had a point. That was something I felt I could shape." This is enough to prove that, at this juncture of his career at least, Peerce

Two Minute Warning.

was a man of some grand design and discriminating taste—one with the wherewithal to deploy that powerful, multipurpose syllable known as "no" (useful to any director of even sporadic discernment). If one is compelled to do a marathon of Larry Peerce's films, his phantom threads will slowly but surely begin to emerge. Directors, if they're of any interest at all, will weave these threads into the fabric of their work. If you watch Peerce's work for any sustained period, one film after another after another, his vision of America as unsteady ground erupts as a fusillade of fire between black and white, rich and poor, armed and unarmed, beautiful and withered, powerful and powerless.

Theatrical Feature Films: *One Potato, Two Potato* (1964), *The Big T.N.T. Show* (1965), *The Incident* (1967), *Goodbye, Columbus* (1969), *The Sporting Club* (1971), *A Separate Peace* (1972), *Ash Wednesday* (1973), *The Other Side of the Mountain* (1975), *Two-Minute Warning* (1976), *The Other Side of the Mountain Part 2* (1978), *The Bell Jar* (1979), *Why Would I Lie?* (1980), *Love Child* (1982), *Hard to Hold* (1984), *Wired* (1989)

Other Notable Works: *The Stranger Who Looks Like Me* (1974), *The Fifth Missile* (1986), *Elvis and Me* (1988), *The Neon Empire* (1989), *Holy Joe* (1999, a.k.a. *Man of Miracles*)

16. The Moviefilm Ethic
The John Badham Vision

This is the adapted, enhanced, and extended script for a video essay titled "Whose Films Are These Anyway?: John Badham from Filmmaker to Moviemaker," which was included on the 2025 Cinematographe Blu-ray release of Drop Zone. *I was originally given the assignment of covering Badham's entire career in at least the basic sense. I was surprised in writing it just how much came out, and how much I discovered upon closer inspection and deliberation.*

John Badham is one of a number of directors behind American cultural landmark motion pictures who are often left in memory's lurch. Glancing over Badham's filmography, a more discerning viewer — one who is keen on deep dives and probing questions — is left puzzled. How does one take a movie like *Saturday Night Fever* (1977), a hardened, streetwise, and often unforgiving realist drama (one that just so happens to feature some of the best dancing ever captured by American movie cameras), and connect that up with later Badham works, especially comedies like *Short Circuit* (1986) or *Stakeout* (1987). Or how do you thread the needle between his morally complex character piece *Whose Life Is It Anyway?* (1981) and high-octane thrillers like *Point of No Return* (1994) or *Nick of Time* (1995)?

Are there two John Badhams? The onscreen credits tell their own story. "John Badham films" quite literally became "John Badham movies" starting with *Stakeout*. Badham himself told me, "We're making motion pictures here, not curing cancer. But I couldn't look at something like *Stakeout* and say it was anywhere near as important as an Ingmar Bergman film, because that to me is a *film*. I know I'm an entertainer." Critic Judith Crist coined the term "movie movie" to affectionately define pictures made with consummate care and skill, which capitalize on entertainment above all. When it comes to Badham though, perhaps it was Eddie Murphy in Frank Oz's *Bowfinger* who put it best: "We're trying to make a movie here, not a film!"

Badham himself winks at us with the idea of movies vs. films. In his action farce *The Hard Way* (1991), our fake movie-within-a-movie, *Smoking Gun II*, about a roguish adventurer who "hates bad guys and loves bad girls" is a very knowing arch parody of the Hollywood genre movie franchise machine, and of the types of movie director outings to which Badham was becoming accustomed. He even manages to sneak in a number of cutting and hyperaware industry in-jokes throughout that fil... a-hem, movie. *Short Circuit*'s Johnny Five likewise loves his deep cut movie references, and the notion of the "Badham in-joke"—something approaching a trope or a trademark—developed over time, but we'll get to that later. *Saturday Night Fever* and especially *Whose Life Is It Anyway?* suggest a more "serious" filmmaker obscured beneath the popcorn-paloozas for which Badham became synonymous.

Critic Lisa Schwartzbaum, in her review of *Drop Zone* (1994), refers to Badham as a "subculture specialist," which is a pretty salient observation. When I brought this up with Badham, he could only say, "She's not wrong." *Saturday Night Fever*, based on a *New York* magazine article entitled "Tribal Rites of the New Saturday Night" by Nick Cohn, is a journey into the heart of Seventies disco subculture and the local club nightlife that was then in full bloom... or, more aptly, full swing. *WarGames* (1983) penetrated the cabal of computer hackers, a still nascent sphere of high-tech nerdery, brainiacs dialed-up and hyperconnected well before the world at large had the first clue about what such a thing even meant. *American Flyers* (1985) is set in the world of professional bicycle racing. With *Short Circuit*, we got to spend time with enterprising, well-meaning robotics engineers attempting to curb the military industrial complex. *Drop Zone*, as Schwartzbaum herself phrased it, is "set in the daredevil society of skydivers." Even the underground networks and specter of counterculture in *Bird on a Wire* (1990), what you might call a kind of Sixties hangover, carry the distinct aroma of subculture as well.

There's something else beyond this grand correlator, though I was personally struck by something Badham himself said when discussing *Whose Life Is It Anyway?* on an episode of Joe Dante's Trailers From Hell: "The point wasn't to make a disease-of-the-week television movie. The point was to explore the question, who controls your own life? Is it the state? Is it the hospital? Is it your own family? Or is it you?" This almost existentially libertarian stance can be applied to other Badham protagonists. In *Saturday*

Tony Manero's brother's parting advice in *Saturday Night Fever* is at the core of Badham thematics of independence and self-possession.

Night Fever, who controls Tony Manero's life and destiny? His parents? The ruffian neighborhood gang to which he belongs? The social class he was born into? Even his adoring fans at his local oasis, the 2001 Odyssey Club, will dare not limit or condescend him, not if he can help it. The parting advice that Tony's brother, the apostate, gives our dreamer hero is at the center of Badham's entire thematic purview: "Are you going to do something with your dancing, Tony? The only way you're going to survive is to do what you think is right, not what they keep trying to jam you into. You let them do that and you're going to end up nothing but miserable."

David Lightman (Matthew Broderick) in *WarGames* desires, and to a certain degree establishes, a life unencumbered by the parents and teachers who deign to suppress his independence. He writes his own rules, for himself and himself alone. But as he discovers, that has its pitfalls too. In *Whose Life Is It Anyway?*, all of this has been made literal. Can a completely paralyzed man, one whose entire being, consciousness, and imagination spoke to him through his hands and his fingers, as a sculptor and as a fine artist, argue for his right to die? Is he in control of his existence? In whose hands does his fate rest? Our director's pointed final shot speaks volumes. In *Short Circuit*, is Johnny Five truly autonomous? Is his so-called "life" his own, as a being whose sentience is in question? Who runs his alleged life? His programmers, marionette operators of a kind, lose access to the strings. Is Number 5 alive?

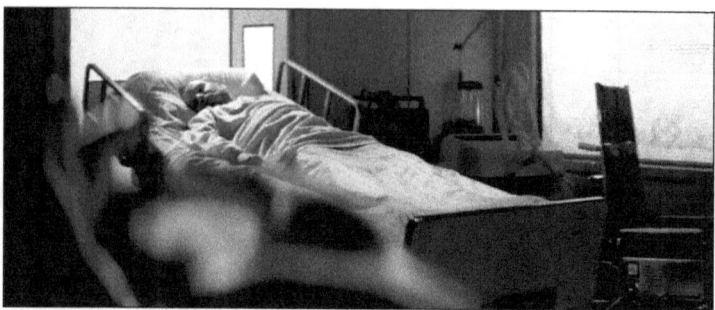

In God's hands? The poetic closing shot of *Whose Life Is It Anyway?*, as framed through a Michelangelo sculpture, adds another dimension to the film's central question.

In *The Hard Way*, does bratty, pampered Hollywood star Michael J. Fox come to actually run hard-boiled cop James Woods' life? Does Woods lose control of his entire existence, and how does he regain it? How can he? Fox wishes to fully become Woods, but quickly goes too far and tramples whatever sense of selfhood that the object of his study once possessed. How does Woods deal with this interloper, who emulates his every move, his every spoken word, and his every breath, in order to score a dream part in a glossy Hollywood movie to be conceived and created a whole world away from the reality he knows? How does he stop this little pisher from moving in on everything he holds sacred, including his would-be girlfriend?

Some have made the argument that Ivan Reitman's *Ghostbusters* (1984) is among the most libertarian of movies, but what of Badham's debut film, *The Bingo Long Traveling All-Stars & Motor Kings* (1976), another story of a systemically oppressed and degraded group of guys who go into business for themselves? Can we sense the connecting threads to these seemingly disparate movies now? It is important to once again remember that auteurism and the auteur theory are not as constricting as its forebears have led us to believe. Badham might have made a single movie called *Whose Life Is It Anyway?*, but from movie to movie, he continues asking that question, except it's more like "Whose lives are these anyway?" Badham is revealed as philosopher... and if you enjoy his movies and buy into the ideas presented herein, philosopher king.

Yet another trope comes into play with Badham: the darkness that lurks beneath charisma. What are the hidden, desperate yearnings of charismatic individuals? Tony Manero is a magnetic presence in *Saturday Night Fever*. He can attract and win over anyone and everyone. He arrives, and the seas part. To quote a line from *Austin Powers* (originally attributable to Raymond Chandler), "Women want him and men want to be him." But Tony is restless and unsettled. Sure, he can turn on the charm and take over a room in the most literal sense, especially if there's an electric dance floor to conquer, but it's still not enough to satiate something more pervasive. He wants more, and the hours he spends daydreaming at the site of the Verrazano Bridge speak of the bridge he wishes to build to a better life, which Manhattan only partly symbolizes.

In *Whose Life Is It Anyway?*, Richard Dreyfuss' quadriplegic Ken Harrison can also easily light up a room, in this case the hospital accommodations he never leaves. He has a joke for every occasion, and the nurses are crazy for him. He's witty, quick to the punch, and deliciously devil-may-care in his attitude and constitution, but all that conceals a despair that no one can reckon with, until all who've come to love him have no choice but to face a terrible void together, only so that he can be left to die alone in a lonely room, laughing to the very end. Talk about gallows humor! It's a powerful film worthy of stacking against great films by more famous directors, staged with aplomb on mostly a single set shot, in anamorphic widescreen. Every staging suggests an unrest, agitation, and imbalance beneath a deceptively humorous surface.

In *WarGames*, Broderick's David Lightman character is a high school badass who always knows precisely what to say to get the class to laugh at the teacher's expense. It's plain to see his intelligence and wit, and, in private, he'll cover his tracks by deviously changing his grades via computer, and then obsessing over the amazing new computer games coming down the pike from the companies he plans to one day conquer. He's above it all, a dreamer not unlike

Tony Manero. Any daily grind, he'll have none of that. He's a born plotter, you might even say a conniver. Even when he gets into trouble with the government, he again manages to quite ingeniously break out of confinement, return as the expert, win over important people including military brass, and outsmart the machines that he himself has unwittingly turned against the entire world. Lightman is a creature of dark charisma, but Badham still manages an endearing, good-natured rendering. That's his charm.

He speaks of directing *WarGames* with a perennial grin, expressing how he pursued a wholly different vision than the original director, Martin Brest, who had been fired: "I couldn't put my finger on what was bothering me about what had been shot. And then it suddenly occurred to me: they're not having any fun. The scene that had Matthew bringing Ally up into his bedroom, there's something dark and evil about the way they're treating this. And yet, I think if I could show a girl how I could break into the computer and change her grade, I would be so excited, I would nearly be peeing in my pants."

It's amazing what a simple change in director can achieve. Relevant to this point is that John G. Avildsen was the original director hired for *Saturday Night Fever*. One does not have to work hard imagining how Avildsen would have rejiggered the story into a potentially overbearing bit of "underdog inspiration porn" in the wake of his raging *Rocky* (1976) success. I personally have no doubt that Avildsen would have completely eliminated many (if not all) of the unflattering aspects of Tony Manero's persona—all of the realism and character complexity in Norman Wexler's script that Badham clearly deemed it imperative to keep. It's ironic that Badham's mise en scène includes a *Rocky* poster in Tony Manero's bedroom, as if to remind us of the type of bowdlerized conquering-the-odds pap we could have gotten instead. (Let the record show that I do love the original *Rocky*, but I am less enthused about where the talented John Avildsen's career went in *Rocky*'s wake.)

In *The Hard Way*, James Woods might not read as traditionally charismatic, but don't tell that to Michael J. Fox, who wants that particular dark charisma for himself. When he requests access to the sensitive details that Woods takes great pains to hide from everyone else, including his would-be girlfriend, he is routinely rebuffed. This should almost be a character archetype: the "Badham charismatic," magnetic outside and somehow tortured on the inside.

The ultra-low angle, ultra-Dutch flash cut is a signature piece of
punctuation in Badham action montage. He uses this in multiple movies,
in high-impact moments with fast cutting.
Top: *Bird on a Wire*. Middle: *The Hard Way*.
Bottom: *Point of No Return*.

Truly, these ideas are also at the center of Badham's *Dracula* (1979), where our Count is charming to the last, including the last drop of blood. An early dinner party scene, during which the ensemble cast first meets the suave and sophisticated blood-guzzling spellbinder (Frank Langella), defines "dark charisma" in the most literal sense possible. The Dracula of lore is transmuted as Badham archetype. We know the rest of the story, of course. This rendition of *Dracula* is one of the most stylish in the annals of Transylvanian cinema, and is generally the more stylish of our director's career, complete with lensing by Gil Taylor, performances by the most capable cast ever assembled for a Dracula flick (e.g. Langella, Laurence Olivier, Donald Pleasence, et al.), and the stormy virtuoso scoring of John Williams, before Badham eventually settled on composer Arthur B. Rubinstein as his semi-permanent musical collaborator. Its muted (almost wholly desaturated) color palette parallels Badham's similar intent on *Whose Life Is It Anyway?*, to "shoot a black-and-white film in color" when the studio vetoed his request to shoot in actual black and white.

Another trope prevalent in the Badham oeuvre is the fish-out-of-water tale, or films about a character or characters adapting to new environments. Surely this is true of *Whose Life Is It Anyway?*, *WarGames*, *Short Circuit*, *The Hard Way*, *Drop Zone*, and *Nick of Time*. In some cases these characters are adapting to a given Badhamian subculture (yes, I just coined the term Badhamian; pretty sure it's a first). There's also the fixation on hardware and software as it presents itself in *Blue Thunder*, *WarGames*, and *Short Circuit*, films in which even the title sequences are technocratized.

The Badham in-joke is another manifestation of his quest to have just a bit of extra fun with his cast, his material, and himself. In the first tier of Badham in-joke, he references other movies, sometimes quite mischievously, such as two cases of one Richard Dreyfuss snubbing another. In a scene in *Stakeout*, Dreyfuss and Emilio Estevez play a movie quote game to pass the time. Between takes, Estevez stumped Dreyfuss with a line from Spielberg's *Jaws* (1975) that he himself had uttered in that film. Badham was so amused, he had them improvise it into the movie. In *Another Stakeout* (1993), Dreyfuss playfully humorously invokes one of his own lines from *The Goodbye Girl* (1977): a hysterical "I don't like the panties drying on the rod!" Extremely wink-wink, kind of lovably devilish too. Badham will even reference his own movies. Sometimes this manifests simply as a conspicuous movie poster in the background, even one from the John Badham movie that immediately preceded it. Or he can veer into full-on pastiche and lampoon, as when the Number Five robot watches *Saturday Night Fever* on television and mimics John Travolta's dance moves. Yes indeed, other Badham movies exist within Badham movies.

Badham sees life as a perpetual struggle for autonomy, independence and personal freedom, with stories revolving around dynamos with demons and designs, caught up in the constant struggle to be free. All this to say, John Badham is never a guy to be counted out. Even if these aspects are subconscious or accidental, there is a clear pursuit that, once you see it, you cannot unsee it. It's pretty easy to see how *Whose Life Is It Anyway?* links up with *Short Circuit*, even if the tones couldn't be more divergent.

An argument I often hear in opposition to my brand of radical auteurism is basically, "Directors need to eat too, so they take jobs often on movies that aren't at all personal, or in any way pursuing their artistic goals." I always retort, the directors worth talking about always either have the power to say no to projects that completely repel them, or they infuse that which interests them into any project's DNA. For as wildly diverse as his resumé is, this is certainly true for Badham. He is a commercial studio filmmaker from head to toe, but in spite of this, whose films are Badham's anyway? His own, completely his own.

Theatrical Feature Films: *The Bingo Long Traveling All-Stars and Motor Kings* (1976), *Saturday Night Fever* (1977), *Dracula* (1979), *Whose Life Is It Anyway?* (1981), *Blue Thunder* (1983), *WarGames* (1983), *American Flyers* (1985), *Short Circuit* (1986), *Stakeout* (1987), *Bird on a Wire* (1990), *The Hard Way* (1991), *Point of No Return* (1993), *Another Stakeout* (1993), *Drop Zone* (1994), *Nick of Time* (1995), *Incognito* (1997)

Other Notable Work: *No Place to Run* (1972), *The Godchild* (1974), *Reflections of Murder* (1974), *Floating Away* (1998), *The Jack Bull* (1999)

PART THREE
THE BRITS

17. A World of Innocent Sinners
The Philip Leacock Vision

I intend to one day direct a documentary film about Philip Leacock and his films. Much of this essay will be the basis for a voiceover script.

Children, when they are in the grip of imagination, are such superb film actors. The intensity of make-believe, of creating a little enclosed world within which there is one reality as distinct and separate from the other reality outside it, is an ancient aspect of human psyche. When you photograph a child gripped in a moment of make-believe, the image has extraordinary cinematic power. The ability to preserve that capacity is what great actors do, and what I think great writers and directors do.

Alexander Mackendrick

Philip Leacock's *Escapade* (1955) culminates in a schoolboy's reading of a letter that states, "Men cannot always see the truth of a simple moral proposition. Perhaps it's for children to lead the way." This is the crux of Leacock, the pivotal and guiding sentiment imparted in a series of films I've come to call his fables. Most palpable is the unabating warmth he nestles between every cut of *The Kidnappers* (1953), *The Spanish Gardener* (1956), *Innocent Sinners* (1958), *Hand in Hand* (1961), and others. He creates robust little communities among children who, in the course of the story, bond with adult societal castaways who nourish their puckish pursuits. These adults often do so because they have themselves never stopped dreaming, and refuse to vacate whatever remains of their own childlike wonder.

It's not merely that Leacock's child characters are hamstrung by a preponderance of adults, and by the adult world in general. Like extensions of the miniature hero in Morris Engel's marvelous *Little Fugitive* (1953), they forge their own private, intricate little worlds in which the stakes are — beneath our noses and almost inexplicably—raised very high very fast. The larger general communities that surround them, which have had some hand in their upbringing, are turned upside down. They are all forced to reckon with a moral clarity they can no longer muster as jaded adults. Though it takes a village to raise a child, it takes that child (or children) to present a clear, uncorrupted moral vision that promises some hope of collective renewal. Innocence is not a commodity or mere virtue in these films—it's a remedy, the freshwater current that purifies the wellspring.

Philip Leacock was my great 2020 Covid pandemic discovery, the subject of my first filmmaker marathon early on in lockdown. Years later, as I write this, the films have tattooed themselves to my soul, and the filmmaker has become one of my principal "pet cause" artists. He and his films are something we decidedly need more of, in this day and age. It's been a goal of mine to turn friends into Leacock fans, and there are normally two movies that do the trick: *Innocent Sinners* and *Hand in Hand*. It's impossible not to smile in the course of both of them. (Frankly, if you don't, you must be made of stone.) When I started the marathon with *Innocent Sinners*, a brilliant adaptation of Rumer Godden's novel *An Episode of Sparrows*, I was immediately struck by a sentiment expressed midway through the film. Twelve-year-old Lovejoy, driven by her quest to create a splendorous Italianate garden in a bombed-out churchyard on very little resources, takes a stroll with Mr. Vincent, who is himself building a dream restaurant he hopes will attract well-heeled clientele. These two creative artists of a kind, misunderstood by those in their immediate environment, seek to transcend circumstance. They can at least understand each other as comrades in like-minded grand endeavors. Immortality might not be in the offing, but with Lovejoy's garden and Mr. Vincent's restaurant, they can be winners and visionary heroes for each other, if just for their day.

"Mr. Vincent, is everyone unhappy?" Lovejoy asks, hoping he will offer some shred of hope. "Everyone!" concedes Mr. Vincent, "But that doesn't stop them from being happy." There is a poignancy in this exchange that touched me deeply on first viewing, and still continues to resonate when I revisit the film.

British critic Mark Cunliffe describes the film as "a metaphor for post-war Britain," with its "call to rebuild society, turning the ruins into something optimistic and beautiful." He recounts a heartbreaking scene in the film thus: David Kossoff's Mr. Vincent "attempts to achieve his dreams of a better menu with the purchase

"Mr. Vincent, is everyone unhappy?" asks Lovejoy in *Innocent Sinners*.

of new white goods and fancy plates, all on [credit] with money he doesn't really possess. The sequence in which his wife brings this uncomfortable truth to the fore, tarnishing his purchase of the plates, fatally cheapening their beauty for him in an instant, is as poignant and heartbreaking as the girl's thwarted efforts at creating her garden from within the devastation of what came before."

This epitomizes the magic and emotional power of Philip Leacock's vision and authorship. This is not to suggest, though, that all Leacock's films are whimsical celebrations of childhood spirit and imagination. In *Reach for Glory* (1962), championed by esteemed British critic and scholar Raymond Durgnat, we get to see the dark side of that same spirit and imagination. In many ways, it is the macabre culmination of a laser-focused thematic pursuit. Durgnat writes that *Reach for Glory* has "another kind of impressiveness, that of everyday experience suddenly clarified by unexpected patterns." Of Leacock's fables of childhood, he argues, "These greyly sensitive, gently bleak, poignant films criticize adult coldness and incomprehension of childish vulnerability and idealism. The remoteness appears in another form: the quiet solitudes of the adult world in which the children seek, diligently, vainly for warmth."

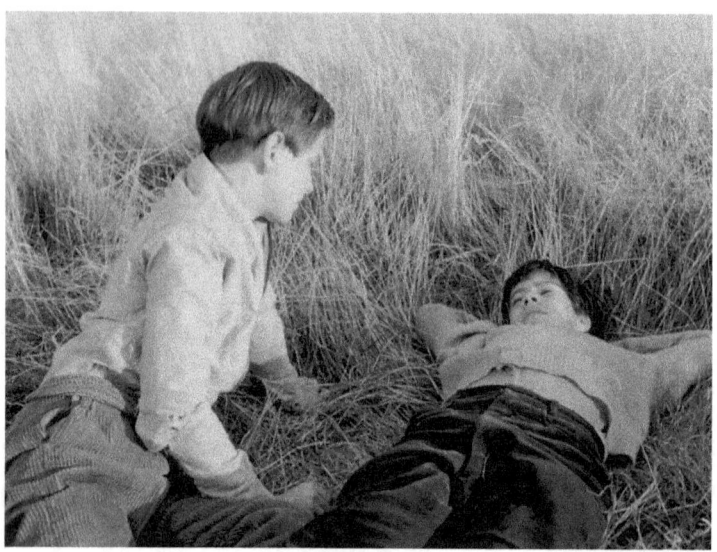

Leacock's masterpiece *Reach for Glory.*

Leacock seems to be known mostly in film circles only as the brother of esteemed documentarian Richard "Rickie" Leacock. Both brothers were brought up in the Canary Islands and educated at British boarding school Bedales. Both also got their start in documentary film, though it was Richard who stayed there and made his name as a pioneer of cinema vérité. Philip's industry path was rather more unusual and circuitous, starting in the Crown Film Unit documentary corps, transitioning to dramatic feature films, then concluding with two decades in television (both episodic and telefilms). While it's an all-too-accepted reflex to sweep him under the rug as "Ricky's less talented brother," I couldn't find that evaluation any less obtuse. There is a beating heart under both his work in features and some of the later telefilms. (And yes, he's yet another glaring omission in Sarris' *The American Cinema.*)

In *The American Vein*, Christopher Wicking and Tise Vahimagi's kindred catalogue of directors who have worked in both movies and television, they file Leacock under the "Elephants' Graveyard" section, which signifies "older talents" who established—and sometimes even distinguished—themselves on the big screen but ended their career (sometimes ingloriously) on the small screen. This, of course, is an unusual reversal of the typical trajectory, which has it that one "graduates" from the small into the big. They write, "Nobody knew what to make of Leacock and his career as a director in England in the Fifties. Was he unusually sensitive to the minds of children, or did his rare understanding of social patterns, as revealed fully in *Reach for Glory* and (unsuccessfully) in the American *Let No Man Write My Epitaph*, indicate that the sensitivity was an excuse, a device to hide from reality? Leacock was once one of [British cinema's] brightest talents, and it is hard to believe it was the light that failed."

It is heartening to know that other critics and historical "beancounters" have seen what I see in his work, but it often strikes me that I'm completely alone in a wilderness of those who have never even heard of him, much less even vaguely admire him (even among cinephiles and cineastes). There is no instantly recognizable classic title, though *Hand in Hand* drums up the most interest and fondness of any of them, at least among Americans. This emphasizes that Leacock's were quiet films that were quietly made and only quietly appreciated in their time. Their defining gentility might have caused them to evaporate next to the era's parade of ferocious box-office spectacles that easily dwarfed them in size, scale, and intensity. The single exception is perhaps *The Kidnappers*, which won special honorary Oscars for its young cast in 1954.

His distinctly documentarian, sometimes neorealistic, aesthetics find their basis in his time serving with the Army Kinematograph Service during World War II. He made his dramatic directing debut with the serial *Riders of the New Forest* (1948), an adventure about two kids who tame a wild pony, but fall into the orbit of a potential horsethief. With *Life in Her Hands* (1951) and

Hand in Hand.

The Brave Don't Cry.

Out of True (1951), two Crown Film Unit "morality play" type dramas sponsored by the British Ministries of Health and Labour, he tackled the overall National Health Service and then, in turn, its treatment of mental illness. Both films were engineered to demonstrate to audiences that the system worked, and that a decent post-war English society was capable of supporting its most vulnerable citizens.

His sometimes documentary-like chronicles of the working class, *The Brave Don't Cry* (1952) and *High Tide at Noon* (1957), echo the work of someone like Jill Craigie, a socialist documentarian who directed two extraordinary dramatic features, *The Way We Live* (1946) and *Blue Scar* (1949), the latter of which vividly documents a Welsh coal mining town. *The Brave Don't Cry*, Leacock's evocative recreation of the Scottish Knockshinnoch Castle mining disaster of 1950, was produced by documentary icon John Grierson for his unfortunately short-lived Group 3 Films, which was set up to fund movies by emerging filmmakers (Lewis Gilbert and John Guillermin were also among the first crop). *The Brave Don't Cry*, originally greenlit under the title *What God Forgot*, establishes a second politically tinged track of Leacock's work. Though it operates partly on a proto-disaster movie wavelength, it never loses sight of the real human drama that undergirds its central crisis. Leacock notably strips the film of a nondiegetic score that would have synthetically heightened the emotion.

A news-conscious British public would have recognized that this was a ripped-from-the-headlines nailbiter fueled first and foremost by its social values. In the real Knockshinnoch disaster, while the majority of the miners were rescued, thirteen did die. When the picture world-premiered at the Edinburgh Film Festival, an audience of invited miners gave it their seal of approval. Though some found Leacock's approach impersonal, the rush to pigeonhole the film as flat reportage is misguided. It's an extraordinary document with much in the way of directorial ingenuity and personality. Leacock's own vim and vigor is mirrored in the miners' indefatigable energy. An almost lyrical sequence in which the trapped miners work to free themselves while singing a Scots work song, reflects Leacock back to us as a man of sound conscience, good humor, and an even keel. However, his personality and generosity of spirit would manifest most appreciably in the later fables.

It is often de rigueur for leftist directors to wallow in a kind of misery fetishism—poverty porn, by another slur—which involves depicting a working class of losers who are destined only to lose. (I find Ken Loach a key offender here, with certain exceptions.) One may call this tireless muckraking, but at too steady a clip, it can become wearying and self-defeating, not to mention demoralizing. Leacock's characters—whether disenfranchised miners or fishermen, or enterprising orphaned children—are permitted to organize, fight, scheme, conspire, build, and often win. He never ennobles shared helplessness, and his outlook is largely aspirational. In particular, *The Brave Don't Cry*, *Escapade*, *The Spanish Gardener*, and *Innocent Sinners*, end with our bedraggled protagonists having accomplished missions that, at times, strike even the audience as impossible or (at best) foolhardy. It's no wonder I latched onto Leacock at the start of the Covid pandemic; I needed a healthy dose of something he was known to provide.

Five years on from *The Brave Don't Cry*, there was *High Tide at Noon*, which, with its story of a poor Nova Scotia fishing village, maintains this similar good humor, especially in scenes like one involving a malfunctioning grandfather clock that will not stop erroneously chiming during a family squabble. [One can imagine the dead-end characters in Don Shebib's Canadian classic *Goin' Down the Road* (1970) having originated from the village in *High Tide at Noon*.] There is a strong, salient documentary ambiance that is detectable despite being fully scripted. In some sense, it is a

Dirk Bogarde and young John Whiteley in *The Spanish Gardener.*

Thomas Hardy *Madding Crowd*-esque story of a young village girl, played by American actress Betta St. John, who is courted by three local men as the community around them faces economic collapse. Though it played in competition at Cannes, it proved both critically and commercially unsuccessful during its run. One critic of its time posited that the lack of children denied Leacock the inspiration he needed to breathe more life into the story. While it does lack the pure poetry of something like Michael Powell's *The Edge of the World* (1937), also about a fishing village, there is far more here than its original notices cared to acknowledge.

On the strength of *The Brave Don't Cry*, he was signed to the Rank Organisation as a contract director. Before taking his post at the studio, he made *Appointment in London* (1953) for British Lion, starring Dirk Bogarde as a wing commander of a Lancaster bomber during the war. This is the film that first establishes a third and final track of Leacock's war films (with the later *Reach for Glory*, a film about children would-be soldiers during wartime, two of Leacock's three tracks intersect). The thematic skeleton of *Appointment in London* is a sort of blueprint for ideas later fleshed out in the superior *The War Lover* (1961), based on Pulitzer Prize-winner John Hersey's novel and starring Steve McQueen and Robert Wagner. Both films are portraits of aerial bombers driven by an obsessive sense of purpose, dodging death at daily intervals. In their tangles with authority, they reckon with the combat machines they have become. One takes heed of a look in the mirror, while the other takes refuge in oblivion.

Leacock's first for Rank, *The Kidnappers* (1953), is the film that widely announced his virtuoso talents with children. It clearly took such a story to fully galvanize his commitment and speak to his abiding sense of morality. It remains one of his most beloved, not to mention financially successful. Said to be J. Arthur Rank's own favorite of his studio's films, it is also one of the titles of his that exported with greatest success. Released in the U.S. as *The Little Kidnappers*, the film was based on the short story "The Scotch Settlement" by Neil Patterson, who also wrote the screenplay. Amid Scots-Dutch settler tensions in an otherwise quiet Nova Scotia colony, two young boys are adopted by their grandparents and aunt after their father dies in the Boer War. They want a dog, but their forbidding, oppressively pious grandfather refuses, so they secretly abduct a Dutch family's unattended baby and raise it as their own, calling it Rover.

John Whiteley and Vincent Winter, the diminutive duo who walked away from the experience with Honorary Oscars, play eight-year-old Harry and six-year-old Davy without a single false or forced note. What's key here is a trademark juxtaposition that would become a familiar point/counterpoint through the rest of Leacock's fables. While the primary drama between the boys and their "pet" plays out, the adult world teems with its own secrets and

The Kidnappers.

conflicts, here in the form of a verboten star-crossed romance between the village's Dutch doctor and the boys' aunt. The severity of the family's world is due in no small part to a bigoted, hard-hearted patriarch whose long, heavy shadow broods over the glum spaces they call home.

Leacock's oppressor figures are always draconian ambassadors of a narrow-minded and often cruel adultness. While *Escapade* (1955) and *The Spanish Gardener* (1956) offer contrasting studies of neglectful fathers who fail their young sons, it is the latter's Michael Hordern as the meddlesome diplomat single father who proves one of the more short-sighted and overbearing tyrants in Leacock's filmography. As he tramples his seven-year-old son's intense but animating friendship with the family's Spanish gardener, as played by Dirk Bogarde, he comes face to face with his own inadequacy as a father and as a man. (The film predictably bowdlerizes the original A. J. Cronin novel's homosexual overtones.) It is because of adult rigidity, backwardness, and rudderlessness that Leacock's children are often forced to take matters into their own hands.

This also occurs in *Escapade*, which climaxes in a very tall, playfully improbable grand gesture. A figure that we the audience never meet or even see, a schoolboy legend nicknamed Icarus, spirits away an aircraft and flies it to Vienna on a "peace mission." The script, written by David Ogden Stewart, largely focuses in its first two acts on the John Mills character Hampden, a pacifist activist so involved in his "causes" that he neglects his wife and, more profoundly, his kids. Thus, it is Icarus who realizes in action what the isolated Mills character can only preach in slogans, no matter the impracticality of Icarus' mission. In the third act of *The Kidnappers*, it is the elder boy, Harry, who stands trial, as a minor, not only for the kidnapping of an infant, but also for the larger prejudicial tensions in the community. The child is designated a potential martyr. Child actor John Whiteley was later cast in *The Spanish Gardener*, and is similarly depicted as the cherubic innocent who shows his elders the way.

The ally is another prevalent figure in Leacock's work from film to film. These are the sympathetic, liberated, and/or starry-eyed adults who act as confidantes and accomplices (to whatever degree of complicity). Sometimes, they too suffer the consequences of the children's actions, as well as their own. The most notable two among this lot are Dirk Bogarde's Jose in *The Spanish Gardener* and David Kossoff's Mr. Vincent in *Innocent Sinners*. However long

The world of children and the world of adults always interact and often collide in the cinema of Philip Leacock, as this shot from *Innocent Sinners* makes literal.

one is punished for dreaming and scheming in Leacock's films, the waters unmuddy in just enough time for mercy and kindness to flow unencumbered.

Innocent Sinners and *Reach for Glory* are Leacock's best films, the former a "lighter" fable, the latter "darker" and heavier. He directed them on either side of a tenure in the United States, during which he helmed four motion pictures. Leacock's close friend, Alexander "Sandy" Mackendrick, had directed *Sweet Smell of Success* (1957) for Burt Lancaster's production company Hecht-Hill-Lancaster. When that instant classic proved a critical and commercial success, Mackendrick got to recommend Leacock to direct the wholesome Hecht-Hill-Lancaster "B" project, *The Rabbit Trap* (1959), starring Ernest Borgnine as another beleaguered father cornered into choosing between career and family. It was the big-screen remake of a "Goodyear Television Playhouse" drama by J. P. Miller, the author of *Days of Wine and Roses*. The material quite obviously couldn't be any more perfect for Leacock, who was by then synonymous with stories about children and family. It received middling reviews and played the caboose of various double features, running a paltry 72 minutes.

Take a Giant Step.

The partnership with Hecht-Hill-Lancaster proved amenable enough that Leacock was placed under five-year contract and signed to direct a second film for the company. *Take a Giant Step* (1959) is fairly novel (certainly for the Fifties) as a drama of an angsty upper-middle-class black teenager living with his parents and grandmother in a predominately white suburb. Upon Leacock's death in 1990, his papers and materials were bequeathed to the University of Wyoming's American Heritage Center. Included was a 16mm print of *Take a Giant Step*, the only one of his films for which he kept a personal copy.

"We shot it in three weeks," Leacock told interviewer Stephen Peet in 1987 for the British Entertainment History Project. "And I don't think we went off the backlot. Universal has a huge backlot and you can do a lot with a good art director, which we had. And… you notice it a bit. There's a rumor that United Artists, who never wanted to make it anyway, destroyed the negative. But I've got a 16mm copy which I bought from them. It's a nice little film. It *is* a little film though."

Because *Innocent Sinners* had ended his contract with Rank, the Mackendrick-engineered deal with Hecht-Hill-Lancaster was perfectly opportune. But his British pictures were always superior to the ones he made in the United States. *The Rabbit Trap* (1959) and especially *13 West Street* (1961) feel awkwardly constrained by sterile, cheap-looking studio sets. Both feel a far cry from the real London streets, or the majesty of the landscapes in *The Kidnappers*, or the villages in *The Brave Don't Cry* and *High Tide at Noon*. The American films generally feel reduced. *13 West Street* is, point blank, Leacock's worst theatrical feature—a leaden, extremely average JD picture that center-stages a hollowed-out Alan Ladd as an astrophysicist targeted by a group of shady young (and very white bread) hoodlums who make a game out of harassing him and his wife (dreadfully played by Dolores Dorn, whose every line-reading is stilted). Rod Steiger is the only one who manages to shine, as the police detective investigating the case.

Take a Giant Step (1959) bears some touches of Leacock's magic, but the barren mise en scène and the obvious Universal backlot city street does give the picture a hemmed-in feel, despite the unique courage of the material. Most of the spaces feel sterile, unlived-in, and artificial. Ruby Dee gives able support as a streetwalker, however, and Leacock's "ally" archetype is aptly embodied by Estelle Hemsley as the protagonist's grandmother, who innately understands the root of the young man's explosive angst and offers a sympathetic ear.

"It takes a village to raise a child" is something that Leacock believes, and this is on full display in *Let No Man Write My Epitaph*, with its warm tenement family.

The best of Leacock's American films, though, is *Let No Man Write My Epitaph* (1960). First of all, consider the cast: Shelley Winters, Burl Ives, James Darren, Jean Seberg, Ricardo Montalban, and Ella Fitzgerald. The film is known in some quarters as a sequel to Nicholas Ray's *Knock on Any Door* (1949), which stars John Derek as Nick Romano, a street tough charged with killing a cop. Leacock's film, only implicitly connected to Ray's, picks up after Romano's public execution, as Romano's illegitimate son is brought up by his addict mother and a tenement full of eccentric characters intent on making sure he does not follow in his father's footsteps. The notion of "it takes a village to raise a child" again looms large.

While *Let No Man Write My Epitaph* is a Columbia picture with, again, some obvious backlot work, the sets don't feel as one-dimensional and limiting as they do on *13 West Street*, or in some stretches of *Take a Giant Step*. Most of all, one takes comfort in the glittering "rabble" that is assembled as a shambling but tight-knit community. The great Arthur Knight wrote of the film, "*Let No Man Write My Epitaph* avoids most of the clichés that have sprung up during the past few years. What makes it arresting is the obvious sincerity that underlies the production, an absence of sordidness or sensationalism for its own sake, and a genuine concern for human values."

Leacock returned to Britain for three final British theatrical pictures: the heartwarming and delightful *Hand in Hand* (1961), the brutal and brilliant *Reach for Glory* (1962), the previously covered *The War Lover* (1962), and the colorful but hollow *Tamahine* (1964). *Hand in Hand* is one of the crown jewels of Leacock's filmography—the story of two ten-year-olds, a Catholic boy and a Jewish girl, who form a fast friendship despite the prejudices of their parents. The message of the film might be obvious, but it is related without the ham-fisted type of "message movie" piety many had come to expect. Most contemporary critics hailed its life-affirming exuberance and unaffectedly humane outlook. Indeed, *Hand in Hand* so moved Jack Lemmon and Eleanor Roosevelt that they were inspired to provide the promotional quotes which grace the poster. It also netted Leacock a Director's Guild of America Award for Outstanding Directorial Achievement.

One scene especially elicits strong emotion. When the children take it upon themselves to learn about each other's culture and religion, the Catholic boy attends the Jewish girl's synagogue on a Saturday morning. He is fearful of being detected, of being castigated as an interloper, of being embarrassed in front of a congregation of intimidating strangers. The pomp of the ritual, the tallises (tallitot), the Torah scroll's removal from the ark, the cantillations

The synagogue scene in *Hand in Hand.*

in another very unfamiliar language, all very daunting to him—and there he is alone, in the men's section, far from his friend, who is seated with her mother. As the rabbi passes by with the Torah scroll, he points to a passage in the boy's siddur (prayer book): "The Lord is with me and I will not fear." As the boy reads, the rabbi smiles, the reassured boy smiles back, and his new friend also smiles, having observed their interaction from afar. In Leacock's films about children, Leacock's unbounding hope for the world, and for the potential of people to grow (especially at tender young ages), renders him exceptional. Sequences such as this are firm cinematic hugs, clearly something he felt the world needed. (In my estimation, something we still very much need.)

Various other sequences in *Hand in Hand* speak to him as cinema's greatest overlooked humanist director. There is an afternoon tea service at the kindly local duchess' estate, the argument over whether a pet mouse is Jewish or Christian, and the search for the proper hat for a pretend African expedition (featuring Finlay Currie as shopkeeper), among others, all to prove that the film is uplifting without ever becoming twee. The story is replete with benevolent spirits, in the mold of the established adult ally archetype. If *Hand in Hand* is an encomium to the joys of childhood, his follow-up, *Reach for Glory,* is the reverse. Based on the novel *The Custard Boys* by John Rae, it is a stern admonition on the dangers of undue violent influence on impressionable minds. Thematically, it is the hellish rejoinder to *Hand in Hand*'s heaven. Raymond Durgnat writes, "In detail, *Reach for Glory* has the rare quality of being at once calmly accurate and devoid of misanthropy (apart from the climax, all the torments are the familiar stuff of everyday experience)."

Reach for Glory follows a group of militarist boys living temporarily in a coastal town during World War II, who take to playing some very twisted and ghoulish war games—including, in a disturbing opening scene, tracking a scared cat as a sort of "enemy combatant" and chasing it off a cliff. Into their midst comes Stein, an Austrian Jewish refugee from mainland Europe, who is scorned and bullied for being different from the rest. Stein is only provisionally permitted to join their ghastly fun and games, but one day, he is brought up on "charges" at a fake court-martial and the unthinkable happens.

As the apotheosis of Leacock's films about childhood, it is the bleakest and most downbeat, but arguably as a result, the most shocking and powerful. Its impact reverberates thunderously well

Reach for Glory.

past the tragic final fade-out. Predictably, many critics made obvious comparisons to *Lord of the Flies*, and though there is validity there, this is not to say that the film lacks for moments when Leacock (again) clearly celebrates childhood as the closest humanity gets to real magic. In many ways, he is incapable of making a film that broods, at least in any unrelenting sense. It is here that the filmmaker's sensitivity proves inviolable, and his allergy to nihilism is incontrovertibly affirmed. It would have been all too easy for another filmmaker to take this material and deliver an unforgiving indictment of humanity as a whole. But that's far off yonder from the Leacock purview. A sequence in which Stein and his closest chum Curlew storm an abandoned house is shot in a loose, almost vérité style that takes a proactive role in their shenanigans. The hyper-kinetic camera is itself merry and frolicsome, wobbling as the boys try on silly hats and then freely sprinting with them as they charge through the long hallways. Friendship, as here between Stein and Curlew, is once again hallowed, as it had been in *Innocent Sinners*, *Hand in Hand*, and others.

The film opens with a title card that states: "During the blitz on London, thousands of children had been evacuated by their families to the safety of remote villages. This film is about a group of these evacuees. They were neither delinquent nor problem children—

Leacock's unleashed handheld camera shares in the merry-making in this scene from his masterpiece *Reach for Glory*.

boys who wanted desperately to be part of the war they were too young to fight." Leacock takes pains in this title card, and throughout the rest of the film, to state that human beings are vulnerable, especially young people, and when they are placed in incubators that foster distrust, paranoia, and reactionary violence, one can never anticipate the depraved, terrible things that can happen. Leacock saw the film as his ultimate anti-war statement, and recognized it as one of his best works. "I'm very proud of it, but it never got anywhere. Unfortunately, it came out almost the same time as Peter Brook's film of *Lord of the Flies*. But it hurt us. [...] It didn't do very much, but it's a film I particularly like." The film did still manage to win Leacock one of the Locarno Film Festival's biggest honors.

Leacock followed up his masterpiece with an agreeable trifle. The innocuous *Tamahine* (1964), shot by Geoffrey Unsworth in color 'Scope and starring Nancy Kwan as a Polynesian teenager sent to live with her uncle in England, was his last British theatrical feature. He would retreat into American episodic television for a number of years, directing "Hawaii Five-O," "Rawhide," "Route 66," and other staples of the era's primetime lineup. He made only a tentative return to movies, first by producing the Henry Fonda oater *Firecreek* (1968) for Vincent McEveety, and then directing one last studio feature, the barely released *Adam's Woman* (1970), starring Beau Bridges and John Mills. The latter, an engaging and well-produced drama set in the 1840s, based on the actual recorded history in its tale of a male prisoner in an Australian penal colony who is manumitted for the purpose of pioneering the frontiers of the Outback, along with a female fellow ex-prisoner he takes as a wife. It never received an American rollout, but played in England and Australian to poor box-office returns. From there, Leacock retired into television permanently.

Some of his early telefilms were of note. *Escape of the Birdmen* (1971), a World War II potboiler, was theatrically released by CIC in Europe. *When Michael Calls* (1972), *Dying Room Only* (1973), and *Baffled!* (1973) were movie-of-the-week thrillers which still live on fondly in the memories of those who caught them upon their original airings. The legitimately edge-of-your-seat *Dying Room Only* prefigures similar later thrillers like *The Vanishing* (1988) and *Breakdown* (1997). With *The Great Man's Whiskers* (1972), he gave us one last fable of childhood, with its charming story of a little girl who writes to Abraham Lincoln, encouraging him to grow a beard. With *Angel City* (1980), a tale of migrant labor camps starring Ralph Waite and a young Jennifer Jason Leigh,

Young Lovejoy and Tip, together in Lovejoy's secret garden, in *Innocent Sinners*.

he made a return to chronicles of the poor and working class, à la *The Brave Don't Cry* and *High Tide at Noon*. There is also a loose trilogy of rollicking Western comedies in this telefilm lot: *The Daughters of Joshua Cabe* (1972), *Wild and Woolly* (1978), and *The Wild Women of Chastity Gulch* (1982), none of which are remarkable but are all harmless diversions.

Leacock did conclude his career on a particularly high note, directing arguably his biggest production in terms of scale. The highly acclaimed *Three Sovereigns for Sarah* (1985) was an American Playhouse epic starring Vanessa Redgrave, Kim Hunter, and Phyllis Thaxter as three sisters accused of witchcraft in Salem. Patrick McGoohan, who had worked with Leacock decades earlier on *High Tide at Noon*, also appears as the Chief Magistrate.

Leacock did not get terribly much time to enjoy his retirement, succumbing to a heart attack in July 1990 while on vacation with his family. He said of his films, "I don't know that I was ever looking for political statement, but I think I was trying to find things that reflected my own philosophy of life, whatever you call it. Something that would encourage a sense of decency really, and I think all those films did that."

There is a scene in Barry Levinson's *Avalon* (1990) in which the Aidan Quinn character Jules muses, "When I was a kid, I used to think the world was made up of big people and little people. And that's the way it would always stay. And I always wondered why sinks were too high and you had to climb up to wash your face. Cupboards, too high. The hole in the toilet was too big. Nothing was made for us! It's just a world of big people and little people.

Hand in Hand.

Philip Leacock.

You never got any older and nobody ever died." Well, one can see how Leacock made his films for those "little people," and for those "big people" who haven't totally lost that childlike sense of wonder. Photo archives are brimming with stills of Leacock down on his haunches taking to his child actors at their level, eye-to-eye. Doing so, rather than speaking to children from one's own height, high above, only became directing gospel later on. It was Truffaut and then Spielberg who popularized the practice. But somehow Leacock innately knew how to communicate with children at this level. (He finds his eastern counterpart in Abbas Kiarostami, in this regard.)

Apart from any academic considerations of his filmmaking voice, inquiries into his craft, and appraisals of his overall cinematics, Philip Leacock was a very special human being, and a great man. This magnanimous quality bled over to his work. One could break down the camerawork and the staging and the editorial patterns, and he was never wanting for estimable talent in these departments. But if men like Leacock wear their hearts on their sleeves, filmmakers like him project it beating with vigor onto the screen. We watch it thump past every shot, every cut, every reel.

He is one of the greatest filmmakers that you don't know, and out of the many filmmakers in this volume, I have a special interest in this particular one. I invite you to discover the sheer magnitude of that greatness.

Theatrical Feature Films: *Riders of the New Forest* (1948), *Life in Her Hands* (1951), *Out of True* (1951), *The Brave Don't Cry* (1952), *Appointment in London* (1953), *The Kidnappers* (1953), *Escapade* (1955), *The Spanish Gardener* (1956), *High Tide at Noon* (1957), *Innocent Sinners* (1958), *The Rabbit Trap* (1959), *Take a Giant Step* (1959), *Let No Man Write My Epitaph* (1960), *Hand in Hand* (1961), *13 West Street* (1962), *Reach for Glory* (1962), *The War Lover* (1962), *Tamahine* (1964), *Adam's Woman* (1970), *Escape of the Birdmen* (1971), *Three Sovereigns for Sarah* (1985)

Other Notable Works: *When Michael Calls* (1972), *The Great Man's Whiskers* (1972), *The Daughters of Joshua Cabe* (1972), *Baffled!* (1973), *Dying Room Only* (1973), *Wild and Woolly* (1978), *Angel City* (1980), *The Wild Women of Chastity Gulch* (1982)

18. A Cinema of Pretenders
The Peter Medak Vision

This is the revised and adjusted video essay script, for a piece included on Severin's Blu-ray release of The Ghost of Peter Sellers.

> Oh yes, I'm the great pretender,
> Adrift in a world of my own.
> My need is such, I pretend too much.
> I'm lonely, but no one can tell."
>
> "The Great Pretender" by The Platters

Peter Medak seems always on the verge of being widely recognized as a director of distinction. His name is more often than not written or uttered in reverence within certain contexts. *The Changeling* and *The Ruling Class*, especially, are perennials with audiences. But still… no critical study text, no book, no retrospective that centers him especially, and not on as many lips as he should be. It's again the age-old stumbling block: many are lazily or myopically not attuned to familiar tropes and trademarks when they exist across multiple genres. Despite the most overt personal artistic flourishes that speak to coherent overall career-wide visions, as if these elements leap out before the audience and shout their presence, the work of many cross-genre filmmakers like Medak still too often goes unnoticed.

When I consider Medak's films, I think of the lyrics of Henry Mancini's song "Charade": "When we played our charade, we were like children posing. Playing at games, acting out names, guessing the parts we played." When you consider nearly every film Peter Medak directed, from his debut feature *Negatives* onward, you'll quickly realize how he centers role-play, dress up, masquerade, cosplay, some mode or manner of impersonation. His is a cinema of grand pretenders. What intrigues Medak, what propels his cinematic eye, is that which happens when all these various masks slip, or drop altogether. Or when the masks cannot be unfastened from the face.

In *Negatives* (1968), a couple sexually tantalize each other by playing dress-up, he as murderer Dr. Krippen, and she as either Krippen's wife Belle or mistress Ethel. Love leaves that masquerade when he gets other ideas, specifically in ditching their Krippen games for a more torrid disguise that excludes her, that of Red Baron Von Ritchhofen. In *A Day in the Death of Joe Egg* (1971), the bizarre games that husband and wife Bri and Sheila play both deflect and reflect the predicament of caring for their spastic vegetable daughter Josephine—this includes voicing Josephine, as to simulate conversations with her. In *The Ruling Class* (1972), Peter O'Toole is a paranoid schizophrenic who believes he is Jesus Christ, and in the course of the runtime rubs up against other masquerades that facilitate his transformation into Jack the Ripper. In *Ghost in the Noonday Sun* (1973), a ship's cook haphazardly assumes the role of captain... with disastrous results.

In *The Changeling* (1980), the central backstory involves a deceitful subterfuge, the switching of a murdered boy with an imposter. In *Zorro the Gay Blade* (1981), the central comedic premise is a double masquerade: one brother taking over for another in the guise of the eponymous masked avenger. In *The Men's Club* (1986), when one of the bordello ladies paints Frank Langella's face with impromptu, ad hoc kabuki makeup, a strange, impossible-to-have-predicted overall shift occurs, one that redefines the male characters' relationship with the reality to which most, but not all, are fated to return after their collective night of sexual bliss. This escape, any escape, will not hold up under a moment's scrutiny. No Medak character's escape, or would-be escape, comes without enhanced gravity. This echoes right back to *Negatives*, with its own sexual role-plays. In *The Krays* (1990), the infamous identical twins in cinematic form represent a familiar playground for Medak, another inquest into identity, its reciprocity, and our human need to pretend as to assert. Assert what? That's up to the masqueraders.

It's not simply about "playing the part" in Medak's world. Characters also routinely surrender selfhood, altogether losing themselves to illusion. In some cases, these identity swaps and submissions to otherness are bound up together. In one scene of *The Krays*, the wife of one of the twins tells her now powerful husband: "Everything about you is different, you know that? Your skin feels different, your body feels different, you even smell different." Transformation: complete. Just a couple of scenes later, she confesses to their mother, "I feel like I'm being taken over.

Peter McEnery's transformation into the Red Baron in *Negatives*.

I haven't got any strength. I don't know who I am. It's not just being married. Sometimes, I wake in the morning and I think, how old am I? What music do I like? What films do I like? I don't know the answer anymore. All I know is what Reg likes, what Reg likes me to like." The symbiosis of individual identity with symbolic character is never complete until there is total dissolution of the individual. Nothing is granular.

While a director like Blake Edwards is similarly preoccupied with masquerade and role play, the nature of Medak's obsession is quite different. Medak is far more invested in the power dynamics in which these masquerade games, gambits, and delusions are rooted. In his world, disguise is tethered to sanity, and that sanity is always fragile, just a hair's breadth away from dissolution. In *Negatives*, when Peter McEnery unilaterally switches personas, it leaves his co-cosplayer Glenda Jackson powerless and impotent, the first expendable pawn in a game that's not hers. What's more, it never really was.

A pivotal scene from *Negatives* lays this out. Theo, having newly assumed his cosplay identity of Red Baron Von Richthofen, presents himself to wife Vivien, who has come dressed as Belle, wife of Dr. Crippen. They are now keen to play very different games, yet only one party is calling the shots as to which one really gets played.

THEO: Van Richthofen, at your service.

VIVIEN: Who?

THEO: You are a fool. You know nothing. It doesn't matter.

VIVIEN: Nothing matters.

THEO: Only games, and the discovery of games. We are quits now.

VIVIEN: Theo…

THEO: (*correcting her*) Baron Von Richthofen!

VIVIEN: Oh, don't say that!

THEO: Your mistake lay in expecting me to remain constant. But you yourself predicted I'd find my own tremendous game. Don't you remember?

VIVIEN: But there's no sex in it! I need you, I want you to want me. I'm "Belle," I'm your wife!

THEO: I don't need you anymore!

Her husband's persona shift is a mirror reverse of the 14th Earl of Gurney in *The Ruling Class*. While the latter becomes a ruthless killer, the former begins as ruthless killer but transitions to another less bloodthirsty and more heroized — but sexless — killer. Medak's social satire is present in the very title *The Ruling Class*. The British class system is lorded over by a cabal that is equal parts fake Jesus and Jack the Ripper, the former as PR and the latter as a matter of course. The shifting and sharing of these principal conflicting characteristics, one being a mask and a pretense for the other's terrible, uncharitable absoluteness, gives way to decrepitude, a swarm of decaying but well-appointed corpses.

In *A Day in the Death of Joe Egg*, husband Bri leaves while Sheila is left to pick up the pieces, again revealing a power dynamic deceptively shrouded by fun and games, even when those fun and games are used to cope, to emotionally survive. Similar to Vivien in *Negatives*, Sheila is left out of all permission structures. Their pranks and antics are an insufficient substitute for something else when one considers that they actually live alone together. Sheila at one point confesses directly to camera, "I join in these jokes to please him. He hasn't any faith she's going to improve, whereas I have, you see." In another scene, their friend Freddie (Peter Bowles), unsettled about their facetious floor show, confronts them: "These jokes… may I say my piece about these jokes? They've obviously helped you see it through. They're useful as an anesthetic, but doesn't there come a point when the jokes start using *you*?"

Alan Bates, Janet Suzman, and their disabled daughter in
A Day in the Death of Joe Egg.

In *The Changeling*, the initial ghostly manifestations emerge as games, a kind of spectral gamesmanship, especially the now famous bouncing ball image, tumbling down the staircase. Politics become of the essence later on, with Melvyn Douglas' Republican senator at the heart of the ghost house's central mystery and central secret. The purview of *Negatives* and *The Ruling Class* looms large all over again. Somehow, you don't expect power to figure into what would normally be weighed as a simple haunted house tale. Even a later work like *Romeo is Bleeding* (1993) renders its story of a double life as a constant game of brinkmanship with seemingly no terminus.

Let Him Have It (1991) presents an interesting offshoot: an illiterate, mentally impaired, epileptic young man stands accused of a murder he did not commit. Though based on a true story (the real subject was later posthumously pardoned), the film gives Medak an opportunity to hang his own thematics on the historical record as he presents it. Derek Bentley (Christopher Eccleston) is tangled up in the various, conflicting ways he has been cast by the press and the public: childlike innocent, dangerous delinquent, scapegoat. Bentley's very demeanor is misinterpreted by the police, the court,

George C. Scott in *The Changeling*.

and other authority figures; his hesitations and verbal repetitions are taken as guile or concealment. His disability claim is seen as a "mask"—a role fashioned to exonerate him. On the flipside, Bentley has fallen in with a group of local boys who have formed a gang. They perform a kind of gangster machismo, lifted from cinema and pulp crime stories. Their posturing gestures and speech are a kind of social cosplay, enacting a self-mythologizing toughness without comprehension of the real stakes.

Though Medak's staging is unadorned, reliant on usually perceptible but elegant zooms, often during moments of mobile camerawork, it is not without character and voice. Never in evidence is a brand of pedestrian, non-active proscenium staging reminiscent of journeymen adapting stage work (both *The Ruling Class* and *Joe Egg* began life as plays). Moments of audacious lens or lighting choice furnish his scenes with sometimes brassy punctuation marks. Though Medak recognizes intrinsic theatricality in works originally written and fashioned for the stage, he opens up his texts for the film form, while having his own way with the material, sometimes to the chagrin of his scenarists, especially *Joe Egg* author Peter Nichols, who gave voice to his displeasure with Medak's interpretation, despite the film version's almost uniformly good reviews. But this was Medak the artist exercising his artistic license over material about which he personally had much to say. Even *Species II* (1998), an otherwise thankless sequel to a moderately successful genre film, gets a working-over by Medak and his favored thematics. Identity itself is rather a costume for the film's alien presence. The alien mimics human behavior, speech, and emotional response. This is a cosplay of humanity itself, and the costume in the film can never come off.

And that's really at the heart of all this. Medak is not merely a functionary in service to sacrosanct texts. A trio of collaborations with Peters on his first three movies—Peter Everett, the novelist of *Negatives*, Nichols, the playwright of *A Day in the Death of Joe Egg*, and Peter Barnes, the writer of *The Ruling Class*—delivered him to prominence. A fourth Peter, Sellers, an international superstar and a comedy ghostwriter of *Ghost in the Noonday Sun*, authored chaos on its set, sending Medak's career into a tailspin. It was his first taste of losing control of a movie he was ostensibly directing, and it took years to recover... and recover he did, especially with a series of films that have since become cult favorites.

As the Mancini song "Charade" continues, "Oh, what a hit we made! We came on next to closing. Best on the bill, lovers until love left the masquerade." Love and power grapple for dominance in the games that Medak's characters comprise and then play to the fringiest edges of sanity, safety, accountability, and vulnerability.

In his documentary *The Ghost of Peter Sellers* (2018), Medak discusses his early upbringing in Hungary under Nazi rule: "I was born in 1937, and Hungary was invaded by the Germans in 1944.

Peter O'Toole and his messianic complex in *The Ruling Class*.

I was seven years old, so I was a very young kid. But I remember when Eichmann came in with his 40 tanks. I walked into my father's study and I overheard his two best friends saying, 'What is to come? We may not survive it.' That's the first time I was scared. So we pretended to be Christians, and you started living with a lie."

His Jewish family pretended to be Christian to escape persecution and worse. He came of age in a time of pretenders, when these putative games had life and death consequences. Even if games were not one's forte, you were cornered irrevocably into playing these ones. Focuses and fascinations are often if not always shaped this way, at this stage of life. There is both safety and danger in illusion, in pretending, and in the art of the lie. This is what makes Peter Medak, beyond merely a director worth an extra second's thought or consideration, one of the most personal filmmakers imaginable, and it's about time the film world recognized this fact and answered to it.

Theatrical Feature Films: *Negatives* (1968), *A Day in the Death of Joe Egg* (1971), *The Ruling Class* (1972), *Ghost in the Noonday Sun* (1973), *Sporting Chance* (1975), *The Odd Job* (1978), *The Changeling* (1980), *Zorro, the Gay Blade* (1981), *The Men's Club* (1986), *The Krays* (1990), *Let Him Have It* (1991), *Romeo is Bleeding* (1993), *Pontiac Moon* (1994), *Species II* (1998), *The Ghost of Peter Sellers* (2018)

Other Notable Works: *The Third Girl from the Left* (1973), *The Babysitter* (1980), *The Feast of All Saints* (2001), *The Dating Game Killer* (2017)

19. Glimpses of Tiger
The Anthony Harvey Vision

This is a revision of a piece titled "Might Be a Giant: In Recognition of Director Anthony Harvey," originally published on my defunct ConFluence-Film Blog in 2013.

It's Oscar night, 1969. An ever-radiant Ingrid Bergman emerges to announce the winner of undoubtedly the most anticipated award of the evening: the Best Actress prize. The critics, the press, and the trades have been publicizing a neck-and-neck race between the seasoned veteran Katharine Hepburn—who has won the coveted award twice previously—and newcomer Barbra Streisand for her starmaking film debut as Fanny Brice in *Funny Girl*. *Variety*'s droll headline roars, "Funny Girl vs. The Lioness." As Bergman opens the envelope, she is clearly flabbergasted. "The winn...," she starts to announce as her voice trails off. A bewildered double-take, followed by a shocked demur, accented with a movement of the hand to cover her mouth in amazement. "It's a tie!" For the first time in Oscar history, two performers are presented with the same award: Streisand and Hepburn, whose Eleanor of Aquitaine in *The Lion in Winter* won nearly unanimous accolades. She is not present to pick up the award herself. Accepting the award on her behalf is her director Anthony Harvey.

Arriving at the podium flanking an overwhelmed Streisand, he holds the statuette in his hands and declares in a distinctly mellow "public school class" British accent, "When I asked Ms. Hepburn what she thought when she had broken the records for nominations, she said, 'I suppose if you live as long as I have, anything can happen.'" The audience murmurs a few courtesy chuckles. He continues, "And I'm absolutely thrilled that it has happened. Thank you." He then steps aside as Streisand takes the podium for her speech, gazing wide-eyed at her statuette and greeting it with a now-classic Streisand salutation, "Hello, gorgeous!" The audience explodes in laughter. They're in love with her. Already, even at the height of his fame, Anthony Harvey had been forgotten with undue haste, his slightly awkward and rare would-be cameo effectively upstaged. It marked a rare public appearance of Harvey, who had himself been nominated for directing *The Lion in Winter*, losing to veteran Carol Reed for *Oliver!* but winning the Director's Guild prize. The die, it would seem, had been cast.

Anthony Harvey launched his career as a film editor on many British productions of the Sixties. Both Stanley Kubrick and Bryan Forbes regularly employed him, namely on *Lolita* (1962), *Dr. Strangelove* (1964), *The L-Shaped Room* (1962), and *The Whisperers* (1966). Both Martin Ritt's *The Spy Who Came In from the Cold* (1966) and Guy Green's *The Angry Silence* (1959) also bear his name as film editor. Kubrick offered him *2001: A Space Odyssey* (1968), but he was itching to transition to directing. He made his debut with the 55-minute *Dutchman* (1967), shot in six days for $48,000. It landed the Critics Prize at Cannes, and also earned Shirley Knight a Best Actress award at the Venice Film Festival. Before Harvey knew it, he was off and running directing an A-list project as his follow-up.

The Lion in Winter (1968), undoubtedly the most prominent, most critically beloved, and most commercially successful film Harvey directed, was not the picture that introduced me personally to his work. At the age of fourteen, I came into possession of the Rank Organisation-bankrolled British Western *Eagle's Wing* (1979) on a pan-and-scan VHS. Little did I know at the time that the film had been beautifully lensed by Billy Williams in anamorphic widescreen and that I was missing almost half the full frame on this shoddy video copy. The epic splendor of the images, cited by even the film's most virulent detractors, was more than a little lost on me, but I still nonetheless took note of its strange pacing — a pace that was particularly at odds with a story that pitted four separate components of a chase narrative against one other. I might have been looking at a Western produced by men fond of regular daytime tea breaks, but I started to recognize a method to the ostensible "madness," inherent in the conflicting rhythmic and narrative elements. In the subsequent years, I came to see most of the other works in Harvey's directorial canon, including *Richard's Things* (1980) and, at long last, *Eagle's Wing* in widescreen. Both inspired the writing of this, the first published essay justifying Harvey's heretofore unawarded status as auteur.

In *The American Vein*, authors Christopher Wicking and Tise Vahimagi cite Harvey's "superb way with extrovert actors (O'Toole, Scott, Hepburn)." At first glance, Harvey would appear

Anthony Harvey was an expert in the two-hander.
All his films revolve around the interactions between two strong-willed
characters, often a man and a woman (not necessarily romantically).

skilled in the art of the two-hander. This predisposition is borne
out in nearly every single one of his films: Shirley Knight and Al
Freeman, Jr. as the subway combatants in *Dutchman*, Hepburn
and O'Toole as royalty-at-odds in *The Lion in Winter*, Scott
and Woodward as quasi-Sherlock and ensnared Watson in *They
Might Be Giants* (1971), Ullman and Finch as illicit lovers in *The
Abdication* (1974), Davis and Dunaway as mother and daughter
in *The Disappearance of Aimee* (1976), Martin and MacGraw
as paramours in *Players* (1979), Sheen and Waterston as cat and
mouse in *Eagle's Wing*, Ullman and Redman as grieving wife and
mistress in *Richard's Things*, O'Toole and Foster as teacher and
protégé in *Svengali* (1983), Nolte and Hepburn as assassin and his
suicidal target in *Grace Quigley* (1985), and Hepburn and Quinn
as ex-spouses in *This Can't Be Love* (1994).

The stories consist largely of pairs thrown together not necessarily out of mutual commitment, love, or the promise of love, but
by expediency, joint utility, the possibility of self-discovery, or
desire for a protracted battle of wits. Most of all, it's what Harvey
reveals about these duos in darkness and in light, and in terms of
another crucial duality.

The true crux of Harvey's films lies, of all places, within the title of Noël Coward's most beloved play: *Private Lives*. The private sphere is sacrosanct in the well-appointed filmic worlds that Harvey forms and fashions. The fragmentation and moderation of human behavior seems to fascinate Harvey as his characters slingshot between public and private. This is most prevalent in those films in which his characters function as public figures, namely King Henry II and Eleanor of Aquitaine in *The Lion in Winter*, Queen Kristina of Sweden and Cardinal Azzolino in *The Abdication*, Aimee Semple McPherson in *The Disappearance of Aimee*, the two Wimbledon-class tennis pros in *Players*, and the eponymous stroke-plagued actress in *The Patricia Neal Story* (1981). While these films especially function within this construct, the others also are suffused with this conceit.

Harvey's gravitation towards material like Tennessee Williams' *The Glass Menagerie* (1973) and Frederic Raphael's *Richard's Things*, despite the authors' exclusive commitment to depicting the lives of ordinary people, is still logical, particularly in the latter case. Both of these are about private lives and, more aptly, inner lives. *Grace Quigley* takes an almost farcical and darkly zany approach to much the same. In *Dutchman* and *Eagle's Wing*, space is used symbolically. The public sphere becomes a proverbial fisticuffs ring in which characters attempt to resolve interpersonal treachery. It is a stage—an unwilling platform—where inner struggle becomes public exhibition. Harvey reveals how private hostilities disrupt and irrevocably alter this public sphere, where space is the currency... a currency that gets gloriously spent.

In other terms, cinematic ones, space is the currency of the director, while time is the currency of the editor. Consider here the richness of Harvey's craftsmanship. The technicians and writers with whom Harvey associated constitute a formidable list of masters. Cinematographers Gerry Turpin, Douglas Slocombe, Geoffrey Unsworth, Freddie Young, Billy Williams, and Larry Pizer, as well as the writers Amiri Baraka (a.k.a. LeRoi Jones), James Goldman, Ruth Wolff, John Briley, and Frederic Raphael have all worked under the aegis of Anthony Harvey as director. (This is to say nothing of the impressive working relationships that had been sustained by Anthony Harvey the editor.) Though not an overt visual stylist, save for Geoffrey Unsworth's soft-focus work in *The Abdication* and Billy Williams' epic panoramica in *Eagle's Wing*, Harvey was always apt at orchestrating subtle visual cues.

Dutchman.

Harvey's directorial debut *Dutchman* is *Who's Afraid of Virginia Woolf?* with the braying, ornery ugliness "turned up to eleven," featuring a younger Taylor and Burton, an interracial version, grappling for control over each other in an unmistakably public arena, with the innocent bystanders as witnesses to the treachery and as silent victims of the drama, much like the audience itself. Also adapted from a stage play, the film is set in the underground New York City of a subway train that doesn't seem to be making its stops. An aggressive and obnoxious firecracker of a woman named Lula takes a seat beside a young black man named Clay. Harvey tempers the early scenes with a reactive zoom lens. In an early shot preceding the meeting of the two characters, Harvey and his cameraman Gerry Turpin choreograph a low-angle zoom from the foregrounded Clay to the backgrounded Lula. With the arrival of subway passenger onlookers in the second act, Harvey locks his focal length for fixed shots. It is a fascinating stylistic departure. The surrounding eyes that have congregated substitute for a more active camera voice, marking a point at which subjectivity turns on itself.

In a quantum stylistic leap from *Dutchman*, Harvey moved on to *The Lion in Winter*, a well-budgeted and handsomely mounted Joseph E. Levine production adapted from James Goldman's Broadway stage

Bette Davis and Faye Dunaway in *The Disappearance of Aimee*.

play. The story involves King Henry II's selection of an heir to the throne, and Eleanor of Aquitaine's struggle for influence in the selection. Goldman is also the film's screenwriter. At heart, the play's and the film's central idea is the human dimension of historical incident. Peter O'Toole championed Harvey as director of the project from the outset. It was he who lured Hepburn to the co-starring role, following rumors that she would retire after Spencer Tracy's death (the two of them had just co-starred in *Guess Who's Coming to Dinner*, for which Hepburn also won an Oscar statuette). Hepburn saw *Dutchman* at O'Toole's behest, stated that the film "grabbed you by the throat, which is exactly the approach that our material needed; not that glossy old MGM stuff, but cold people living in cold castles." She remained steady friends with Harvey for the rest of her life, and starred in two later Harvey productions.

Cinematographer Billy Williams, who shot the Harvey-Hepburn collaboration *The Glass Menagerie*, remembered of the rapport, "She had an extraordinary relationship with Anthony Harvey. Their relationship was like an aunt with a favorite nephew, in that she was kind of protective of him, and he was anxious to please her all the time."

Staging is of the essence in *The Lion in Winter*, even more so than in its stage incarnation. As an ensemble piece, every room in its castle location could be considered a smaller theater within the castle's (and the film's) larger theater. The perfect example is the key scene that intimates a scandalous love affair between Richard the Lionheart (Anthony Hopkins in his sophomore film role) and King Phillip II (the debuting Timothy Dalton). As the two men are about to liaise, O'Toole's Henry II intrudes, prompting Richard to hide behind a nearby curtain. Richard becomes voyeur to a conversation between Henry and Phillip. The contrasts of the initial intimacy, the interruption of that intimacy, and the ensuing voyeurism all speak to Harvey as one who moderates and mines the levels of complexity in a favored theme, how the private impacts and even transforms the public, even at such an early stage of his directing career.

As in Fred Zinnemann's *A Man for All Seasons* (1966) and Peter Glenville's *Becket* (1964, in which O'Toole plays the same character as in *Lion*), while the fate of a nation hangs in the balance within the film's narrative, focus is not lavished on cold, impersonal epic pomp that would have plagued a more Samuel Bronston-esque production. In Harvey's film, periodic scenes feature all characters together, but they will resign themselves to direct confrontations in hideouts within the larger space. Excepting Mike Nichols' *Carnal Knowledge* (1971), *The Lion in Winter* proved the last successful prestige production that Joseph E. Levine's now-defunct Avco-Embassy Pictures mounted.

Though he was offered tidy sums to direct *Nicholas and Alexandra* (1971) and *Cabaret* (1972), Harvey followed up *The Lion in Winter* with *They Might Be Giants*, a nutty ripping yarn of a comedy starring George C. Scott and Joanne Woodward, and produced by Paul Newman (under his Newman-Foreman Productions banner). It is in this film that an opening-up of Harvey's thematic thread of public vs. private occurs. The film tells the story of a widowed Manhattan lawyer named Justin Playfair who, in a fit of paranoid delusion, believes himself to be Sherlock Holmes. He garbs himself in deerstalker attire and takes to the streets in search of his nemesis Moriarty. His concerned brother hires female psychoanalyst Dr. Mildred Watson to treat him. Soon, she is drawn into his infectiously exciting world of "adventure, danger and intrigue" against her better judgment. As Holmes/Playfair also lures a cast of "Bleecker Street irregulars" into his fantasy world, it becomes more and more apparent that these irregulars do not just inhabit this world, but own it as well. The *They Might Be Giants* universe is one based in the fanciful, where public and private become blurred and ultimately indistinguishable.

If *The Lion in Winter* is about the existence of the binary of public and private, and their reciprocal shifting and sharing, *They Might Be Giants* is about the destruction of the binary. At the final fade-out, it asks a question common to the theater of the absurd: Does it matter to which reality we subscribe? The film, quite befittingly, has become a cult favorite over the years, even though its original box-office returns were somewhat discouraging.

The film that was to be Harvey's riposte to the comedic anarchy of *They Might Be Giants* proved an unqualified disaster that was shut down by the studio. I like to believe there is an alternate dimension in which films like *A Glimpse of Tiger* were actually completed and exist to be viewed. But short of that, we have to settle for Herman Raucher's source novel and the various records of its outrageous production history. This was a comedy to star Elliott Gould as a sort of New York bohemian urban guerrilla who variously believes he is Dracula or the "Mad Bomber of London." He ensnares in his shenanigans a naïve Indiana girl just off the bus; Kim Darby was cast in the role. One can, with very little effort, see the connecting tissue between *Giants* and *Tiger*. They would have certainly made a dynamic duet of far-out farces involving merry madmen in Manhattan. Much of the overall blame, judging from the published record, is placed on Gould, who "went crazy" according to one source, and started behaving erratically to the point it became untenable to continue shooting. In my own time with Gould, he seemed to still place blame on Harvey. One interview has Gould bemoaning the fact that Harvey started "directing before I even show up" (referring to the fact that the director selected the costumes without his consent as co-producer on the project). Other sources claim that distinguished friends of Gould's, namely Keith Carradine, David Carradine, and Barbara Hershey, would regularly show up to disrupt the proceedings (mostly by hassling Harvey).

Harvey carried the trauma of *A Glimpse of Tiger* with him as a sort of untreated gaping psychic wound (though he diplomatically stated years later that it was "water under the bridge"). He elected to pick up the pieces of his career by retreating into the comfortable and the comforting. *The Abdication* (1974), adapted from a play by British dramatist Ruth Wolff, is perfectly aligned with the Harvey signature in terms of subject matter and theme. It is a big, old-fashioned style piece, shot by Geoffrey Unsworth as a lollapalooza of soft focus, heavy fog, and wide lenses. Pauline Kael remarked that the film is "embalmed in such reverence for its own cultural elevation that it loses all contact with the audience." She is not lacking a valid point here, and the rest of its contemporary reviews were not much better. While *The Abdication* avoids the risible historical pageantry of Liv Ullmann's other star vehicle of the time, *Pope Joan* (1972), it couches many long, unwieldy dialogue scenes in an intermittent frisson of heavy style. Judith Crist of *New York* magazine was essentially the only major critic to take a shine to it.

Both *The Abdication* and the big-event telefilm *The Disappearance of Aimee* (1976) surface as dry treatments of their historical sources. Any thrill of the latter is in watching the collaboration and arguable chemistry between Faye Dunaway and Bette Davis (who did not get along on Harvey's set, to say the least). *Players* (1979) is the nadir of Harvey's career. Ex-Paramount head Robert Evans' personally supervised the making and marketing of this pet project, casting ex-wife Ali MacGraw as a tennis pro who falls in love with another pro at Wimbledon. The male lead is Dean Paul Martin, a real-life tennis pro who gives a dreadful performance, one that no crafty director nor editor could rescue. Even in the most de rigueur work, however, Harvey's burgeoning fascination with private lives in public contexts is still palpable. Much was made in the press at the time of the release of *Players* of the fact that Harvey was one of the first to be offered the job of directing *Love Story* (1970), after Larry Peerce (*Goodbye, Columbus*) rejected the offer. Both had "no faith in the script." Evans came back around to Harvey on *Players* because, to Harvey's recollection, "The screen tests I did with Ali on *Love Story* were better than anything she did in the picture. Bob tells me I would have made five or six million dollars by now if I'd stuck with it."

Harvey returned to form with two exquisite consecutive works: the Western *Eagle's Wing* (1979) and the melodrama *Richard's Things* (1980). Both mark his return to the British film industry after a short tenure in Hollywood and American television. It's on the merit of these two pictures alone that Harvey is worth serious study; in both, a clear, dominant style conjoins with a newly evolving but long-in-development thematic spine. The sense of "public" in *Eagle's Wing* is novel for Harvey within his own context. He is attentive to the idea of the land—this particular land—as sacred space. And in this sacred space, public and private merge in ritual alignment, albeit in a way different from how public and private are blurred in *They Might Be Giants*. These are whole new grounds for exploration. We witness a communion, and various bids at communion, in painstaking real time. Cinematographer Billy Williams' vistas are not there simply for picture-postcard snap, crackle and pop. Harvey's pacing of his shots is very deliberate, as if he has opened his eyes to other presences locked inside the images, approaching them with a new, unwavering gaze.

Eagle's Wing is an almost oneiric film about the very meaning and spiritual weight of land, depending on through whose eyes we choose to perceive it. The images must answer to that, and do. The film plays out visually, mostly without spoken dialogue, almost as not to rustle up unwanted spirits and intrusions. It's the Harvey film that is closest to silent cinema aesthetics—one could watch it with the audio turned off and come away having had a robust experience. With a spare script by John Briley, *Eagle's Wing* is perhaps an apotheosis for Harvey as director, while *Richard's Things* in response is his striking, calculated diminuendo. Harvey remembered what drew him to the project: "*Eagle's Wing* was a film with a very thin script in a way but it had a very strong story. It didn't have much detail and no dialogue at all, except for the first ten minutes between Harvey Keitel and Sam Waterston. It was very much a director's subject. The moment I read *Eagle's Wing* I knew very clearly the kind of things I wanted visually, and talked to Billy Williams for days about it. It's about the way we spend our lives reaching for the unobtainable. We search for something which is, sadly, seldom found. The impossible dream, if you like."

At one point in the film, in what could be seen as a microcosm for the whole story, Martin Sheen's character, Pike, invades a ritually sanctified space during the foiled ritual slaughter of the mystical white horse that gives the film its title. The encounter ends in the accidental death of the Indian priest, followed by Pike's appropriation of the beautiful steed, just spared ritual death. The horse is used by the white man for utility, to traverse the space, but in this scene, it is intimated that such an animal assumes ritual and spiritual meaning beyond the practical. The ensuing duel between warrior White Bull (Sam Waterston) and fur-trapper Pike becomes allegory, as two men grapple for dominion over the prized horse. With a posse recruited from a nearby hacienda in hot pursuit, it becomes a four-way struggle.

Eagle's Wing also alludes to colonial (read: Christian) spirituality. At one point, White Bull traps a scorpion first with a tribal trinket decorated with feathers and beads, then exchanges the trinket for a large crucifix-topped chalice-cover pilfered from a hacienda-bound stagecoach he has just ambushed. I am rather partial toward Tom Milne's review of the film in *Time Out London*:

Harvey's masterpiece *Eagle's Wing* is not only a "British Western" but also largely plays without dialogue, as almost a silent film.

"This is unusual not only as a first-class Western made by a British director, but in being virtually a silent movie as an Indian and a white man (Waterston and Sheen), each a failure in his own world and determined to prove otherwise, pursue a strange, obsessive duel for possession of the glorious white stallion that gives the film its title. Quirkishly funny as the duel evolves into a sort of medieval quest attended by its own rituals and chivalries, the film gradually weaves its concentric subplots (various other parties tag along behind, driven by their own passions) into a plaintively spiraling lament for lost illusions. Marvelously shot by Billy Williams, it's weird, hypnotic and magical."

Eagle's Wing is one of the few Westerns that ends with a tearful white man in defeat. As White Bull blazes off into a wide-open plain, kicking up thick white dust, Pike overlooks the victor's escape from a see-all vantage point and mournfully whimpers, "Help me... please... help me." It is a fitting way to end what is Harvey's best film, and what I believe is his "testament film" (the one-film summation of a director's technique, the work that signifies "what cinema means" to that director). It is Harvey's best because it so clearly exemplifies everything he had been working towards throughout his entire directorial career. *Eagle's Wing* and *The Lion in Winter* mark the only occasions that Harvey uses the 'Scope (2.35:1) aspect ratio. *Eagle's Wing* particularly loses its visual and overall artistic soul when it is reformatted to fit the standard television screen. The contrast for me is personal. When I first saw the film on pan-and-scan VHS, I thought it was "fine"—merely another chase film with some unusual twists and flourishes. When I finally viewed it on DVD in its proper dimensions, I realized what a masterpiece it is.

In another in a series of film-to-film departures, *Richard's Things* is based on a novel and screenplay by Frederic Raphael, author of John Schlesinger's *Darling* (1965) and *Far from the Madding Crowd* (1967), Stanley Donen's *Two for the Road* (1967), Kubrick's *Eyes Wide Shut* (1999), and the BBC miniseries "The Glittering Prizes" (1976), which was also based on his own novel. Harvey's drama, featuring Liv Ullmann (yet another Harvey alumnus from her work in *The Abdication*) in a colossally challenging lead role which won her the Best Actress prize at the Venice Film Festival, can easily be and has been lazily displaced into the "average lesbian soap opera" camp. Andrew Sarris, scholar and *Village Voice* critic of the time, was among the few to note its subtle power, writing, "I am hopelessly hooked on the scintillating blend of sensuality and sensibility expressed through the intense rapport of Liv Ullmann and Amanda Redman. Oh those lips and those eyes. Ullmann has never acted as eloquently and emotionally in English. Magic is worth celebrating."

The film tells the story of Kate Morris (Ullmann) who, after twenty years of marriage, receives word that her husband Richard died on a business trip. The hotel register reveals that he had been traveling with another woman. Kate tracks her down her rival and uncovers the secrets of her husband's double life. However, as the two women talk about their respective relationships with Richard, it becomes a kind of exorcism for both of them — one that soon develops into a physical relationship. Where *Eagle's Wing* filled its canvas with breathtaking visuals and largely dialogue-free sound design, *Richard's Things* conversely fills its canvas with the motion picture equivalent of "the talking cure," i.e. scenes that are driven by mutual psychoanalysis and a kind of symbiotic therapy between the two women. The film's cinematographer, however, is Freddie Young, who lensed expansive epic productions like *Lawrence of Arabia* (1962), *Doctor Zhivago* (1965), and *Nicholas and Alexandra* (1971). Young is no stranger to dialogue-driven films that originated as stage plays, the main contemporary one being Robert Enders' *Stevie* (1978), starring Glenda Jackson.

Superficially, the film sounds Bergmanesque: a brooding, *Persona*-adjacent study of love between two women in the wake of trauma. Whereas *Eagle's Wing* finds spiritual communion born from struggle in a land defined as sacred space, *Richard's Things* sees

Richard's Things.

spiritual communion spring from infidelity and untimely death. In tone, the film feels like a cousin of John Schlesinger's *Sunday, Bloody Sunday* (1971), which is fitting for many reasons. Both Schlesinger and Harvey were gay men and were especially sensitive to aspects of the human psyche too often overlooked by heterosexual directors. The question in *Richard's Things* is not one of space, as it had been in *Eagle's Wing*. The spatial world in *Richard's Things* is almost entirely private, although a key scene in a supermarket early in the film, in which the jilted Ullmann slips an incriminating personal item into her rival's (and eventual lover's) shopping basket may momentarily indicate otherwise—i.e. private hostility brought out into the open.

On the whole, however, the idea of public vs. private is slightly more of an abstraction in the film, but not any less of a thematic presence. Ullmann's last words, in voice-over monologue, allude to public illusion and presentation. As she drives off into an uncertain future, we leave her in the film exactly as we first encountered her, in the driver's seat of a car as she tells us, "My pleasure will come from being what people believe me to be, and from not quite being it. I shall never be suspected of being other than what I appear, and I shall appear to be exactly what I am." Fade out, "mic drop" as my generation says. This deceit as conceit is pure Anthony Harvey. A signature is boldly inked.

Roger Corman's New World Pictures distributed *Richard's Things* in the United States, after it had played in competition at the Venice Film Festival and won Ullman the festival's Pasinetti Award for her performance. The film presaged Robert Towne's *Personal Best* (1982), which arrived two years later to critical acclaim and box office death. As that film's gay male counterpart *Making Love* (1982) likewise proved, audiences were not yet ready for such an envelope to be pushed. In the case of *Richard's Things*, audiences predictably avoided it and critics didn't get on board en masse.

Grace Quigley (1985) started as a script by A. Martin Zweibak, entitled *The Ultimate Solution of Grace Quigley*. It had been a pet project of Hepburn's for eleven years when Golan and Globus of Cannon Films agreed to finance it, and Harvey agreed once again to stand at her side as director. Featuring Nick Nolte as a beleaguered hit man faced with administering euthanasia for pay, *Grace Quigley* is notable as a tonal departure for Harvey. It defies his other works, even the wild and woolly *They Might Be Giants*, the gleeful anarchy of which is taken to another (or at least an alternate) level. The characters on Nolte's mercy-kill list are fond of gathering

Anthony Harvey directed Katharine Hepburn in four films. He also enjoyed the closest of friendships with her, all the way up until her death.

for what could only be described as "death parties," where they air their joy at the prospect of facing the eternal void, making it well known how miserable their lives are.

The film premiered at the Cannes Film Festival in May 1984 at 102 minutes, to the most dismal of notices. Originally slated to play in-competition at the festival, its cold reception from the programming committee relegated it to an out-of-competition slot. Theatrically released in America a year later, in May 1985, the film came and went without a whisper. It was twice re-edited: 87 and 94-minute versions surfaced, one of them having been edited by screenwriter Zweiback (who had directed a single feature himself, 1971's *Cactus in the Snow*). Every version had a different ending. Curiously, Leonard Maltin pans Zweiback's version, calling it an "abysmal misfire that manages to be both bland and tasteless," yet in the same review calls the 94-minute director's cut of the film "a touching, funny and surreal black comedy about the problems of the elderly and the right of choice." It goes to show you what a little editing can do! It was Hepburn's final leading role in a theatrical motion picture, and it was also Harvey's final theatrical picture as director. *Grace Quigley*'s troubled post-production and stormy reception signal a confounding (but nonetheless interesting) picture.

Svengali.

Harvey's television works are conspicuously well-staffed. The first-class talent on display in front of and behind the camera routinely suggests prestige. One only need to glance at the cast and crew rosters on *The Glass Menagerie* (1973), *The Patricia Neal Story* (1981), *Svengali* (1983), and *This Can't Be Love* (1994) to see how they exceed expectation for the average telefilm. Cinematographer Billy Williams said of his time shooting *The Glass Menagerie* (1973), "I remember having a discussion with Tony Harvey, who insisted that the movie was actually going to be released as a movie. And so when we shot the picture, we framed it for 1.85 [aspect ratio], because we all felt that the film was going to come out in the cinema as well. It was a good picture, beautifully played. But apart from a showing at the London Film Festival, it never went into the cinema. And I was told afterward, it was because the producers refused to pay the actors the extra fee to release it as a movie. So it was never shown that way."

Harvey, for his part, explained, "We had the most marvelous screening at the London Film Festival. But for some unfathomable reason, the producer David Susskind simply will not open it theatrically, although Kate and everyone agreed to waive their fees. Baffling!" *The Glass Menagerie* nevertheless became the definitive film adaptation of Tennessee Williams' classic play, easily usurping Irving Rapper's 1950 big screen version, until Paul Newman's 1987 movie adaptation came along to contend.

With its pedigree, *Svengali* (1983), starring Peter O'Toole and Jodie Foster, always seemed a shoe-in for theatrical exhibition in other territories after its premiere on CBS. With its scoring by

John Barry (including a soundtrack of catchy original pop songs) and lensing by Larry Pizer, it was groomed for life beyond the small screen (maybe even covertly by the filmmaker)—and so it was that the film was a moderate hit during its 1985 run in Italy. In the middle of post-production, Harvey got into a near-fatal car accident. He lamented, "I hadn't been in the hospital but a week when CBS started cutting the movie, seriously harming it. All the more fragile moments are gone, and so are the exterior scenes that opened up the story."

It's odd that it took Harvey so long to realize a film about the performing arts, because his thematics are a natural fit for stories such as the one in *Svengali*. There's another apt comparison to a John Schlesinger picture in the offing here, in this case *Madame Sousatzka* (1988). In *Svengali*, the rigorous vocal coaching of Jodie Foster by the domineering Peter O'Toole is, in the Harvey context, the idea of "the private" training for the public, and by extension, a private that nurtures the public. "What goes on here is just you and me! No other influence can come between us!" fumes O'Toole's character Anton. The ineffable and the private, with its shared affirmation and attendant intimacy, affects artistic performances for the benefit of others, as in the scene where Foster records her first album and is unable to deliver until O'Toole belatedly turns up in the studio. With Harvey as an expert with the "two-hander," as mentioned earlier, much of the runtime is spent establishing chemistry

This Can't Be Love.

that resonates in light of these pursuits. That chemistry does register, with O'Toole praising Foster as a "gutsy little bird" at the time of the film's airing. (The actor was also effusive to the press about having been creatively reunited with his friend Harvey for the first time since *The Lion in Winter*.) It's as a result of O'Toole and Foster's curious harmony that, generally, I consider *Svengali* one of the most purely entertaining of all Harvey's pictures.

Harvey had all kinds of designs on, and ideas for, other projects that never saw daylight. Years before John Huston's *Under the Volcano* (1984), he was attached to an adaptation of the Malcolm Lowry novel as a Robert Evans production. At one point, he told a reporter, "I'd like to make a musical with some kind of edge, some kind of point to it. And I have great admiration for Patricia Highsmith for the way she gets into people." He also floated a "love story in the *Brief Encounter* mold," but one could argue he got somewhere close with *Richard's Things*. He officially ended his career with *This Can't Be Love* (1994), once again starring Harvey's ever-willing Ms. Ubiquitous, Hepburn, this time paired with Anthony Quinn. They play two former movie stars who shared a brief but bitter marriage in the Forties. In reuniting decades later, they discover that little if anything has changed. Once again, it's the story of the private lives of those living in the public spotlight, and how the one sphere of existence affects, and/or affected, the other. In one scene, the discovery of an unpublished, unflattering memoir manuscript is a casus belli—secrets consigned to be aired as dirty laundry, a sin and spectacle common in Harvey-land. Hepburn's and Quinn's characters know the deep, dark things about each other, the messy particulars that their adoring public, past and present, will never know—just the type of dynamic that clearly excites Anthony Harvey.

In Harvey's *Guardian* obituary, columnist Ronald Bergan breaks with the cold objectivity normally afforded most newsprint remembrances, relating a visit he made to the home of Katharine Hepburn in her final years. Displayed prominently in her parlor was a photograph of Harvey directing her with Peter O'Toole on *The Lion in Winter*. Bergan remembers "her eyes lighting up." "Dear Tony, looking so young and thoughtful," she told him, beaming with tenderness. "A real English gentleman and a brilliant director. One of the best I've ever worked with." Certainly no small praise, in light of her collaborations with Cukor, Hawks, Ford, Capra, Huston, Stevens, and Lean.

There is a myth among hardened auteurists that "actors' directors" of Harvey's ilk are anonymous because they are slaves to text, and to nuts-and-bolts craft, regardless of how difficult such a craft can be to hone well, let alone master. It is a rare skill, one that takes time and ample experience to develop and train like a muscle, yet it is routinely disrespected in such conversations. Thus, artists like Anthony Harvey got shortchanged. He is precisely the type of director who hides in plain sight. But no matter how famous or historically renowned his characters are, they are never myths or untouchable deities, the type that Mozart in *Amadeus* disparages as figures "so lofty it sounds as if they shit marble." There was a dynamic there that Harvey individually—with concerted specificity!—pursued as to put it under the microscope of his art. When his films were not historically rooted, he still looked for means of consistent thematic exploration in modern stories. All streams flowed into one current, and that is the definition of an auteur. The fact that Hepburn adored him is the sweetest of bonuses, but a bonus nonetheless. That it remains his epitaph is probably how he would have wanted it.

Theatrical Feature Films: *Dutchman* (1967), *The Lion in Winter* (1968), *They Might Be Giants* (1971), *A Glimpse of Tiger* (1973, unfinished), *The Glass Menagerie* (1973), *The Abdication* (1974), *The Disappearance of Aimee* (1976), *Players* (1979), *Eagle's Wing* (1979), *Richard's Things* (1980), *The Patricia Neal Story* (a.k.a. *An Act of Love*) (1981, with Anthony Page), *Svengali* (1983), *Grace Quigley* (1985, a.k.a. *The Ultimate Solution of Grace Quigley*), *This Can't Be Love* (1994)

20. To Cast a Skyward Gaze
The John Guillermin Vision

Most of this text was originally the script for a video essay on the 2024 Imprint Films Blu-ray release of The Bridge at Remagen, *titled "To Cast a Skyward Gaze: Making the Case for John Guillermin."*

Bloodied, bruised, grizzled, and otherwise depleted men often look upward to the heavens at some point during a John Guillermin film. In recognition of something lost, of what should be and isn't, of the mystery of what lurks beyond our natural world, at a dream deferred or extinguished, in some cases literally, as in his biggest hit *The Towering Inferno* (1974). These moments are emotionally and psychologically framed in the same way David Lean's heroes gaze into the distance, at a vanishing point beyond any number of horizons, or the way Steven Spielberg's heroes gaze in wonder, shock, and awe at something off-camera—something we cannot see, or haven't yet seen. In all cases, reverence is the refrain. For John Guillermin, it's an acknowledgement of something bigger than ourselves, an encounter with our own mortality, and for a moment, perhaps some ability to transcend it. It's as if a theoretical passport is about to get stamped, and you get to go one way, or the other, with all the stakes of life and death itself.

The consensus on Guillermin was that he was "difficult," or at best temperamental. The word "irrascible" crops up more than once in any research. Producer David Wolper didn't mince words or brandish euphemisms when he called him a "pain in the ass" on the set of *The Bridge at Remagen* (1969). *Deliverance* author James Dickey even called him megalomaniacal. Orson Welles, who worked with him on *House of Cards* (1968), went right for the jugular, referring to him as "one of the truly outstanding incompetents." All the while, Joseph Losey cited Guillermin as one of the few British directors with a "signature," putting him in a distinguished class with Carol Reed, Alexander Mackendrick, Lindsay Anderson, and Seth Holt. Raymond Durgnat, who called Guillermin's stylings

Guillermin's characters regularly cast their eyes to the heavens.

"dashing," notes that a French critic described him as "the Paganini of the mise en scène."

Whether the collective impression of his "difficult" persona is based on mere reading of the various accounts, or my personally encountering people who worked with him directly who often elect to "plead the Fifth" so to speak, a portrait certainly gets painted. David Cairns, on his Shadowplay blog, recalls a friend of his who worked with Guillermin listening to a review calling a Guillermin film "nasty, slick, and superficial," and retorting, "That's John!" That aside, while he's not widely or traditionally considered one of the so-called "great" directors, or an auteur on *terribly* many lips, John Guillermin did develop a cultivated cult following, and he has now been written about, by serious scholars such as Neil Sinyard and Olaf Möller (who published an appreciation in *Film Comment*). Their case for him is perspicacious, intelligently framed, and sometimes quite passionate. All this was enough fodder to comprise a volume of critical essays written on his work, edited by his widow, Mary Guillermin.

So what is there to John Guillermin? What's he all about? According to one obituary published upon his death in 2015 at age 89, quote, "Regardless of whether he was directing a light comedy, war epic, or crime drama, Mr. Guillermin had a reputation as an intense, temperamental perfectionist, notorious for screaming at cast and crew alike. His domineering manner often alienated producers and actors. But Mr. Guillermin's impeccable eye and ability to capture both intimate moments and large-scale action scenes usually overcame that reputation." Neil Sinyard observes, "Perhaps this variety of output was the reason behind the critical underestimation. He seemed capable of turning his hands to anything; he was a difficult director to pigeonhole, and auteurist critics have always struggled with the idea of versatility."

Durgnat's work on Guillermin is worth exploring further (as his writings on British cinema probe the deepest on directors such as Guillermin). When he writes that it's possible that "many artists endeavor to fit their style to their subject, so that one has really to ascribe auteur *status* to chameleons like René Clément in France, Alberto Lattuada in Italy, or John Huston in the U.S.A.," he notes that "the British cinema offers two such directors: Alberto Cavalcanti and John Guillermin."

Nick Redman, a film and soundtrack historian powerhouse that the wider cinema community misses greatly, describes him in the opening of Mary Guillermin's volume on her husband: "John

Rapture.

Guillerman was, even in his eighties, an irrepressible life force, funny, cantankerous, profane, sophisticated, urbane. A gentleman of the old school, a pilot in the RAF during World War II, and later an eloquent filmmaker of taste and judgment—his movies speak for themselves, and also for him, for he is there inside them, his personality tumbling out in every reel."

To his dying day, Guillermin insisted that his arty melodrama *Rapture* (1965) was his best film. I personally concur that *Rapture* is indeed his masterpiece, as indeed beyond being "arty" it is also, more importantly, artful, a compelling, expressive, and expressionist character-driven film—in Mary Guillermin's words, "the only film he directed that wholly satisfied his vision as an artist." His defenders and the scholars who have made him their pet cause insist that *The Blue Max* (1966), which came immediately after it, was his testament film (the term "testament film," according to French cineastes, being defined essentially as the clearest distillation of a director's style and thematic focus).

His Seventies filmography is rife with big budget genre outings, the tentpole productions of the era, namely *The Towering Inferno* (1974) and the Dino De Laurentiis remake of *King Kong* (1976). Though one could make the argument that these two pictures feature certain hallmarks of Guillermin's constitution, personal pursuit, and style of directing, they seem more the manifestations of their producers' brands, especially in the case of Master of Disaster Irwin Allen (namely "spectacle, spectacle, and more spectacle"). His *Shaft in Africa* (1973) is the rather thankless third in a successful, culturally groundbreaking trilogy that set the standard for a whole new genre.

Smack dab in the middle of these "big look" pictures is a stop-over in Canada, where he directed *Mr. Patman* (1980), the offbeat psychological study of male psych ward nurse losing his own mind, starring James Coburn in the title role. In the full blush of its tax shelter era, Canada gave Guillermin one of his last opportunities to devise a much simpler offbeat character piece, though not one that critics valued, or that audiences got around to seeing in any appreciable way. Though it died a quiet death on the nascent home video market (under the title *Crossover*), *Mr. Patman* is idiosyncratic (and in some ways singular) in how it depicts psychosis. It is more subdued in comparison to the high style of *Rapture*, but casts the same eye toward psychic survival. When stacking the two films against each other qualitatively, however, the inadequacy of *Mr. Patman* becomes palpable.

Guillermin's by then erratic career coda-ed with thankless assignments that flopped as epically as they attempted to play. I'm referring to *Sheena* (1984) and the hideous, ill-fated sequel *King Kong Lives* (1976), produced during a period of mourning for its director, following the untimely death of his son Michael. That is not to say that *Sheena* in particular as a widescreen spectacle altogether lacks visual appeal, with its ravishing 'Scope frames and stagings. Guillermin rarely if ever lacked visual flair, but whatever issues that cropped up in the later pictures resulted from intractable scripting issues rather than a bankruptcy of visual imagination.

How did Guillermin wind up on these Seventies and Eighties mega-movies? He had proven his mettle for directing to such scale on the war sagas *Guns at Batasi* (1964) and *The Bridge at Remagen* (1969), as well as a trio of George Peppard action-adventure extravaganzas: *The Blue Max* (1966), *P.J.* (1967), and *House of Cards* (1968). As Olaf Möller writes in his *Film Comment* piece, he "hit his stride at the end of the Fifties, just as a post-studio style of filmmaking was arising. For the admirers of these idioms, Guillermin's meticulously executed and unapologetically classical works were anathema." And that style of work stuck for him.

There is art in such Guillermin outings, but the artistic and auteurist meat of his career is found most conspicuously in his films of the Fifties and Sixties. He couches his favored theme of heroism, especially untenable heroism among a once-esteemed class of men now grappling with the need to merely survive, in big and burly genre-oriented motion pictures, ones that are disproportionately melancholic.

In a comedy like *Waltz of the Toreadors* (1962), ostensibly a typical Peter Sellers vehicle of its time, there's an anomalous melancholy as a kind of palimpsest under the broad romp-ish exterior. Durgnat identifies a "misanthropic edge" to the film. Sellers plays a vaguely Blimp-ish officer with many a romantic complication, and rather than overaccentuate the character to caricatured proportions, under Guillermin's direction he realizes a more unaffected, humanized, and Livesey-ish Blimp figure. The dance sequence that gives the film its title is a marvel of camera movement and staging, in that Guillermin has us constantly on the move, swooping above the waltzers, dancing in swift circles around our principals, tracking them to the outer bailey, dutching the angle almost severely, only to readjust at the musical coda. He then cuts back to reveal the expanse of the exterior in what, by all objective measures, is a painterly composition. No average Sellers comedy, this — and even more so during a sober, poignant dialogue scene between Sellers and Margaret Leighton, in which they air regrets about their marriage.

Guillermin's restless camera is also in evidence in *Town on Trial* (1957), featuring a master-stroke signature sequence with a striking (and novel for its time) point-of-view gaze that places us behind the eyes of a killer stalking his prey. This prefigured the likes of De Palma, Carpenter, and Argento by quite a number of years. In another scene, a series of whip-pans introduces a group of suspects. Yet, his patient, static introduction to the Richard Attenborough character in *Guns at Batasi* (1964) stands in contrast. Much of a director's job, after all, is knowing innately when to move the camera and when not.

Rapture's camera language is active and imaginative. Perhaps one might even call it extroverted. From the very first scene in the movie this is apparent. An elaborate, hyper (almost drunken) two-minute-long take frantically tracks the flurry of activity at a wedding reception hall, rivaling anything that a De Palma and Scorsese would achieve later on. The average shot length in *Rapture* is conspicuously extended, relative to other films in release at the time. The boldness of its style and overall storytelling approach is often likened to the work then coming out of the French New Wave. While the camerawork and chiaroscuro monochrome lighting by

Left: Guillermin's camera floats and dances in this eponymous scene from *Waltz of the Toreadors*. As Peter Sellers whisks his lady outside, the camera dutches to both sides, then lands on a painterly wide shot.

Marcel Grignon feels redolent of—or at least adjacent to—the style of Raoul Coutard (especially when held up against Tony Richardson's *Mademoiselle*, another contemporary Gallic retreat for a British director), *Rapture*'s true roots feel more planted in the Ingmar Bergman films of the Fifties, principally *Summer Interlude* (1951) and especially *Summer With Monika* (1953).

Via a pastiche of Euro-art-film tricks and tropes, Guillermin positions his story as a spiritual confessional. In the film's final scene, his childlike heroine once again casts her eyes to the heavens, the camera spinning directly above her. It's no wonder Guillermin felt as close to *Rapture* as he did, and it's astounding that a major Hollywood studio, in this case 20th Century Fox, underwrote such an outwardly "arty" picture. One can only suppose that its majestic vistas of the Brittany coast buttered up Francophile studio head Darryl Zanuck, who also had a hand in casting Patricia Gozzi (of *Sundays and Cybèle*) as the lead.

Sinyard notes that Guillermin's endings are "more equivocal than affirmative." The best his heroes can achieve are pyrrhic victories. At the end of *Waltz of the Toreadors*, a suicidal Sellers, holding a pistol to his head, is thwarted by the arrival of a silhouetted figure in a wide shot. It's the pretty young thing who's been hired as his new maid. We realize that a familiar, likely destructive, and (in its way) "vicious" cycle is to repeat—or is it just another trip around a wearying merry-go-round. At the end of Guillermin's other collaboration with Sellers, *Never Let Go* (1960), the crooked Sellers character is arrested following a brutal brawl, while a bruised and bloodied Richard Todd returns home to an empty flat with his eye swollen shut—a winner disfigured. For any other director, this final accent mark would be superfluous and the film would have ended with a final orchestra hit at the fighting grounds (in this case, a garage). For Guillermin, the horrible gravity and the cost of a struggle is most essential, even when the character's objective has been fulfilled. Judith Crist quipped in her review of the World War II caper *The Bridge at Remagen* that if the audience had not known beforehand, one would be hard pressed to guess from the film who won the war. Even Lieutenant Stachel's blaze of aerial glory at the end of *The Blue Max* is an escape from accountability that ends in death.

Möller elaborates, "In his cool, unflinching cinema, tired, traumatized men in desperate situations fight with dour determination for a few shreds of dignity. There's nothing conventionally uplifting about his films. His tales of violence, grimy glory, and defeat

Guillermin plays with Dutch (canted) angles, Y-axis placement, and reflections throughout his masterpiece *Rapture*.

Guns at Batasi.

conceded with stoicism, don't make for easy viewing experiences. At their finest, Guillermin's films are howls from the soul's darker recesses. Theirs is a savage heart."

From *The Blue Max*:

VON KLUGERMAN: We are about to honor your dead.

LT. STACHEL: So I see.

VON KLUGERMAN: Well, aren't you coming? It's an order.

LT. STACHEL: Why?

VON KLUGERMAN: Because our commanding officer has made it one. He believes in chivalry.

LT. STACHEL: Chivalry? To kill a man then make a ritual out of saluting him, it's hypocrisy. If they kill me, I don't want anyone to salute.

VON KLUGERMAN: They probably won't.

LT. STACHEL: Alright, let's get it over with, shall we?

In *Never Let Go* (1960), Richard Todd is an ordinary man so consumed with day-to-day survival that he attempts to be his own hero, at great personal cost, because the authorities are too hidebound, complacent, or impotent to proactively help in any way. In Guillermin's world, the cost of being quixotic is blood, guts, and very little glory. When scolded by his wife to let it go ("You're not meant to push and shove your way through life; you're not tough enough"), Todd's character is only emboldened. His chastening, and resulting diminishment as a man, is a motivator. He appears to be on an inevitable collision course with death, or at best defilement, at the hands of cast-against-type gangster Peter Sellers. Sinyard writes that, though people were accustomed to Sellers' comic persona and were "unwilling to adjust to this new example of versatility," it was a characterization "unnervingly close to his unstable and occasionally violent personality" (as the public only learned of his now notorious erratic behaviors after his death). It took true perspicacity on Guillermin's part to tap Sellers for the role. With the menace made vivid (his use of severe, low-angle close-ups being crucial), he effectively orchestrates a sense of dread as hero and adversary draw inexorably closer to the final confrontation.

Rapture centers on a pathologically lonely girl obsessed with dolls, scarecrows, and a coterie of inanimate friends, who winds up at the center of a survival-driven escaped convict's possibly sinister desires. *The Bridge at Remagen* follows two battalions, Allied and Axis, who race to a confrontation at a bridge that can end the war, but is surviving the battle less important that surviving the war itself... and who among them is cut out for heroism by this point?

From *The Bridge at Remagen*:

BARNES: I know it's been a hard blow. It's always a shock to lose a buddy, a man you worked with and fought with. I mean, we're all human. I guess what I'm trying to say is, I realize Captain Colt was your friend. He was my friend too.

The Bridge at Remagen.

Even in a later, lesser picture like *Sheena*,
Guillermin's use of widescreen is dynamic.

HARTMAN: Bullshit.

BARNES: Would you care to rephrase, lieutenant.

HARTMAN: You don't have any friends out here, major.
Neither do I. We can't afford it, neither one of us.

Tarzan's Greatest Adventure (1959) is the most rough, ready,
and rugged of the Tarzan movies, and the melodrama of the
diamond smuggler villains, men so obviously lacking in honor
(especially the kind of honor Guillermin prized, even in his characters' defeat), often takes center stage.

These aspects do not just crop up in, but altogether *prop* up
Town on Trial, *The Whole Truth*, *I Was Monty's Double*, *Guns at
Batasi*, *The Blue Max*, *P.J.*, *House of Cards* and other Guillermin
films. There's little in the way of uplift. All are the testament of a
man with a stubborn dark side—a deep, so often fleeting melancholy, a depression that fueled his overall artistic ethic, his ethos,
and the individual moments he dared to wax poetic. It's all in those
eyes, cast to heaven, that ask questions we can't hear with our
ears, but rather in the darkest recesses of our souls—a passionately
agonized transmission.

Afterword: I might not beat the drum for Guillermin as rigorously as I do for others covered in this overall text. But though I
find him wanting in comparison with the top-tier class of genre-
fluid auteurs like Sidney J. Furie or Franklin J. Schaffner (he
might need a special secret ingredient, a middle initial J.—I jest,
of course), I certainly think he deserves further attention. It's all
for the better that Guillermin doesn't match Furie or Schaffner's
chameleon proficiency, because he clearly did his best work well

before hitching his wagon to Hollywood. The more I researched the video piece I created for Imprint, the more I became convinced. I'd certainly much rather watch Furie's *Gable and Lombard* or Schaffner's *Sphinx* (their flops) than *King Kong Lives* or *Sheena* (Guillermin's flops) but a voice and an imprint is nevertheless present. I have yet to see many of his earliest films, so he shall remain a subject for further study.

Theatrical Feature Films: *High Jinks in Society* (1949), *Paper Gallows* (1950), *Smart Alec* (1951), *Two on the Tiles* (1951), *Four Days* (1951), *Bachelor in Paris* (1952), *Miss Robin Hood* (1952), *Operation Diplomat* (1953), *Shop Spoiled* (1954), *Adventure in the Hopfields* (1954), *Thunderstorm* (1956), *Town on Trial* (1957), *The Whole Truth* (1958), *I Was Monty's Double* (1958, a.k.a. *Hell, Heaven or Hoboken*), *Tarzan's Greatest Adventure* (1959), *The Day They Robbed the Bank of England* (1960), *Never Let Go* (1960), *Waltz of the Toreadors* (1963), *Tarzan Goes to India* (1964), *Guns at Batasi* (1964), *Rapture* (1965), *The Blue Max* (1966), *P.J.* (1967), *House of Cards* (1968), *The Bridge at Remagen* (1969), *El Condor* (1970), *Skyjacked* (1972), *Shaft in Africa* (1973), *The Towering Inferno* (1974), *King Kong* (1976), *Death on the Nile* (1978), *Mr. Patman* (1980, a.k.a. *Crossover*), *Sahara* (1983, fired), *Sheena* (1984), *King Kong Lives* (1986), *The Tracker* (1988)

21. Mod Man Out
The Clive Donner Vision

This is the first publication of this essay, written especially for this volume.

Face it, it's a filthy stinking world… but there are some smashing things in it. And I want them!

Jimmy Brewster (Alan Bates) in
Nothing But the Best (1964)

Andrew Sarris was something of a Clive Donner enthusiast, once naming his *What's New Pussycat* (1965) the second best of its year, topping other offerings from Losey, Antonioni, Godard, and Polanski which were further down his list. He professed to having seen the film four times, remarking that "Each time I find new nuances in the direction, the writing, the playing, and, above all, the music" and emphasizing "This is not the movie it seems at first glance." He praised Donner as a "gifted stylist with an eye for contemporaneous detail" who "seems to be emerging as Britain's answer to Vincente Minnelli." What was the nature of such an esteemed critic's love of such a frothy, featherweight farce that was flayed in other critical quarters (even as it raked in box-office dollars)? Well, he marveled that Donner "tried to use comedy to be serious about sex, which is something you can't yet do in a 'serious' movie." Woody Allen, for his part, was politely disgruntled about what Donner (and especially producer Charles K. Feldman) did to his original *What's New Pussycat* script: "I kept thinking, just get out of my way and let me show you how to do this." (The debuting Woody was a few years off from actually directing a script of his own, though he did remark to interviewer Eric Lax that Donner was a "very sweet guy.")

Because of Sarris' unique, often full-throated advocacy, I'm going to continue referring back to him and his reviews at various points in this study.

The schizoid rhythms of this Maestro of Mod's late sixties pictures synthesize a brassy rhythm and screwball logic all their own, always with a moral vision that hardly seems germane to all the pizzazz. The sexual exploits of *What's New Pussycat* and *Here We Go Round the Mulberry Bush* (1968) rouse in our heroes any number of anxieties and misgivings about the permissive Sixties, even as they reap the boudoir benefits of it. Yet neither film feels the unbearable weight of a sermonizing director's moralism beating off its back. It was with those two films in particular that Donner made his name as the reigning British lord-purveyor of the swinging sex farce – a sort of stylistic cousin to Richard Lester. (Lester won the Cannes Palme d'Or for his own Swinging London sex farce *The Knack... and How to Get It*, the same year that his would-be cousin's *Pussycat* meowed... uhh, I mean bowed). But Donner walks, runs, jumps, and—only occasionally—stands still in a style that is breezy rather than preachy, and punchy rather than suffocating. The characters' doubts and their wafflings are what make Donner the Swinging London zeitgeist's most compelling and, from today's vantage point, most complex directing talent. The lusty fumes emitted from his moral stands are not at cross-purposes, but rather, they more resemble something like a cross-examination.

"It remains to be seen if the prophet can avoid being swallowed up by his own revolution," Sarris poses in *The American Cinema*. "With Donner, it is not so much a question of aesthetics versus ethics, as of decorative complicity versus dramatic conflict." Though he publicly started shuffling off the Donner train by 1968, remarking that the "mod mushiness" of the director's *Mulberry Bush* marked "an ominous turn in [his] career," Sarris did make sure to include Donner in his *Interviews with Film Directors* book. This interview focused entirely on *Pussycat*, with Donner alphabetically flanked on either side of his chapter by Cukor and Dreyer. Needless to say, Sarris had Donner keeping distinguished but perhaps otherwise wholly unlikely company—truly, the mod man out.

Around the time of *The American Cinema*'s publication, Donner had released his reviled first American film *Luv* (1967), from the Murray Schisgal play, starring Jack Lemmon, Elaine May, and Peter Falk. This certainly ain't no Arthur Hiller-style romp that bore the stamp of a Ray Stark or Neil Simon. Its vaguely Catskills quasi-dadaism found a Carnaby Street inflection with Donner at the helm, resulting in confusion and dismay. Clive Donner unmistakably put his own zany, almost cartoon-like, and very "with-it" stamp on the affair. I can personally verify that a summer 2024 screening of Quentin Tarantino's personal 16mm pan-and-scan print (likely a television station copy) at the New Beverly went over like gangbusters when it played alongside May's *A New Leaf* (1971). I'll note that a few weeks after that screening, I was given a ride by a veteran Los Angeles actor who loves Murray Schisgal and has nothing but rancor for the *Luv* film adaptation. Considering that the New Beverly audience was predominately young, there may very well be a generational divide here—the youth largely don't know Schisgal, thus are divorced from any potential point of comparison. The film's ability to exist independently from its source has nearly six intervening decades to thank for any new lease on life.

Most of all, Donner's films consider the absurd (and absurdist), devilish detours on the road to success, privilege, and contentment (including sexual/romantic contentment). This is particularly the case in *Nothing But the Best* (1964), starring Alan Bates as an deviously enterprising young lad who, desiring upward mobility, is given lessons in conniving refinement. Donner's own road to success was paved for a, shall we say, pleasant drive. Much like his contemporary Anthony Harvey, Donner got his wings as a director during his time as an editor—both have impressive resumés working for some of Britain's greatest legends. His salad days were as illustrious as one's salad days could be, first spent as editing trainee under the Archers on *The Life and Death of Colonel Blimp* (1943) at age 17. He then edited for the likes of Carol Reed and David Lean, before building himself up as the indispensably skilled scissor-and-cement wizard behind many a Fifties British classic: the beloved motorhead comedy *Genevieve* (1953), the *Cabaret* forerunner *I Am a Camera* (1955), and the Alistair Sim *A Christmas Carol* (1951), which he later remade for television in 1984 with George C. Scott.

His early directing efforts, programmers for J. Arthur Rank, are not much at all in line with the style and thematics he would develop in the decade that followed. *Heart of a Child* (1958) feels, in too many ways, like the Philip Leacock classic that Leacock never got to actually make, with its story of a beleaguered boy's devotion to his beloved St. Bernard dog. The film did introduce Donner to Donald Pleasence, who played the key role of Mac in Donner's breakthrough, the film adaptation of Harold Pinter's *The Caretaker* (1963). Produced independently and completed with the

The Caretaker.

help of monetary contributions from a distinguished roster of industry luminaries like Richard Burton, Leslie Caron, Noël Coward, Harry Saltzman, Peter Sellers, and Liz Taylor, *The Caretaker* was released within months of Joseph Losey's formative and now classic Pinter project *The Servant* (1963). Both are cutting investigations of class, power structures, and master-and-servant dynamics in classic Pinteresque fashion. While they were met with rapturous critical acclaim, only Losey's masterpiece gets playtime today, though *The Caretaker* is the play that "made" Pinter and established him in the international theater scene. It remains today one of his most popular and often performed works.

None of the principals in *The Caretaker*—including Robert Shaw, Alan Bates, and Pleasence—accepted payment for their work, because they were committed to just getting the film version made after the studios and distributors rejected it. All had profit participation, but it was a true labor of love for everyone involved. Relative to Donner's boisterous later films, this one is conspicuous for its restraint and its nervous tranquility. For lack of a music score, Donner instead had composer Ron Grainer design a vibrant soundscape that firmly embeds us in the film's claustrophobic and even hermetic world. As a consequence, we are forced to live inside Pinter's trademark pauses and silences. Whereas another director might have scored the film in the manner of, for instance, John

Barry on *Séance on a Wet Afternoon* (1964), with its silky, ethereal tensions, Donner never hits us with a sonic flinch, whether dulcet or dissonant. He locks us in, fully immersing us in the space, the situations, and the dynamics of both. This is, of course, not to fault Losey for his use of jazzy Johnny Dankworth in *The Servant*; for all its similarities, *The Caretaker* is a film of different needs and predilections. The former needs to ripple out while the latter needs to breathe.

It is in Donner's decoupage that he transcends the staginess such material risks. The cinematographer here is Nicolas Roeg (who would go on to shoot *Nothing But the Best* for Donner as well). Whether a shot lingers, cuts to one character or another, to a two-shot, or to a wide master, the mise en scène and editorial logic work in concert uncommonly well. Penelope Gilliat in her review for *The Observer* wrote, "A lot of films made from stage sources deserve the ritual snobbish abuse about photographed plays, but I hope *The Caretaker* doesn't come in for it. Every line in it involved rather delicate decisions of filmmaking, and Clive Donner and the cameraman have taken them impeccably." The British Film Institute's head of special collection Janet Moat posits that Donner "deploys a non-musical soundtrack, close-ups, and two-shots to unsettling and menacing effect."

Drama critic Michael Billington observes, "While retaining the structure and themes of the original play, it also improves on it. Pinter pared down the dialogue. At the same time, Donner used the camera to lend the action a social context, and to remind us that the three characters exist not only in the room, but also in the harsh, bleak, unforgiving outside world. You can see them, if you so choose, as God the father, God the son, and God the holy ghost—or ego, superego, and id, but the film establishes that they are first and foremost real people in a real situation." Indeed, many of Roeg's camera moves are almost whispered, as if the operator is some sort of ghost or spectral hand, especially in the scenes involving Robert Shaw's psychiatrically scarred Aston. His monologue about electro-shock treatments is just as riveting as the famed U.S.S. Indianapolis monologue he would deliver twelve years later in *Jaws* (1975).

Charity almost inevitably exposes cruelty and condescension. Class is as primal as earth, air, fire, and water in the cinema of Clive Donner, especially in this early stage. *Some People* (1962), one of the better "trad, dad" rock musicals of its time, is another excursion into the working class and society's unseen, in its way. It's not

Alan Bates and Denholm Elliott in *Nothing But the Best.*

quite like other contemporary British youth pictures, in that it started as a documentary concept. Donner felt such a piece would only resonate for those with sympathy for the Duke of Edinburgh's Award Scheme—recognizing lower-income young adults who succeed in "social self-improvement"—so he made the case for a fiction feature that won out. Rather than do what had already been done by Karel Reisz with *We Are the Lambeth Boys* (1958), a direct cinema docudrama from the Free Cinema movement about a youth club in south London, *Some People* is a simple but effective proto-"garage band" musical with flourishes of style that would have otherwise been shafted in favor of capital-M Message. (The music ain't bad either!) Ray Brooks (the lothario in Lester's *The Knack*) and David Hemmings (who would later headline Donner's *Alfred the Great*) head up the young cast.

Never was class consciousness and social climbing more salient for Donner than in *Nothing But the Best*. Adapted from the short story "The Best of Everything" by Stanley Ellin and given a right working-over by Frederic Raphael, one year off from his success on John Schlesinger's *Darling* (1965), the film cross-stitches a gnarly satirical grit and sardonic warp that would become essential to Donner's tonal approach and overall style moving forward—and he would achieve this in collaborating with many first-tier screenwriters, including Woody Allen and Larry Kramer. Because the film was a staple of Bravo and Encore programming back in the 1990s (which is when I first saw it), the Millicent Martin title tune became an earworm for me in the decades that followed, for whatever strange reason (along with the cornball Sinatra-knockoff song by Jack Jones from the opening titles of Edward Dmytryk's *Anzio*, also a programming staple of that time).

What comes into play here is Donner's biting refinement. In this particular case, an indolent aristocrat as played by Denholm Elliott takes on an impetuous and increasingly devious pupil who acquires a cutthroat taste for the jugular all too easily—a handsome opportunist who wants to fly high and never leave the sky. The "biting" part is there on the page, thanks to Raphael, while the director never lacks for the "refinement" part, especially in one pivotal scene, a grisly murder implied only by a splattered gob of shaving cream on a mirror. Alan Bates' Jimmy Brewster is the perfect Ted Kotcheff-type character, a natural born climber looking to break out of his current station by any and all means available... and necessary. In its mordant wit, and its tongue-in-cheek disdain for privilege and upward mobility, *Nothing But the Best* is a kind of New Wave-midpoint sine qua non for the Angry Young Man cycle's transition into something far colder and more cynical, with pictures like *Negatives* (with its twisted perversions and subversions), *Two Gentlemen Sharing* (chockful of the aforementioned Kotcheff's Canadian cynicism), the work of Peter Collinson, and most crucially, Lindsay Anderson's *if....* (with its whiff of bloody revolution at the hands of radicalized schoolboys). Donner might have migrated to, and set up shop in, comedy territory after his celebrated Pinter adaptation, but he offers something far more caustic when he starts playing for laughs here. In highlighting the chasm that yawns between not only ambition and reality, but ambition and consequence, Donner digs down to show us how mod soil—which lays the ground for a garden of pleasures, delights, and privileges—also has traces of radioactivity. *Nothing But the Best* ends with a discovery of Brewster's crime, met with his foxy smirk, followed by a title card that reads "The End is a phrase which usually closes other people's stories: it never applies to one's own."

Something also at play in Donner is how he deliberately roots many of his films firmly in their locations, whether it be the bonechilling Hackney in *The Caretaker*, London's affluent, turned-out Richmond area in *Nothing But the Best*, the ever-festive cluster of Paris arrondissements in *What's New Pussycat*, and the sleek glass-and-steel modernist post-war "pop-up town" Stevenage in *Here We Go Round the Mulberry Bush*. All carry distinct character that plays into each film's own character; the places are themselves players.

Many bedroom doors slam in the third act of *What's New Pussycat.*

Even a curiously designed traffic interchange in Stevenage is put to good graphic use, as it gives the *Mulberry Bush* title sequence animators an orb shape on which to geometrically superimpose the first of their psychedelic lettering ("Clive Donner's film of"). And even when the drama is mostly constrained to a single interior, as in *The Caretaker*, it remains rather a marvel how attuned Donner always is to locale, conscious of a specific environment's importance in his narrative construction.

Producer Charles K. Feldman, onetime agent, was a longtime Hollywood fixture that historian Nathaniel Thompson accurately labeled a "more is more" personality with "a fondness for mayhem and excess." He took a meeting with Donner after the successes of *The Caretaker* and *Nothing But the Best*, giving him four scripts to read and consider, including ones for *The Group* (1966, later directed by Sidney Lumet) and *Casino Royale* (1967). (It seems as though Donner was one of few contemporary directors who didn't have a hand in that infamous Bond-sploitation fiasco.) Donner was drawn immediately to *What's New Pussycat* and a deal was inked. Originally slated as a vehicle for Warren Beatty, it was rewritten and overhauled when Beatty bailed and Peter O'Toole replaced him. With the Art Nouveau, Aubrey Beardsley-style kitsch of its titles and transitions, courtesy of the Richard Williams Studio, the madcap romp is Donner's rally cry against sexual repression, a purpose he expresses in his interview with Sarris. "We are, or should be, moving into a period where sex is having the bogeyman trappings removed from it," he stated. "Everybody thinks more, plays more, talks more about sex, sexuality, and in sexual terms than they ever admit to themselves in public. [...] Dirty jokes have always been an outlet. I think that younger people today just talk about it and don't really bother with dirty jokes."

Peter O'Toole's character Michael James does not actively seek a life of constant, "on-demand" sexual extravagance, nor is he tempted by satyrdom. The film's many women quite simply come to him, without much effort on his part. He seeks to shake off his "unbearable lightness of being" in favor of commitment to Carole (Romy Schneider), yet is hampered at every turn, partly by his horndog Viennese shrink (Peter Sellers) but mostly by a bevy of beautiful and neurotic ladies. As in Tony Richardson's *Tom Jones* (1963), a bawdy megahit that snagged all the major Oscars the year that *Pussycat* went into production, a bag of cinema tricks keeps pace with the Rabelaisian ribaldry, and feeds into a kind of controlled meta anarchy. Fourth-wall-breaking, title cards, and over-cranked motion-heavy silent-film shots rule the roost in Richardson's film. Donner harvests his own novelties. In one scene of *Pussycat*, as O'Toole pontificates about monogamy, Donner flashes the text "Author's Message" in the title's swirling typeface. There are a number of breaks in continuity as well, all to emphasize—once again—the absurd (and absurdist) detours on the road to success, privilege, and/or contentment. This is the pulse of all Donner's work. I'm not about to take Sarris' nearly evangelical

Here We Go Round the Mulberry Bush.

tack here, but I can at least agree with him to some degree that there is more to *Pussycat* than most have ever given it credit for, especially when viewed in the larger context of its director's oeuvre (not to mention the fact that the laughs still come steady and true).

It makes the most sense to weigh *Pussycat* together with *Here We Go Round the Mulberry Bush*, as the wacky odysseys of sexually frustrated men twitterpated in scene after scene by a rolling roster of buxom "birds." O'Toole easily gets his, and he gets it much too much, while foppish *Mulberry* lead Barry Evans, a callow cross between Davy Jones and Manfred Mann's Paul Jones, is a virgin monomaniacally driven by his hormonal quest for that first carnal rite of passage. This era of British cinema never wanted for sexcapades, bearing in mind Lewis Gilbert's cultural landmark *Alfie* (1966) and Michael Sarne's less successful but charming *Joanna* (1968). Rakishness for its own sake isn't necessarily what Donner pursues for himself as thematic practitioner, though. Again, there is the moral vision and the sense that ceaseless pursuit of such conquest dries out as to become stultifying. This idea prefigures later British films like Damian Harris' *The Rachel Papers* (1989) and Randal Kleiser's *Getting It Right* (1989)—though, of course, we know that the cinema never lacked for "losing virginity" sagas ever since the censors loosened their iron grip. At the end, Barry Evans' Jamie has matured enough to start weighing the possibilities of connubial bliss, just as O'Toole's Michael finally ties the knot with Carole at his own denouement.

Betwixt *Pussycat* and *Mulberry* came *Luv*. From the very outset, *Luv* establishes that no Donner film in the prime of his career is truly complete without a specially designed carnivalesque title sequence with comic-book romance imagery. Full disclosure: I love *Luv*, and in rewatching the film to write this piece, I laughed just as much as I had at the New Beverly over a year ago. It warms the cockles of my absurdist comedy-loving heart. In opening up a single-set play (under Mike Nichols' direction) into a multi-location feature film, many faulted screenwriter Elliott Baker, whose taste for bold bursts of slick, no-holds-barred comic anarchy had goosed Irvin Kershner's *A Fine Madness* (1966) the year before. But placing the gleefully unhinged *Luv*'s mad, mad, mad, mad comedy stylings on a continuum with Donner's earlier work, it could scarcely fit in more. He makes the Schisgal source his own. Though *Luv* is less overtly horny that the Donner films that flank it, and is more innocent in the ways that count, the name of the game is still wife-swapping, with a dash of homosexual panic, and

Donner transforms Murray Schisgal's *Luv* into a daffy cartoon.

even homosexual curiosity, as clearly hinted between Lemmon and Falk. Sarris, in his dismissive but polite review, likens the characters to "ill-mannered giraffes." (Only the august Penelope Gilliatt gave *Luv* full critical support.)

Our director lunges for a cartoon aesthetic in *Luv*, epitomized by its overarching broadness, its comic excess, its graphic aggressions (the camera contorts in the opening scene, and in one moment, an array of animated daggers rains into frame), and its kinetic 2.35:1 'Scope slapstick stagings and compositions. Like others might, at least in a cursory sense, I think of Frank Tashlin, the greatest of all cartoonists turned live-action directors. *Luv* is a glitter bomb of a movie—one either likes the momentary spectacle and doesn't mind cleaning up the mess, while others would rather spare themselves the aggravation.

Sarris' comparison with Minnelli is apt here, because the film's color work is exquisite in its design in many scenes. In *Mulberry Bush* the following year, a mushrooming blush of pinks and purples pervades even the scenes played to grotesquely absurdist heights, especially one involving Denholm Elliott mugging during a wine tasting. It might very well be that these bold hues suspend and sustain the picture in an outlandish alter-reality during these more overstated bits. The reveries of *Mulberry* also take great pains to push color and, more generally, saturation values, to their very limits.

Here We Go Round the Mulberry Bush.

In *Luv*, animated pink hearts magnify into frame. Primary-colored wardrobe selections offset the drab suburban spaces in the film's first half, while May's red dress in the second half positions her as the mark of two lovelorn bulls, with all their proverbial bullshit. To some not negligible extent, Donner did paint with color, and his use of it (with a kind of defined color syntax) is quite meticulous. "All my films are color-controlled," Donner told interviewer Roy Fowler in March 2000. "I have a great belief in color control."

Donner did clash with Elaine May on the set of *Luv*. She would demand retakes of scenes shot days before because she didn't like her performance (or her memory of the performance). May's biographer Carrie Courogen accounts, "It didn't take long for *Luv* to come to a grinding halt, an entire crew waiting as production staff flitted between Elaine's trailer and the director's bay and back again in desperate attempts to talk her down from the ledge." Donner went on the record stating, "The devastating thing about Elaine is that she is better at everything—writing, acting, directing—than almost anyone I know." Lemmon provided his own situation diagnosis: "She's touched with genius, like Judy Holliday. She approaches a scene like a director and writer, not like an actor, and she can go so deep so fast on a scene. Her mind works at such a great speed that it's difficult for her to communicate with other actors." As Sarris had it in his notice, "She comes off like Rosalind Russell with a Ph.D."

The dearth of acclaim in the wake of *What's New Pussycat?*—or even some more hushed measure of encouragement—ensured that Donner's time in the auteurist sun (or at least one prominent critic's auteurist sun) had reached its terminus. It would appear that Donner didn't meet the moment—or specifically, the challenge as lain out by his chief critical champion, who predicted that the film anticipated a sort of sharp decline into empty style. It was with *Alfred the Great* (1969), a critically and commercially disastrous MGM megaproduction, that Donner confirmed his worst suspicions; any assertive critic's defensive posture came to appear beyond the pale, no matter the skin in the game. Sarris did manage to muster up a few pale compliments in his review of the film, calling Michael York's performance "more [Rolling] Stones than Rock of Ages." I personally say that this can be said of the whole film.

Alfred the Great (1969), like Tony Richardson's *The Charge of the Light Brigade* (1968), was a mod shot at a roadshow-style historical epic. Both presuppose that the "British invasion" craze, and the prevalence of Britophilia on the world stage at the time, extended to wide interest in re-enactments of long-buried history, with some new modern allegorical underpinnings. Both had the biggest budgets ever granted to British productions up to that time. Richardson's film was perceived as the commentary on the Vietnam War that the filmmaker himself intended it to be. Though critics and audiences struggled a bit more in decoding *Alfred the Great*, the story of a ninth-century monarch who abandons his religious training to fight Danish invaders, Donner's film probes a very contemporary type of duality, between monastic idealism and worldly violence, or more specifically, between hippiedom's spiritual yearnings and the bloody demands of realpolitik (i.e. anti-establishment revolution in the Sixties sense). While both flopped, it was Donner's film that was dismissed as muddled and

A bold use of color and 'Scope in *Alfred the Great*,
Donner's favorite of his own films.

Alfred the Great.

ponderous. Donner never retreated from an opportunity to artic-ulate his aims to journalists, however. In speaking to Bert Reisfeld for the *Los Angeles Times*, Donner stated that he made *Alfred the Great* "because of the inherent youth problem." Alfred, to him, "turned the destructiveness of youth into constructiveness," and "like so many students today, he advocated peace, but at the same time proclaimed violence in order to redo the world."

No one could argue that Donner's style is still present. It's not soft-headed in the way that Franco Zeffirelli's later, fairly similar *Brother Sun, Sister Moon* (1972) proved to be. Again, Donner is working with 2.35:1 'Scope, and it's a "big look" picture in the Franklin J. Schaffner mold. In fact, the "visionary men outside their own time" model upon which Schaffner branded himself is, arguably, at play here as well. But this is Donner's world, where color is king, and a Sixties ethos veils even the tiniest crevice of screen space. We again have an artisanal title sequence, this time at the end. Striking primary colors punctuate vast Ireland landscapes of brown and green. Donner regular Fergus McDonell's sharp, disruptive, sometimes disjunctive cutting in the more frenetic sequences recalls the work on earlier pictures, especially *Nothing But the Best* and *Pussycat*. Donner lamented in his interview with the British Film & Television History Project that the audience broke out in unintentional laughter at its world premiere, largely because of the demotic nature of the dialogue. "I put a lot of myself into that one," Donner stated. "I loved doing it. It's a very political picture, very complex. Really, I put my heart and soul into that picture and I was shattered when people laughed at it. None of us saw it coming." He took care to point out that the film played far better in mainland Europe and elsewhere in the world than it did in America and Britain. In the same interview, he recalled that the *Alfred* script as originated by James R. Webb was "a very American-type script, with typical Hollywood period-piece stuff, and I don't say that admiringly. [Webb] was just too old Hollywood and couldn't break out of it." In recounting how he rewrote and transformed that script with British television writer Ken Taylor, he admitted it was his favorite among his own films.

A three-picture run of flops—*Luv*, *Mulberry Bush*, and *Alfred*—slammed the brakes on Donner's theatrical directing career. He retreated for years into television and directed stage production in the West End, before resurfacing with a woeful Hammer send-up, *Old Dracula* (1974), with David Niven in the title role. I take very little pleasure quoting Ebert in much of any context, but he was right in observing, "When you think what a truly great bad movie Niven might have made of all of this, it's a shame he merely made a terrible bad movie." There are remnants of the Donner of yore in *Old Dracula*, however, particular in its literally show-stopping, pseudo-mod, Sixties-style party scene.

Two television productions later in the decade, *Rogue Male* (1976) and *She Fell Among Thieves* (1978)—both of which got theatrical rollouts in other territories—were stylish, elegant, and always well-appointed. Donner's eye for color and movement had not dimmed by the time he had arrived at this later stage of his career. *Rogue Male*, a remake of Fritz Lang's *Man Hunt* (1941), reunited him with Peter O'Toole, screenwriter Frederic Raphael, and Harold Pinter (who acts rather than writes here). Its story— of the hot pursuit of a game hunter, appropriately named Hunter, who perilously takes aim at Adolf Hitler in 1939 before Britain's entry into the war—does not really thematically line up with most of the work that had come before, but it remains one of the best British telefilms of its time. Raphael, for his part, ignored the Lang original and went back to the Geoffrey Household novel. Most striking is the film's tight editing, evocative of Hitchcock's orchestration of tension. *She Fell Among Thieves*, starring Malcolm

She Fell Among Thieves.

McDowell as a British lord cum amateur detective who matches wits with improbably named villainess Vanity Fair as he investigates her diabolical inheritance-swindle scheme, sees Donner's return to delightfully entertaining, sophisticated camp. One cannot say the same about the camp in the dire Hollywood comedy *Charlie Chan and the Curse of the Dragon Queen* (1981), starring a woefully miscast Peter Ustinov, playing the iconic title role in yellowface. The less said about that one, the better. A self-flagellating Donner cursed the film in later interviews as the product of a sleazy snake-oil salesman, saying he "should have known better." He was also offered the director's chair on the all-star British pirate comedy *Yellowbeard* (1983), but in later years said he was grateful he declined, all things considered.

With *The Nude Bomb* (1980), Donner broke back into Hollywood following his Waterloo on *Luv*, but though this "Get Smart" movie is zany, it's more of a Mel Brooks "zany" than a Clive Donner "zany." Donner's brand of "zanefulness," if you will, had long since fallen out of style, though it certainly does some service in keeping the energy at peak. Various well-heeled television productions surround these later pictures, most notable of which were well-worn and oft-adapted classics like *The Thief of Bagdad* (1978), *Oliver Twist* (1982), *The Scarlet Pimpernel* (1982), *A Christmas Carol* (1984), and *Arthur the King* (1985). An HBO production *To Catch a King* (1984), starring Robert Wagner and Teri Garr, is more in the mold of *Rogue Male*, with its wartime caper of two Americans who attempt to thwart the kidnapping of the Duke of Windsor. It proved to be a massive theatrical success in, of all places, Finland.

Donner's final theatrical feature, *Stealing Heaven* (1988), starring Derek de Lint and, once again, Denholm Elliott (in his third Donner collaboration), falls more in line with *Alfred the Great*. But with its steamy tale of medieval romance and hippie-infused courtly love, it resembles something more like John Huston's *A Walk With Love and Death* (1969). In this case, the paramours are philosopher/logician Peter Abelard and his student Héloïse d'Argenteuil, two hapless souls who find comfort in each other's arms as they fight the restrictive conventions of their time. In his *Los Angeles Times* review, Michael Wilmington writes that *Stealing Heaven* "suggests the Sixties: a decade of turbulence, idealism, sex, and riot," and that the characters are "a quintessentially Sixties pair: long-haired beauties trapped in a cloistered society, battling the hypocrites and the meanies, the crooked parents, frigid nuns, cops, and sneering churchmen, who want to stifle their passion." He makes another keen observation when he quips that Donner, whom he types as "a king of high-style naughty camp," "may be nostalgic" for the era in which he made his best known and most admired films. He even name-drops a few of the titles. Indeed, no truer words were uttered about Clive Donner, who came of age as an artist in the Sixties and then got stuck there, either by design or (more likely) by circumstance. There is fine craftsmanship in *Stealing Heaven*, but it lacks the edge and the angst of even the director's more lighthearted Sixties offerings. From an auteur perspective, *Stealing*

Peter O'Toole takes aim at Hitler in *Rogue Male*.

Heaven is beyond the shadow of a doubt a Clive Donner motion picture. The colors and cutting patterns and stylistic mien—all there in this swan song. A Donner film is a Donner film; he's one of the easiest-to-spot-with-the-naked-eye auteurs in this volume, next to Sidney J. Furie.

To pluck Clive Donner out of the Sixties unprotected and in his purest state of being is to ensure he appears largely lost. There is often general talk, pablum perhaps, of individuals who fit into the decade hand in glove. Cinematically, this description suits Donner more than any filmmaker I can think of offhand. He lost his footing when the trappings of sexual liberation and free love dissolved into fashionable disillusionment. However, the films of his made in that shimmering era in which he stepped out and made himself known waft a positively "smashing" breeze—that most breezy of all breezes. Lester and Donner, along with Tony Richardson, are atavistic in their way. They resurrected tropes of a much earlier form of cinema—modes and manners of big-screen storytelling (and early experimental cinema) altogether absent in the long interim between themselves and a flickering, long gone past, at least within the English-American idiom. And they did so as a way of saying, "Yes, it was fraught and often frightening, but don't forget we had fun, too." In that respect, Donner is a historian as much as he is a director. For as much as he's been smeared as a smut peddler, and a connoisseur of concupiscence, he opens a precious, priceless window to an unrepeatable time. A smashing time, indeed.

Theatrical Feature Films: *The Secret Place* (1957), *Heart of a Child* (1958), *Marriage of Convenience* (1960), *The Sinister Man* (1961), *Some People* (1962), *The Caretaker* (1963), *Nothing But the Best* (1964), *What's New Pussycat?* (1965), *Luv* (1967), *Here We Go Round the Mulberry Bush* (1968), *Alfred the Great* (1969), *Old Dracula* (1974), *Rogue Male* (1976), *Spectre* (1977), *She Fell Among Thieves* (1978), *The Nude Bomb* (1980), *Charlie Chan and the Curse of the Dragon Queen* (1981), *To Catch a King* (1984), *Babes in Toyland* (1986), *Stealing Heaven* (1988)

Other Notable Works: *The Three Hostages* (1977), *The Scarlet Pimpernel* (1982), *Oliver Twist* (1982), *A Christmas Carol* (1984), *Arthur the King* (1985), *Dead Man's Folly* (1986), *Not a Penny More, Not a Penny Less* (1990)

22. The Wonder Cabinets of Muriel Box and Wendy Toye

This is the first publication of this essay, written especially for this volume.

Within the last year, I found myself in the position of having to program a short film for two visiting friends. A feature had been screened already, and time-wise, there was only room for a short film, if I could procure one. I selected Wendy Toye's "In the Frame," the first segment in the anthology film *Three Cases of Murder* (1954). To say they found the film mesmerizing and immersive is apt, considering that the story sees characters breaking out of and projecting themselves into a particular museum painting. It was the perfect film to show before we wrapped our evening. The very next day, I was taking one of those friends to lunch, where he was to meet Joe Dante for the first time. When Joe learned that we had screened "In the Picture" the previous evening, he was delighted. "Wendy Toye was a really special talent," he told us, "And that's such a great film."

Muriel Box was always a presence on the Fifties British cinema scene for me. I had procured a VHS copy of her *The Truth About Women* (1957) when I was but a teenager, and found it a strangely mature and melancholic comedy. That a woman directed it did not entirely register at the time. It certainly caught my attention when her work received a full retrospective at the 2018 San Sebastian Film Festival. That same retrospective was brought to the British Film Institute with some fanfare in 2023. It is heartening to see the Box filmography receive renewed attention and praise, because for many decades, she had fallen between the cracks of cinema history, not merely because of society's longtime built-in nearsightedness toward female directors, but also because of the limited availability of her films. In the United States, this scarcity unfortunately persists.

Admittedly, Toye and Box make for a playfully named duo (they never collaborated, but were certain kindred spirits). But to behold their respective work is to take notice of mighty artists in film that equally subverted gender expectation. In terms of their pure cinema hocus-pocus, they made more than a passing nod to the marvelous plasticity of the Archers' great films, replete with enough of the elements that made the work of Powell and Pressburger special. In fact, Box was Michael Powell's secretary early on when he was making "quota quickies," while Toye at one point nearly collaborated with the famous filmmaking team. They are the great toy box of their nation's cinema history, though the toy here is never simply a disposable plaything, and the nature of the box is more Chinese or Russian than it is British (Box especially loved stories within stories).

Their presence on the scene, and in this period of British film history, is nothing short of miraculous, if one considers the odds. Michael Balcon at Ealing Studios famously believed that women could not run film crews. There had been female screenwriters of British cinema, but female directors were that most rare and even endangered of species. The noted socialist and feminist documentarian Jill Craigie had succeeded in making two distinctive fiction hybrid features, *The Way We Live* (1946) and *Blue Scar* (1949), surveying the everyday lives of the working class, before retiring back into documentary. She resurfaced sporadically to pen the screenplays of films by prominent male directors. The Australian-born Margaret Thomson established herself as a documentarian for the Crown Film Unit before directing one fiction feature, the science-fiction comedy frolic *Child's Play* (1954) for John Grierson's Group 3 Films. The short-lived Group 3's failure certainly did not help her climb out of the documentary short "ghetto" afterwards (though she had helped filmmaker Philip Leacock coach the child actors in his *The Kidnappers*). Box and Toye were anomalies, the only two British female directors of their time with anything resembling endurance. This is never to say that they had it easy, even once they had cemented themselves in the industry.

It is an objective truth that Toye did her best work in the short form. The "In the Picture" segment of *Three Cases of Murder* and her masterpiece *The Stranger Left No Card* (1952) both feature Alan Badel as beguiling, decadent tricksters, or more descriptively, deceitfully benign chaperones to twisty treachery and diabolical doings. My friend, film historian David Del Valle, writes, "There are two short films that shine like beacons in the fantasy landscape of British cinema, that I now consider landmarks of their kind. They have left a lasting impression whenever I think of distinctly

Shades of Powell and Pressburger are noticeable in this sequence of "In the Picture" from *Three Cases of Murder.*

English filmmaking." A third beloved short, the Christmas classic *On the Twelfth Day…* (1955), also exemplifies the innovations she made with zippy, succinct material that was short on minutes but never ideas.

The comparison to the Archers is not one made in vain. "In the Picture"—with its languorous, almost hypnotizing "trip" of being projected into the story's central painting via the use of a distended and palpably uninterrupted move into the brushstrokes of a house door—is especially redolent of Powell and Pressburger in films like *The Red Shoes* (1948) and especially *The Tales of Hoffman* (1951). But possible influence aside, Toye gives them a life of their own, and we eventually come to recognize that the vision belongs to her and her alone. As evidenced in this scene, and a later one in which Badel exits the painting by shattering the museum's replacement glass encasement (a striking image, just as impactful as the iconic opening eye shot in the Archers' *A Matter of Life and Death*), Toye was a visionary of a rare breed. Compositionally, the film is always "on" and very proactive, with its canted frames and weighted geometries; the eye never dims, nor averts its gaze. If that were not enough, the cinematographer is Georges Perinal, who worked with the Archers more than once. Film scholar Caroline Merz says, "Not for nothing has she been compared with Powell and Pressburger, for her exuberant exploitation of the cinema's greatest powers of fantasy, and her openness to the links between cinema and the other arts of painting, music, and ballet."

Toye's background as a dancer and choreographer is entirely relevant. Her work in this arena caught the attention of impresario Sergei Diaghilev, who rewarded her with a place in his exalted Ballets Russes. It was there that she first met Jean Cocteau. One can strongly sense the latter's influence on her short film work as well, à la *The Blood of a Poet* (1932) with its story of an artist transported through a mirror into an alternate dimension. Cocteau was president of the Cannes festival jury that awarded *The Stranger Left No Card* its short film prize. Toye's measured and meticulous cutting to Alfven's "Swedish Rhapsody" suggests, even to those unaware of her background, the instincts of a musician or dancer. There is a steady hand, guided by a devoutly musical wit. Understanding rhythm and movement, whether movement of character or camera, in conjunction with her musical cutting, is intrinsic to Toye and her artistry. Film historian Dr. Josephine Botting observes, "I think perhaps the most important thing that her dance experience and love of dance brought to her filmmaking was her real sense of music. She could listen to a piece of music and visualize a piece of movement, or even a narrative."

The Archers' influence on Muriel Box is most apparent in *The Passionate Stranger* (1957), originally released in America as *A Novel Affair*. Today, it's precisely the type of romantic comedy that someone like Nancy Meyers would delight in remaking: a female romance novelist titillates her sexy chauffeur with the scintillating portrayal of him in her latest tome, as her dishy Valentino lover. It is in its daring, experimental blend of monochrome and color sequences that we are reminded quite vividly of *A Matter of Life and Death*, with its heaven and earth delineations. In this case, though, the melodrama creative/imagined world—the novelist's and readers' reverie—is in color, while real life is black and white. Box transposes *A Matter of Life and Death*'s chromatic partition of physical/metaphysical. This was a costly and time-consuming experiment that wreaked havoc on post-production process. Because the color change-overs in those days had to come at the end of each reel, this determined the length that each section could run, causing quite a number of headaches.

Simon and Laura (1955), a Box film that preceded *The Passionate Stranger*, also considers how illusion and fantasy are distorted projections of the tough realities we have trouble confronting. The premise is the stuff of great farce: a husband and wife (played by Peter Finch and Kay Kendall) have unchecked rancor for each other in their private life, but must present to the public as the model couple on their hit television show. This is a farce that deals in the theme of consumerism, ribbing television and its often fraught relationship with the public at large. Its depiction of this "cool medium" predates Marshall McLuhan's landmark *Understanding Media* by about a decade. Though on a cursory level, Box's target is television as a medium on the whole—the way it misrepresents, the way it packages illusion, and the growing public overindulgence of it—Box explores at a deeper level how the notion of private self either informs or counters public image. [Anthony Harvey, another director covered in this volume, also weighs the reciprocity between public and private, albeit in a different way.] Box is drawn to films-within-films and shows-within-shows, which critic Rachel Cooke likens to "puzzle boxes." She cites *Simon and Laura* and *The Passionate Stranger* as prime examples. In both, Box interweaves fiction and reality to the point that they seem co-dependent.

Toye's features, only in minor contrast, are fluffy, frothy, and frilly affairs, though still always charming and easy to enjoy. In two cases, *All for Mary* (1955) and *True as a Turtle* (1957), there are

Kay Kendall and Peter Finch wage furious battle as a pair of married TV stars in Muriel Box's *Simon and Laura.*

couples on vacations ("on holiday" to use the British-ism) during which high-larious complications ensue. These were just the type of pictures that promised Fifties British audiences a bit of escapism in far-flung, exotic locales. In that sense, they were marquee-perfect. There is also the big boisterous family comedy *Raising a Riot* (1955), with Kenneth More as a clueless father to a young brood who has to figure out how to care for them (and the family's mischievous pooch) when his wife ventures off to Canada to visit her sick mother. The best of her features is certainly *The Teckman Mystery* (1954); its precise short timing and carefully articulated decoupage evoke the best qualities that distinguished her short films, especially its finale Tower of London sequence.

Toye's skill with tonal transition, most present in *The Stranger Left No Card*, which slips from arch whimsy into cold-blooded homicide without blinking, is mirrored in the work of Muriel Box. *Eyewitness* (1956) perhaps best typifies this. One never expects the breathless shifts between tension and humor, the latter best epitomized by Ada Reeve, who steals all her scenes as the ill-tempered elderly lady in the hospital bed next to our damsel in distress for much of the runtime. It's a very Pressburgian wit, and temper of wit.

Her final film, *Rattle of a Simple Man* (1964), arguably her best (a contest between *Rattle*, *Passionate Stranger*, and *The Truth About Women*), operates similarly vis-à-vis tone. It is predominantly a two-hander between Harry H. Corbett and Diane Cilento (a returning cast member for Box). The level of banter, courtesy of playwright Charles Dyer (later of *Staircase* fame, or infamy), might suggest the type of fast and furious Ealing or Rank comedy, or whatever else had competed with her own comedies in the previous decade. But the prevailing mood is redolent of the kitchen sink dramas that were becoming increasingly dominant in the era as the culture noticeably changed. If you ask me, Box answers to this well and rises to the moment.

With *Rattle of a Simple Man*, I was personally reminded of the American film *A Cold Wind in August* (1961), an independent picture directed by Alexander Singer that was championed by some important critics of the day—but of course forgotten today. In both *Rattle* and *Cold Wind*, potentially stage-bound material is well cinematized. Both stories involve "loose" women, a sex worker and stripper respectively, who are unleashed upon sexually inexperienced men. Box's film is notable for the pathos and moments of gravitas that it hangs on its most jagged crimps, all in a putatively comedic stream. Furthermore, it gives her grounding to needle the constructs of masculinity that she always deemed satirical red meat. Film scholar Caroline Merz notes that the film can be

The Teckman Mystery.

Rattle of a Simple Man.

seen as "a woman's reply to the eulogies of the northern working-class male made famous in the social realist dramas of writers like John Osborne in the 1960's."

The film that Box called "personally significant to me above all the others" is, like *The Passionate Stranger*, based on her own original concept, co-scripted with husband Sydney Box. *The Truth About Women* (1957) is not the bawdy, potentially trashy picaresque of sexual conquest that it might first appear to be. In film terms, this is not akin to the American *A Guide for the Married Man* (1967) or *What a Way to Go!* (1964) but rather something more like John Guillermin's handling of Jean Anouilh's *Waltz of the Toreadors* (1963). It is not merely because the latter is British. There's something sharp and melancholic about *The Truth About Women*, even when it goes broader. The Guillermin hits a similar pitch, with unexpectedly poignant scenes woven into an ostensibly comedic framework. Each of the women we encounter in Box's film is a new station in an evolutionary chain of self-realized, self-conceptualized independent woman.

Box had always self-identified as a proud feminist, and her memoir *Odd Woman Out* recalls her militancy, the risks that militancy carried when she was at her busiest in the industry, and how she imbued her work with a constant appetite for gender subversion. Laurence Harvey in the lead feels almost upstaged in many of his scenes, by the likes of (again) Cilento, Eva Gabor, Julie Harris, and Mai Zetterling (well before she herself became a filmmaker). In fact, Harvey is often the butt of many of the film's jokes, rather than the sexual Adonis hero in control of his own story's humor. The flashback structure plays him as more of a Clive Candy of *Life and Death of Colonel Blimp* type of figure (in admittedly dreadful age makeup), than a plaintive Don Juan who feels nostalgia for his sordid past mostly in his loins rather than his heart.

There is merit in many of her other works, along with clear thematic throughlines. One of her earliest, *Street Corner* (1953) is a historically intriguing and progressive-minded documentary-esque slice-of-life drama about female cops. Other Box films build a framework around ideas of mythmaking (*The Happy* Family, *This Other Eden* especially), tribalist pride and the folly of nationalism (*Eden* again, along with *The Happy Family*), battle of the sexes (*To Dorothy, a Son, Simon and Laura, Passionate Stranger, Rattle*), and the give-and-take between public and private life (ditto the same titles). Others like *Subway in the Sky* (1959) and *Too Young to Love* (1960) feel perfunctory and suffer from the type of passionlessness that was rare for Box. The *Passport to Pimlico*-esque *The Happy Family* (1952) and *This Other Eden* (1959) are effective in their "fight City Hall" disdain for the "public good" as it is manipulatively defined and re-defined by inflexible bureaucrats, ideologues, and doctrinaires. Box was, after all, a seasoned skeptic with a sidelong glance and a beatific smirk that became her.

This Other Eden.

The Truth About Women.

As a matter of course and a foregone conclusion, Box and Toye never faced a smooth-sailing ride through the film industry. They both retired from directing for the screen in the early-to-mid Sixties. At various points, Box especially had to confront those who found the notion of a woman film director distasteful or objectionable, and some of those individuals were woman. Kay Kendall and Muriel Pavlow were both "uncomfortable" with a woman director. Jean Simmons went out of her way to get Box fired off *So Long at the Fair* (1950) for the same reason. Box's screenwriting Oscar (shared with husband Sidney) for *The Seventh Veil* (1945) cut no ice with Simmons or any of these other hostile parties—the idea that a woman was incapable of commanding a crew and "making her day" was so internalized as to be almost gospel. Both of the women profiled in this chapter proved them so fiercely wrong. Box, for her part, turned to spearheading Femina, the first feminist British publishing company, dedicated to books by and about women. When Toye retired, she went out in a blaze of glory with another brilliant short subject, *The King's Breakfast* (1963). Plenty of other creative avenues awaited her; she returned to the stage, directing operas, musicals, and the television specials that recorded the efforts (her *Orpheus in the Underworld* being of particular note). She died in 2010 at the age of 92, while Box departed in 1991 at 85.

David Del Valle laments that Toye "would never again tap into her talent for imaginative and macabre subjects which, sadly, is our loss." Historian Pamela Hutchinson marvels that "she worked on films that are art and ballet and mime and performance and poetry, a very interesting strain of British film; the fact that she could make these marvelous creations, you just wish she'd made so many more."

As Melanie Williams, the author of a forthcoming Muriel Box monograph, put it, "That Box was able to make such eloquent and well-crafted films spanning a wide generic range which all spoke subtly but firmly of her feminist concerns is miraculous," but that "the prospect of having to shadow box against misogynist superstition had begun to seriously pall."

The good news is that the toy box still dangles ample playtime before us, especially now that their works are emerging on new home video releases. (Box in particular has been the subject of renewed scholarly attention from a growing array of advocates.) Their mazes of light and shadow still beckon us to wander, to linger, to reflect, to dream, and to rediscover.

Muriel Box's Theatrical Feature Films: *The English Inn* (1941, short), *The Seventh Veil* (1945, script, uncredited director), *The Happy Family* (1952, a.k.a. *Mr. Lord Says No*), *Street Corner* (1953, a.k.a. *Both Sides of the Law*), *The Beachcomber* (1954), *To Dorothy, a Son* (1954, a.k.a. *Cash on Delivery*), *Simon and Laura* (1955), *Eyewitness* (1956), *The Passionate Stranger* (1957, a.k.a. *A Novel Affair*), *The Truth About Women* (1957), *Subway in the Sky* (1959), *This Other Eden* (1959), *Too Young to Love* (1960), *The Piper's Tune* (1962), *Rattle of a Simple Man* (1964)

Wendy Toye's Theatrical Feature Films: *The Stranger Left No Card* (1952, short), *The Teckman Mystery* (1954), *Three Cases of Murder* (1954, segment: "In the Picture"), *Raising a Riot* (1955), *All for Mary* (1955), *On the Twelfth Day...* (1955, short), *True as a Turtle* (1957), *Orpheus in the Underworld* (1961, TV), *We Joined the Navy* (1962), *The King's Breakfast* (1963, short), *Follow the Star* (1979, TV)

PART FOUR
THOSE ABROAD[*]

---

[*] Essays on directors who stepped out of their established comfort zones for sustained periods.

22. Elective Vicissitudes
The Radical Exiles of Jules Dassin

This is the revised and adjusted video essay script for a 2021 piece included on the Imprint Films Blu-ray release of Up Tight!

> None are more hopelessly enslaved than those who falsely believe they are free.
>
> Johann Wolfgang von Goethe,
> *Elective Affinities*

Andrew Sarris, in *The American Cinema*, cheekily refers to the films Jules Dassin made in exile as his "Mercourial Period," a pun in reference to his partnership with, and then marriage to, Melina Mercouri. He writes of "a career that verges on the grotesque," before driving the stake into Dassin's heart by stating that "Dassin's softheaded social consciousness has never obscured his minor talents." He faults the "lumpy proletarianism of *He Who Must Die*" and "the ludicrous escapades of *Never on Sunday* and *Phaedra*." Again, Monsieur Sarris et moi must part ways. On this occasion, it's a pretty bitter parting.

There's one especially extraordinary later Dassin film I wish to spotlight. *Up Tight!* (1968) might appear an anomaly in the context of the latter part of Dassin's career. It's the work of a longtime exile come home, albeit temporarily, during the apex of a social and political maelstrom. The fierce distortions in America's funhouse mirrors were made flesh (as a surreal scene from *Up Tight!* makes literal). The grotesquerie of pointless war and inequality was made manifest. *Up Tight!* is the extraordinary film into which Dassin, the inveterate dissident, channeled his indignation and disillusionment about the land he left behind, after the drunk-on-power sociopaths of the anti-communist crusade put a target on his back. He rebounded in record time, relative to blacklisted expat comrades Joseph Losey and Abraham Polonsky, not only building but fortifying a robust career as a newly European auteur, no alias required.

His first full, major post-blacklist venture, *Rififi* (1955), repurposed and reinvigorated many of the film noir tropes he had a hand in mainstreaming, in films like *Brute Force* (1947), *The Naked City* (1948), *Thieves' Highway* (1949), and *Night and the City* (1950). When he won the Cannes Best Director prize for *Rififi*, he was reborn into another filmmaking ecosystem, and could stand on a new pair of artistic legs. Amid that year's festivities along the Croisette, Dassin met Mercouri, who would go on to star in nine of his films. Together, they built a home together, in Greece, where he died peacefully at the age of 96 in 2008. He had become such a lover and aficionado of all things Greek that local officials called him "first-generation Greek."

Ever the political outcast in his birth country, Dassin eventually found himself in exile from his adopted country, following a Greek military junta known as the colonel's coup. This was later the subject of his 1974 film *The Rehearsal*. When he arrived stateside to make *Up Tight!*, the world was going mad. And by the time he finished and released the film, it already had. Need I remind you, dear reader, that 1968 was a worldwide battleground. In January, the opening salvo in the Tet Offensive. In April, the assassination of Dr. Martin Luther King, Jr. In May, France shuts down, the Cannes Film Festival is cancelled, the nation's streets roil with conflict; meanwhile, Dassin's actors go before the camera. In June, the assassination of Bobby Kennedy. August brought the Democratic National Convention protests and skirmish in Chicago. The Soviets invade Czechoslovakia. In November, Nixon wins the Presidency. In December, Paramount opens *Up Tight!* to dead-on-arrival business.

The film never had even a whisper of a chance in such a turbulent environment. The FBI had closely monitored every stage of production, harassing those involved right up to the eve of its premiere. Crew members and studio functionaries had ratted out the filmmakers' "activities" to the Cleveland FBI field office, which is all the more ironic because the film was a remake of John Ford's masterpiece *The Informer* (1935)—specifically, the story of an unemployed alcoholic who betrays his revolutionary comrades by ratting out their charismatic leader in the immediate aftermath of Martin Luther King, Jr.'s assassination. Dassin's film had cast actor and civil rights activist Julian Mayfield, the film's co-writer, as its own informer. How undelightfully meta of Uncle Sam! Dassin

Up Tight!

could never catch a break in the old red, white, and blue. This type of Big Brother behavior would echo later on, during the production and release of Ivan Dixon's *The Spook Who Sat by the Door* (1973), another celluloid powder keg about black revolution that was suppressed and barely exhibited. In that case, the film disappeared off the circuit for well over a decade.

On a personal note, when I first caught up with *Up Tight!*, around 2007, it was on a degraded tape-sourced bootleg copy recorded off a television broadcast, presumably from the Eighties. This so-called "version" altogether eliminated a key set piece, the funhouse sequence. I only came to know of the sequence's existence and its place within the film when I attended a 35mm screening at Film Forum New York circa 2010, with the incomparable Ruby Dee in attendance. I sat there stunned as it played, all the more so considering that someone at the network in question saw fit to eliminate it entirely from their broadcast. Not a single trace of it remained on said tape copy. It just proved to me that the film had remained incendiary to the powers that be, decades after it first hit theaters. Or!—that a touchy, thin-skinned white scissorhands contingent had taken offense at its implications about race relations, especially in voicing a call to revolt that would displace even self-identified allies to the cause. What would showing this scene to the television audience entail? This wasn't a sex scene, a burst of profanity, or a moment of violence, gratuitous or otherwise. No, this bit was undoubtedly censored for politics, for its admittedly playful innuendos about pandemonium and blood in

The too-hot-for-TV funhouse sequence in *Up Tight!*

the streets. That studios used to back and release "dangerously" political movies like this is nothing short of marvelous, if you ask me.

At one point in the film, a revolutionary reads the riot act to another voice begging for moderation: "When you're born black in this country, you're born dead. Don't talk to us about being killed. We know about that. You do your thing, and we'll do ours. But get this straight: I don't know about a revolution without arms. And I don't know about a revolution that doesn't punish its enemies." In an interview later in his life, Dassin planted his flag, stating, "I think I'm a crook at heart. And also, I guess, what's left of the old rebel in me is that I like authority being conquered."

Up Tight! was certainly a conspicuous departure for the director, born of a desire to harness the high-voltage currents of the civil rights struggle. The activists and politically alert citizens of the era dared to ask, what did the struggle for racial justice mean, and where did it stand, after the horrific deaths of so many of the movement's most inspiring figures in the cause of racial justice? Malcolm X, Medgar Evers, Louis Allen, James Chaney, Andrew Goodman, Michael Schwerner, Dr. Martin Luther King, Jr. (and, later, Fred Hampton). Was there no other recourse beside revolution? Beside militancy and revolt? As Malcolm X once asseverated, "By any means necessary." And what is to be made of the sell-out? The turncoat? Of whomever is not ready to make the move?

Conspicuously absent from *Up Tight!*, in the context of Dassin's whole career, is Melina Mercouri. It's one of only two

Dassin films from 1955 onward that do not feature her, the other being his final work, *Circle of Two* (1980). She was off with Norman Jewison making *Gaily, Gaily* (1969) in Chicago while Dassin toiled away in Cleveland on *Up Tight!* Many of Dassin's post-*Rififi* post-exile films could be called earthy, frothy celebrations of life, love, sexuality, all things Dionysian. One thinks immediately of *Never on Sunday* (1960). Both *Up Tight!* and *He Who Must Die* (1957) were salient commentaries, fearless declarations of a political identity, pictures that wore their provocations on their sleeves, without ever veering off into agitprop. And never were they without the shadings that deepened any discussion about them.

He Who Must Die is a Nikos Kazantzakis adaptation about a small Anatolian village staging an Easter passion play, which becomes ground zero for a battle of wills between the Christ-like and the merely Christian. The hypocrisy of church leaders is a casus belli in a spiritual war of attrition with pointed political ramifications. The film's unabashedly socialist bent, which originates at the top with Kazantzakis himself, and was then spiced and enhanced by Dassin's own leanings and loyalties, ensured the film would never circulate in late Fifties America. It was Dassin's favorite among his own work—the perfect vehicle for his political expression, anticipating the third rails that he would hit and trigger a little over ten years later with *Up Tight!* Incidentally, *He Who Must Die* is Dassin's only film shot in widescreen 'Scope, and it is a marvel of anamorphic eyescan, the shot-by-shot staging and editing process (and art) of carefully guiding the eye through the

Up Tight!

expansive width of a frame without strain. It's a pity he never shot other films in this aspect ratio.

The tragedy is that *Up Tight!* quickly slipped into obscurity, but today, the film is more potent than ever before, as fresh clarion calls are sounded throughout the United States of America, in the new struggle for equality and civil rights. In his documentary *Is That Black Enough for You?* (2022), film critic Elvis Mitchell and his interview subjects weigh the film's impact as a historical document.

SAMUEL L. JACKSON: Is that the one that's like a remake of *The Informer*? I knew what *The Informer* was, so when I saw *Up Tight!*, I knew exactly what it was!

BARRY JENKINS: *Up Tight!* is this super subversive political thriller from the late Sixties. The fact that they did this and they didn't get… I mean, I'm sure they ended up on some FBI J. Edgar kind of list, because is it out there. And it's very relevant to the time we're living in right now. It's *such* an amazing film, and nobody's seen it. And people should watch it.

There's an immediacy felt by all when *Up Tight!* is brought up for discussion. The film is unique in this regard. The term "ripped from the headlines" is a phrase that was used, re-used, and abused in early Hollywood trailers and promotion. Dassin went at least one better: his extraordinary *Up Tight!* is ripped from the pages of our living history. In the words of Julian Mayfield's character Tank in *Up Tight!*, "There's where it's at! That's beautiful! That's power! Real power!"

Jules Dassin's "Post Exile" Theatrical Feature Films: *Rififi* (1955), *He Who Must Die* (1957), *The Law* (1959), *Never on Sunday* (1960), *Phaedra* (1962), *Topkapi* (1964), *10:30 P.M. Summer* (1966), *Survival 1967* (1968), *Up Tight!* (1968), *Promise at Dawn* (1970), *The Rehearsal* (1974), *A Dream of Passion* (1978), *Circle of Two* (1980)

24. Phantom America
The Anglophone Louis Malle in Seven Pictures

This is the revised and adjusted video essay script for a piece included on the Imprint Films Blu-ray release of Pretty Baby.

> It's hard to stay an outsider after all the time I spent [in America]. I never wanted to become an American citizen, which I suppose would have been easy for me. I felt there was no point in it. When I came to America, I was in my forties. Although I decided to stay all those years, I felt it was important for me to keep a slightly different angle, to try to stay an observer of the American scene.
>
> Louis Malle, *Malle on Malle*
> (edited by Philip French)

For years, I thought I shared a special artistic kinship with Louis Malle. His work spoke to me because, at the time, I thought it suggested the types of films I would one day make, once I established myself and scored larger budgets. I was just a film student then, though; I hadn't really developed what you'd call a sensibility at that point, let alone cemented it to any degree. It took making a few early features to realize how different Malle and I were, especially when I took into consideration his vision of America, my home country. He looked at it as a bewildered émigré; I looked at it as an inured native. Fundamentally, we didn't differ over a sense that the United States is the only country to "go from barbarism to decadence without once passing through civilization," as Oscar Wilde put it. For a while, I guess I was more interested in the civilization part. Was it there at all? I was trying to find pockets of it where I could, where they existed. When Malle arrived here, he turned his lens on both the barbarism and the decadence. In some films, it's only the barbarism, others the decadence, and occasionally, they're mixed together into a bitter red, white and blue cocktail.

Pretty Baby.

As I enter middle age, I find myself aligning more with Malle's vision of America as not just a decaying monument, but a monument to decay. But I've got to still live here, in America, even when things stop making sense. I've got to hold out hope for those aforementioned pockets of civilization. But in unmasking a nation that had such big plans, a land of the overpromise and underdelivery, Malle reveals to us the scratchy flipside of "La Vie en Rose," that beloved anthem to Paris, Malle's old stomping ground. In his Anglophone pictures, we have "La Vie en Gris"—life in gray. Gray is meant in a few ways: overcast, depleted. But also, gray as in complex, as in not simply black and white. It's a shade with which most European filmmakers paint when they come here to the US. They spend their screen time trying to parse the various shades, to make sense of all that gray means, to them and to the woebegone locals they always encounter.

Film critic Roger Ebert recalled in 2005, "When I told a French film official last autumn that I had just seen and admired *Elevator to the Gallows*, I received not a smile but a scornful 'Pffft!' Perhaps Malle alienated his countrymen by moving to America, by marrying Candice Bergen, by taking on so many American stories like *Pretty Baby* (1978) and *Alamo Bay* (1985). Malle did not follow his New Wave origins into ideological extremities, like Godard, but like his German contemporary Fassbinder frankly desired large audiences."

So, with that in mind, how well did he score those larger audiences? Did he walk the tightrope of commerce and art, the trapeze act that so many directors have muddled or altogether botched? In 1977, David Picker, then a Paramount Pictures exec, lured Malle to the States and put him to work with the always formidable Polly Platt, an art director and general creative force fresh off her divorce from Peter Bogdanovich. Malle, for his part, was an internationally recognized, Oscar-nominated director eager to show us America through his eyes. As a stranger abroad, he had taken us on a tour of another faraway land in his six-and-a-half-hour documentary epic *Phantom India*. Would he now deliver *Phantom America*?

Polly Platt asked Malle, "Other than our movies, what else about America do you like? What interests you?" His love of jazz got them to New Orleans, and a book of old turn-of-the-century photographs pulled the rest of the creative weight, conceiving what would eventually become *Pretty Baby* (1978), a consummately controversial entryway into the American motion picture ecosystem, about a turn-of-the-century artiste photographer smitten with a 12-year-old child prostitute. Malle's New Orleans is a pretty evocation, a Renaissance or Belle Époque painting that captures the light and beauty, courtesy of Sven Nykvist's camera. But also on moody display are the darker themes of human exploitation, human weakness, depravity, the illusion of innocence, the corruption of beauty, purity as deception. Sounds, I don't know, almost uniquely American, doesn't it?

In 1980, Malle brought himself up to date, with a gritty, modern saga of barely functioning broken dreamers. In *Atlantic City*, what many consider Malle's finest American effort, decay is omnipresent. It's America as Grey Gardens. Every character in the film is fueled by disappointment—chronic disappointment, lifetimes of disappointment. Life for them is itself a weigh-station for an assured and more ultimate disappointment. Cue Peggy Lee arriving at the pearly gates singing "Is that all there is?" There is a more plot-driven aspect of *Atlantic City*, involving a stolen supply of cocaine, but it's nothing more than a McGuffin really, in this ghost story about the living. "They had just legalized gambling in Atlantic City," Malle explains. "It was very controversial, and there were all these stories about 'Will the mob move in?" Two casinos had just opened and they were building several more. We saw for ourselves all the contrasts, all the gloss. The rest of the town was literally a slum. Before they legalized gambling, Atlantic City, which had had a glorious past in the 1920s and 1930s and 1940s, had almost become a ghost town."

The rundown America of artist-abroad Louis Malle in
Atlantic City and *My Dinner With Andre*.

Malle and screenwriter John Guare have populated their ghost town with should-have-beens, could-have-beens, would-have-beens, legends in their own minds, dreamers by any other name. The New Jersey of the cinema seems a haven for them, as in *On the Waterfront* (1954), for example. Nathanael West gives us a kind of West Coast equivalent in his *Day of the Locust*, with the parasitic hangers-on at the San Berdoo bungalow complex. Malle's vision, however, while never pristine, is never misanthropic, but neither is it sentimental. In all these cases though, I think of Langston

Hughes: "What happens to a dream deferred? / Does it dry up / like a raisin in the sun? / Or fester like a sore— / And then run? / Does it stink like rotten meat? / Or crust and sugar over— / like a syrupy sweet? / Maybe it just sags / like a heavy load. / Or does it explode?" Pretty self-explanatory, even though the title of this poem is "Harlem" not "Atlantic City." All this will not stop Burt Lancaster's Lou from rhapsodizing the city as it was in a bygone era. What is still present, he fails to mention, are the gangsters, but long gone is the romance and the atmosphere:

> LOU: It's all shit now. It's a shame you never saw Atlantic City when it had floy floy. Remember the song "Flatfoot Floozy with the Floy Floy"? Hep cat in the zoot suit. Floy floy, that was something special. Atlantic City had floy floy coming out of its ears in those days. Now it's all so goddamn legal. Howard Johnsons running a casino! Tutti fruitti ice cream and craps don't mix. Yes, it used to be beautiful, what with the rackets, whoring, guns.

Louis Malle's follow-up, *My Dinner With Andre* (1981), tracks with all this. While it might have appeared less ambitious on the page—after all, it's two guys in a restaurant booth talking for two hours—it's actually a sweeping epic of words, a globe-trotting story of an economically advantaged but existentially discombobulated American artist's struggle to find and feel life, both his own and also life as a concept. In an upscale Manhattan restaurant, in the type of bourgeois environment Malle knew very well, as evidenced in his earlier French pictures, especially *Murmur of the Heart* (1971), our title character Andre Gregory speaks of mystical encounters, hallucinations, spiritual and creative awakenings, and literally being buried alive. All the while, Wallace Shawn, our surrogate, or foil if you will, is on another wavelength entirely.

Shawn tells us in his opening narration:

> The life of a playwright is tough. It's not easy, as some people seem to think. You work hard writing plays and nobody puts them on. You take up other lines of work to try to make a living—I became an actor, and people don't hire you. So you just spend your days doing the errands of your trade. Today, I had to be up by ten in the morning to make some important phone calls. Then, I'd gone to

My Dinner With Andre.

the stationery store to buy envelopes. Then, to the Xerox shop. There were dozens of things to do. By five o'clock, I'd finally made it to the post office and mailed off several copies of my plays, meanwhile checking constantly with my answering service to see if my agent had called with any acting work. In the morning, the mailbox had just been stuffed with bills. What was I supposed to do? How was I supposed to pay them? After all, I was already doing my best. I've lived in this city all my life. I grew up on the Upper East Side and when I was ten years old I was rich, I was an aristocrat, riding around in taxis, surrounded by comfort, and all I thought about was art and music. Now, I'm 36, and all I think about is money.

Once again, we're surrounded with American decay, as made manifest when Wally enters a subway car with every inch covered in graffiti and crud, as if the trains themselves are made of the stuff, not merely littered with it. But do Wally and Andre touch any ugly reality from their temporary perch at this quasi-Café des Artistes? At least one of them, the pragmatist, must eventually return to it.

The conversation takes us to a variety of places, and on a rewatch, you can feel the dialogue launch backward in the runtime to the images of Wally during the prelude. This expositional overture documents the rundown Manhattan of Ed Koch's early mayoral years. A conversation takes us lands away, which for me evokes Emily Dickinson: "To take us Lands away, / Nor any Coursers like a Page / Of prancing Poetry—/ This Traverse may the poorest take / Without oppress of Toll—/ How frugal is the Chariot / That bears a Human soul." In this case, Dickinson is rhapsodizing books and the act of reading, but with some liberties, her thoughts may be applied to the probing exchange in *My Dinner With Andre*. With Andre's words as a magic carpet, we leave Manhattan and America, a crumbling city in a crumbling land, as captured by Monsieur Réalisateur Malle. Andre's warnings and admonitions about the city's oppressiveness offer a stark juxtaposition. When we do finally land back in New York, Wally remembers the way things all used to be, on his ride home:

> All the other customers seemed to have left hours ago. We got the bill, and Andre paid for our dinner. I treated myself to a taxi. I rode home through the city streets. There wasn't a street, there wasn't a building that wasn't connected to some memory in my mind. There, I was buying a suit with my father. There, I was having an ice cream soda after school. When I finally came in, Debby was home from work, and I told her everything about my dinner with Andre.

A melting pot of a motley crew in Malle's *Crackers*, shot in San Francisco.

An uglier side of America in *Alamo Bay*.

The odd-film-out in this "Phantom America" lineup is really *Crackers* (1983), shot in my onetime San Francisco neighborhood. Though Malle admits he more or less got cornered into directing this heist comedy, almost by accident, the film still has a taste for the rabble and the riff-raff. As one critic quipped, "All Wallace Shawn gets to do is have dinner without Andre." But let's further consider these characters. The laconic Wally, in the role of Turtle, does indeed either eat or look for things to eat nonstop, but he lives under a bridge in a makeshift... habitat, for lack of a better word. Jack Warden runs and lives above a crummy pawnshop in the rundown Mission District. Donald Sutherland is a loser who thinks he's a winner, yet another character who would have felt right at home in a movie like *Atlantic City*. Sean Penn is a loafing amateur musician. Trinidad Silva is an undocumented immigrant. A farcical heist seems natural and logical, by default. Yet for all the hardscrabble lives on display, the kitschy Michael MacDonald opening title tune assures us that "they've got more than [they] need." The film flopped both critically and commercially, raking in a scant $130,000 on a $12 million budget.

A year later, Malle bounced back—at least critically—with *Alamo Bay* (1985), his darkest, ugliest vision of America, a narrative complement to his two American documentaries, *God's Country* (1985) and especially ...*And the Pursuit of Happiness* (1986), which examined the immigrant experience in Eighties America. Set on the Texas Gulf Coast amid a local race war between Vietnamese immigrant and white supremacist shrimp boat fishermen, *Alamo Bay* is the portrait of a country whose poor and disenfranchised see equality and equal opportunity as oppression. Indeed, the film resonates today and is very prescient of today's America. This is also explicitly his most "American" picture, complete with an original Ry Cooder score against a depleted heartland.

The late Eighties saw a brief and mostly successful return to his French homeland, for the hit *Au revoir les enfants* (1987) and the comedy *Milou in mai* (1990). In France, he could make a tentative return to the bourgeoisie, as in both these cases. Harsh reality can break through the shell of privilege, but never the decay that makes it truly ubiquitous. The same can be said of *Damage* (1992), Malle's only cinematic trip to Great Britain. It's telling that, with the British, he concentrates on the monied class, the ruling class, specifically a member of Parliament, his family, and most critically, his mistress. There is not a whisper of decay, no hardscrabble characters, no rust, graffiti, or blight. To invoke Don King, "only in America." In *Damage*, only in human behavior alone, or more accurately misbehavior, can one find rot. (I've always felt that *Damage* reads more like a more mannerly Roman Polanski film than a Louis Malle.)

Wally and Andre return in Malle's final film, *Vanya on 42nd Street* (1994). In a dilapidated theater, the New Amsterdam on West 42nd Street, he makes one last cinematic visit to the United States. And it is in some ways a fitting end, despite his death the following year, at the age of 63, being untimely. There is safety in theater. It's a shelter from almost all storms — America's last fortress. In *Vanya on 42nd Street*, theater sanctifies a space that has seen better days.

Wally and Andre return in Malle's final film.

In many ways, it's a valedictory statement, as if to recite, "We are the music makers, / And we are the dreamers of dreams, / Wandering by lone sea-breakers, / And sitting by desolate streams; / World-losers and world-forsakers, / On whom the pale moon gleams: / Yet we are the movers and shakers / Of the world for ever, it seems."

Anton Chekhov can and does exist in the rattiest of artistic temples. Likewise, dreamers, music makers, romantics, movers, shakers, gluttons, roses among weeds, deadbeats, reprobates, and the otherwise defeated, might stand a chance in this crazy country, the one they call an experiment. Can they chip away at the gloss to carve out a space between all the barbarism and decadence that Malle reveals to us? Maybe, on some level, Malle and I *were* pursuing the same thing after all: a life in gray, in Louis Malle's Phantom America.

Louis Malle's American and "Post-America" Theatrical Feature Films: *Pretty Baby* (1978), *Atlantic City* (1980), *My Dinner With Andre* (1981), *Crackers* (1983), *Alamo Bay* (1985), *God's Country* (1985), *...And the Pursuit of Happiness* (1986), *Au revoir, les enfants* (1987), *May Fools* (1990), *Damage* (1992), *Vanya on 42nd Street* (1994)

25. The Great Ecstasy of Tree-Climber Otto, or
How I Learned to Stop Worrying and Love Late Preminger (with a Peek into Late-Career Stanley Kramer)

This is the revised and adjusted video essay script for a piece included on the Imprint Films Blu-ray release of Hurry Sundown.

They called him Otto the Terrible, but he was also Otto the Gadfly, Otto the hipster, Otto the shark, and Otto the king of publicity. But his blanket nickname should be Otto the Present. In many ways, Otto was as ubiquitous in the culture as Alfred Hitchcock. He was on every talk show, made every public appearance, and crafted his persona carefully in many headlines. You might say he dug the spotlight. Personally, I was obsessed (and I do mean obsessed) with Preminger's later work when I was in high school. The later careers of other classic Hollywood directing icons didn't wear the filmmaker's perceived growing pains on their sleeves as did Preminger's final curious movement. Later Preminger is always a minefield for most audiences. I've always been fascinated watching Otto the Terrible out on the limbs that, in all likelihood, can't support his hefty weight.

"Hey, Otto, what are you doing up there?" He just looks at you like you've asked the dumbest question in the world, and replies defiantly "Exshperimenting. Vat else?" The branch snaps and he plummets ever so ungracefully to the ground, landing right on that Mr. Clean dome of his. As he brushes himself off, he points up to another branch and exclaims, "Now I try dat one!" Otto, the tree climber!

Others would call his later work an enigma, but I think his purview and intent were crystalline. He essentially crops the vast widths of the often sweeping canvases on which he built his larger-than-life name as a director, to refocus on much more intimate stories that were incongruous relative to much of his earlier canon. These new films were stories of survival, heterodoxy, rapprochement, and personal liberation, just as the nation and its culture were experiencing liberation writ large. They are defiantly idiosyncratic, renewed calls for tolerance in a world ever more entrenched. He also shoots in the 1.85:1 aspect ratio, after an almost straight run of shooting wide for 'Scope screen sizes.

His *Tell Me That You Love Me, Junie Moon* (1970) found facially scarred Liza Minnelli making house with two other rejects of society, and fending off a campy, cruel world in no short supply of predatory skeptics, tormentors, and bullies. And when I say campy world, there are widely faulted scenes, like the one with Kay Thompson as Minnelli and company's dowager landlady, who lives in an imported castle. But these scenes are calculated to effect, as to further pit our outcasts against an outright grotesque and overwrought display of insensitivity and inhumanity outside the walls of the home that the film's three misfits created for themselves.

In *Such Good Friends* (1971), Dyan Cannon confronts a similar grotesquerie in a not-so-dissimilar bid for self-respect. In that film's funniest sequence, a blood drive turns into an impromptu, bitchy cocktail party... without the cocktails. This is the kind of absurdist sequence Buñuel or Fellini might have staged, had they been ugly Americans. Preminger's savage insider vision of a smarmy, snarky, sniping Manhattan upper crust is a jet-black satirical bacchanal of cheaters, climbers, hangers-on, parvenus, pseudo-intellectuals, debutantes, debutantes-in-training, pariahs, and other patsies of privilege. And the film itself is in turns awkward, tart, biting, ham-fisted, salient, broad, subtle, and black as death, written in poison pen by Elaine May under the pseudonym Esther Dale. But in the film's unpredictably sober finale, death comes knocking for one of this rabble's number, with guilt and emerging self-awareness that open the door to Cannon's ultimate deliberation.

I perceive definitive analogs in the respective canons of Otto Preminger and Stanley Kramer, both of whom were Jewish and renowned as politically progressive liberals. Their taste in material was startlingly similar, even if their approaches to staging were quite different. Both men were social and thematic lightning rods, but it was Preminger who "wrote" his pictures in cinematic longhand, from a formalist perspective. In order of the most appropriate, there's *Tell Me That You Love Me, Junie Moon* and Kramer's *Bless the Beasts and Children* (1971). Within just one year of

Preminger's *Tell Me That You Love Me, Junie Moon* and Kramer's *Bless the Beasts and Children* assayed the hippie ethos with sensitive dramas about unlikely brigades of misfits who are derided for being different from the rest.

each other, Kramer and Preminger make markedly sensitive dramas about misfits and outcasts who join forces to fend off a society that won't have them, or deride them for being different. These are two very hippie ethos-inflected pictures, and they are most remarkably in sync with each other. Both also exude a lot of unexpected sexual tension.

Then there are Preminger's *Rosebud* (1975) and Kramer's inscrutable *The Domino Principle* (1977). These are their respective penultimate films, which are trenchant topical political thrillers that the critics tore to shreds. *Rosebud* is, in one way, a "bitter herbs" historical sequel to Preminger's *Exodus* (1960), insofar that it concerns itself with the notion of aftermath, i.e. the burgeoning bitter and bloody clash between the Israelis and Palestinians as perpetuated by punitive cycles of violence, terrorism, and revanchism. *The Domino Principle* indexes heavily on the paranoid conspiracy thrillers that sprang up in the wake of Watergate, though Kramer's reputation as "The Message Man" shoots itself in the foot here, as no one on God's green earth understood what Kramer was attempting to say or do with such a confusing concept. (I'm convinced that, somewhere, there are men in white coats who are still studying what happens to their subjects when they attempt to explain the plot of *The Domino Principle*. Talk about "conspiracy brain"!)

With penultimate inevitably comes ultimate. Kramer's *The Runner Stumbles* (1979) and Preminger's *The Human Factor* (1980), are strangely complementary and somewhat more muted swan songs. Both are humbler bounce-backs from the slings and arrows of *Rosebud* and *The Domino Principle*. Forbidden relationships corner precarious lovers into untenable and tragic situations. With that in mind, the weepy theme song for both pictures could be "There's a Place for Us" from *West Side Story*, though Preminger's in particular has a harder edge and a sardonic British humor as supplied by the Graham Greene source novel and Tom Stoppard's adaptation. Both were also made on lower budgets relative to their previous efforts. Preminger even pawned his art collection to finish his. One can bring Preminger's *The Cardinal* (1963) into this conversation, too, as a point of comparison to *The Runner Stumbles*, in terms of how each filmmaker frames the Catholic Church.

And how about Kramer's *Guess Who's Coming to Dinner* and Preminger's *Hurry Sundown*? Both made in 1967, a formative year for the civil rights struggle. Both filmmakers pursue hot-button dramas about race and interracial relations. Kramer's film is a hit, while Otto's movie flops, but both make history. Kramer stages a passionate movie kiss between a black man and a white woman—filtered through a rearview mirror and minimized in the frame, but it still stirred controversy. Meanwhile, Otto becomes the first director to shoot in the Jim Crow South with an integrated cast and crew. *Hurry Sundown* is really the bridge between classic Preminger and this late Preminger period I've identified.

Of course, we have the comedy extravaganzas: *It's a Mad, Mad, Mad, Mad World* (1963) and *Skidoo* (1968). Kramer and Preminger were never known as comedy directors, but when they stepped out and made their Sixties comedy extravaganzas, they went all out with who's-who all-star casts and some crossover players. Arnold Stang and Mickey Rooney appear in both. Once again, Kramer's is widely regarded as a comedy classic, while Preminger's is appreciated by some diehard auteurists, but remains widely lambasted, so much so as to now be a punchline all its own. You could also enter Kramer's *R.P.M.* (1970) into this particular discussion, as *Skidoo* and *R.P.M.* see aging directors turning their lenses on the counterculture, the hippie movement, and in Kramer's case, hippie activism.

They also both made epic courtroom dramas: Otto's *Anatomy of a Murder* (1959) and Stanley's *Judgment at Nuremberg* (1961), both recognized as two of the best of their respective directors' careers. Stanley Kramer produced *The Juggler* (1953) but didn't direct it (though he did personally shepherd the project into production), and

Otto and the *Skidoo* gang.

Preminger's *The Human Factor* and Kramer's *The Runner Stumbles*, respective final films about star-crossed lovers kept apart by a cruel world.

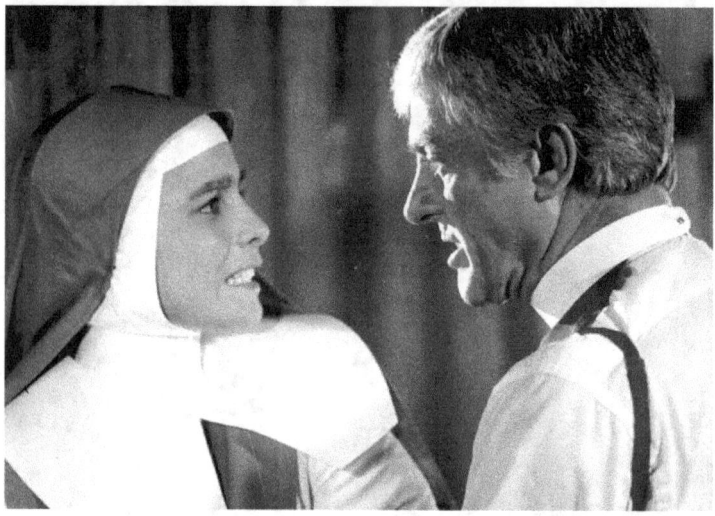

like Otto's *Exodus* (1960), it examines the founding of the state of Israel, and living there in its earliest days. No one else was really drawn to making comparable films on this particular subject. Certainly there was Melville Shavelson's *Cast a Giant Shadow* (1966), but that came some time later with mixed results.

With Preminger's *Saint Joan* (1957) and Kramer's *Inherit the Wind* (1960), it's a bit more of a stretch, perhaps, but both were adapted from stage successes, and both deal in charges of heresy while tastefully skewering intolerance and hidebound religious conservatism.

With Stanley's *Ship of Fools* (1965) and Otto's *In Harm's Way* (1965), we have character-driven epics set largely at sea both just before and early into World War II. Both were also based on highly successful bestselling novels. The only ones for which I don't sense any reciprocals or analogs are Otto's *Advise and Consent* (1962) and *Such Good Friends*, and Stanley's *Oklahoma Crude* (1973) and *The Secret of Santa Vittoria* (1969). It does not ever seem like the two men were in competition with each other, though who really knows with the highly competitive Otto, whose *Exodus* was in a race with *Spartacus* (1960) to be the first to break the blacklist by hiring screenwriter Dalton Trumbo.

But what set Otto apart? It's truly this: You couldn't ever really count him out. He refused to be consigned to any ash heap when some gale force winds shifted against him. Yes, late Preminger is left to be blindly and blithely dismissed by carping critics who would rather lampoon an aging director for expanding his comfort zones and attempting to remain relevant, even amid some admittedly awkward directorial spasms (cue up the clip of Burgess Meredith dancing in nothing but a loin cloth in *Such Good Friends*, Jane Fonda's saxophone fellatio in *Hurry Sundown*, Carol Channing stripteasing for Frankie Avalon in *Skidoo*, or Jackie Gleason's acid trip in the same).

His directorial hallmarks were still present. Those elegant tracking shots, the long takes, those virtuoso movements, the objective lens, the stacked compositions, the themes of space and land and justice and ritual and process. This final movement of his career adds another theme: the perils, the pitfalls, and the awkward grace of liberation.

Otto Preminger's "Late Experimental Period" Theatrical Features: *Bunny Lake is Missing* (1965), *Hurry Sundown* (1967), *Skidoo* (1968), *Tell Me That You Love Me, Junie Moon* (1970), *Such Good Friends* (1971), *Rosebud* (1975), *The Human Factor* (1980)

Stanley Kramer's Late Career Theatrical Features: *Ship of Fools* (1965), *Guess Who's Coming to Dinner* (1967), *The Secret of Santa Vittoria* (1969), *R.P.M.* (1970), *Bless the Beasts and Children* (1971), *Oklahoma Crude* (1973), *The Domino Principle* (1977), *The Runner Stumbles* (1979)

26. No Words for the Dead
Reanimating William Castle's Oddball Swan Song

This is the adjusted and revised script for a video essay titled No Words for the Dead: Reanimating William Castle and the Historical Path to Shanks, *featured on the* Shanks *Blu-ray release from Cinématographe in 2024.*

> From the very beginning, I craved recognition and applause, constantly needing to prove myself to someone – anyone. I had now achieved all that and more, but I was still hungry. Never having had the luxury of a bigger star for my films, I had been forced to build my little empire on ingenious showmanship.
>
> William Castle

The term "high concept" gets bandied around a great deal in discussing cinema that challenges the elastic boundaries of traditional form. It becomes an expression not simply of a story with an easy-to-pitch, succinct, attention-grabbing premise, but one that stretches the contours or evokes earlier iterations of cinema storytelling.

Gene Kelly was an early purveyor of high-concept studio filmmaking. In 1952, he sold MGM on an entirely dialogue-free dance musical called *Invitation to the Dance*, which he pitched as a celebration of ballet and mime. The film sat on the shelf for years because the studio was mortified about its lack of box-office potential. One exec told him, "Dance, especially ballet, is longhair at best, homosexual at worst." The skittish MGM brass made it a condition that he star in the film, as his initial plan was simply to direct a pack of unknown dancers without so much as even making a cameo. Kelly, of course, had no choice but to accept. It was, at the time, the studio's second longest-running shoot, having started in

M·G·M presents **Invitation To The Dance** Color by Technicolor

August 1952 and wrapping June of 1954. That's twenty-two months. The fears, it turns out, were well-founded. *Invitation to the Dance* flopped both critically and commercially when it finally premiered in May of 1956. Bosley Crowther, in lambasting the picture, exemplified the majority opinion in complimenting Kelly for his gumption in even attempting to mount the project, while deeming his material somewhat less than captivating or compelling. *Invitation to the Dance* can now be experienced as an historical experiment—an elaborate, feature-length extension of the musical fantasia detour sequences in films of his like *An American in Paris* and *Singin' in the Rain*.

Kelly's ambition wouldn't give up the ghost when, just six years later, he attempted nearly dialogue-free, silent movie-style storytelling again with *Gigot* (1962), starring Jackie Gleason as a completely mute, slow-witted, but warm-hearted janitor and vagabond who befriends a little girl, the daughter of a prostitute. There's not much in the way of plot, but Gleason conceived the story himself, in the hope that Orson Welles would direct. The final film, ultimately taken on by Kelly, was aggressively re-edited by studio executives. One contemporary critic branded it, "A grotesque piece of self-indulgence, the arch example of the clown who wanted to play Hamlet. Plotless, mawkish, and wholly unfunny." The film was such a flop that Dick Zanuck at Fox refused to approve Gleason to star in *The French Connection* when his name was floated for the role of Popeye Doyle. (What a different movie that would have been!) Methinks Friedkin would have had an issue getting Gleason to chase his perps on foot. I will note that I'm a major proponent of *Gigot*, which I've always deemed misunderstood and ripe for rediscovery.

The European art film throughout the ages would occasionally take stabs at experimental use of language and communicative sound, or a lack altogether thereof. The most radical example is perhaps Claude Faraldo's *Themroc* (1974), the "story" of which is performed in grunts and gibberish by game actors like Michel Piccoli and Miou-Miou. Yes, the film is in an invented, cacophonous "language" reminiscent of cave people. Jean-Luc Godard, of course, took cracks at spoken language, its quirks, its absurdities and its limits, on more than one occasion at many junctures of his career. This proclivity culminated in his use of so-called Navajo English subtitles in *Film Socialisme*. His subsequent film was the aptly titled *Goodbye to Language*.

Other English-language directors took big swings at silent movie-style in the current and extended age of the talkie. Chaplin and Buster Keaton held onto silent cinema aesthetics for many years following the advent of sound. The most commercially successful examples post-Chaplin and post-Keaton were both affectionate pointed tributes to the silent era: Mel Brooks' *Silent Movie* (1976) and Michel Hazanavicius' *The Artist* (2011). Other efforts,

Gigot.

though, saw mostly withering commercial results. Peter Bogdan-ovich accented his stage-to-screen adaptation *Noises Off* (1992) with broad silent comedy brush strokes. Martin Ritt's purely visual storytelling hewed close to the aesthetics of the early social conscience cinema of the silent era with his labor drama *The Molly Maguires* (1970), the opening sixteen minutes of which run without dialogue.

No example, however, was more conspicuous—or in point of fact, downright extraordinary—in its yearning regard for silent cinema than William Castle's *Shanks*, an almost how-did-this-get-produced oddity released by Paramount in 1974. The coup of the production, if one is to call it that, was unusual. Iconic mime artist Marcel Marceau stars as Malcolm Shanks, a mute puppeteer of the dead, a reanimation hobbyist, who takes a young girl under his wing as he endeavors to create a kind of corpse puppet show, using a departed Frankenstein-like doctor's novel "remote-con-trol-corpse" invention. The film is part silent comedy, part classic horror, part puppet show, part mime act, part Dada-ist experiment, but 100% original. Castle was famous or infamous for his exhi-bition gimmicks, like buzzers under seats for *The Tingler* (1959), plastic skeletons floating over the audience for *House on Haunted Hill* (1959), democratizing his villain's fate for *Mr. Sardonicus* (1961), unleashing an axe-wielding Joan Crawford on the crowd gathered to see *Strait-Jacket* (1964), and so on. His gimmick for *Shanks* wasn't, shall we say, extracurricular. The very casting of Marcel Marceau, whose hijinks are juxtaposed with silent movie intertitles, was all the gimmick Castle needed for what ultimately marked his last outing as director.

Joe Dante, of course, pays tribute to Castle, with John Good-man's "Lawrence Woolsey" character in his masterpiece *Matinee* (1993). When I approached Joe, and asked him if he'd consider going on camera to discuss *Shanks*, he replied simply, "Hmm... don't really have much to say about that one." *Shanks* has always been one of the more overlooked entries in his filmography, the unloved Castle movie, but there's something almost ineffable that I personally find intriguing about it. I personally see *Shanks* as not merely a valedictory address, the filmmaker's capstone statement, but the closest thing approaching a personal artistic testament that Castle ever committed to celluloid. We are made to look at puppetmaster Malcolm Shanks as showman, as an avatar for Castle himself—Castle the puppetmaster, Castle the gimmick-spinner, Castle the shadow-tamer—a man who himself reanimated many

Marcel Marceau puppeteering the dead, as Malcolm Shanks in *Shanks*.

corpses throughout an illustrious career of profitable and popular genre exercises.

The art, no matter how shambolic, is customized, nothing if not unique to the individual artist. This is Castle as classicist, as Old Industry man, one at odds with the trends that sought to subvert all classical models, as the New American Cinema was succeeding in doing at the time. The motorcycle gang entering the picture is a metaphor for the rise of the new paradigm (the "easy riders" come to wreak havoc), a hostile takeover by a posse that seeks to pervert Shanks' beloved technology, just as the young guns had upended Castle's industry. They too shamble along, with the death of the gangleader they mourn, which comes with a new ruddlerlessness.

This is just as the New Hollywood was beginning to lose some of its footing, so one sees some allegory. Yet the film still manages to avoid bitterness or sour grapes. On the contrary, it's Castle's Biblical "Here I am" moment for his cinema, his brand, his stamp. "I reanimate corpses, too, and do ghastly things to you in dark theaters, and you love it," he seemed to be reminding people.

To weigh Castle's visual classicism, let's put a hypothetical into action: If one applies desaturation and tinting to many of Castle's scenes in *Shanks*, it would become easy to mistake it for a proper silent film. Mimicking silent film tropes is affectation that many directors try and fail at achieving, because they overlook or inadequately scrutinize the type of staging and blocking specific to early cinema. There were some contemporary critics who faulted Castle for his objective, often flat camerawork, as if the lens is perpetually gazing upon the action as something akin to a stage play. His cinematographer, Joseph Biroc, tends to pump excessive light into interior spaces, as a general rule (consult any Robert Aldrich color picture shot by Biroc, and you might see what I mean). Thus, the added help of Alex North's unique, Oscar-nominated score completes the picture with a heightened literacy and historicity.

Castle had a refined taste for the high concept, or an unrefined taste, depending on whom you ask. Did his tack, his approach, elevate… or degrade? Did it elevate by degradation, and is that why his schtick was as fun as it was to so many moviegoers? He innovated the very term "high concept" in ways that people still have fun discussing, so why wouldn't a final go up at bat lack that spirit? He proved that the durability of the term extended beyond anything spoken. It's all in the show.

William Castle's Later Theatrical Films: *The Night Walker* (1964), *I Saw What You Did* (1965), *Let's Kill Uncle* (1966), *The Busy Body* (1967), *The Spirit is Willing* (1967), *Project X* (1968), *Shanks* (1974)

27. Voluptuous Immobility
Martin Brest and His Gray Ghosts (with a Peek Into the Later Films of Luchino Visconti)

This is a revision of a piece titled "Voluptuous Immobility: Death and Legacy in Luchino Visconti's The Leopard *and Martin Brest's* Meet Joe Black," *originally published on my defunct ConFluence-Film Blog in the spring of 2017.*

> All Sicilian expression, even the most violent, is really a wish for death. Our sensuality, a wish for oblivion. Our knifings and shootings, a hankering after extinction. Our laziness, our spiced and drugged sherbets, a desire for voluptuous immobility, that is... for death again.
>
> Prince Don Fabrizio Salina
> (Burt Lancaster) in *Il Gattopardo*
> (*The Leopard*) (1963)

When I finally got around to a belated viewing of Martin Brest's now infamous *Gigli* (2003), a full decade after its doomed theatrical release, I approached the film with the naïve hope and an arrogant confidence that the hullabaloo of negative press and critical rancor that surrounded it amounted simply to much-ado-about-nothing. "The hoi polloi is so often wrong and their cruel dismissals so often unwarranted," I pep-talked myself. Basically, I was hoping for a *Heaven's Gate* kind of situation. (Yes, despite its still dubious reputation, I am a staunch defender of *Heaven's Gate*, and have cheered its recent reappraisals with a big gloating bellow of "I toldja so!")

With director Martin Brest behind the camera on *Gigli*, how bad could it be, really? I was almost trancing myself before showtime. After all, this was the same Martin Brest who gave us the mischievous but compassionate *Going in Style* (1979), the skillfully orchestrated *Beverly Hills Cop* (1984), the uncommonly witty *Midnight Run* (1988), and the flawed but perfectly likable *Scent of a Woman* (1992), with all its emphatic "hoo-ahs."

I watched maybe about an hour of *Gigli* before I just couldn't bear it anymore. It is rare for me to not finish a picture once I start it. In all candor, *Gigli* stands right, left, and bloody center as a towering monument to bad taste; I frankly found myself dumbstruck by its singular, near indescribable awfulness. I also felt stupid looking back at my earlier hope and confidence. So alas, it was indeed for good reason that critics were sent into paroxysms of rage and indignation. And their invective was nothing if not colorful: "A hypnotic black hole of a movie that sucks reputations, careers, and goodwill down its vortex," wrote the *Toronto Globe and Mail* critic. Unfortunately, it also sent Brest into "Salinger-esque" retreat and early retirement. A now retracted December 2014 *Playboy* article by Matt Patches attempted unsuccessfully to trace Brest after his disappearing act. The apoplectic response to his movie was perhaps too much to handle, though it was also reported that Brest had the movie taken away from him and re-edited. As much as I'd like giving him the benefit of the doubt, I find it hard to imagine that anyone or anything could improve upon the woeful material on display in the release version. (Sorry, Marty, wherever you are.)

Brest, like Michael Cimino in his day, became a poster boy for the perils of Hollywood largesse. The worst side effect of the *Gigli* fallout, however, was that it gave newly minted Brest skeptics and detractors license to further deride his previous effort, *Meet Joe Black* (1998), the film I would surely call his most elegant and aesthetically refined. It might not be fashionable to lavish it with such praise, but I'll lay my cards on the table without compunction. The ravishing *Meet Joe Black* is one of my "crusade pictures," that is, the misunderstood or outright dismissed films that I defend to the bitter end. It is also one that I have recommended to people, especially those who know it only by reputation. Without shame, I have repeatedly proclaimed it a *film maudit* ("cursed film," but beyond that, one worthy of re-evaluation).

Just as much a reinterpretation and extrapolation of Luchino Visconti's *The Leopard* (1963) as it is a remake and re-envisioning of Mitchell Leisen's *Death Takes a Holiday* (1934), its purported source, the three-hour *Meet Joe Black* was of course accused of prolixity across the board — mostly because it more than doubled the length of Leisen's "original," adding a number of subplots, thematic

Princes with their handsome harbingers of change in
Meet Joe Black and *The Leopard*.

threads, and unexpected narrative detours, not to mention skillfully protracted dramatic movements. The word is "protracted" rather than "distended." Distension implies strain, whereas protraction implies premeditation. The math works out just fine, because *Meet Joe Black* is just one-half *Death Takes a Holiday*, no more and no less. Needless to say, the great Mitchell Leisen's story, a genteel high-concept farce, is a much more streamlined treatment.

With its $90 million price tag and the expected starpower that comes with all those zeroes—boasting Brad Pitt at his most "beefcake" in the lead role—it has become habit and de rigueur to overlook *Meet Joe Black* as a real piece of cinema and to simply accept it as just another Big Bad Studio Film, a flop at that. At this juncture, it is perhaps apropos to note the apocryphal: the film actually did go into profit, thanks to the predictably discerning European audience. Stateside, it made back about half its negative cost, whereas it made double that across the pond. American studios and American audiences traditionally reject alternative, daresay subversive, treatments of cinematic duration.

The film's relative intimacy suggests a perceived imbalance in the expected reciprocity between a movie's length and its flair for spectacle. On the latter front, Brest finds spectacle in Academy Award winner Dante Ferretti's exquisite design, and the "saffron glow" of cinematographer Emmanuel "Chivo" Lubezki's rendering of that design. The European audience has never been discomfited by epics of pure intimacy, as Americans have. On the contrary, they have lauded them.

The European epic to which I most compare *Meet Joe Black* does indeed offer that traditional historical epic sweep typical of three-hour length. Luchino Visconti's *Il Gattopardo* (*The Leopard*) is based on Giuseppe Tomasi de Lampedusa's posthumously published saga of Italy's Resorgimento ("Resurgence"), during which Giuseppe Garibaldi and his "redshirts" battled the royalist army for the unification of a fractured Italy in 1860. The novel and the film tell the story of Sicilian aristocrat Don Fabrizio Corbera, the prince of Salina, who simultaneously resists, and then in good conscience, welcomes the political groundswell that sweeps the land. He also realizes with great sadness, however, that he will have no place within the new society it births. When the prince's firebrand nephew Tancredi, previously a redshirt, intends to marry Angelica, the daughter of a nouveau riche beneficiary of the revolution, the film culminates in a nearly hour-long dress ball sequence during which she is introduced to the local aristocracy.

The dress ball is symbolic of the end of an era, the last gasp of decadence, the well-festooned Viking funeral given a newly irrelevant man, internally aflame in a sea of faces he labors to recognize his place within. The prince is a "leopard," the member of a mournful dying breed who can neither take comfort or refuge in denial, nor bargain his way out of the new, bitter reality. This dress ball is, of course, perfectly analogous to the 45-minute birthday ball that caps off *Meet Joe Black*.

Both Visconti's and Brest's films are pristine portraits of opulence and privilege. Both are about the nature of legacy, and both are about fear—specifically, fear of the loss of that legacy, opulence, and privilege. Both Burt Lancaster's Sicilian prince and

The opulent sets of Martin Brest (above) and Luchino Visconti (below).

Anthony Hopkins' communications magnate William Parrish are gray ghosts, onetime men of excellence, patricians of astonishing taste and class and acumen, cornered into a fate that withers them into hollowed-out relics (Al Pacino's character in *Scent of a Woman* is also a "gray ghost," a term actually used in the dialogue of a second-act scene of that film, as are the trio in *Going in Style*.) Hopkins, the recently defrocked and humiliated chairman of the board of his own communications empire, knows that his death awaits at party's end. It has been agreed upon by both parties: himself and the handsome grim reaper who has breezed into his charmed life.

At an earlier point in the movie, Hopkins' worldly, dyspeptic William Parrish angrily laments, "I don't want anybody buying up my life's work, turning it into something it wasn't meant to be. A man wants to leave something behind, and he wants it left behind the way he made it, with a sense of honor, of dedication, of truth. Okay?" One can certainly see how *The Leopard*'s Prince of Salina could relate to Parrish's dilemma. They are both newly convicted prisoners of an unforeseen ignominy. And beyond that, the Joe Black/Angel of Death character is the Prince's death dream (and death wish) manifest. About midway through Lampedusa's *The Leopard*, the prince launches into a soliloquy about death: "Sleep, my dear Chevalley, eternal sleep… that is what Sicilians want. And they will always resent anyone who tries to awaken them, even to bring them the most wonderful of gifts. And, between ourselves, I doubt very strongly whether this new Kingdom has very many gifts for us in its luggage."

The prince speaks of the desire for "voluptuous immobility," in other words, the luxury of a dirt nap. As an aristocrat who knows only the best of everything, the Prince understands and can perceive the ultimate "luxury" left unspoken and unconsidered. As stated in the novel's closing line, "Then all found peace in a heap of livid dust" (translation: Archibald Colquhoun).

Both the Prince and William Parrish find their final respite in dances with respective young women: for the former, his nephew's fiancée (Claudia Cardinale); for the latter, his youngest daughter, Susan (Claire Forlani). The women's respective romantic partners could be argued as analogous. If William Parrish's daughter Susan is smitten with Brad Pitt's reaping Joe Black, is the Alain Delon character in *The Leopard*, Tancredi Falconeri, the Garibaldini, an angel of death in some figurative sense? Bracketing the Prince's acceptance of Garibaldi's revolution, he covets Tancredi's youthful idealism, just as much as he is amused and dismayed by it. Tancredi's now oft-quoted line, "If things are to stay as they are, they must change," is met with a quiet, acquiescing grimace on the prince's part; there is an inconvenient truth in his nephew's nifty slogan. The whimsicality and callowness of the Joe Black character conforms with how the prince sees Tancredi, who is a solemn but impetuous usher of the inevitable, just as Joe Black is for Parrish.

"Nunc et in hora mortis nostrae. Amen." ("Now and in the hour of our death. Amen.")—the opening of Giuseppe Tomasi de Lampedusa's novel *The Leopard*.

Many Visconti scholars have argued the emotional and psychological proximity he shared with his protagonist in *The Leopard*. He knew what the prince's calamitous loss meant in a very direct sense, despite his own loss being self-imposed. Born an aristocrat himself, and a descendant of Milan's ruling dynasty, Visconti renounced these roots to align himself with the Italian

The princes' last dances with beauty,
in *Meet Joe Black* and *The Leopard*.

Communist Party. He lived this most wholeheartedly in his earliest films, especially his breakthrough film, *La Terra Trema* (1948), the neorealist documentary-drama anthem to the residents of a poor fishing village in rural Sicily. Though he remained the cultivated, urbane individual renowned for directing lavishly designed operas (and formatively shaping the career of legendary opera diva Maria Callas), he remained politically committed, and this is appreciable in his films up to and including his classic *Rocco and His Brothers* (1960), likewise an epic of supreme intimacy.

With *The Leopard*, Visconti made a leap towards the more formally epic, with all an epic entails, including pomp and visual extravagance in surplus. At the time of release and its subsequent winning of the Palme d'Or at Cannes, this leap was perceived as an unexpected but glorious left turn. *The Damned* (*Il Caduta Degli Dei*, 1969), the saga of a German industrial dynasty during the rise of Nazism, and *Ludwig* (1973), a biopic of Bavaria's mad king and builder of extravagant dream castles, both saw him continue down the path of directing films that indicted decadence while also putting it on unfettered display.

On a personal note, Luchino Visconti is my own favorite Italian director. I count many of his films, including *La Terra Trema*, *Senso* (1954), *Rocco and His Brothers*, and *The Leopard*, as favorites among my pantheon. I find that I connect with him most on an emotional level, as his films not only consider the aforementioned loss, with remarkable transference. There is no more powerful film, in this regard, than *The Leopard*. His ability to project that sense of loss on a dramaturgical level is matched, indeed augmented and poeticized, by his abilities as a cinematic technician, scenarist, and craftsman.

Beyond *The Leopard*'s various narrative parallels to *Meet Joe Black*, there exist clear stylistic and visual ones as well. Shallow focus, diaphanous lighting, and sure, steady-as-she-goes camera movement, all especially present in the climactic set pieces, speak to a refined sense of decoupage in both films. I would not be the least bit surprised to learn that Brest consciously took cues from Visconti in his own film. He appropriates Visconti tropes for an unmistakably Hollywood-engineered and financed film, produced for mass consumption (with some degree of schmaltz at the denouement, as to throw the popcorn crowd a bone after three hours), but his aesthetic approach is scrupulously tasteful in ways that few other pieces of modern Hollywood product are.

How many Martin Brests do we really have left in today's mainstream Hollywood machine? Most of the auteurs working today succeed in spite of the system, but seldom within it. Within only lies the safety of anonymity. This is why I cannot countenance any digs made against *Meet Joe Black*, clearly one of the most personal and profoundly cinema-literate big budget efforts of its time or any time. Do I have any minor misgivings? Perhaps— but I do feel the subplot relationship between Joe Black and the Jamaican elder contributes to a cumulative effect that bears fruit. *Meet Joe Black* has far more than a greeting card's depth in its commentary to say about life and mortality, and these other dimensions are perhaps fit for another essay. I love it as much as I love the arguably more sophisticated *The Leopard*. One may think the comparison herein vulgar or upstart-ish, but these are things I say at play, take them or leave them. I do believe that Brest himself was conscious of the parallels. *Gigli* or no *Gigli*, Martin Brest unabashedly gets my support, for his individuality and his precision. The problem is that when he had to go, he didn't go in style—and as evidenced in his work, that's not like him.

Martin Brest's Theatrical Feature Films: *Hot Dogs for Gaugin* (1972, short), *Hot Tomorrows* (1977), *Going in Style* (1979), *WarGames* (1983, fired and replaced by John Badham), *Beverly Hills Cop* (1984), *Midnight Run* (1988), *Scent of a Woman* (1992), *Meet Joe Black* (1998), *Gigli* (2003)

Luchino Visconti Post-Neorealism: *The Leopard* (1963), *Sandra* (1965), *The Stranger* (1967), *The Damned* (1969), *Death in Venice* (1971), *Ludwig* (1973), *Conversation Piece* (1974), *The Innocent* (1976)

Appendix: Capsule Case Studies

Allan Arkush: The best phrase to describe Allan Arkush's filmography is "Mosh Bosch"—that is, an Hieronymus Bosch action painting of a mosh pit in a messy, raucous rock 'n' roll zen state. Much like his lifelong friend Joe Dante, Arkush has picked up a *Hellzapoppin'* (1941) influenced taste for often meta anarchy and a very pop-ish, madcap kind of tomfoolery. Arkush made too few feature films, though one should take into account telefilms like *Shake, Rattle and Rock* (1994), *Elvis Meets Nixon* (1997), and the miniseries event *The Temptations* (1999). His underseen comic quasi-memoir *Get Crazy* (1983) is based on his wild, wacky days as an usher and backstage hand at the Fillmore East. It's a woolly, glorious, gag-a-minute "shit-riposte" to the fevers of his classic *Rock 'n' Roll High School* (1979).

Though his *Heartbeeps* (1981) was an unqualified disaster in its day, I find more and more people who earnestly and honestly love the film, tuning into its strange, almost religious waves, as a paean to the ability of any sentient being to find love. (Note: That doesn't mean that most don't hate it and find it woefully misguided, but it does have some devotees.) Arkush dismisses the whole affair as "youthful hubris" because he had envisioned it as his take on Frank Borzage's *7th Heaven* (1927), about pure souls who find each other, but... with robots. Whatever one comes away with, it is a "failed experiment" at the very least, and this particular writer/critic thinks there's nothing really all that wrong with that. *Caddyshack II* (1988) was his Waterloo but, so shoot me, my brothers and I grew up watching this one more than the original (which we don't like very much) and easily preferring it. To this day, we still quote lines to each other. Just goes to show you, it takes all kinds.

Robert Altman: I'm the type of guy who believes that even when Altman is bad, he's good. And that's all I got to say about that.

Ari Aster: I'm agnostic regarding Aster. I think he's talented but fatally undisciplined. Others can channel similar angst with a similar depth of intimacy without getting so constantly tangled in the weeds, tripping on both those weeds and himself. For instance, in *Beau is Afraid*: If I were Aster, by the time I was re-reading my script in pre, and noticed pages and pages of (often redundant) block text that Mama LuPone would have to rattle off, with whatever degree of intensity or conviction—and imagined that in actual screen time, no matter how well-staged—I'd feel it imperative to liberate my material a bit from my own solipsism. Re: the misanthropy, this ain't nothing either. He's misanthropic to a fault, and not always in a way that's entertaining or, at base level, intriguing. It's always cynicism on parade, dancing the mashed-potato, hanging from the rafters, oozing from the floorboards, and hiding in the Bisquick.

Part of what bothers me is I'm not sure if Mr. Aster is capable of any true feeling. Everything just seems to be a shit-post or a troll, sometimes both. That might be some folks' cup of tea though. I prefer misanthropy when it comes from the likes of, for instance, Silvio Narizzano (and yet still nothing in *Eddington* manages to be as fucked up as something like Narizzano's *Redneck*, as much as I think Aster would like it to be). Too much of his work seems like an empty exercise in trying to outdo himself and others with the outrage and the button-pushing, without much of an endgame. I found that to be true of his career-making student short *The Strange Thing About the Johnsons* (2011), which is expressly designed to appall. I could never work on such a wavelength, honestly. It takes years to make a film, and if I'm doing it even 40% for the thrill of offending, I'd find my time better spent doing something else.

In terms of his most recent, *Eddington* (2025), when a film-maker concocts such a gory, balls-to-the-wall, epic, all-American burlesque, it seems to me that a statement should be more in the offing. Is it that tech has turned us into stratified classes of zombies, a gambit which paves the way for its overall takeover, while the dangerously malcontent byproducts it creates wait in the wings for their time to strike? Most of all, Mr. El Director needs more self-discipline if he is ever really going to develop into a filmmaker with staying power. He even admitted as much in a recent interview. As is, he is heading into flash-in-the-pan territory, because outrage-manufacturing only stays fresh for so long.

Paul Bartel: A filmmaker after my own heart, a pioneer of the Vantablack comedy (steps beyond the standard dark comedy, the next level up from that being "jet-black comedy") and a surprisingly poised stylist who traffics in deliciously devilish films designed to stir moral outrage among professional pearl-clutchers. The tidal wave of gallows humor is buttressed by a more cultivated and discerning taste for the perverse. Bartel is a wicked, crude but paradoxically classy, chop-licking purveyor of cinematic id. He is the John Waters of a more elegant, even aristocratic bearing (I tend to enjoy Bartel much more than Waters). I can imagine Bartel at table sipping Dirty Shirleys with Silvio Narizzano, yucking it up in the afterlife somewhere. Neither cared to placate anyone less than prepared to accept their most delectably depraved visions. It's telling that an early Bartel screenwriting credit, for his friend Charles Hirsch, is titled *Utterly Without Redeeming Social Value* (1969), a designation that the censors doth bestowed, as it set the pace for a career, and it was never less than gleeful about it: *Private Parts* (1972), *Death Race 2000* (1975), *Eating Raoul* (1982), and *Scenes from the Class Struggle in Beverly Hills* (1989) are the best of his films. I'm also quite fond of a number of sequences in *Not for Publication* (1984) and *Shelf Life* (1993).

Hall Bartlett: An image of Bartlett that leaps to mind from watching his films is of a silver-haired, 60-ish hipster wearing a turtleneck with love-beads and an ankh, speaking unaffectedly and unironically about peace and love. The picture for which he is most known is the live-action adaptation of *Jonathan Livingston Seagull* (1973), On IMDb, Hall Bartlett is defined on his biography page as an "American experimental filmmaker, writer, producer and director. Many of his films deal with social issues, such as racial tension, teenage angst, life in prison, and so on." The Turner Classic Movies site describes him as "a filmmaker with a mystical bent, a love of nature, and an interest in minorities and the oppressed. A highly respected filmmaker in Europe, Bartlett never quite achieved a really outstanding or important film, but his oeuvre does occasionally suggest the chances post-war independent filmmakers could take in terms of subject matter."

The New York Times called *Changes* (1969), his masterpiece in my opinion, "one of the most imaginative, haunting and artistic movies yet made. It is a remarkable film and—more than that— a remarkable experience." Talk about a rave! As my friend, critic Nathaniel Thompson, observes in his review, "*Changes* is about as perfect an example of how much experimental filmmaking was impacting American theaters in 1969." It's a soulful (and nearly plotless) entry in the pantheon of Sixties counterculture cinema. Starring Kent Lane, Bartlett's stepson by his second wife (actress Rhonda Fleming), the film takes a different sort of look at dropping out from society. One can, in a number of sequences, sense the influence of Bruce Conner and Kenneth Anger. *The Sandpit Generals* (1971), released by AIP in America as *The Wild Pack*, is a tale of homeless orphans in Brazil that also starred Kent Lane. It became a major cult film sensation in, of all places, Russia. Both *Changes* and *The Sandpit Generals* possess a dignified, nongimmicky, and (considering Bartlett's age) strangely unaffected hippie sensibility. The pop-existentialist, New Agey, hippie-dippy *Jonathan Livingston Seagull* was daring if, for no other reason, because it featured an all-seagull cast. But what of the films Bartlett made before he fully realized himself as a geriatric hippie-whisperer?

At his outset, Bartlett formed his own production company in 1952 and produced the Oscar-nominated *Navajo* (1952), a documentary about a Native American boy who runs away from white culture when he is dragged off to school. Over the next few decades Bartlett drifted into and out of the studio system, helming the prison melodrama *Unchained* (1954) for Warners. And then, oh boy, there's *Zero Hour!* (1957), the film that inspired *Airplane* (a parody which actually credits Bartlett). *Drango* (1957) is not a Western, as it's often credited, but a "Southern" that uses the Western tropes. He filled multiple roles beyond simply directing his Sixties pictures, including the campy mental asylum melodrama *The Caretakers* (1963), starring Joan Crawford as a nasty nurse. The message-y but well-intentioned *All the Young Men* (1960) pitted a latter-day Alan Ladd against a rising Sidney Poitier in a racial drama set during the Civil War. Bartlett went out on two films, *The Children of Sanchez* (1978), another Anthony Quinn Zorba-knockoff-athon mostly known for its Grammy-winning Chuck Mangione music, and *Comeback* (1982), which told the fact-based story of an Australian reporter attempting to rescue a Laotian girl from the Pathet Lao Army, in the aftermath of the Vietnam War. Public disputes between Bartlett and star Michael Landon led to two distinct versions being released. It was NBC that broadcast the Landon recut as *Love is Forever*. The clusterfuck prompted his retirement.

Noel Black: Black was first known for *Skaterdater* (1965), a ubiquitous short in its day. Picked up for distribution by United Artists, it was perhaps the only work of its kind to go into profit. But following an auspicious feature debut with the sleeper hit *Pretty Poison* (1968), a stunningly intelligent small-town thriller starring Anthony Perkins and Tuesday Weld, he had what was perhaps the most precipitous fall from grace of any upcoming director in the history of American cinema. His two immediate follow-ups were films that flopped so resoundingly that his career never recovered. *Cover Me Babe* (1970) doesn't "work" per se, but it's fascinating as artifact. To wit, it's the first film—or at least the first major studio film—to be set at a film school, with film students as its principal characters. It was also Robert Forster's own follow-up to his role in Haskell Wexler's *Medium Cool* (1969); his character is an extension of that film's news cameraman, still pressing his face to the eyepiece of a CP-16 in scene after scene. He's a downright bastard in the picture: a toweringly arrogant, far beyond pretentious, and (one could feasibly argue) sociopathic experimental cinema iconoclast—a real "jewel" of a human. His fierce unlikability is no doubt just one reason why it tanked. Writer-director Floyd Mutrux pops up in the cast, as an ashamed-of-being-gay student filmmaker who gets cruelly mistreated by our "hero." Black went on the record saying the film should have never been made. When I met Robert Forster (through Karen Black) back in 2008, I mentioned this film to him. He shot me a very curious look, as one would.

Jennifer on My Mind (1971) was Black's next. I'd never say it's a "good" film, but I think I "get" it, so I'm not going to join the chorus of those who say it's a disaster (which seems to be a majority). Very odd, yes, but disaster? Sheesh. Someone's review on Letterboxd made me chuckle: "Puff of cigar smoke: 'Let's do *Love Story* meets *Panic in Needle Park*! Is Erich Segal available?'" There's a smidge of truth to that. Our young hero has to awkwardly cart his lady love's corpse around throughout much of the runtime. A large part of the movie feels like a puppydog-eyed lovestruck-and-lovelorn *Weekend at Bernie*'s with a drug message, absent the absurdism and increasingly extravagant necro-comedy set pieces. Peter Bonerz, Chuck McCann, Renee Taylor, baby Barry Bostwick, and yes, Robert De Niro (as a "gypsy cab driver"—oh the irony!) turn up too.

The rest of Black's career is unremarkable (including being fired off the Shirley MacLaine picture *A Change of Seasons*), though it wasn't for lack of ambition. Black had planned to adapt Saul Bellow's *The Adventures of Augie March* and make a biopic of Railroad Bill. He tends to favor stories about guys who make their own rules, especially when pressured by the normies that orbit them. Christopher Wicking and Tise Vahimagi's *The American Vein* notes his unique "sense of intimacy with freaky characters."

Bill Brame: With only four directorial efforts to his name, Brame is one of my favorite skid-row exploitation/grindhouse/camp directors. There's no bio of him out there, even on the internet—he's just *that* obscure. He was the type of guy who would start making a period piece and then either forget he's doing period, or simply says "Fuck it" (which is only a part of what makes his *Baby Needs a New Pair of Shoes* such a gas). Brame made his fortune as an editor, having toiled in the cutting room on Howard Hawks' *Red Line 7000* (1965), Roger Vadim's *Pretty Maids All in a Row* (1971), and Ted Post's *The Harrad Experiment* (1973), among a handful of others. He made his directorial debut with *The Cycle Savages* (1968), a biker flick with one humdinger of a premise: Bruce Dern, hot into his AIP tenure, plays Keeg, a fierce, "heavy," shade-wearing rider who supplies nubile young ladies for his brother's white slavery racket. That brother is played by Casey Kasem (oh but of course, dear reader!). It's one of the more grisly, wackadoo, and blissfully un-self-aware in that, a-hem, "cycle" of pictures, if you'll forgive the lame pun.

Free Grass (1969), a.k.a. *Scream Free*, is a counterculture happening with a wholly arbitrary *West Side Story* fixation in that it stars Richard Beymer ("Tony"), Russ Tamblyn ("Riff"), and Lana Wood (Natalie's sister). The poster proclaimed, "The stars of *West Side Story* together again!" The film itself, however, had nothing else whatsoever to do with Sondheim and Bernstein's beloved musical. Beymer and Wood need cash, so they agree to help Tamblyn smuggle grass from Mexico to L.A. Sounds like *Easy Rider*, no? (They were released concurrently.) When Beymer objects to narcotics agents being killed, Tamblyn puts LSD in his drink, tries to burn him alive, and has Lana kidnapped. It's Bad Trip Time! Incidentally, Casey Kasem appears in this one too, as a dope dealer (oh but of course, dear reader!). If you dig psychedelic cinema, this one is pretty far out, in both awful and wonderful ways. *Miss Melody Jones* (1972), a.k.a. *Ebony Dreams*, stars Philomena Nowlin as a young woman willing to do almost anything for fame and fortune in Hollywood. Sounds like a familiar premise, right? The only element that renders it a bit more unique is that she realizes the key to her success might involve passing herself off as white. She has voice that could shatter mason jars from a distance, but the best part of all is that she plays an actress who, apparently, so deeply impresses the tone-deaf and bat-blind industry honchos she comes to work for. Some of its video boxes, with its pistol-toting, fro-topped heroine promising blazeroo action, would lead you to believe it's a *Cleopatra Jones* or *Coffy* type of affair. It's not. It is horribly acted, but does have a number of campy charms though.

As mentioned earlier, *Baby Needs a New Pair of Shoes* (1974), a.k.a. *Jive Turkey*, starts as a period flick, with '40s and '50s automobiles buzzing by while actors decked out in old suits and nifty fedoras parade around them. But Brame seems far more preoccupied with disguising what looks like a small Ohio town as Harlem to notice when his meager period trappings start to betray him. There are more inadvertent anachronisms in this film than there are advertent ones in Alex Cox's *Walker* (1987). But, if you go with it, the film spins you into a weird delirium with strokes of sheer insanity, which translate, by some quirk of fate, to a cock-eyed almost-brilliance. Watch for a brutal transvestite mobster named Serene who kills with her high-heeled shoes. The opening promises "This is a true story," though if that disclaimer appeared at the end, it would raise eyebrows and/or stir some chuckles. And, as Nathaniel Thompson notes, "The jolting slo-mo massacre scene over the opening credits is a much more aggressive and stylish curtain raiser than you usually saw around this time." *Baby Needs* is his best film for every one of these reasons.

Peter Collinson: In his later career, Collinson is kind of a version of Lindsay Shonteff, with more money and more horse-sense. There's more to Collinson beyond that, but if you consider his globe-trotting cloak-and-dagger excursions, it becomes an interesting parallel. No one loved low-angle shots more, and as my friend Nathaniel Thompson told me, "Peter Collinson perfectly embodies the Seventies British mindset in basically every way, and he seems to fancy the idea of social systems as destroyers, or at least antagonists." Howard S. Berger, who provides the Blu-ray commentary on Collinson's film *Fright* (1971) points out that many of his films revolve around women held captive in distinctively (and oppressively) men's worlds. This is certainly also true of *The Penthouse* (1967), *Straight on Till Morning* (1972), *Innocent*

Bystanders (1973), *Open Season* (1974), and *Tomorrow Never Comes* (1978), which all involve the taking of female hostages. Collinson is a subject for further study, and he might be covered much more fully in a second volume of my essays, if there is one. This capsule write-up has identified some recurring tropes and trademarks, but has still managed to overlook his finest works: *Up the Junction* (1968), *The Long Day's Dying* (1968), *The Italian Job* (1969), and *The Earthling* (1980).

Lance Comfort: A subject for further study. This is a British director who intrigues me more than many/most of the others in his generation. His *Live It Up!* (1963) is not a flawless pop musical, but again, it's got lashings of style. As evidenced by *Eight O'Clock Walk* (1954), *The Man in the Road* (1956), and *Tomorrow at 10* (1963), there is something more to Mr. Comfort, and one day, I will get to the bottom of it, and him.

Brian De Palma: I love De Palma for his free-form, free-for-all counterculture comedies. *Murder a la Mod* (1967), *Greetings* (1968), *The Wedding Party* (1969), *Hi, Mom!* (1970), and *Phantom of the Paradise* (1974), and even the reviled (and studio-mutilated) *Get to Know Your Rabbit* (1972). These constitute my sweet spot with this most beloved of auteurs. And for a genre I don't really jibe with, I unusually delight in his gangster films: *Scarface* (1983), *The Untouchables* (1987), and *Carlito's Way* (1993). As for the Hitchcockian works, I vary. I think *Sisters* (1973) is the most evocative distillation of the Brian/Alfie ethos, while still managing to infuse the film with the De Palma's interest in voyeurism, duality (or the "dueling dualing"), erotic obsession, and the vagaries of a fractured psyche. *Carrie* (1976) is so in-the-culture that any grievance one could have about it is entirely moot. Nearly my whole life, I've never quite been able to wrap my head around the incredulities of *Dressed to Kill* (1980), even when I'm feeling more generous; though I applaud that film's formal and stylistic bravado. I might be more amenable to De Palma some days more than others. I recognize that he's consummately cinematic, and that he thinks so purely in those terms, but I find his material a bit wearying sometimes (and this is certainly not to say I'm a prude). But this is more personal taste than objective appraisal, obviously—it's a question of material I'm often not all that keen on.

Disney Live Action Directors of the Sixties and Seventies: When I was a kid, becoming aware of directors and the important role they played on the movies I watched, I started keeping a mental index of assorted names I'd see in the opening credits, attempting to detect traces of personality.

Robert Stevenson (*Mary Poppins, Bedknobs and Broomsticks*, countless others) was kind of the Disney live action John Ford, drawn to the studio's films that assayed themes of family, tradition, and ritual. Norman Tokar (*Savage Sam, Follow Me, Boys!, The Ugly Dachshund, The Happiest Millionaire*) struck me as the most creature-friendly, including the "friendly" but very real alligators in *Happiest Millionaire*, and the four-legged lovables in *Ugly Dachshund*, among others, so he's kind of the Clarence Brown of the stable. One might even say the alligators reach Hawksian levels in their treatment, à la *Bringing Up Baby*, but I'll settle on Brown.

Vincent McEveety (*The Million Dollar Duck, Superdad, Herbie Goes to Monte Carlo*) always struck me as the Richard Lester of the Disney stable—his cuts were faster and were occasionally trickstery. I admit there might be nothing here, but Disney was a place to begin for me, way back when. This isn't a wanton attempt to twist your melon, dear reader, but think of it as an amusin' little musin' using a swatch of my own biography.

Cy Endfield: I've heard and read multiple critics and historians extol Endfield through the years. There were Pierre Rissient, Jonathan Rosenbaum, Gavin Lambert, and Raymond Durgnat, just to name a few. With the publication of Brian Neve's biography *The Many Lives of Cy Endfield* in 2015, someone finally put pen to a loose tangle of thought, theory, and opinion. There weren't many films you'd call "famous" except for *Zulu* (1964), which placed 31 on the British Film Institute's Top 100 British Films of All Time. As one of a number of American directors who departed for Europe in the early Fifties because of the blacklist (among them were Joseph Losey, John Berry, Jules Dassin, and Carl Foreman), Endfield made his name in his adopted country with muscular genre pictures distinguished by their salient political underpinnings.

Along with *Zulu, Hell Drivers* (1958), the story of a cutthroat trucking company, is his best post-blacklist picture—a film I first saw on VHS in the early aughts under the American title *Hard Drivers*. Stanley Baker became Endfield's avatar, his residing spirit and star-as-canvas, casting him in five films, the last of which was the blistering survival saga *Sands of the Kalahari* (1965). As for his pre-blacklist work, *Try and Get Me!* (1951), also known as *The Sound of Fury*, a fresh take on Fritz Lang's scorching vigilante noir *Fury* (1936), is undoubtedly his best and most touted, with the journo saga *The Underworld Story* (1950) coming right up behind. It's fascinating that he coda-ed with *Universal Soldier* (1971), starring George Lazenby immediately after his one Bond outing, just as he was in the throes of an existential crisis that precluded him from a second go strapping on the Walther PPK and ordering up a shaken-not-stirred martini. In Endfield's swan song, he plays a laconic, emotionally wounded, but still tough-as-nails mercenary who, mirroring Lazenby's reality, undergoes an existential crisis of his own, from which he is reborn as a pacifist. The film is almost like a personal press kit for Lazenby, considering his nascent emotional investment in the peacenik counterculture currents of the time. He even financially invested in the production once the backers got wind that the director wasn't shooting the script he first presented to them, and pulled out. Endfield appears in the film in a supporting role.

The vagaries of the biz had clearly gotten to him by then (especially after Roger Corman radically recut his previous film *De Sade*), so he took a page from his *Universal Soldier* protagonist's book and dropped out himself, making a name in other disciplines, especially his invention of the first pocket word-processing system, the MicroWriter. The man was a renowned polymath. Cinematically, *Universal Soldier* was an odd way to go, but a very "Endfieldian" and meta-textual way to go, nevertheless. He was never precious about departures; even when he had to leave his birth country during the McCarthy era, he did so without looking back. He spent the rest of his days being honored at festivals and attending career retrospectives at a number of venues, including at the Cinémathèque française in Paris. What a subject, this Mr. Enfield!

John Farrow: The lion's share of my deepened education on John Farrow came as a result of working on a tribute box-set, put out by Imprint Films. I had the privilege of pretty much co-producing the entire set and I was struck by the baroqueness of his shots and his extended takes. By all accounts, he was a rather f-ed up human being, but a cut-above-the-rest talent when it came to active, interesting, and always dynamic staging for camera. Farrow would never be counted as a "sensitive" director—he was too much an

Australian sailor to ever throw his masculinity in the backseat, but I find him more palatable than others of his ilk. His three-film run of *The Big Clock* (1948), *Night Has a Thousand Eyes* (1948), and *Alias Nick Beal* (1949) are my three favorites, but there are more where those came from.

Emerald Fennell: Many of the self-style "cool kids" of my own millennial generation who think they're socialists (but are actually just cravenly middle-class suburban kids cosplaying as "revolutionaries," or at least peacocking the shallow aesthetic of revolution) think Emerald Fennell is some kind of cinematic antichrist. It's become fashionable to dunk on Fennell as some nepo-baby fraud. Honestly, only makes her more attractive to me. I also sense a divide between gay and straight audiences when it comes to appreciation of *Saltburn* (2023). My gay male film-nerd friends had a gay old time, while their heterosexual male counterparts were driven to apoplectic seething and indignation. To a lesser extent, this is also true of *Promising Young Woman* (2021). We'll see where she goes (as of this printing, she is set to release *Wuthering Heights*), but I'm intrigued, and so is my husband, who preferred *Promising* to *Saltburn*. I just want to present a diagram of a human body to her most aggravated and beady-eyed detractors and ask them, "Where on this diagram did Fennell's films hurt you?" Post-script: I recently saw an insult directed at her that went, "Her filmmaking makes sense when you know her father sells ornate, tacky, stupid, expensive jewelry." Jesus H, remind me to never take you wet-blanket killjoys to a drag show. They said the same of Mitchell Leisen.

Richard Fleischer: It is impossible for me to put Fleischer in a class either with or above the likes of Schaffner, Furie, or Guillermin. I can and do enjoy many of the films, but still cannot fathom a director who gives us something as dire as *Doctor Dolittle* (1967), then turns around to fill in for other director brothers who got fired off their productions. He seemed to be Hollywood's favorite ringer, having replaced John Farrow, John Huston, Michael Campus, Richard C. Sarafian, and Sidney J. Furie. These are just the guys we know of. I guess it's a living, but I don't look kindly upon it from an auteurist point-of-view. I think the closest he got to true auteurship was with his trilogy of serial killer films: *Compulsion* (1960), *The Boston Strangler* (1968), and *10 Rillington Place* (1971). I know he's got his defenders, and I hear them, but I'm not anywhere near listing him as someone as important as others I've personally defended and championed. I do love what he did with something like *Mr. Majestyk* (1974), however— coloring an Elmore Leonard potboiler with a kind of adjacent working man saga, a sympathetic eye cast in the direction of the film's undocumented migrant farmers. He could be capable of certain small but noble transcendences. I'm never going to argue with films like *20,000 Leagues Under the Sea* (1954) and *Fantastic Voyage* (1966) as first league entertainment.

Theodore J. Flicker: *The President's Analyst* (1967) had critics and counterculture audiences standing to attention. His Second City background gave the satire in the film the all-important punch. It was so potent that the real US government put Paramount execs on the defensive, and on notice, in advance of the release. Then it seemed like we never really heard from him again, though he kept working. Canadians of a certain generation have his *Jacob Two-Two and the Hooded Fang* (1978) burrowed into their psyche from childhood, for better or worse. *Up in the Cellar* (1970) is indeed a curious follow-up to *The President's Analyst* and is... *interesting*, at least as another anti-establishment farce about sticking it to the man, in this case a university president (whereas in *Analyst*, it was big government and its handmaidens). He then gets lost in the wilderness and resurfaces, like so many similar promising but sidetracked talents of his era (Noel Black, Barry Shear, David Greene), on television.

John Ford: I'm thinking of a BoJack Horseman line: "When you're looking at something or someone through rose-colored glasses, all red flags just look like flags." It's probably something we're all guilty of, but thus is subjectivity, which is really what this book is about. I recognize I'm a minority view here, but I belong to an actually quite distinguished fraternity that finds *The Searchers* (1956) pretty dire (Truffaut being just one). I don't connect with Ford as so many others seem to. I find him much too invested in the most jaundiced American mythopoetics. Outside his landscapes, I formally don't find him terribly exciting, and I much prefer the Fonda pictures to the Duke ones. But just on the overall, in terms of the Western, I'm far more emotionally and intellectually invested in Anthony Mann (with *Bend of the River* and *The Furies* especially), Howard Hawks (with *Red River* and *Rio Bravo*), Nicholas Ray (with *Johnny Guitar*), or Budd Boetticher (with *The Tall T* or *Ride Lonesome*), than I ever could be with *She Wore a Yellow Ribbon* and its like-directed siblings. Ford's co-star in Griffith's *Birth of a Nation* (1915), Raoul Walsh, also holds far more allure for me. I'm also left uncharmed by his humor, which unfortunately plays an all too outsized role in too many of his pictures. At least there is a humor, though, because when he goes all reverential, I'm left even more uncharmed. Of all his films, I most prefer *Young Mr. Lincoln* (1939), *The Grapes of Wrath* (1940), *They Were Expendable* (1945), *My Darling Clementine* (1946), and provisionally *How Green Was My Valley* (1941).

William Frawley: If Frawley had only directed *The Christian Licorice Store* (1971), a Floyd Mutrux-scripted mood piece with which I've been obsessed for the better part of two decades, he'd be worthy of discussion next to other figures Sarris might have classified as "expressive esoterica." Most would have you believe that Jacques Demy's *Model Shop* (1969) is the very height of the "existentially stymied dude driving around L.A." movie, but I'm here to tell you that, for me, the grand prize on that front goes to James Frawley's *The Christian Licorice Store*. It's a moody, structurally languorous, radically almost anti-narrative (similar to the Demy) little film that captures time and place almost as a tone piece would, courtesy of the illusory Mutrux script and an alternatingly mournful and jaunty score by Lalo Schifrin. The draggy dirge-like main theme is right in step with the Sixties and Seventies chic of "living in doubt." Plus, *Model Shop* doesn't have cameos from Jean Renoir, Monte Hellman, Tim Buckley, James B. Harris, Theodore Flicker, tennis star Butch Bucholtz, and agent Mike Medavoy. Its languorous artiness, bold elliptical patterns, odd rhythms, and a "story" that never insists upon itself, are pretty unique in American movies, even of the time. It is inscrutable in its way, and fascinating. Meandering, perhaps to a fault, but a compelling character study.

Kid Blue (1973) is similarly meandering, a mostly action-free neo-Western with a patently odd vibe. Frawley was fashioning a style of pacing and European languor all his own, but we never got to see where it went, because his next picture, *The Big Bus* (1976), an admittedly quite hilarious disaster movie parody, took him on a detour that saw its terminus with *The Muppet Movie* (1979), a film I grew up with and still love. The latter two seem to speak to his background and training as a Monkees man, working under BBS Productions in the Sixties before breaking into cinema with *Christian Licorice*, a film *The American Vein* describes as "an expensive post-Monkees home movie." But where he might have gone had he stayed the course after those first two features, I'm only left to imagine.

David Greene: Greene was focused on the idea of perversion, not necessarily sexual perversion, but the perversion of roles, totems, and institutions. His work has undergone a kind of micro-renaissance in this age of digital accessibility. His 1969 film *I Start Counting* received a great deal of enthusiastic renewed attention and a bunch of salutes and accolades following its rollout on Blu-ray in both the US and UK. The disc companies have also thankfully dug up *The People Next Door*, which likewise has many admirers. He's a very interesting director, very under-the-radar, and you could make an auteurist argument for him. I see a through-line. There's the idea of "perversion" and not necessarily in a sexual sense, although that can occasionally play into things. In his true crime double-header, *Fatal Vision* is the perversion of fatherhood, *Small Sacrifices* is the perversion of motherhood. *I Start Counting* is the perversion of brotherhood or siblinghood (and a traditional or "normal" coming-of-age), *The People Next Door* is the perversion of family overall (or the family unit) and by extension a culture in decay, *The Strange Affair* is the perversion of law, order, and social orthodoxy (the social order), *The Shuttered Room* is the perversion of community, *Sebastian*, with Dirk Bogarde, is the perversion of logic, *Friendly Fire* is the perversion of patriotism and faith in country, *Hard Country*, you might argue, is the perversion of provincialism (and the idea of normalcy and expectation). His *Godspell* is, interestingly, a reversal of all of this. That film is the sanctification of a perverted or polluted space. And *Gray Lady Down* is the hardest to read through this prism, as it feels more like a standard issue disaster pic. David Greene style?

(Discuss.) Early films exhibit more overt stylization. Purveyor of psychedelia in the late Sixties. This persists up until *Godspell*. As he moves on in his career, they become more tempered. *Gray Lady Down* is his most anonymous picture, plays like a standard disaster film, not that there's anything wrong with that per se. Retreated into or relegated to television in the late Seventies. Stayed in television until his death in 2003.

Tom Gries: It's rare when a director makes something as good as *Will Penny* (1968) and follows it up with something as unspeakable as *Fools* (1970). But then, to weigh *The Glass House* (1972), a masterful telefilm justifiably released into theaters later, along with the flawed but fascinating *Journey Through Rosebud* (1972), Gries had... something going on. His *Breakheart Pass* (1976) is one of the better Charles Bronson outings. I fail to comprehend how someone can climb such heights yet surrender so completely to dreck. I guess this is just the nature of directing in his time. His major television events, *QB VII* (1974) and *Helter Skelter* (1976), the latter of which also had a theatrical release in certain territories, are the best of their kind—true prestige productions with ample respect paid to their sources, and some technique to savor as well. Gries is a fascinating case study because when he was "on" he was *really* on. Unfortunately, there are just as many examples of Gries in "off" mode.

Ulu Grosbard: Not a big filmography, but an idiosyncratic one. I've always been partial toward *Who Is Harry Kellerman and Why Is He Saying Those Terrible Things About Me?* (1971), as a fractured comedy that indexes heavily on Resnais cutting, sparked my stream-of-consciousness memory, anxiety, and reverie. It's just the type of cockeyed movie that rouses my appetite. His debut, *The Subject Was Roses* (1968), seems to inaugurate a thematic focus, despite the Frank D. Gilroy source play reigning supreme. In the context of later works like *True Confessions* (1981), *Falling in Love* (1984), *Georgia* (1996), and *The Deep End of the Ocean* (1998), *Roses* pokes and prods at an unusual chain of family dynamics, with family members separated or otherwise challenged by professional ethics, artistic integrity, long-term separation, or simply growing estrangement. The need for personal autonomy reverberates with the characters in each. There are lines that, once defined, cannot be crossed, lest their worlds become completely destabilized. *Straight Time* (1978) is a magnificent character piece overlooked in its time, with Hoffman (much like in *Harry Kellerman*) a stranger in his own world.

Bill Gunn: What can one say about an arthouse horror landmark like *Ganja & Hess* (1973) that hasn't already been said? Gunn is invested in the idea of the fractured self, in a way no audience is, or was, used to seeing on screen. He made only three pictures— that is, if you count (as I do) the astonishing *Personal Problems* (1980), an intimate three-hour epic of black middle-class longings made expressly for the video format. He interiorizes the video art in a way no one had attempted by that point. When Kino Lorber re-released it, I was overwhelmed by Gunn's customized, rough-and-ready brand of heightened (and largely improvised) American kitchen sink realism—all this from a man I only knew from a vampiric masterpiece. Yet I could still trace colloquial cadences, shadings, rhythms, and textures connecting the work back to *Ganja*. It is a treasure. Writing about it, I feel a strong hankering to revisit it. Soon after, I had the distinct privilege of seeing his unreleased debut *Stop* (1970), regarded as one of the most coveted "lost" films of all time. I now possess a rare (in fact, beyond rare) video copy of the film, and have screened it for friends. Its hypnotic, somehow mournful eroticism—a sensuality of body contours and curves—is confrontational, thorny, frank, and shocking (enough so in its day to earn an X rating). I cannot imagine why the issues around the film have not been resolved by now, as it is simply an extraordinary film, one that has gained urban legend status over the decades it has remained out of circulation. Bill Gunn is an American treasure known by too few, and he's certainly one of the filmmakers I most wish had given us more.

Hugo Haas: I named the woebegone hero of my second feature (and university thesis film) *A Trip to Swadades* (2008) in part after Hugo Haas, skid row cinemagician extraordinaire. We shot that film on Super 16mm black and white negative, unexposing on purpose and "pushing" the stock in processing to induce extra graininess. I wanted the type of grungy, low-rent look reminiscent of the vintage low-budget works of someone like Haas. When I explained this to Henry Jaglom at the time, he was flabbergasted. His brother Michael, who acted in many of Jaglom's films as Michael Emil, would take Henry to Amos Vogel's Cinema 16 in Fifties New York, and Michael expressed a special love for the films of Hugo Haas that were sometimes shown there. Henry had not heard anyone even utter his name since those days. Critic Dennis Dermody referred to him as "the Skid Row Orson Welles" and writes, "If ever there was a director who deserves critical re-evaluation, it's the Czech-born Hugo Haas, who wrote, produced, directed and starred in over a dozen movies in the 1950s." Precious few of his movies are available on home video. Leonard Maltin's *Movie & Video Guide* often rate his films "BOMB," his bottom-of-the-barrel designation, and Ira Konigsberg in *The Complete Film Dictionary* writes off his work as "dreary, low-budget melodramas usually focusing on an inevitably doomed encounter between a crude middle-aged man and a young temptress." In the early aughts, I spent an untold number of hours tracking down bootlegs of his films, and then further hours in front of the telly watching them. They're flimsy on any number of fronts, but there is something special about Haas' often female-controlled melodramas and noirs (when I say "female-controlled," I mean that the women often yanked and jerked the marionette strings on hapless male leads). Underneath any superficial traits, there is an an honesty about them in terms of craft and pursuit, even at their most ragged. I'm especially fond of his 1951 noir *Pickup* (1951), though I do love his final film *Paradise Alley* (1962) for how it envisions run-and-gun filmmaking—his brand of filmmaking—as community-building. He's awaiting a full study and maybe a volume two of *Adventures in Auteurism* would one day do the honors. As Dermody puts it, "His moody, character-driven tales of losers and lost souls are taut, well directed, and endlessly fascinating." I've encountered more than just Dermody among a cabal of Haas lovers in my travails.

Randa Haines: In the 2010s, there was a glut of articles spotlighting pioneer female filmmakers past to present, and nearly every single one of them forgot to so much as even mention Randa Haines. Catching *Children of a Lesser God* (1986) on an airplane within the last few years, I was struck by how cinematic it was. Either I forgot or I wasn't paying attention to that dimension of it on the first go-round. One thing is clear, she loves salsa music, as it crops up in *The Doctor* (1991), *Wrestling Ernest Hemingway* (1993), and most appreciably, *Dance With Me* (1998). As far as pioneering female directors go, she never hit the heights of a Joan Micklin Silver, nor maintained her consistency, but she's got a saucy humanist personality that it is all too easy to commend.

James B. Harris: A beneficiary of Kubrickian trickle-down fame, but also a directing talent in his own right. The works are few and far between: the *Dr. Strangelove* complement *The Bedford Incident* (1965), the sui generis modern fairy tale *Some Call It Loving* (1973), the down-and-dirty James Woods double-feature *Fast-Walking* (1982) and *Cop* (1988), and the Wesley Snipes crime saga *Boiling Point* (1993) really stand as a contender for a filmography like no other. I got to meet Harris once (still ticking, as of this writing, age 98) thanks to my friendship with the late F. X. Feeney. He seemed ecstatic to meet someone who didn't regale him with questions on Kubrick, but on the films that *he* directed. I could have spent all night just on the beautiful and wholly its-own-animal *Some Call It Loving*, but our conversation splayed all over the place. Never did I want to ask him about Kubrick. I knew that was already on the record. "I want to know about you, artist James B. Harris." He might be a full study in a volume two.

Howard Hawks: Nothing but respect, but I often get the sense that the muckety-mucks put on happy glasses and read certain things into his staging and aesthetics that just aren't there, or are unremarkable comparable to other period or genre analogs. I feel this is mostly prevalent in films such as *Monkey Business* (1952) and *Gentlemen Prefer Blondes* (1953). But do I love the Hawksian female? You bet your keester! I love revisiting *Bringing Up Baby* (1938) and *Ball of Fire* (1941) with some regularity, and I'll take *Only Angels Have Wings* (1939), *Red River* (1948), and *Rio Bravo* (1958) over anything on offer from a certain Mr. Ford. I even endorse *Red Line 7000* (1965).

Alfred Hitchcock: I mostly prefer his early British and early American films. While I personally find far, far, far more pleasure in Hitchcock than in Ford, I bristle at certain mannerisms and certain overpowering fetishes found especially in the later works of the Fifties and Sixties. The craft is always impeccable, but with the ogle-the-blonde sagas (*Vertigo*, *The Birds*, *Marnie*), there is a spiritual disconnect for me, the late Robin Wood and his writings be damned. I can still remember how excited I felt seeing *Psycho* (1960) for the first time as a boy however, and I'll be the first to defend *Topaz* (1969) from its detractors. So, with certain exceptions, I'm very pro-Hitch up until the mid-Fifties or thereabouts. As is the case with Kubrick, I cannot tolerate the critic-proofing of Hitchcock, and I feel completely alienated from the Hitchcock cultists who believe in hard-and-fast blasphemy laws. And at this saturated point in history, I'd rather read film books on anyone but him.

Waris Hussein: Here we have a very humane director, who may very well be a subject for further study, and a prime pick for a full chapter in a potential volume two. Years ago, I introduced my friend and longtime cinematographer to both *Quackser Fortune Has a Cousin in the Bronx* (1970) and *Melody* (1971). I have to credit that friend with the notion that Hussein is the closest Britain ever got to a Hal Ashby, at least as evidenced in his first three features: *A Touch of Love* (1969, a.k.a. *Thank You All Very Much*) was his big screen debut.

There's a kind of grand whimsy upon which he appends bigger (and deceptively simple) ideas about non-conformity, the challenging of authority, and the fudging of social expectation via grand gestures. Like John Badham, he writes paeans to the individual. *Quackser* and *Melody* in particular are parables ("What if an uneducated bloke made his own cottage industry out of literal horseshit to avoid a depressive existence working at the local mill—a man who made his own luck?" or "What if two twelve-year-olds pursued marriage?"). *A Touch of Love* beholds an independent single mother-to-be, in a time that doing so was quite uncommon, even scandalous.

He retired into television for decades after *The Possession of Joel Delaney* (1972), his first and only American film, a surprisingly class-conscious horror thriller starring Shirley MacLaine. Class struggle emerged ever so gingerly in *Quackser* and *Melody*, then exploded upon itself in *Joel Delaney*, one of the most socially alert and disturbing such items of its time. His later feature *Sixth Happiness* (1997) returned to form with another whimsical story of social defiance through individualism. He also directed Liz Taylor and Richard Burton's last production *Divorce His/Divorce Hers* (1973), a dual-perspective drama of divorce. *Doctor Who* fans may delight in Waris Hussein because he directed the first episode ever of the series, but few if any discuss his marvelous but all too brief feature film career.

John Huston: John Huston is a great director, and anyone who'd say different, I'd never trust (and that includes Mr. Sarris, when he classifies him in his "Less Than Meets the Eye" chapter, which I find almost grotesque). What can I say that hasn't already been said? Yes, he's a great director, without question. He always know where his shot is. Next...

Peter Hyams: Hyams' films are easy to spot visually. Smoky, low-light compositions, with carefully accented highlights. These are usually engineered by the director himself (Hyams is his own cinematographer from *2010* onward). There are also the physical signs as they exist in the script: the existence of a company called ConAmalgamate (which even appears in the Herb Ross-directed *T.R. Baskin*, which he wrote and produced), a guy or shop or business named Spota the course of the runtime. Hyams is that most idiosyncratic of popcorn-paloozists. Hyams loves his conspiracies, his outlandish means of vanquishing them, his shadowy cabals, his rathskeller-esque sets. He gets short shrift, but if you're truly a cinema omnivore, it's impossible not to like the guy and what's he's put out.

Henry Jaglom: Jaglom seems to incite a great deal of anger or passion. There's very little in-between, you either dig his cinema or you don't. The same could probably be said for the man himself. I've had my ups and downs with him over the last couple of decades of mostly steady contact, but he's sui generis. I do consider him a friend and I've never met anyone like him, and never will again, however long I last on this earth. Every encounter—and there have been many over the years—goes unpredictable places conversationally. No one I've ever known is more into what makes people tick. He probes with unequaled vigor, and his pursuit is aggressive. Even when I get exasperated, I'm stimulated, and never get too agitated.

In 1971, Peter Bogdanovich and Henry Jaglom appeared on film critic Molly Haskell's public access talk show in advance of the premieres of their films, respectively *The Last Picture Show* and *A Safe Place*, at the New York Film Festival. In conversation, Bogdanovich recounted how he worked a day on Henry's film playing a juggler, but Henry cut him from the final movie. "I think Henry just wanted that for his scrapbook," Bogdanovich quipped. There's something to that. Henry at his best makes what I call "scrapbook cinema." Some refer to his aesthetic as "home movie"-esque but that's a glib and much too simplistic way of describing his métier. His Eighties films especially exemplify his sensibility. The "Jaglomian Ethic" crystallized around this time. You see Henry's friends and acquaintances captured in pressure-cooker environments wherein they bare their souls, wax philosophical (sometimes badly or awkwardly, sometimes profoundly), work out some animus or anxiety or complex, and reveal odd talents and hobbies (e.g. Michael Margotta's training of his pigeon in *Can She Bake a Cherry Pie?*, Maggie Wheeler's dolphin and chimp coaching in *New Year's Day*, Nelly Alard's cultivated physics metaphors in *Venice/Venice*, the various musical talents on display in *Someone to Love*, Henry's hilarious brother Michael Emil's sexually "enlightened" counsel on multiple pictures, etc).

The films feel intimate not just because of what the people on screen reveal about themselves, but because so much feels like Henry keeping a scrapbook and bearing his own soul through others, by virtue of what he uses in the edit. It's the compulsive holding-on of moments, familiar to many filmmakers—a kind of custom auto-documentary. Alan Berliner and Ross McElwee try to liberate formal documentary storytelling, in their own way, though not too dissimilar first-person testament, but Henry stages it in fiction. One person's trash is another's treasure, just as one person's fascination or exhilaration is another person's irritation. You'll find revelation or self-indulgence, and maybe sometimes a mixture of both.

I always ask myself when I'm watching a film, is this work something that only the cinema form could achieve or harness? Could this given film only exist as a film, or could it be something else in some other medium entirely? Essentially, how "cinematic" is it? It's a simple but occasionally complex litmus test. To many, "talkie" films are inherently un-cinematic, by definition. Perhaps you'd say Henry's films are not "polished" in the classical sense, and sometimes they can be messy, but honestly, he wants it messy. When Josh and Benny Safdie programmed a film series at BAM, New York, in 2010, they called it "Emotionally Sloppy Manic Cinema." It's a great phrase and apropos here, because Henry at his best is the messy voice of a generation—maybe not *his* generation or *the* generation, but *a* generation. I understand what he pursues, why he pursues it, and I think he has something to say, whether or not one is open to hearing it. For many of his films, you'd find a pithy, effective summary in the title of a Czech New Wave picture: *A Report on the Party and the Guests* (1966). He creates its own class of essay film, of social document, of "actuality drama" (to co-opt Allan King's term), of film form and content. The fact that the work divides only enhances its potency.

Lamont Johnson: Pauline Kael's horse, once upon a time. A subject for further study. I've seen most of the films. I need to give him a closer look, though I am particular fond of his one-two punch *The Last American Hero* (1973) and *You'll Like My Mother* (1973), along with his telefilms *My Sweet Charlie* (1970), *That Certain Summer* (1973), and *The Execution of Private Slovik* (1974). He never really turned out to be cinema's "love's young dream" as Kael predicted, but she was right for vesting some of her hopes in him. Sometimes it's just the circumstances and the fickle fumes of fate that sideline a promising talent.

Jeremy Paul Kagan: I've long been intrigued by Kagan, who is sometimes credited as just Jeremy Kagan. Few directors so explicitly gave voice to the angst and weltschmerz of post-Sixties radicalism, specifically the process of de-radicalization. Like Joan Micklin Silver with her brilliant post-counterculture couplet *Between the Lines* (1977) and *Chilly Scenes of Winter* (1979),

Kagan addresses the dissipation and sense of anticlimax acutely felt by those poised begrudgingly at a woebegone generation's exit door. His characters are often societal misfits, living artifacts of an earlier time, who wind up paradoxically disenchanted with their own (often wistful) disenchantment. This is felt most profoundly in *Katherine* (1975), *Heroes* (1977), *The Big Fix* (1978), and later, *Conspiracy: The Trial of the Chicago 8* (1987).

His MIA student AFI thesis, *The Love Song of Charles Farberman* (1971) is described as "an episodic tragicomedy of a lawyer, his wife, the people of East Los Angeles, and a viola, all intermixed as the lawyer seeks refuge from the establishment's injustices." This seems to tie in, as a historical checkpoint. Even his Chaim Potok adaptation *The Chosen* (1981), while in no way about the Sixties, nevertheless speaks to a theme of "de-radicalization"—it ends with Robby Benson's Satmar Chasid character rejecting the foregone promise of a severe, radically cloistered life, as the heir apparent to his rebbe father's "throne," and sees him comfortably step away from the extremity within which he was raised.

I see *Katherine*, *Heroes*, and *The Big Fix* as an informal trilogy of character pieces about the human leftovers who now tread suspiciously still waters. *Katherine* stars Sissy Spacek as a fictional Patty Hearst surrogate, a wealthy debutante who rejects the privilege and advantages of her upbringing. The film deftly uses a Fosse-esque faux documentary framing device. *Heroes* stars Henry Winkler as a manic Vietnam veteran suffering from PTSD, who breaks out of a VA hospital and pairs up with a sympathetic fellow traveler (Sally Field) on a cross-country road trip to reunite with the other men in his unit. The comic neo-noir *The Big Fix* is the true apotheosis of the three, in that it stars Richard Dreyfuss as an ex-Sixties student radical and now gumshoe investigating a political smear campaign that, in short order, spurs a murder case. It's Phillip Marlow-meets-Jerry Rubin… or a Yippie Sam Spade, take your pick. Kagan's sensibility is distinctly Jewish-American. *The Chosen* is perhaps Kagan's most beloved theatrical picture (in contention with *The Journey of Natty Gann*). The film's sober depiction of the struggle between the post-war Zionists and the Satmar anti-Zionists is unique in the annals of Jewish-American cinema. As something of a self-appointed scholar of Jewish religious cinema, I cannot think of another picture, let alone one produced by an American studio, that interprets this historical schism.

Years later, Kagan returned to the American shtetl with *Crown Heights* (2004), a limply humanist drama set during the 1991 Crown Heights Riots. His *The Journey of Natty Gann* (1985) was the first American film to win a Gold Prize at the Moscow Film Festival. It's a Depression saga—produced by Disney, no less—that paints a vivid picture of the era's farmhouses, police stations, hobo camps, reform schools, and boxcars. My mentor Paul Sylbert was the production designer. Other films include the misbegotten sequel *The Sting II* (1983), the fencing drama *By the Sword* (1991), the oddball college comedy spin on *The Hunchback of Notre Dame* called *Big Man on Campus* (1989), and the social drama *Shot* (2007).

Jonathan Kaplan: Along with Jonathan Demme and Joe Dante, Kaplan is perhaps generally the most loved among the directing crop to have emerged from Roger Corman's New World Pictures era. For Corman, Kaplan delivered *Night Call Nurses* (1972) and *The Student Teachers* (1973), before departing to MGM to collaborate with Roger's brother Gene Corman on *The Slams* (1973), with Jim Brown. His *White Line Fever* (1975) and *Truck Turner* (1976) are among the wittier entries in the Seventies B action canon, both with a clear-cut working-class moxie. Upon Kaplan's recent death, filmmaker Tim Hunter, a friend of Kaplan's, told IndieWire, "He was big-hearted, exuberant, smarter than anyone, and he always knew what felt most real, on and off a set. A lot of his best films are about working and blue-collar class heroes." As the son of the blacklisted film composer Sol Kaplan, there's a lineage for this—one obituary referred to him as a "red diaper baby." He's kind of a political sibling to fellow Corman alum Demme, who received more laurels and gold for his lifetime of work. His breakthrough was the high-water mark of all contemporary alienated youth movies *Over the Edge* (1979)—catching it on TV as a teen was certainly memorable, because it was uncommonly attuned to its material in a way that led me to imagine its director as being the same age of his subjects. I recently revisited *Unlawful Entry* (1992), one among a glut of early nineties thrillers. I filed it away as an unremarkable potboiler the first time I saw it years ago, but this time, I sensed a larger statement about class and privilege that hit me hard. Along with *Edge*, acknowledge *Heart Like a Wheel* (1983), *The Accused* (1988), and *Love Field* (1992) as his finest works, but it's often remarkable how he supplies genre works with the luxuries we've too often convinced ourselves they cannot afford.

Philip Kaufman: It was a joy getting to know Kaufman at parties thrown by Tom Luddy and the Telluride Film Festival when I lived in San Francisco. Outside of Annette Insdorf's study, there are no books on him. I couldn't think of a better man to turn to turn to when I needed a little shot in the arm. When my film *Overwhelm the Sky* (2019) was playing well in test screenings at a near three-hour length, I asked him for advice. Over cocktails at Lucasfilm at the Letterman Center, he dished it out… and I wound up winning the fight to keep my movie my own. Because, in those days, I wore a black porkpie that complemented my scraggly dark beard, he nicknamed me "the rabbi of noir," and would proceed to call me rabbi whenever we crossed paths moving forward. But it's beyond obvious to say that the man who directed *Invasion of the Body Snatchers* (1978), *The Wanderers* (1979), *The Right Stuff* (1983), *The Unbearable Lightness of Being* (1988), and others deserves more than the scholarly class has given him.

Larry Kent: If I do a volume two of this book, Larry Kent will certainly get a whole chapter. It is a relief that many of his historically vital Canadian indie features are getting renewed circulation: *The Bitter Ash* (1963), *Sweet Substitute* (1964), *When Tomorrow Dies* (1965), and *High* (1967). There is equally fine work among his later films, especially *Mothers and Daughters* (1992) and *Exley* (2011).

Irvin Kershner: I once heard one of Irvin Kershner's directing contemporaries say, "Kershner could turn a 'Go' picture back into a development deal." He made a great deal of hay later on with franchise fare: *The Empire Strikes Back* (1980), the outside-the-007-canon remix *Never Say Never Again* (1983), and *Robocop 2* (1990). Indeed, he was the only-ever competent director of actors who got anywhere near the *Star Wars* franchise, and it shows. The contrast between Lucas' direction of performers, and Kershner's far more delicate, meticulous approach to them, couldn't be more stark. But I'm the most interested in the early films, especially *The Luck of Ginger Coffey* (1964), *A Fine Madness* (1966), *The Flim-Flam Man* (1967), *Loving* (1970), and *Up the Sandbox* (1972). Or have that read: Kershner's "smaller," more modest, character-driven films. Before the post-Vietnam era sparked a number of dramas and thrillers casting veterans as ticking time bombs, the men in Kershner's Sixties films were time bombs and renegades who couldn't use war or combat trauma as an excuse for their behavior. These guys were pretty much cranks, kooks, cons, and loose cannons—in many cases, coots and codgers well before their time. They "assume the position" with abandon. We missed *that* Kershner once he got big.

Randal Kleiser: Randal is a friend, and I know he's proud of his work as a director of popular mainstream cinema. If he has any kind of auteurist signature, it involves training his camera on beautiful people in the full bloom of youth, doing the things the admirers of that youth want to see them doing. *The Blue Lagoon* (1980) and *Summer Lovers* (1981) are the most conspicuous here. Two other personal films of his, *Getting It Right* (1989) and *It's My Party* (1996), intimate that there's more to the guy who gave us *Honey, I Blew Up the Kid!* (1992). Randal once told me that he was excited to pay tribute to the British New Wave comedies of the Sixties with *Getting It Right*, and I think it's a lovely little film too easily overlooked in his filmography, smack dab in the middle of the anonymous blockbusters. And seeing him get so intensely personal in *It's My Party* is revelatory. You have to separate the wheat from the chaff with Kleiser, but there might be more here.

Andrei Konchalovsky: We speak too little of Konchalovsky's extraordinary American period, in which most of the films were produced by Golan and Globus at Cannon. *Maria's Lovers* (1984), *Runaway Train* (1985), *Duet for One* (1986), and *Shy People* (1987). Jonathan Rosenbaum, a major proponent of *Shy People,* once described Konchalovsky as "a Soviet director who makes commercial American movies that somehow manage to be commercial, American, Soviet, and serious, all at the same time." As to the "Soviet" descriptor, he identifies the most Russian elements in these films as "allegorical, mystical, poetic, pantheistic, and fairy-tale." He has a point, as you see these elements as much in the Cannon films as you see it in his epic *Siberiade* (1979), a nearly five-hour epic of twentieth-century Siberia.

There is something very Russkie about Konchalovsky, even when (only ostensibly) tempered by the likes of screenwriters like Gerard Brach, Paul Zindel, Edward Bunker, and playwright Tom Kempinski. I remember personally having conversations with Tom Luddy about his love and advocacy for Konchalovsky, including during his critical years at Cannon (around the same time Tom helped Godard score the now famous "napkin contract" with Golan and Globus for *King Lear*). Konchalovsky had the critical brass and the movie-world power-brokers in his corner. For a director who seemed so intent on casting off the shackles of Communist Mother Russia in these works (especially *Runaway Train*), he is now back in Putin's Russia cheerleading "dear leader" and his Ukrainian invasion, not to mention running interference on Stalin's legacy. A bit of a head-scratcher, though Rosenbaum notes that Konchalovsky was careful never to surrender his Soviet citizenship during those American years. The man, methinks, is and/or was a bit of a conundrum. For as confounding as Konchalovsky is, the politics of his filmmaker brother Nikita Mikhalkov (*Burnt by the Sun*) are far worse, even dystopian.

John Korty: Korty's *A Christmas Without Snow* (1980), shot in his native San Francisco, features one of my favorite soliloquies in any film, delivered by John Houseman: "Mrs. Burns is right, of course. You are amateurs, unlike certain pseudo-professionals like myself who insist on slave wages. Your voluntary and steadfast attendance at these rehearsals fully qualifies you for any definition of the word 'amateur.' What Mrs. Burns and many others are wrong about is the meaning of the word, which has to do with motivation, not quality. Remember 'amo, amat, amas,' the Latin verb 'to love.' The meaning of 'amateur' is 'he or she who does a thing for the love of it.' There is no higher reason for singing than the love of doing it. In that respect, you do qualify as amateurs. And I salute you for it."

Korty's picture is one of the most effective pieces I know about community, specifically one's artistic family, and the ties that bind people who create together. The rest of his body of work—principally *The Crazy Quilt* (1966), *Funnyman* (1967), and *Riverrun* (1970) especially—all have an unmistakably handmade quality that is rare, even as it's become easier with digital technology to make personal cinema. I knew John a bit and attended his memorial service a few years back. The refrain of all the eulogies was the disbelief that one man could be such a one-stop shop in an era when that was nearly unheard-of. He edited his films himself in a remodeled shack that was originally a barn on his property. He was giving and generous, and wanted to see other people succeed in the craft and, by extension, the biz. An uncommon gent.

Stanley Kubrick: Kubrick, to me, is like the genius father who never took me fishing or to the fair. The man is obviously brilliant, and I understand the adulation (in a way that I fail to understand that of Ford or Malick). But as much as I'm always entertained by his films, and for as much as his craft is impeccable, I cannot really emotionally penetrate him. The older I get, the more I am sure that *Barry Lyndon* (1975) is his best. If you told me as a teenager that I'd one day believe that, I would have told you to screw. I detest *Full Metal Jacket* (1987), and will always implore people to search out the film which at least partly inspired it, Sidney J. Furie's *The Boys in Company C* (1978), which I believe is superior in every way—including in what it says about the futility of war, and how innocent boys are transformed into meat-grinder cogs.

The thing that bugs me the most is how Kubrick packages psychosis as something to emulate, as a kind of demento mystique of "cool"-ness. I flash to a muscular bald-headed Iowa man I once met, who was rather scary and imposing and had a *Clockwork Orange* tattoo that he liked flashing around. Let's just say it was a picture. Whatever admiration one has for that film, or for the colorful insults of R. Lee Ermey in *Full Metal Jacket*, the need for fans to emulate these things for any reason (including humor) disturbs me. It's all in Kubrick's seductive presentation, and something about it doesn't sit well with me. That said, I still take great pleasure in decoding *Eyes Wide Shut* (1999), and *2001: A Space Odyssey* (1968) always gets my noodle spinnin' right round, baby, right round. And like a few other artists mentioned in the introduction to this book, I resist critics and scholars who build critic-proof fortresses around Kubrick. Yes, I said my piece. I'm not going to deny he's great, okey-doke?

Mitchell Leisen: Leisen has what I call "a flair to remember." He is in the same school of gay auteurs as my beloved Silvio Narizzano, and he's one of my most treasured artists of the cinema. Earlier this year, when scrubbing through Mitchell Leisen's imagery for a video piece, he reminds me why I never tire of just *looking* at his work—especially his Forties films, where he gets very flamboyant with color and design and haberdashery (and, when without color, he seems to innately understand the precise grayscale shadings/gradations). There are so many gay directors in my personal pantheon, all who do this type of thing to one degree or another: Leisen, Rapper, Cukor, Minnelli, Visconti, Narizzano, Jutra, Fassbinder. What can I say, I love my gay or "queer" directors. And there are other directors in that personal pantheon who, while not gay or openly queer, also imbued their works with this well-appointed sense of flair: Losey, Ophüls, The Archers, Furie, even some Preminger. All these guys are painters at heart, at their best. I like pictorially arresting filmmakers who, in varying doses, subvert "trad" masculinity. I relish classic movies where women are three-dimensional and have rich interior lives, and are a more assertive presence than their male co-stars. Some of the more Manly auteurs fall rather flat for me. I love *Johnny Guitar* and *The Furies* more than I could love most anything by the sexually regressive Ford. Ray's and Mann's films tend to surprise me more, viewing after viewing. Most of all, I want sensitivity, and not as entirely extrapolated from chivalry or valor. As a boy, I was an extra in a dreadful remake of *Diabolique* (1996), and Kathy Bates had one great line in it: "Testosterone… they should put it in bombs." Leisen's stylistically feminine wiles are best expressed, from a design point of view, in ravishing later works like *Frenchman's Creek* (1944), *Kitty* (1945), and *Golden Earrings* (1947). From a purely experiential perspective, the eye-popping *Lady in the Dark* (1944) rivals some of my beloved Archers' Technicolor brush-stroking. My personal favorites of Leisen's, though, are *Remember the Night* (1940), *Hold Back the Dawn* (1941), and *To Each Their Own* (1946). Billy Wilder and Preston Sturges, who wrote many of Leisen's best scripts, were both cruel in using sometimes homophobic language to scornfully dismiss what Leisen "did to" their work, but it's hard to imagine the films being any better if they had been the ones directing them. And if you ask me, Leisen made them all the more visually dynamic and further attuned to mise en scène. Those who know, know. David Chierichetti's fabulous Leisen biography reveals how, for years (and even still today), we routinely neglect one of the greatest directors of his era.

Joseph Losey: One of the best to ever do it. Better scholars and historians than I have explained how and why. I need not spill any more ink here doing what they've already done exceedingly well. He is in my Pantheon for a reason, as he is in others'. "Vox populi, vox Dei" is a sort of path of least resistance, and certainly not a maxim in which I put much stock, especially when it's applied within critical consensus (I'm a rebel, but with a cause here). But in his exalted status, Losey proves that, just often enough, majority rule gets it right.

Sidney Lumet: I most object to Lumet's canned leftism, which he opens like a tin of Campbell's tomato then microwaves for a minute. You go back to bed at 3am with horrid indigestion. In other words, it's a squishy, generically package-able leftism, especially in something like *Daniel* (1983). But worst of all is that I find his staging for camera uniquely unexciting. Whenever anything interesting happens on screen, it's just the striking of a pose. Lumet is a real bête noire of mine, I'm sorry to say.

Not long ago, I heard two Sidney Lumet tales that confirmed long held suspicions. In my interview with John Badham, *The Wiz* (1978) was discussed. Badham was originally up to direct, but left in disagreement over the casting of Diana Ross, and other creative decisions taken in advance by Berry Gordy and Motown. They hired a jobbing Lumet. All's well that ended well, as Badham delivered the still-fabulous *Saturday Night Fever* (1977), which launched his career.

The staging of the dance and musical sequences in *Saturday Night Fever* vs. *The Wiz* couldn't offer a more plain contrast. One director's staging is dynamic and propulsive, the other's is flat as a pancake. In *The Wiz*, cameras are always perched at a distance like it's live TV special or the recording of a stage performance. It conjures the image of some guy in a booth frantically instructing the operators in real time. Badham told me that, though he left the project, his friend Rob Cohen stayed behind to produce (Badham and Cohen later formed their own company). Cohen and others tried to get Lumet to shoot more coverage and stage the musical sequences more dynamically. He actually told Cohen point blank, "I wouldn't know how to do that," and refused to be given advice on how to improve, or work more synergistically with his team, i.e. folks who might have had good ideas vis-à-vis. He chewed out anyone who questioned his authority. Motown and Gordy came to regret hiring him. Badham told me, "Whatever strengths Mr. Lumet had as a director, he didn't know what he was doing on that particular movie."

The other story hit the cutting room floor on the documentary *King Cohen* (2018). On *Guilty as Sin* (1993), Larry Cohen was the screenwriter. He had written a really visual, "cinematic" opening for the film. Lumet didn't shoot it all as written, in the interest of saving time (Lumet was obsessed with bringing in films ahead of schedule, like it was a race, and this compulsion was on overdrive with this production). Cohen was on the set for some of it... until he wasn't. Cohen watched Lumet sleepwalk through the shoot days, shooting lifeless rewrites of scenes in his script was heartbreaking to him, as he had admired some of Lumet's films. The final straw came when Cohen watched helplessly as Lumet was staging shots so that you could clearly see that Toronto was doubling for Chicago (with the CN Tower in the background clearly visible). Cohen offered to go to Chicago to get some b-roll and second unit footage of the city; Lumet was so dismissive that Cohen never returned to set and just wrote it all off (almost wishing he had directed it himself, his way). His opinion of Lumet changed forever. Add to this that my first mentor, production designer Paul Sylbert, never had a kind word for him.

I love *Dog Day Afternoon* (1975) because of a humor and humanity that simply had to have been in Frank Pierson's brilliant original script, but the rest? I think Lumet is best when he has a lighter touch. The heavy films hem and haw and speechify, and swing sledgehammers at the audience. His staging, even in plain old chamber drama, drives me up a wall. I have actually used examples throughout his filmography to illustrate to a film class what *not* to do. I just don't like his "playing for the cheap seats" actors-in-search-of-a-tantrum constitution in directing performance. I find that he overmodulates and winds his actors up to a point of bad opera, then shoots it poorly or perfunctorily. There are examples in, especially, *Prince of the City* (1981) that induce major cringing, especially an early scene when we are framed well above and far behind Treat Williams' head at great length, as if this ugly shot is a "one-er" that holds the screen. Among Lumet's class of directors, Mike Nichols certainly knew how to do a one-er and keep it interesting. So did Frankenheimer and Penn, but it seems to me that Lumet never really graduated from his training in live television.

Looking at *The Pawnbroker* (1965), *Bye Bye Braverman* (1968), and *A Stranger Among Us* (1992), I also realize he is likely my least favorite Jewish director when it comes to Jewish material. Everything is a crusty virtue signal. His "Jewish films" are the biggest sledgehammer affairs of all. *A Stranger Among Us* especially is point-blank one of the worst films I've ever seen (in the top 10), a total disgrace, unspeakably ghastly, somehow managing to be both silly and dehumanizing. *Bye Bye Braverman* is so aggressively contrived, cloying, and so irritatingly cutesy about its own overt Jewish "personality" that it's difficult to appreciate even that swell Sixties Brooklyn scenery. Compare it with, say, *The Plot Against Harry* (1969; not released until 1989) and you start to realize Lumet's artistically crippling tone-deafness. *The Pawnbroker*? Kael and Sarris, in a rare moment of alignment, were both correct about it. Stereotypes all over. The film's Jews are stony, dour, anguished, and torturedly one-dimensional, without exception. The people of color are easily manipulable, devious, or antisocial. The principal gay character is an abusive predator whose tackily implied afternoon tryst with a young nubile boytoy is designed strictly to heighten audience antipathy—one almost expects a "Boo! Hiss!" title card to drop in. One can applaud Steiger's efforts and editor Ralph Rosenblum's experimental cutting without endorsing the other nonsense Lumet engineers. I'll let the record show that my mentor Paul Sylbert, and his twin brother Dick Sylbert, didn't think much of Lumet either. The one thing he had in his corner: taste for material... enough of the time.

Radley Metzger: Metzger is my softcore and hardcore artist of choice. I respect someone like Russ Meyer, but in terms of the blending of high-art with X or XXX erotica in the general sense, I pick Metzger every single time.

Robert Mulligan: It is nearly impossible to imagine how the man who directed *To Kill a Mockingbird* (1962) has been counted out in even middling American auteur studies, but he has. Strangely enough, I find it's the French who make the arguments for him (Lionel Lacour being key), though there is one notable American—a lone voice in the wilderness. Peter Tonguette writes in his 2025 *Wall Street Journal* appreciation, "From *To Kill a Mockingbird* (1962) to *Summer of '42* (1971) to *The Man in the Moon* (1991), Mulligan attended to the universal states of childhood and adolescence, and the timeless condition of love at any age, but particularly youth. When he strayed from these themes for a picture or two, he found his way back to them. He developed a cinematic style that was in keeping with his poetic rather than didactic sensibility: expressive, lyrical, aligned with the internal dramas of his characters." Indeed, Mulligan was never the finger-on-the-pulse type that his protégé and producer Alan J. Pakula became. I appreciate his pack of coming-of-age type films, *The Pursuit of Happiness* (1971), *Bloodbrothers* (1978), and *Clara's Heart* (1987) included, but I tend to evince a bit more interest in films he made outside of that track, namely *Baby, the Rain Must Fall* (1965), *The Other* (1972) and *The Nickel Ride* (1975), which suggest a harder edge that counters and even pushes against his usual sentimentality (and, by extension, his sentimental lyricism). *The Nickel Ride* especially hints at what Mulligan could do with a purely cinematic language outside of the safety of his lyricism— and it also owes a great deal to Jason Miller, a compelling screen presence who never got enough play. Mulligan's troubling alcoholism is very much on the historical record. Perhaps the lyrical, romantic film presented life as he might have wanted it to be, and films like *Nickel Ride* and *Baby, the Rain Must Fall* a life as he knew it to be, unfiltered through a much darker side. In any event, I do see how Mulligan as subject is a worthy pursuit.

Floyd Mutrux: America has so little frame of reference for someone as individual as Floyd Mutrux. *Dusty and Sweets Magee* (1971), *Aloha, Bobby and Rose* (1975), and *American Hot Wax* (1978) constitute the most solid triple claim to Seventies filmmaker-ly street cred. I have examined Mutrux's scripts and I found it fascinating that he specifically notes needle-drops on the page, even on *The Christian Licorice Store* (1971), directed by William Frawley (who used almost all of them in his final cut). *The Hollywood Knights* (1980), however, seemed a bit of an anemic *American Graffiti* clone, and he avoided the director's chair until his (to date) final film, *There Goes My Baby* (1994), which was one of a number of victims of Orion's bankruptcy. Mutrux's L.A. is a vision—strugglers, stragglers, strivers, pranksters, and the like. Another artist I wish had given us more... but what he did give us is substantial, and I'm thrilled to include him here.

Jean Negulesco: Negulesco pretty much never makes anyone's list of favorite or best classic Hollywood directors. Historians, scholars, and critics have in general forgotten or rejected him. Andrew Sarris writes, "Negulesco's is the most dramatic case of directorial maladjustment in the '50s. His career can be divided into two periods: BC and AC, or Before CinemaScope and After CinemaScope. Many of his BC films are rather competently and even memorably made. Everything AC is completely worthless." Ouch. Harsh. Dare I say bitchy? But who could call a deliciously glossy soaper like *The Best of Everything* (1959) worthless? Besides that, his 'Scope films handsomely exemplify his impressive background and portfolio as a painter.

Negulesco's road to directing feature films was a tortured one. He was replaced by John Huston two months into shooting *The Maltese Falcon* (1941) and suffered a similar fate with *Singapore Woman* (1941). His big break came when he landed the directing job for *The Mask of Dimitrios* (1944), starring Sydney Greenstreet and Peter Lorre. It proved a financial boon for Warner Bros. and led to further assignments. *Humoresque* (1946) is the one I'd argue his masterpiece, the tale of a rising young violinist and his tempestuous, ultimately, ill-fated relationship with an unhappily married alcoholic socialite. It could have been hackneyed soap opera under a lesser talent. In 1948, Negulesco signed as a contract director for 20th Century-Fox, a studio where he found a pace more to his liking. His first assignment was *Road House* (1948), a noir with Ida Lupino and Richard Widmark. From 1953 onward, Negulesco effectively reinvented himself as a director of more glossy entertainments. *How to Marry a Millionaire* (1953) and *Three Coins in a Fountain* (1954) both exemplified the well-heeled pulp of the studio brand, with the latter's theme tune playing on endless loop (even today, in some quarters). He may have lost some of his teeth after the migration to Fox, but there is still some bite in his 'Scope staging for which few auteurists ever cared to credit him. Worthless? Another Sarris injustice, if you ask me. Just adjust your specs and take a closer look.

Paul Newman: We speak enough about Newman the actor (and I'm certainly not telling anyone to stop) but we need to speak more of Newman the director. Moments, images, and scenes from *Rachel Rachel* (1968), *Sometimes a Great Notion* (1971), *The Effect of Gamma Rays on Man-in-the-Moon Marigolds* (1972), and *The Glass Menagerie* (1987) are seared into my movie-brain forever. Anyone who can direct the drowning scene in *Sometimes a Great Notion* is something at least close to a master.

Frank Oz: Frank Oz never gets credit for being one of America's finest farceurs. His farces tend to center around charismatics who bewitch others in the act of concealment, whether it be of a deceitful scheme (*Dirty Rotten Scoundrels*, *Bowfinger*, *Housesitter*), a neurosis or psychosis (*What About Bob?*), or a life-altering secret (*In & Out*, *Death at a Funeral*). His stagings are overall basic but sometimes ring of Blake Edwards (in his boldest and brashest moments, especially *What About Bob?*), Lubitsch (especially in *Dirty Rotten Scoundrels*), and Preston Sturges (as in parts of *Bowfinger*, especially in its warmer moments, and *In & Out*'s small-town Americana). I think Oz loves these directors, and makes conscious choices in airing toward them. Oz is rightly venerated for the Muppets and for his characterizations of Yoda, Fozzy, Miss Piggy, etc, but his brush strokes as a big-screen comedy director get short shrift even as the films themselves live on fondly in audiences' minds.

Gordon Parks (Sr. and Jr.): I created a video essay for the long-awaited Blu-ray release of Gordon Parks, Sr.'s *Leadbelly* (1976), one of the great blues films of all time. By the time Parks Sr. made his feature motion picture debut, with an adaptation of his novel *The Learning Tree*, he gave autobiographical heft to the type of historically significant images of the Jim Crow south he'd snapped for *Life* magazine. Many looked to Gordon Parks as renaissance man, the consummate artist, spanning multiple media, including not only photography and filmmaking, but music, choreography, and writing, in both prose and poetry. As a photographer, he shot filmically, and there was life and a pulse poking in and vibrating at the edges of the stills, as well as a not dissimilar life of movement—movement in all its meanings and with all its ramifications—that haunts the edges of his Panavision frames.

Shaft gave its black target audience the type of hero they never had or held at the cinema before. Along with *Sweet Sweetback's Baadasssss Song*, it minted blaxploitation as its own genre and form. The notion of folk hero becomes prevalent, and quite readily so. It's too easy to pin themes of social justice, racism, and Black Power upon the work of a trailblazing black filmmaker like Gordon Parks, and though it is consistent with the nature of his earlier still photography work, it's much too surface and superficial in a deeper study or interrogation into his motion picture output, at least in their basic form. Even the white title heroes in *The Super Cops* (1973) read as Parksian folk heroes. *Leadbelly* further explores the Gordon Parks cinematic folk hero archetype in a slightly more bildungsroman fashion, not quite in the manner of *The Learning Tree*, with its coming-of-age lyricism, but rather in terms of recreating the wealth of experience that defines any artist. A life lived springs forth from works that reflect that, directly or indirectly. There's a root to any sensibility, to any approach, to any métier, especially within the blues genre, a form which sprang from hardship, oppression, cycles of struggle, and gin joint-by-way-of-prison existences where the beat goes on, or rather grinds on and on and on. Parks Jr. also seemed to hone in on his father's thematics, customizing them for himself, and emerging with *Superfly* (1972) and *Thomasine & Bushrod* (1974). One can only imagine where Parks Jr.'s career might have gone if he had lived rather than died young in a tragic accident.

Frank Perry: I became obsessed with Frank Perry just around the time he started getting further coverage and exposure as an overlooked auteur. He started getting screened more in the latter part of the 2010s, including by Tarantino at his New Beverly Cinema. I wanted to cover Perry in book form at one point, but I was beat to the punch by another author. Many tend to claim that his films were better when they were written by his onetime wife, Eleanor, whom he divorced in 1970. Yes, *David and Lisa* (1962), *Ladybug Ladybug* (1963), *The Swimmer* (1968), *Last Summer* (1969), *Diary of a Mad Housewife* (1970), and their Truman Capote short story films have panache. *Last Summer* is my particular favorite among those, but of course, who could argue with the greatness of *The Swimmer*? All these pictures effortlessly flex a kind of elegance found in *New Yorker* fiction. But the other worthy films that Frank directed without Eleanor should not be dismissed, especially *Play It As It Lays* (1972), *Man on a Swing* (1974), and *Rancho Deluxe* (1975). *Man on a Swing* was a major influence on my own *Overwhelm the Sky* (2019)—I had my cinematographer and lead actor on that picture watch it for prep.

The camp stylings of *Mommie Dearest* (1981) and *Monsignor* (1982), Perry's two Frank Yablans projects, have merit unrecognized among the wide swath of the viewership that thinks of them only as howlers. I'm also considering how filmmaker Frank Perry had a penchant for making "companion films"—I realized this when seeing the New Beverly schedule for "Frank Perry Month" and realizing how and why they paired certain films together. There are the two filed under "Youth": *Ladybug Ladybug* and *Last Summer*. We then have "struggles and inner lives of modern urban women," one for New York and another for L.A.: *Diary of a Mad Housewife* and *Play It As It Lays*. Then there are the "Westerns of a different breed": *Doc* (1971) and *Rancho Deluxe*. With *Man on a Swing* (1974) and *Dummy* (1979), there's a true-crime double feature. Of course, we have "Camp Yablans" (double meaning): *Mommie Dearest* and *Monsignor*. *Compromising Positions* (1985) and *Hello Again* (1987), his two final narrative features, are both feminist farces. Finally, at the heart of Perrylandia, "Great American Short Fiction": *The Swimmer* (1968) and *Trilogy* (1969).

Ernest Pintoff: Most remember Ernest Pintoff for his film *The Critic* (1963), a short satire on modern art written and narrated by Mel Brooks, which won the Oscar for Best Animated Short. Horror-teur Jeff Lieberman (*Squirm*, *Blue Sunshine*—another suitable case for study and praise) cites Pintoff as his mentor in the biz. I personally am most interested in Pintoff's independent features, all of which defy easy description (42nd Street grindhouse vérité neo-noir?), but I am here, dear reader, to give it a whirl.

Pintoff's skid row aesthetic somehow crystallizes into a stroke of style. He began his animation career in 1956. Before *The Critic*, Pintoff earned another Oscar nomination for his animated short *The Violinist* (1959), narrated by Carl Reiner. As part of NBC's "Experiments in Television" in the late Sixties, he directed the documentaries *This is Marshall McLuhan: The Medium is the Massage* (1967) and *This is Sholem Aleichem* (1969). His feature debut as director was *Harvey Middleman, Fireman* (1965), riddled with slightly soft, out-of-focus shots and little technical foibles, indicates a skid-row budgetary bracket, but it sports a broad, zany swagger that suggests (rather than references or explicitly riffs on) Richard Lester in his early *Running Jumping Standing Still* era. Furthermore, like Frank Tashlin just before him, it outwardly suggests the filmmaker's background in animation. It takes aim at refried American lily-white "normalism" via a consciously absurd story of a fireman who falls in love with a girl he saves, only for her to stage another fire to rouse another savior fireman's twitter-pation. Pintoff also composed his own score for the picture, which runs a scant 75 minutes and was picked up by Columbia Pictures for distribution. It was fairly well-reviewed; in his original *Village Voice* review, Andrew Sarris writes, "Ernest Pintoff has devised a reasonable number of bright gags. I think some of his pop color is appropriate for a Freudian fire engine motif. I would like to see him make another try with a more charming protagonist and a less caricaturist conception."

Who Killed Mary Whats'ername? (1971), starring Red Buttons as a diabetic ex-boxer investigating the death of a hooker, is another effort that wears its scant budget on its sleeve, proudly. The New York of the film, like his later neo-noir *Blade* (1973), is pure, unfiltered Mayor Lindsay-era grime, matched that same year by Ivan Passer's *Born to Win*. Pintoff surprises in how effectively he interprets a typically New York-style societal indifference that would metastasize on screen later on in something like *Taxi Driver* (1976). The same year, he delivered *Dynamite Chicken* (1971) anticipated the "variety show flick" subgenre (à la *Groove Tube*, *Tunnelvision*, *Kentucky Fried Movie*) and features Richard Pryor as an ad hoc tour guide trough a hodge-podge of songs, skits, parodies, and old movie clips. John Lennon, Andy Warhol, Al Goldstein, Joan Baez, and The Ace Trucking Company all turn up, sometimes all too briefly.

The great John Marley gets a rare starring role as the title character in *Blade*, a very ragged, extremely clumsily shot (but interestingly so) killer-on-the-loose thriller that is uniformly shot in jerky handheld like a documentary. One constantly gets the sense that the cinematographer, an actual vérité documentarian named David Hoffman, is catching a "reality" as it happens, even when the dialogue seems to ape standard TV policiers. Scene after scene, the frame consistently readjusts multiple times for queasy compositions and weird zooms that are artless, impulsive, utilitarian. The New York of the film is, again, a dark, dank, dirty, gritty, grimy, sleazy, overcast hellhole. Pintoff filled out the rest of the Seventies with television work, directing episodes of "Hawaii Five-O," "The Six Million Dollar Man," and many others. He made a single telefilm called *Human Feelings* (1978) starring Billy Crystal, Armand Asante, and Pat Morita. It's a Borscht Belt-y comedy that feels "Pintoffian" in the *Harvey Middleman/ Dynamite Chicken* sense. He returned to drive-ins with *Jaguar Lives!* (1979), *Lunch Wagon* (1981), and *St. Helens* (1981), which seems to live on fondly for those who caught it on television way back when. It's easy to get the sense that the later pictures were work-for-hire efforts, but nevertheless, one does occasionally get hints that what we have is an animator transmitting an animation "animus" (if you will) into a live-action arena. In much of his work, he's a poor man's New York grindhouse Frank Tashlin.

Albert Pyun: On the basis of a single period in his filmography, a run that includes *Radioactive Dreams* (1985), *Vicious Lips* (1986), *Dangerously Close* (1987), and *Down Twisted* (1988), I've developed an interested in the "Pyuniverse." Cannon productions, if they weren't known largely for their schlock quotient, were groomed for the attempted arthouse rebranding of the company circa 1985. Golan and Globus were able to attract world-class filmmakers for specialty products by subsidizing them with money from the schlock. Jerry Schatzberg, Franco Zeffirelli, and John Cassavetes were just three of the directors who made higher profile pictures for the company. But films like *Runaway Train* (1985), directed by Andrei Konchalovsky, successfully straddle the line between Cannon pulp and Cannon arthouse. It feels to me that something like Pyun's *Dangerously Close* was attempting to do something similar, but didn't quite live up to the promise, at least in its time. Marrying genre whims to high style, while striving a bit more for thematic purpose and artistic weight (of some caliber anyway), is what intrigues me about these individual works.

On a visual level alone, *Dangerously Close* is one of the most fascinating high school films in a decade saturated with them. I will defer to Felipe Furtado, a critic I follow on Letterboxd, who writes, "Most of the best Albert Pyun movies are fantasy films set in some kind of junkyard futuristic world, but what *Dangerously Close* proposes is, what if an elite school in Reagan's USA is pretty much already that? Our first step towards extinction. It is a strange marriage between Cannon junk and Pyun's very heightened idea of artifice." I'll sign on the line and drink to that! Furtado is unusually quite keen on Pyun, including his goofy intergalactic punk musical *Vicious Lips* (1986), which he calls "well imagined, beautifully shot but super cheap; one of those films of his where he finds the right synthetic post-human headspace and just goes all-in." Again, cheers! He saves his superlatives for *Radioactive Dreams* though. "Wildly imaginative, suggesting the overworked mind of a twelve-year-old on heavy drugs, slapdashly put together in a nearly experimental way and absolutely in love with every form of pop culture detritus it can possibly gaze upon."

It's sometimes the lovably (and lovingly) cheap quality of many of his works that gives him an allure and a certain mystique. I find him a strangely very passionate filmmaker. I have it on good authority from a friend of the departed Pyun's, Michelle Kisner, that he "would sacrifice wherever he could in his, in most cases, minuscule budgets to ensure he could shoot in his beloved and preferred format, anamorphic widescreen Panavision, because he saw how it lent the films a look, a gloss, a size, and a scope that set him apart from most of the comparative product of the time." Kisner likewise counts herself a fan: "He was a true film lover and loved what he did." Say what you will about the quality of many of his films, but he had a vision and a style. And though he made his films on a much smaller scale than he might have liked, he worked sometimes brilliantly within the constraints he had.

Dick Richards: On the strength of *The Culpepper Cattle Co.* (1972), *Rafferty and the Gold Dust Twins* (1974), and his Raymond Chandler noir, *Farewell, My Lovely* (1975), Dick Richards is a director of some distinction. My friend and fellow historian Howard S. Berger posits that Richards "seems to prefer the study of youthful ambition and contemplation with middle-aged re-examination and re-evaluation." He identifies that, in Richards' world, good intentions are met with disappointment and disillusionment. This is certainly true of the first two named above, and is present to a slightly lesser degree in the Marlowe film, in which Mitchum's private eye is a cynical, salty old street dog who opens the film by stating that he is starting to more acutely feel the impact of aging. Pauline Kael calls Richards a "real southpaw" and notes that he "shows a feeling for momentary encounters; what might be throwaways for another director are his most acutely realized moments." I'm also quite partial towards his go at the slasher genre, *Death Valley* (1982), which certainly pursues the above theme that Berger floats. Richards is in a pack with Richard C. Sarafian, Lamont Johnson, and William Frawley. The early Seventies opened up opportunities for them to create distinctive, heady filmic odysseys with personality to spare, but with the *Wars*-ification of Hollywood, they lost whatever leverage they might have enjoyed at one time. It should be noted that, like Howard Zieff (who was more successful in comedy), Richards was an accomplished ad man before he became a filmmaker, having risen to prominence as a TV commercial whiz, authoring campaigns for Coca-Cola, Volkswagen, Polaroid, and other high-profile companies. His work was celebrated and won every major advertising award. From the auteurist persepective, it is useful to note that he seemed to get much out of a standing collaboration with a single screenwriter, David Zelag Goodman.

Stuart Rosenberg: It would seem *Cool Hand Luke* (1967) is Rosenberg's one masterpiece, though that doesn't mean his filmography is lacking for other fine and sometimes even great work. *Pocket Money* (1972), *The Laughing Policeman* (1973), *Brubaker* (1980), and *The Pope of Greenwich Village* (1984) are the MVPs of the next tier down. I'm also quite fond of *The April Fools* (1969), despite the improbable casting of, and strange chemistry between, Jack Lemmon and Catherine Deneuve (I'll also note Jack Weston's "This train don't stop at cookie" being a favorite laugh line). Rosenberg is often muscular with his ideas, especially in works like *WUSA* (1970) and *Brubaker* (1980), the latter of which he took over from Bob Rafelson. His direction of an all-star mega-cast in *Voyage of the Damned* (1976) lifted the production out of the Lord "Low"/Lew Grade ghetto and into Oscar contention. For someone branded a journeyman by default, he had an uncommon sensitivity and a political pugilist stance that puts him a cut above others who might be dismissed (or merely overlooked) similarly. Something like *Move* (1970), a shaggy Elliott Gould counterculture-adjacent comedy, might feel anomalous three years after his triumph on *Cool Hand Luke*, but the Rosenberg brand of outsider operates within a given system longer than is tenable, tolerable, or palatable (think the Paul Newman pictures in particular) until they break loose to strike out on their own—and even the comedies work within that framework. Jack Lemmon's escape from his civilization at the end of *The April Fools* sets a pace for the rest of Rosenberg-ia.

Herbert Ross: Ross was in the Neil Simon business for so long, it's almost audacious to ask if any life existed outside such a writerly-minded canon. Outside of Simon, he made *The Last of Sheila* (1973) and *The Seven Per-Cent Solution* (1976), which are A-plus sophisticated potboilers. But then there are the dance films: *The Turning Point* (1977), *Nijinsky* (1980), *Pennies from Heaven* (1981), *Footloose* (1984), and *Dancers* (1987). Ross hailed from a choreographer background, and his truest self comes out when he stages dance. Even *The Secret of My Success* (1987) has a kind of amiable but feral kineticism. You've got to wade through a lot of "Neil Simon is the auteur here" works to get to the other stuff, but there just might be something there.

Richard Rush: Rush's ethos is "punk before punk." His "damn the man" and the torpedoes full-speed-ahead gusto endows the run of *Psych-Out* (1968), *Getting Straight* (1970), *Freebie and the Bean* (1974), and *The Stunt Man* (1980) in particular. It's a pitch he's able to effortlessly hit that prefigures a brand of rebel-vigor that would take hold in the culture only later on. The wild, wild Sixties could give it a home only so much. His camera language is certainly consistent: constant movement, fevered zooms, rack focuses, racks, racks, and more racks.

Richard C. Sarafian: Bertrand Tavernier and Jean-Pierre Coursodon were cautious fans of Sarafian in their *50 ans de cinéma américain*, and they are the best critics to invoke here. They write that *Vanishing Point* (1971) is "both the complement and the antithesis of Monte Hellman's *Two-Lane Blacktop*, and it contrasts with the opacity of Hellman's film, handled with an elliptical speed that makes the story more coded than it seems." They also remark that *Man in the Wilderness* (1971) is "one of the major Westerns of the decade and reverses the theme of the previous film. Gerry Fisher's epic photography, just as inspired here as with Joseph Losey, gives nature as womb-and-tomb arbiter of the hero's destiny (as in

Vanishing Point) all its strength and its soul." They were slightly less enthusiastic about *The Man Who Loved Cat Dancing* (1973), citing "an incompatibility between a theoretical, badly constructed scenario by Eleanor Perry, and ambitious staging which seems only to tease." They detested *Lolly Madonna XXX* (1973), which they label "a festival of histrionics." And they don't care to comment on the rest of his features that followed, including *The Next Man* (1976), *Sunburn* (1979), and *The Bear* (1984).

I'm interested in the notion of the "hero's journey" in Sarafian's films of this period. Sarafian men don't merely brush up against the elements, but they are given a means of existential rebellion. As Tavernier and Coursodon note that Sarafian is a kind of inverse to Monte Hellman, this lies in a sense that Sarafian's hero's journey is a suicide mission that gives the hero a window into demiurgic fulfillment. It is a shame he couldn't develop these ideas further with projects that suited his abilities better. Like Lamont Johnson, he was another case of a system unable to answer to more offbeat talent.

Joseph Sargent: Two of his big screen potboilers, *Colossus: The Forbin Project* (1970) and *The Taking of Pelham One Two Three* (1974), are magnificent, stand-outs among their respective genres. But then there's *Jaws the Revenge* (1987). I run in circles that make weirdly sophisticated arguments for the Oedipal threads in his infamous *Jaws* sequel. This is so deep in the weeds as to suggest a place where the sun never shines. His television films were the best of their kind: *Tribes* (1970), *Man on a String* (1971), *The Man* (1972), *Sunshine* (1973), *Hustling* (1975), *Playing for Time* (1980). He was a Modigliani of the telefilm format, if one should ever exist. I hate to say "You gotta give the guy credit" but I do. I'll leave it to you to be open-minded.

Peter Sasdy: Sasdy might be the subject of a full case-study chapter in a possible volume two of this book, if I ever get around to it. But I need to do a full retrospective deep dive, to help me get more detailed. Until then, here's a capsule study. Justin LaLiberty, curator of Cinematographe (and someone whose opinion I respect) writes, "*Hands of the Ripper* has the fortune of being directed by Peter Sasdy, who is responsible for my personal favorite Hammer feature, *Taste the Blood of Dracula*. Sasdy is great at keeping everything in check. He maintains a near constant air of tension, tosses in quite a few surprisingly severe scenes of violence, and even manages to get some very convincing performances out of actors most wouldn't think twice about casting. It is one of the better Hammer films and perhaps the best Jack the Ripper related film of note."

Film critic David Edelstein once wrote to me stating, "*Hands of the Ripper* is very good and very sick. The themes and performances in his *Taste the Blood of Dracula* (1970) work really well, and it would have been the best Dracula with a slightly better script and ending. It hurt that Lee didn't commit until the last second so Drac's vengeance doesn't make a lot of sense. His *The Stone Tapes* is *excellent* and very scary."

I cannot fathom how his sci-fi Western *Welcome to Blood City* (1977) is still unavailable on digital, with no acceptable transfer in sight (it was originally shot 2.35:1). The widely circulated pan-and-scan is simply unwatchable, so the people ranking it on sites like Letterboxd... I must ask, what are they ranking it off of? That pan-and-scan? If so, that is hardly fair. For the lack of an acceptable transfer in circulation, I'd put this in the pile labeled "few have *really* seen beyond rare, scattered screenings on 35mm." There's also: *Nothing But the Night* (1972), *Doomwatch* (1972), *I Don't Want to Be Born* (1975, which Severin Films head David Gregory swears by), and the ill-fated *The Lonely Lady* (1983), which prematurely ended Sasdy's movie directing career.

Jerry Schatzberg: Schatzberg's initial trio *Puzzle of a Downfall Child* (1970), *The Panic in Needle Park* (1971), and *Scarecrow* (1973) automatically render him an important director. *Puzzle* redefined for me what film editing was capable of expressing when I was a freshman in film school. The post "initial trilogy of brilliance" work? *Sweet Revenge* (1976) doesn't lack for certain charms. *Honeysuckle Rose* (1980) is one of the better on-the-road films about traveling musicians (it's the source of Willie's "On the Road Again" after all). *No Small Affair* (1984) might be a serious contender for the smartest teen sex comedy of the Eighties. His remake of a 1966 Italian film based on the same novel, *Misunderstood* (1984), is at least a little misunderstood. *Reunion* (1989) uses anamorphic widescreen to often great graphic effect. But entirely by virtue of his first three features, he's a master filmmaker.

Michael Schultz: I'm clamoring for a book on Michael Schultz. I'm not the one to do it, because I feel a black author would much better reflect the ethos. But on the basis of his masterpiece *Cooley High* (1975), which I feel is far superior to *American Graffiti*, along with the skillfully assembled populist ensemble piece *Car Wash* (1976), the raunchy labor comedy cum Wertmuller remake *Which Way is Up?* (1977), and the just plain fun *Krush Groove* (1985), I think there is a fascinating study here for some enterprising author. He is no doubt an auteur, a genius at mixing highbrow and lowbrow elements into very tart but delicious cocktails that will have you drunk on immaculately mixed spirits that should never mix.

Barry Shear: I'm not the first or the only one to single out Barry Shear as a "he coulda been a contender" director. He only made four theatrical features, but you never sensed some schlub at the controls. Shear was a special case. In *Time Out*, critic Thom Rhodes writes, "*The Todd Killings* (1971) establishes a micro- cosm of American matriarchal society, and then tosses in a suit- ably bourgeois Manson figure to stir it up. Shear's astounding film goes beyond the alienation, bikini beaches, and campus revolt of earlier 'youth pics' to a hardcore nihilism, and it spells out the message underlying the long Hollywood heritage of misogynistic, latent homosexual heroes. Mounted like true tabloid journalism, as sensational as anything of Sam Fuller's, it's a genuinely provocative account of the souring of the American dream."

Geoff Andrew, also in *Time Out*, says of *Across 110th Street*, "As directed by Shear, who made the highly impressive *The Todd Killings*, it's a gutsy affair, given a distinct lift by the Harlem loca- tions." *Time Out* also complimented Shear's *Wild in the Streets* in terms of its flair, claiming it is directed with "great verve." Leave it to Christopher Wicking and Tise Vahimagi to give us a take on the whole enchilada in *The American Vein*: "*Wild in the Streets* brought Shear up front; *Across 110th Street* was a welcome reminder that he deserved critical attention; *Deadly Trackers* (which he took over when Samuel Fuller was fired) was a convenient excuse to forget him again. His TV work is, however, consistently remarkable, and while he continues to work with formula shows, he seems to invest them with an almost immediately recognizable quality. Such shows highlight Shear's capacity to handle action and other plastic values. His understanding of pace, rhythm, angle, cutting, etc. place him, if not on the same level as Don Siegel, not far below. On the TV ladder, he is rungs higher than most."

I sit here typing, wishing he had given us more, but what he gave us suggested a Fuller fetus, elevating the seediest dime-novel affairs with class and perspective on America as it stood when he was working. Shear is buried treasure. Get digging, and dig him!

Steven Spielberg: The venom directed toward Spielberg by people who, in the same breath, venerate John Ford and everything he does, is utterly incomprehensible and absurd on its face. I grew up on Spielberg, and his work is part of a spiritual biography for me. But his vocabulary is extrapolated from Ford, someone the cognoscenti has sanctified – and Spielberg's *The Fabelmans* (2022) even admitted to it.

Consider that his first three movies, three of his very best, are hot-pursuit pictures not terribly unlike *The Searchers*: *Duel* (1971), *The Sugarland Express* (1974), and *Jaws* (1975). His doe-eyed Americanism in recent years is part a reflection of Ford and the Kramer message films of his youth. Purely in terms of emotion—straight up and not on the rocks—his poise in eliciting feeling from the audience is a gift approaching god-like. Manipulation? Perhaps, but with a fine touch. He often gets blamed for ruining the industry with his *Jaws* arrival; this judgment is dropped ad nauseam among a class of terminally online film bros. I place far more blame on comrade George's shoulders there. When his mother once joked that she should have had her uterus bronzed for having birthed such an icon, one can laugh and then understand the why and wherefore. Best of all, though, like him or hate him, the work is never not intensely personal to him. He's not the long-in-the-tooth amusement park technician Lucas always was or, at least in time, became.

Victor Stoloff: One thing is clear about Stoloff: the dude really loved therapy, psychoanalytics, and the talking cure, as demonstrated in *Intimacy* (1966), *The 300-Year Weekend* (1971), and *Why* (1973). No one's ever heard of him, and one day I feel like I want to do a full excavation and microscopic examination. Both *The 300-Year Weekend* and *Why* are extended scripted group therapy sessions on film. It's not everyone's thing, certainly, but you marvel that they were ever made at all. *Intimacy* is the strangest of all domestic dramas. Another subject for further study.

Joseph Strick: Strick hails from my birth city, Pittsburgh, Pennsylvania. He was born in Rankin, the next borough over from where I grew up, in Swissvale. From such humble beginnings, he went on to adapt some hoity-toity literary properties like James Joyce's *Ulysses* (1967) and Henry Miller's *Tropic of Cancer* (1970). Bertrand Tavernier wrote of him with unchecked rancor, but even at his most foolhardy, there's a sheen to Strick's ambition that I've appreciated, even when it falters. He was apparently not such a nice man, from everything I've heard, but as a fellow east-Pittsburghian, I have some sense of pride that such a dreamer emerged from someplace as now-rundown as Rankin.

David Swift: Swift is of note because of how he tends to pattern himself after Frank Tashlin, especially in *Good Neighbor Sam* (1964) and *How to Succeed in Business Without Really Trying* (1967). Something like Tashlin's *Will Success Spoil Rock Hunter?* (1957) is formally more bold, but the way Swift skewers the advertising industry—or big American corporate business—and the way he roasts American plasticity and its conservative image-cultivators feels like something in the Tashlin wheelhouse. I personally believe that *Good Neighbor Sam* is one of the best studio comedies of its time. I'd even say there's a dash of Blake Edwards in there too. *Love is a Ball* (1963), with Lucille Ball and Glenn Ford, plays like an Edwards romantic farce that he turned down. Look at the cutting patterns and compare. That influence is also present in Swift's *Under the Yum-Yum Tree* (1963), and not merely because of Jack Lemmon's presence. His Hayley Mills at Disney outings, *Polyanna* (1960) and *The Parent Trap* (1961), suggest another track of his oeuvre altogether. A subject for further study, in any event.

J. Lee Thompson: J. Lee Thompson has a case of John Guillermin's Syndrome. An impressive early resumé (*Yield to the Night, Ice Cold in Alex, The Guns of Navarone, Cape Fear, Return from the Ashes, Eye of the Devil*) and an almost inexplicably trashy later resumé (*Death Wish 4: The Crackdown*, Cannon's *King Solomon's Mines, Kinjite*). A funny thing happened on the way to retirement for Mr. Thompson.

James Toback: It's hard to think of a director I detest more than James Toback. Yes, *Fingers* (1978) is a fine film and it seems to be that *The Gambler* (1974), which Toback wrote, owes a great deal to director Karel Reisz. But I constantly get the sense that the rest of his filmography consists of electronic press kits for himself, all repurposed as a tool to "cruise chicks." And the fact that he leaves a trail of tears and litigation in his wake, in terms of the dozens if not hundreds (thousands?) of women who have accused him of harassment and sexual malfeasance, I have a hunch I'm right. I avoid Toback films the way that backwards-cap football-bro tailgaters avoid Henry Jaglom films. My mentor Paul Sylbert, who designed *The Pick-Up Artist* (1987) for him, didn't have terribly nice things to say either. A critical study of his films should also be titled *The Pick-Up Artist*, or "the pick-up hack" if you consider the women who didn't dig said artistry. Toback is the dreaded "toxic masculinity" in celluloid form. As such, you inject it into your eyes as "pure shit," as they say in the narcotics world.

Paul Williams: Here we have one of the Seventies' best kept secrets. Only seven features, including four between 1969 and 1978 that are terrific: *Out of It* (1969), *The Revolutionary* (1970), *Dealing, or the Berkeley-to-Boston Forty-Brick Lost-Bag Blues* (1972), and *Nunzio* (1978), starring my friend David Proval. I got to know Williams a bit through that friendship. I love him as a sort of self-styled guerrilla who infuses a devil-may-care bluster into each film. One can look at a later film like *The November Men* (1993), a politically charged thriller that one can imagine the FBI investigating Williams for making—and if you know Paul for any amount of time, you say, "This is such a Paul Williams joint." When I corralled him for a 2020 Zoom seminar to speak with budding filmmakers, he was broadcast from a hacienda in the jungles of Brazil. It was picture perfect. I think of a John Cassavetes story: J.C. was stationed on the floor of his editing suite with a big camera, grabbing insert shots staged impromptu. When someone entered and asked what he was doing, he said, "You know me, I'm crazy" and continued shooting. That's Paul Williams!

Michael Winner: I often wish his staging for camera didn't seem so arbitrary so often, especially once he enters the Seventies. Even within the contours of Charles Bronson cinema, the Michael Winner of *The Mechanic* (1972) feels—in a number of ways—different from the Winner of the Cannon and *Death Wish* flicks. It's hard to completely fault any director capable of the films he made in his early British period, namely *The Girl-Getters* (1964), *The Jokers* (1966), and the best of those, *I'll Never Forget What's'isname* (1968). Winner did his best work with Oliver Reed. His bridge to the American market, *Hannibal Brooks* (1968), led to his high-water mark on *Lawman* (1971). One constant is his relish for controversy. He was a favorite of talk show hosts for his chutzpah and his ineffably posh uncouthness. He was notoriously irascible on set and his Eighties are marked by a brand of sordid excess that entertains with boundlessly vulgar, savage spectacle. Winner's foxy smile and his mischievous raised brow lingers over each outing. One's individual mileage may vary. The limp comedies on which he ended his career are bizarre in the context of humdingers like *The Wicked Lady* (1983) or *Death Wish 3* (1985).

Robert M. Young: Young had a feel for the lumpenproletariat, if you will, and a flair for stories centered around them (all the more ironic it is then that a film called *Rich Kids* is smuggled into his filmography amid *Alambrista!*, *The Ballad of Gregorio Cortez*, et al.). No one much discusses him as an auteur or even filmmaker of note, though Criterion has so far inducted two of his films into the collection. His work with Michael Roemer (now undergoing his own resurgence) lends him further glimmer.

Howard Zieff: It was in Howard Zieff comedies that audiences saw a distinct, lovable Borscht Belt sensibility re-emerge in wider, more popular form. There's a Borscht Belt swagger that sashays across a number of his formula comedies, and a couple more heartfelt endeavors; it's in the delivery of lines that the spirit of that humor, with its unabashedly Jewish tenor. I am particularly fond of *Slither* (1972), *Hearts of the West* (1975), and *House Calls* (1978), but I also find myself checking back in with others like *The Dream Team* (1989) at a pretty regular clip, when I need a pick-me-up. The American-Jewish humor is alive in well in Zieff, the man who gave us "Mama mia, that's a spicy meat-a-ball!"

Fred Zinnemann, William Wyler and George Stevens: Mike Nichols once mused on the auteur theory, "I think there were these French guys with cigarette ashes all over them, and that they basically misunderstood the whole thing. The first thing they misunderstood is the so-called 'pantheon' of great directors, because as we know, the French people have some bizarre perception of our movies, like they think Jerry Lewis the greatest. Howard Hawks is a wonderful director, but he isn't the greatest director Hollywood ever knew. The guys with the cigarette ashes on them, ignored our greatest directors, and humiliated George Stevens, William Wyler, Fred Zinnemann. Billy Wilder became fashionable again later. But the tragedy is that Wyler, Zinnemann, and Stevens, that they just weren't part of the froggie conspiracy."

Wyler, to me, is superior to Hawks, yet indeed, he was shunned by the French auteurists. I've met and worked with Catherine Wyler, who is fond of reminding anyone who'll listen that her father was of French bearing and liked to quip, "I'm one of the few Americans who can actually correctly pronounce the word 'auteur.'" To me, Wyler's films are about cushy, comfortable, sometimes self-identified anti-violent or non-violent characters who are cornered into acting, sometimes with the violence they dread or abhor. Most of his Fifties films revolve around this idea. Think *The Desperate Hours* (1955), *The Big Country* (1958), and *Ben-Hur* (1959). His *Friendly Persuasion* (1956) specifically centers on a non-violent religious sect suddenly thrust into a very real, very violent world. Earlier pictures like *Mrs. Miniver* (1942) get at this as well. *The Best Years of Our Lives* (1946) profiles the veterans of the necessary violence, with the women of the story now forced to act for themselves, in various ways and to various degrees. Cracking Wyler's earlier pictures is a fun feat unto itself, but yes, he is a great director, and an auteur as he would correctly pronounce (in both senses of the word "pronounce"). "Life has us do things we wouldn't otherwise like or find ourselves doing, and the way we make do shapes one's experience of it," he tells us in film after film. This is certainly a coherent way of looking at the world, which is unique to him and him alone as expressed in the collected work. Wyler is, point blank, the greatest American director of the classic era, and the undisputed best when it came to performance. Also, he was more visually dynamic and innovative than many of the figures that the French auteurist forebearers lionized. Zinnemann's auteurist neglect is likewise sinful. My friend Julie Kirgo argues Zinnemann's focus on marriage.

As for Stevens, I'll take *Shane* (1953) and *Giant* (1956) over virtually any Ford Western, and I see more in those two as well. And who on God's green earth would ever argue with *A Place in the Sun* (1951)? We can thank the French on one level, but on another level, I feel they have done some kind of disservice.

Conclusion and Self-Analysis

No matter what I felt or thought, no matter what I tried to accomplish or how, the director would ultimately have his way. That was what I had to face and accept. They didn't cry "Author! Author!" in the movies. They never had. Now they cried "Auteur! Auteur!"—even if the auteur fucked up the picture.

Arthur Laurents, screenwriter and playwright

So, page after page, all this talk of "auteur this" and "auteur that"— "What does it all *mean*, Basil?!"

I was recently on a Zoom call with Australian director Simon Wincer, for my day job. He recounted how, in the wake of his having directed *Phar Lap*, *Free Willy*, and *Operation: Dumbo Drop*, a studio executive proclaimed that he could now be "Hollywood's large mammal guy." The name Simon Wincer had, by some curious course of events, become synonymous with compassionate films about large, lovable creatures—whales, elephants, horses, etc. He laughed about it then, and still laughs now. Wincer knows it's important to keep a good humor in this crazy business, and he's never lost sight of how fortunate he's been. He's worked ceaselessly since his humble beginnings, and carved out a fine life.

So listen here, I have no illusions about how directors sometimes stumble onto their brands. In some cases, it is indeed unwittingly and/or by chance. Sometimes, yes, a director needs a job and takes the first gig available. You make the movies you can make, when you can make them. This is axiomatically true, even for myself as an independent feature filmmaker. I get a bit more of a hand in guiding my own way and calling my own shots overall, but the projects that actually get produced are dictated by circumstance and the way the stars align.

Robert Altman speaks to something that many filmmakers do: "The filmmakers who influenced me, I don't know their names, because I would go and see a film and hate it, and say, 'I've got to remember never to do anything like that.'" Kubrick is claimed to have operated similarly, with many recounting, "He didn't always know what he wanted, but he always knew what he *didn't* want."

I'm an "appreciator" above all. Because I'm a historian and critic who makes his own movies, I understand the process of what goes into making a coherent movie. I do know what I do not want, and that is as much a political question as it is anything else—the latter is just part of my issue with Ford. Sidney Furie did not wish to be connected with me and was not initially interested in a book until he learned that I was a filmmaker myself. "You know what we directors go through, and you understand more than some critic who has never lived it," was his attitude. In his mind, I'd have "rachmunes" (Yiddish for "compassion" or "mercy"), a word he actually used. He does have a point. As a result of my having directing a number of narrative features and having experienced the day-to-day as the "general-in-command" on a movie set, I'm a little more understanding and forgiving when a movie, or movies, by certain directors don't work or add up, or when they fail to come together. It is said that no one sets out to make a bad movie, they just happen (though, having worked long enough, I can think of a few examples to counter this truism).

If I can sense ambition or risk or some level of artistry, my benefit of the doubt is never in short supply. I'm never going to throw out Larry Peerce's *The Incident* or *Goodbye, Columbus*—and what I perceive as accents in his personal style—because he later gave us *Hard to Hold* and *Wired*. And I'm going to look to find the things that interest me in works like *Ash Wednesday*, rather than groping for wisecracks and verbal fireworks. I see the stitching, and that's enough. A true cinephile, and by extension cineaste, must be omnivorous rather than closed-minded. I always wish to be as good an audience as I can be.

I've met and befriended so many film directors in my life so far. I'm lucky in that respect. You can learn so much by breaking bread with even the most overlooked or work-a-day directors. I think many critics, and even the most august scholars, lack a sense of this, outside of swank private audiences with the lions they've anointed and, in some cases, empowered. They can be unsparing and unforgiving of others outside the winners circle, even when they skillfully untangle the type of on-set tangles that would flummox even the most poker-faced among us.

So, to conclude, let us return to the religious analogy from the opening. I've attended many filmmakers' "churches and syna- gogues," including at any number of movie palace "temples." What have I taken with me? And how has my being a steady congregant affected me, the films I've made, and my own sensibility? As a filmmaker, I can say that we all take these things with us and repurpose them, filter them through our own lens or prism of experience and culture, to make sense of them for ourselves. I've had a steady diet of films for the last forty years of my life. Favorites have changed hands, influences have blown through my door and then rushed out. Whereas I was still being sculpted as an artist, and as an individual, in my formative years, I have a sturdy sense of who I am today. By the time most people hit their forties, they are at least something closer to a fully formed person.

Jean Cocteau once said, "An artist cannot speak about his art any more than a plant can discuss horticulture." Fine, I'll be the talking tree about to lecture folks on George Washington Carver and Rachel Carson. And I won't slap you when you take my apples, à la *Wizard of Oz* — I'll just give 'em to you.

In my case, I'm a man grown old before my time. That might be why The Archers (Michael Powell and Emeric Pressburger) are my favorite filmmakers of all, and why their *The Life and Death of Colonel Blimp* (1943) is my single favorite film of all time, if I were forced to name just one. But I began somewhat differently. My first feature film, *Sophisticated Acquaintance* (2007), was shot in film school, and it wore its influences on its sleeve. I mixed a Peter Watkins with an early Ken Russell (his BBC biopics especially) sensibility and added some No Wave no-budget tropes à la James Nares and Amos Poe to tell the story of author Klaus Mann's "short life and long death." It's a film I somewhat enjoy watching back today, because it's very much a young man's movie. I really thought I was going to redefine the form in some way, that's how impetuous I was. I merged drama, mock-documentary, essay, and experimental "poetic" filmmaking into one 75-minute feature product.

A Trip to Swadades (2008) saw my first foray into a cinema of the aged and addled. My early films could be grouped into a program called "Premature Nostalgia." I had saudades (the root of the title) for a time that had passed long before I was even born — and also for a period of culture that had long since evaporated. My characters were men past the age of 70, communing over a mutual inability to reconcile new realities with the halcyon (and maybe falsely rosy) memories of what's come before. The theme of memory and the power of memory is major with me, for whatever reason.

The Idiotmaker's Gravity Tour (2011) was another in this run: an aging ex-hippie, with intense nostalgia for his youth, goes to India looking to right a major wrong from his past. If Shirley MacLaine had her go at me, I'm sure she would rule I was once a Canadian-Jewish *alter kocker* who lived happily in his own time, somewhere in the mid-twentieth century. Memory and Jewish identity is likely why Joan Micklin Silver is so precious to me as an artist. Whether it's Charles remembering his idolized past with Laura in *Chilly Scenes of Winter*, or Gitl's struggle to understand and acclimate to the New World in *Hester Street*, I feel like I really "get" Joan's work—and I also think that's why we personally got along so well and enjoyed each other's company as friends.

By the time I got to San Francisco, I was looking to spread my wings a bit more as a filmmaker—and to stretch my clay feet out of troubling, tricky, or potentially treacherous patterns. My style was always observational and improvisatory, with a special love of naturalistic dialogue, to the point it could be achieved seamlessly and without editing room headaches. I still believe that the film form presents artists with possibilities to record sometimes astonishing, and most of all truthful, moments that cannot be contrived or repeated. That means experimenting with how far structured improvisational acting can take an entire film. One cannot do multiple takes on stage, but one can do as many takes as one needs in cinema, and cull together a scene from even the smallest gestures in each of those takes. That's how I work. I'm not impugning scripted filmmaking—great (or talented at the very least) directors can do and have done so much with screenplays by the best writers. But I just have a different métier, one for which I've been both applauded and attacked (it matters not, because I'll continue doing things my way).

Raise Your Kids on Seltzer.

With *Raise Your Kids on Seltzer* (2015), I wanted to shoot in proper, "native" 'Scope, having been inspired by Sidney J. Furie from the time I was a kid—and by then, having met and befriended him. That film emerged from a time of trying to understand where my own parents were in their marriage, and how newly married friends were dealing with the transition. I sold it as a film about cults, but truly, it is a film about marriage, and about control as an element in any intimate relationship. I continue to be fascinated by how it divides the audiences for whom it has screened; the men are sympathetic to the husband, and the women are sympathetic to the wife, almost without exception. . I noticed this at screening after screening, and it verified to me that I did a real groovy job on the material. It's not a flawless work, by any means, but it was precisely the film I needed to make at that time.

Ezer Kenegdo (2017) I have a hard time watching now, partly because it features me in the lead role, playing a version of myself at a problematic point in my life. But it was lovely collaborating with Josh Safdie, a filmmaker I respected well before he broke out with *Uncut Gems* (2019). There was an understanding I felt toward the work ethic at his now defunct Red Bucket Films that I wanted some insight into. As much as the film is an inquiry into the complex relationship between Poles and Jews, it is also an awkward portrait of me at a confused time, as a "frum" Chassidic Jew straddling the secular art and film world while simultaneously keeping kosher and immersing in the joys and rigmaroles of Yiddishkeit. (For what it's worth, I've backed off that level of observance, but still attend shul weekly.) Again, my thematic refrain is the past—broadly, much like Joan Micklin Silver, "old world vs. new world."

Overwhelm the Sky (2019) is the film I see as my personal best, and it seems the critics agreed. With this loose adaptation of *Edgar Huntly, or Memoirs of a Sleepwalker*, an early American novel, I took great joy in hanging all my obsessions and stylistic preoccupations on a piece of American Gothic. Alexander Hero was cast in the lead, because he evoked everything I loved about the heroes of the Seventies Canadian films of directors like Don Shebib. I also thought the way that the camera gazed at his angular Scandinavian physiognomy owed itself to the monochrome Bergman classics that cast themselves in my memory.

Furie's compositional work is once again always with me, but I also like to think that Rivette (at his most Borgesian), Losey (at his most mainland Europe-y), and my perennial love for *Zabriskie Point* (especially in the desert finale) are also in the final product.

Sidney Furie taught me in practice how one can invigorate something as basic as shot-reverse-shot "over-the-shoulder" scenes. Top image from his *The Entity*, and bottom two from my *Overwhelm the Sky*.

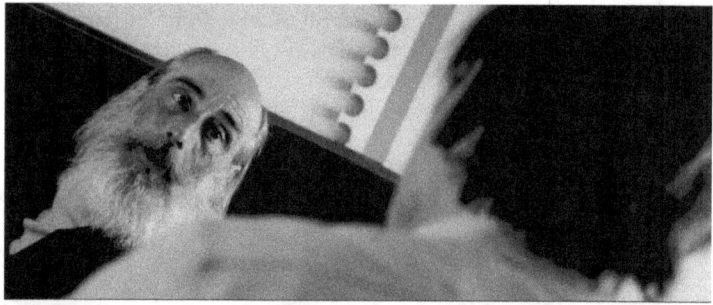

Many thought I was channeling David Lynch (and many reviews of my film name-drop him, betting on him as an influence), but it was not conscious of me if he was. It might have just come out that way. The visual vocabulary, staging, and cutting patterns are Sidney Furie's, if anyone's.

With Covid, I had to slow down my production of narrative features, and I retreated into documentary and essay-form cinema, which is where I'm currently situated—and quite happily, I'll add. If it hadn't been for my full immersion in the documentary and essay films, almost all of which have been on cinema subjects, this book might not exist, at least in this form. I'll re-emerge in narrative someday. I do have two features in post, both having presented certain conundrums that I have the privilege of solving thanks to the gift of time and control. The best way to make a film is to have no one—money men, studios, etc.—breathing down your neck. So few filmmakers seem to understand (nor have they ever known) such privilege. My friendships with the indie "mavericks" Henry Jaglom, Rob Nilsson, and Jon Jost have been the most formative in my development, as they have also been lucky enough to enjoy the same artistic freedom, not to mention more of a sense of self-reliance relative to the industry at large.

Jost, for one, is the ultimate Emersonian filmmaker—he shoots, directs, edits all by himself, a one-man band. Coppola once said that he looked forward to the day when "a little fat girl from Ohio will make a beautiful film and be the next Mozart." He's of course referring to the democratization of the medium, something we have very much realized by now. But Jost realized that for himself long ago. I think that, out of the many individuals I've met in my years in the business—good or bad, selfless or selfish—the Josts and Nilssons and Jagloms are the types I most aspire to be. Like or hate their films, these are men in charge of their own cinematic destiny. What they've put on the screen is never more or less than exactly what they've wanted to put there. They've also all lived colorful lives. How could any filmmaker's filmmaker not want to model him/herself after that?

In any event, these are the movies I've made, and the movies that made me, and how they travel on my life's road hand-in-hand. You are what you "eat" or consume, and you are what you enjoy—and, more importantly, find value in. As a filmmaker, you take it all with you. The most offbeat or customized elements should emerge and re-emerge without fear, or need to reinforce canons or mainstream tastes, no matter how refined or widely praised. Film lovers and filmmakers need to find their own ways, singular to themselves, if the work is ever going to be fresh, new, individual. Nowadays, by and large, new "product"—or "content"—is decidedly not. This is not mere heterodoxy, but a plea to find oneself through omnivorous viewing habits, as not to become another homogenized voice.

Once upon a time, it was difficult to marathon any director's films, unless one had an inside track at an archive or museum collection. One had to rely on the endorsement of tastemakers with those advantages. Now, almost everything is available. We all have the privilege of access and playback, plus the gift of remotes with "pause" and "rewind" buttons for ease of closer inspection. Expand your palate! No excuses! Don't rely on others to curate your own tastes. There is a big, wide world out there—thousands of filmmakers and millions of films—at your fingertips. Go and explore! I hear more and more that every movie is somebody's favorite, which is as it should be.

Narrative Feature Films: *Sophisticated Acquaintance* (2007), *A Trip to Swadades* (2008), *The Idiotmaker's Gravity Tour* (2011), *A Simple Game of Catch* (2012), *Raise Your Kids on Seltzer* (2015), *Ezer Kenegdo* (2017), *Overwhelm the Sky* (2019), *Countercurrents* (2025), *Even Just* (in post-production), *Precious Wheels Above* (shooting)

Non-Fiction Feature Films: *It's a Zabriskie, Zabriskie, Zabriskie, Zabriskie Point* (2023), *Cruel, Usual, Necessary: The Passion of Silvio Narizzano* (2024), *Now, Irving Rapper* (coming in 2026), *A World of Innocent Sinners: The Fables of Philip Leacock* (coming within the next two years)

Short Films and Short Video Essays of Choice: *Charles at the Threshold* (2006), *Collection of Chemicals* (2009), *Ceiling-Head Angel* (2010), *Paralyzed Segments: Suzanne Pleshette Tangled Up in Codes* (2022), *Cinema of the Pilpul: A Talmudic View of Early Holocaust Cinema* (2023)

Afterword by Daniel Waters

It was a deceptively simple exercise. Once a day, during the pandemic lockdown, this guy on Facebook, a "friend" I don't recall making or meeting was posting his ten favorite movies corresponding to a letter in the alphabet. The problem was this Kremer dude was not picking the right movies, at least according to me. And Planet Earth. I mean, no room for *Lawrence of Arabia* in L? No Network in N (don't get Kremer started!)? Here was a champion of the Odd, the Truly Transgressive, and the Not Widely Known. I duly harrumphed and resisted, but took it as a point of P Pride when one of my deep, secret celluloid crushes. *Puzzle of a Downfall Child* made an appearance—hey, I can be a freak too.

The "friends" became friends without the quotations, and if there's anything we Daniels enjoy more than making films, it's watching films, reading about them, writing about them, kvetching about them. I'm one of those annoying cinephiles who thinks he's seen everything and knows everything. Kremer tenderly slaps the shit of cinephiles and cine-folk like me. His knowledge is vast and idiosyncratic. I've always known if he ever sat down to write a book on Film, capital F, it would be a monster, thrilling and terrifying in detail and ambition.

Adventures in Auteurism is indeed a beast, both a warm hug and a terrorist act, conjuring giddy memories of the readings of our voracious youth, but going way beyond sober Sarris stratification and wily Kael heroine chic. If you think the title promises ho-humpteenth rehashings of Welles, Scorsese, Tarantino and Hitchcock—glance to the table of contents and feel the burn. This is a book for the directors (mostly) without books, all the unusual suspects, the ones dismissed as journeymen, the ones with schizoid IMDb pages of big swings and whiffs not always under their control.

So many movies! Kremer overwhelms with secret stunners you've never heard of, films you remember as decent that may be masterpieces (like Harvey Hart's *Shoot*, which this book inspired me to see), and notorious laughingstocks that still possess a certain something—I can't say Daniel defends Larry Peerce's Belushi biopic *Wired*, but he sure does make it sound fascinating.

[And I'll just say the fact that there is a movie where "Telly Savalas is accidentally castrated by a camper hitch as he frivolously drowns the family of five inside said camper" and I don't know it, destroys me.]

Kremer's opening salvo on Canadian Directors is a notably exhilarating balm. As a McGill University student in 1980's Montreal, Canadian cinema was a Saul Rubinek-infused fever dream where I experienced the strange and wonderful and not-so-wonderful, but always off-American-kilter. The section confirms I did not imagine the exquisite madness and there's so much more to explore.

Kremer's archeology travels the rest of the world. Again though, his main destination is the Island of the Misfit Toys, an all-out counter-mythology of filmmakers and filmmakers to be discovered and rediscovered. (Oh the joy to find someone else who thinks *Meet Joe Black* is something of a masterpiece and the funhouse mirror sequence in Jules Dassan's *Up Tight!* is one of the greatest scenes ever.)

In addition, Kremer brings fresh points-of-view to the party—Jewish, gay (I don't recall Andy and Pauline being able to so brilliantly dissect a bullhorn rape, as in Silvio Narizzano's *The Sky is Falling*), and most of all, humanist. It's the depth of feeling that dazzles throughout. Scenes are "tattooed to my soul" and lines "resonate every time I revisit."

Yes, the book's secret weapon is its warmth, with the author many times breaking bread and befriending the subject and their collaborators, unearthing dimensions your usual critic/scholar alone in a study can only hope to achieve.

Ultimately, my reactions to *Adventures in Auteurism* mirror my reaction the first images of the universe from the James Webb telescope—hushed, helpless awe with a little confounded anger that I'll never be able to figure it all out. I guess it's best to just surrender to the infinity of the cosmos. And to the magic of film. Keep reading, keep watching, keep creating, keep kvetching. This is the business we've chosen.

Daniel Waters is an Edgar Award-winning screenwriter known for Heathers *(1989),* Batman Returns *(1992), and* Demolition Man *(1993). For many years, he was one of Hollywood's most in-demand script doctors.*

Acknowledgements

First thanks should go to Gerald Peary. In wishing to access more of my video essay work as packaged on home video releases, he suggested I gather together my pieces on overlooked directors and publish them as a compilation of print essays. It was he who planted the seed of the idea. I will note, Gerry has historically been a fierce American advocate of Canadian cinema himself. The next round of thanks should go to Paul Cronin, who immediately contacted me and expressed keen interest in publishing such a volume, as soon as I floated it publicly and started tinkering with it.

I also wish to thank Saul Rubinek, as I did in the Acknowledgements of my Sidney J. Furie book years ago. Saul ignited a chain reaction. As soon as I evinced an interest in "deep cut" Canadian cinema circa 2009, I contacted my friend Wendel Meldrum (to whom this book is dedicated) who then put me in touch with Saul. He was generous with his time and believed that I could do something of importance—or, at least, of use—for his birth country's cinema heritage. It was Saul who pulled the strings to get me in touch with Sidney J. Furie (a filmmaking hero of mine, then and now), which in turn spurred a friendship and mentorship that persists to this day—not to mention a first-of-its-kind book on Furie, published in 2015, of which I'm still exceedingly proud.

Additional gratitude to my buddy, Canadian filmmaker Paul Lynch, who has supported and encouraged all my projects the entire time I've known him. Paul, as the Italians say, cent'anni. Or, as my own people say, "to 120 in good health!"—here's looking at you, my good friend!

A hat tip to Toronto Jewish Film Festival head Stuart Hands, who has helped me score so much in the way of Canadian buried treasure over the years. With this book, he helped me get in touch with Harvey Hart's daughter Bethelene Hart. (Thanks to Bethelene, as well!) Stuart also supplied me with rare copies of Hart's early CBC television dramas, which proved of great research value. On that note, thanks also to Julie Kirgo for furnishing me with a now rare out-of-print Blu-ray copy of John Guillermin's masterpiece *Rapture*, on which she does stellar audio commentary duties… next to the great (and terribly missed) Nick Redman.

To my foreword and afterword writers, the legendary Joe Dante, and the one and only Daniel Waters. I consider you both friends, but as I step back for a moment look at both your names on the cover of my own book, I have to just pinch myself. You've done me such a great honor! Thank you.

Also, to my buddy and sometimes partner-in-crime David Del Valle. Our open-ended cinemaniacal conversations over pecan sandies at Bolt in Hollywood were always enriching, and often informed my approach. Occasionally, he even clued me into possible blind spots.

A moment of appreciation for Karen Black, who, in her time, put me in touch with George Kaczender and Ivan Passer, both of whom are profiled in this text. Karen, George, and Ivan are all gone now, but I felt far more equipped writing about them thanks to Karen's always available helping hand. She is so missed in my life.

And to Joan Micklin Silver, also greatly missed. Joan, our friendship was far too short, as I only met you in your final years. But I'll go to my own grave cherishing those kitchen table conversations over English muffins and tea, and I will rest just a bit more easily knowing that your work will continue to get discovered.

Thanks to Josh Hibberd and Justin LaLiberty for the steady flow of work at Imprint Films and Cinematographe. I was awarded the time to write many of the pieces featured herein, and given respect as a film scholar. It was my honor to be featured on so many of your disc packages.

This book reads all the better because of the diligent work of copy-editor Daniel Rosenthal, and once again, Mr. Cronin of Sticking Place Books. Corrections and typesetting were fast, super smooth, and highly enjoyable thanks to Paul, who even made the process fun (and that's kind of a first for me). It's such a joy having written something so important to me for his imprint.

I remember the morning that I checked my email to find that graphic designer Scott Saslow had sent me twelve options for the cover design. Opening the document, I was just stunned. Scott, you're a wizard with posters and covers, for now multiple labels and publishers; I fully intend to continue our collaboration over multiple projects, so thank you tons for your marvelous taste.

No film scholar's Acknowledgements section is complete without proper thanks to the Academy of Motion Picture Arts and Sciences' Margaret Herrick Library. In the particular case of the Irving Rapper chapter, I must also thank USC's Warner Bros. archives. (Stay tuned for my Irving Rapper documentary!)

Above all, without the love of my husband, Evan, this book wouldn't be what it is. Endless thanks for holding down the fort while I finished this thing, babe. I love you more than words can express. You are, as always, the director's director and I'd be lost without you in my life.

Index

Sticking Place Books (stickingplacebooks.com) is a New York-based publisher specializing in cinema, offering interview books, memoirs, critical and historical studies, screenplays, and essay collections. Our titles include:

Lessons with Kiarostami, edited by Paul Cronin

In the Shadow of Trees: The Collected Poetry of Abbas Kiarostami

Still Film Crazy (After All These Years) by Patrick McGilligan

It's Only a Movie by Bruce Joel Rubin

Three Visionary Screenplays by Bruce Joel Rubin

Playing Among the Stars: Conversations with Damien Chazelle by Nathan Réra

The Magic Eye: The Cinema of Stanley Kubrick by Neil Hornick

A Shared Cinema: Conversations with Michael Ciment by N. T. Bihn

The Naughty Bits: What the Censors Wouldn't Let You See in Hollywood's Most Famous Movies by Nat Segaloff

Mexico: The Aztec Account of the Conquest by Werner Herzog

Werner Herzog/Rogue Filmmaker by David LaRocca

De Palma on De Palma: Conversations with Samuel Blumenfeld and Laurent Vachaud

Publication as Autobiography: Occasional and Forsaken Texts— and Endangered Cinema Species by Scott MacDonald

Filmmakers Thinking by Adrian Martin

Secret Cinema: The Rise and Fall of the Blue Movie by John Baxter

Casualties of War: An Investigation by Nathan Réra

Hollywood on the Tiber by Hank Kaufman and Gene Lerner

What Made Cinema? Essays on Visual Culture and Early Film by Ian Christie

Travels in the Cities of Cinema: Conversations with Jonathan Rosenbaum by Ehsan Khoshbakht

Camera Movements that Confound Us by Jonathan Rosenbaum

Upon Open Sky by Guillermo Arriaga

Ambrose Chapel by Brian De Palma

Russian Poland: by David Mamet

The Archival Impermanence Project by Ross Lipman

These Fragments I Have Shored Against My Ruin by Caveh Zahedi

Cinema Now and Then: Conversations with James Naremore
by Craig S. Simpson

Circle of Lions by Anthony Ray

Peace of Mind: A Paul Williams Anthology, edited by Paul Cronin

Flashbacks: A Passion for Film by Peter Cowie

Haneke on Haneke: Conversations with Michel Cieutat
and Philippe Rouyer

Darkness Visible: The Cinema of Jonathan Glazer by John Bleasdale

Let Me Dream Again: Essays on the Moving Image by Luke McKernan

O Brother, What Might Have Been: Three Lost Screenplays
by Preston Sturges

Mister Everywhere: Conversations with Pierre Rissient
by Samuel Blumenfeld

Every Movie is a Miracle: A Colloquy Between Leonard Maltin
and Nat Segaloff

High Contrast Hollywood by Julian Upton

Charles Chaplin's The Freak: The Story of an Unfinished Film
by David Robinson

Jump Cuts, Tracking Shots, and Scherzos by David Sterritt

A Cinephile Under the Influence: Conversations with David Sterritt
by Mikita Brottman

My Life is the Cinema by Esfir Shub

I Killed Bette Davis by Larry Cohen

HeadHunter by Larry Cohen

I Loved Movies... But: Conversations with Joseph McBride
by Danny Peary

A Reluctant Film Critic by Gerald Peary

The Zen of the Director by Peter Markham